Philosophical Aspects of Globalization: A Multidisciplinary Inquiry

Contemporary Russian Philosophy

Editor

Alyssa DeBlasio, *Dickinson College, Carlisle, PA (USA)*

Editorial Board

Marina Bykova, *North Carolina State University, Raleigh (USA)*
Alexander Chumakov, *Lomonosov Moscow State University (Russia)*
Mikhail Epstein, *Emory University, Atlanta (USA)*
William Gay, *University of North Carolina at Charlotte (USA)*
Boris Groys, *New York University, New York (USA), and The European Graduate School / EGS, Saas Fee (Switzerland)*
Vladimir Kantor, *National Research University Higher School of Economics, Moscow (Russia)*
Ruslan Loshakov, *Uppsala University, Uppsala (Sweden)*
Natalya Shelkovaya, *Volodymyr Dahl East Ukrainian National University (Ukraine)*
Mikhail Sergeev, *University of the Arts, Philadelphia (USA)*
Igor Smirnov, *University of Konstanz, Konstanz (Germany)*
Karen Swassjan, *Forum für Geisteswissenschaft, Basel (Switzerland)*
Vladimir Zelinsky, *Catholic University of Sacred Heart, Brescia (Italy)*

VOLUME 2

The titles published in this series are listed at *brill.com/crph*

Philosophical Aspects of Globalization: A Multidisciplinary Inquiry

Edited by

Alexander N. Chumakov
Alyssa DeBlasio
Ilya V. Ilyin

In collaboration with

Ivan A. Aleshkovski and Mikhail Y. Sergeev

BRILL

LEIDEN | BOSTON

Cover illustration: The Gulf of Mexico, United States, photographed by NASA and made available in 2015 via unsplash.com.

Names: Chumakov, A. N. (Aleksandr Nikolaevich), editor. | DeBlasio, Alyssa, editor. | Ilyin, Ilya Vyacheslavovich., editor.
Title: Philosophical aspects of globalization : a multidisciplinary inquiry / edited by Alexander N. Chumakov, Alyssa DeBlasio, Ilya V. Ilyin ; in collaboration with Ivan A. Aleshkovski and Mikhail Y. Sergeev.
Description: Leiden ; Boston : Brill, 2022. | Series: Contemporary Russian philosophy, 2406-0070 ; volume 2 | Includes bibliographical references and index. | Summary: "Globalization is a defining characteristic of our contemporary world, with a reach and impact affecting all nations and peoples. Philosophical Aspects of Globalization is a collection of essays by leading contemporary Russian philosophers, scholars, and scientists concerned with addressing pressing issues of globalization from a philosophical point of view. The thirty-four authors who have contributed to this book represent a range of approaches and subfields of Global Studies in Russia, including topics such as theory of globalization, globalization and the environment, history and geopolitics, and globalization in cultural context. When compiled together in a single collection of essays, their work offers the English-speaking reader a comprehensive picture of new directions in Russian Global Studies in the twenty-first century, as well as demonstrates the importance of questions of globalization for philosophical inquiry in Russia today"– Provided by publisher.
Identifiers: LCCN 2022014359 | ISBN 9789004515499 (hardback) | ISBN 9789004516007 (ebook)
Subjects: LCSH: Globalization–Philosophy. | Globalization–Russia (Federation) | Philosophy, Russian.
Classification: LCC JZ1318 .P486 2022 | DDC 303.48/2–dc23/eng/20220511 LC record available at https://lccn.loc.gov/2022014359

Typeface for the Latin, Greek, and Cyrillic scripts: "Brill". See and download: brill.com/brill-typeface.

ISSN 2406-0070
ISBN 978-90-04-51549-9 (hardback)
ISBN 978-90-04-51600-7 (e-book)

Copyright 2022 by Alexander N. Chumakov, Alyssa DeBlasio and Ilya V. Ilyin. Published by Koninklijke Brill NV, Leiden, The Netherlands.
Koninklijke Brill NV incorporates the imprints Brill, Brill Nijhoff, Brill Hotei, Brill Schöningh, Brill Fink, Brill mentis, Vandenhoeck & Ruprecht, Böhlau and V&R unipress.
Koninklijke Brill NV reserves the right to protect this publication against unauthorized use. Requests for re-use and/or translations must be addressed to Koninklijke Brill NV via brill.com or copyright.com.

This book is printed on acid-free paper and produced in a sustainable manner.

Contents

Foreword: Philosophy of Globalization in Today's Dialogue of Civilizations IX
Preface XIII
Notes on Contributors XXI

PART 1
Globalization in the Focus of Interdisciplinary Research

Globalization from the Philosophical Point of View 3
Alexander N. Chumakov

Globalization as a Holistic Process
Philosophical and Methodological Aspects 23
Boris I. Pruzhinin and Tatiana G. Shchedrina

The Age of Competing Globalizations 37
Vladislav L. Inozemtsev

Globalization and Global Processes: The Algorithm of Development 51
Arkady D. Ursul, Ilya V. Ilyin, and Tatiana A. Ursul

The Historical Logic of Globalization 65
Tatiana L. Shestova

International Cooperation under the Conditions of Globalization: A Holistic Assessment 76
Tatiana A. Alekseeva and Ivan D. Loshkariov

PART 2
Philosophical and Sociocultural Aspects of Globalization

The Role of Global Studies in the Development of a Sustainable Security System 99
Ilya V. Ilyin and Kristina S. Leonova

The Pandemic and the Crisis of the Global World 110
Alexey A. Gromyko

The Globalized World under the Prism of COVID-19 124
   Victor B. Kuvaldin

The Twilight of Neoliberal Globalization
Alternatives to the Dead-Ends of the Proto-Empire 140
   Aleksandr V. Buzgalin

The Concept of "Political Globalization" and Global Challenges 163
   Olga G. Leonova

PART 3
Nature, Society, and Humans in a Global World

Sustainable Development of Civilization and the Global Environmental Problem 181
   Victor I. Danilov-Danilyan

Harmonization of the Biosphere and the Technosphere as a Global Problem of Modernity 196
   Nizami M. Mamedov

Natural-Historic Aspects of Globalization 210
   Valery V. Snakin

Global Digital Society and the Problems of Social Adaptation 224
   Aza D. Ioseliani

Globalization Aporia: The Hegemonic "World State" versus Cosmopolitanism to Come 236
   Edward V. Demenchonok

PART 4
Russia in the Global World: Philosophy, History, Geopolitics

Russia in the Projects of the Coming World Order 255
   Yury D. Granin

Ways for Evolving Russia's Current Civilizational Choice in the Context of Globalization 271
   Igor K. Liseyev

Globalization, the Great Russian Revolution of 1917, and the
Transformation of the World System
A Historical and Philosophical Perspective   291
    Leonid E. Grinin

The Structures of Social Solidarity in Contemporary Russia
Evolution and Perspectives   307
    Anastasia V. Mitrofanova

The Philosophical Potential of Russian Cosmism in the Context of
Contemporary Interdisciplinary Global Studies   323
    Alexander M. Starostin

PART 5
Humanistic Aspects of Global Civilization

Civilizational Values in the Age of Global Social Transformations   335
    Ivan A. Aleshkovski and Alexander T. Gasparishvili

Towards a Theory of Global Security   346
    Igor F. Kefeli

Modern Challenges of Global Sports Development
A Philosophical and Methodological Analysis   358
    Vladislav I. Stolyarov and Sergey G. Seyranov

The Dialectic of Civilization
From Ethnic-Religious to Global Civilization   372
    Ilham R. Mamedzade and Tair M. Makhamatov

The Essence of Globalization in the Spiritual Dimension   387
    Anatoliy G. Kossichenko

Religion in the Globalized World
Philosophical Reflections   402
    Mikhail Y. Sergeev

Index   419

Foreword: Philosophy of Globalization in Today's Dialogue of Civilizations

Today, when, in the context of globalization, national interests prevail over the common interests of humankind, it is extremely important that the dialogue of civilizations should not halt but continue to develop. It is equally important to take into account the achievements and developments of the previous decades, in terms of the interactions between different countries and peoples, in order to preserve the ideals of a humane, just and democratic society for the future. The international academic community is one of the most important pillars of the panhuman civilization; at present, the fate of almost all aspects of global development depends on its internal and external resources. The forms and tools of interaction that have developed in world science are one of the main values of humankind and, possibly, one of the most important factors in maintaining a relatively stable balance of modern international life.

In this regard, the present collective monograph, *Philosophical Aspects of Globalization: A Multidisciplinary Inquiry*, is of particular interest. First, the authors represented in this collection are leading Russian scientists, experts in various fields of global research, many of whom are still unknown to the Western reader. Second, the book presents the Russian scientists' original generalized views of nature and of the history of global processes, their development, and their consequences. All this is very valuable, both from a scientific and a cultural point of view. There is no doubt that the book will be useful and interesting not only for professionals, but also for a wide audience.

Regrettably, the current dialogue of civilizations is increasingly conducted in raised tones. Books like this one are very much needed and wished for. Its measured, reasonable, and tolerant style of presentation makes this book a globally significant source for the study of the theory and history of globalization. It also charts a path towards a better mutual understanding, and a sound basis for establishing a constructive dialogue.

Deep-level globalization studies have been carried out in Russia for a long time. As early as the Soviet period, a serious school of global studies was established in Russia. The systematic and planned nature of Soviet science, which provided for a wide coverage of the issues studied, enabled a comprehensively study of many subjects of global importance (the World Ocean, fresh water, atmosphere, climate, raw materials and energy sources, biodiversity, demography, etc.). At the same time, conclusions were drawn, and generalizations made, in line with the Marxist theory, which absolutized the class approach and reduced the recipes for solving global problems to the struggle against capitalism.

In the 1990s, when the post-Soviet space opened up to the world economy, the era of multifaceted globalization began, and the term "globalization" became widespread in public and political discourse. The direction of global studies was then established in world science, shaping the substantive study of the global-scale phenomena and processes. In Russia, the topic of globalization turned out to be in great demand. Conclusions that had been aggregating for a long time, yet found no expression under the monopoly of Marxism, burst forth into the space of ideological freedom, creating a synergistic effect of an intellectual explosion. It was precisely the explosive nature of Russia's globalization studies in the 1990s and around the turn of the millennium that led to numerous breakthroughs in the stagnant repositories of knowledge, with huge volumes of accumulated but scarcely used information. New Russian research began to acquire international significance. The free access of Russian scientists to foreign information and the acquaintance of the world scientific community with the results of Russian research were among the factors accelerating scientific development at the advent of the twenty-first century.

Probably for this reason, Russian science has become one of the main springboards for the development of the philosophy of globalization. It is quite telling that it was on the initiative of Russian scientists in 2003 that the *Global Studies Encyclopedia* was first published, in Russian and English, in Russia.[1] In 2006, a *Global Studies Encyclopedic Dictionary* was published in Russia.[2] Both of these publications, authored by 647 leading scientists from fifty-eight countries, played an important role in the formation of global studies as an independent branch of scientific knowledge. In 2014, the *Global Studies Encyclopedic Dictionary* was republished by Brill, becoming an important factor in raising the standards of international research into the diverse aspects of globalization.[3]

This publication, which features the forefront of contemporary Russian global studies, is one of the finest examples of multidimensional globalization research to emerge in the past decade. The main virtue of this book is *systematicity*—a quality that, unfortunately, has all but disappeared from

---

1 Alexander Chumakov, William Gay, and Ivan Mazour, eds., *Global Studies Encyclopedia* (Moscow: Raduga, 2003).
2 Alexander Chumakov and Ivan Mazour, eds., *Global Studies: International Interdisciplinary Encyclopedic Dictionary* (New York: Piter, 2006).
3 Alexander Chumakov, Ivan Mazour, and William Gay, eds., *Global Studies Encyclopedic Dictionary*, with a foreword by Mikhail Gorbachev (Boston: Brill, 2014).

modern collective monographs. *Philosophical Aspects of Globalization* is not just a collection of selected articles on globalization written by core specialists, but a monograph that systematically covers various aspects of globalization at a single level of philosophical and methodological generalization. This approach has enabled the editors to collect and present an extensive empirical material from specific spheres of scientific globalization studies (economics, sociology, political science, etc.), which makes this book a kind of textbook on globalization as such, and a highly valuable and convenient resource for subsequent research. The structure of the book reflects nearly every aspect of the world globalization studies agenda, which makes its contents both balanced and topical.

I would like to congratulate the editors, as well as the authors of this book, on the creation of a valuable, informative, and structurally elegant specimen of modern scholarly literature, certain to make a serious contribution not only to the development of international academic discourse on globalization, but also to the modern dialogue of civilizations. Academic books like this one allow people and nations to better understand the world we live in—and therefore, to better understand one another.

Dr. Walter Schwimmer
President of the International Institute for Social and Economic Studies
Secretary General of the Council of Europe (1999–2004)
Vienna, Austria

Preface

The present volume, which we began in 2019 and completed work on in the summer of 2021, is a collection of articles by leading contemporary Russian philosophers and scholars concerned with addressing questions of globalization and its impact from a philosophical point of view. Globalization is a fixture, even a defining characteristic, of our contemporary world. In the work of this volume's thirty-three contributors, globalization comes forth as multifarious in its features and in the extent of its reach; and yet, in all the varied scholarly approaches presented here, we see how the processes that comprise globalization have a direct influence on the social, economic, political, and cultural development of all nations and peoples across the globe. Still, there remain many unanswered questions as to the origins of globalization or the nature and extent of its positive and negative consequences. For instance, the question of *when* globalization began is up for debate, while analyses surrounding *why* globalization began present an even more diverse picture of this field of inquiry, including views that range from describing globalization as an objective and law-governed historical process to a trajectory initiated by individual actors on a global scale.

The lack of consensus in the field, and the very flexibility and volatility of the term itself, poses serious challenges for global and transnational thinking—i.e., not only for conceiving of problems on a global scale, but for applying integral and transnational thinking to decision-making at the micro and macro level. Global thinking has perhaps never been more urgent than right now, the middle of March 2022; as we write this introduction, the stability and future of Europe—and of the entire world—is under serious threat. In our nuclear age, the global worldview, and its associated forms of thinking, must serve as the foundation for international relations and decision-making at all levels. This volume is one attempt to put forward an approach toward philosophical solutions to the most urgent crises of globalization.

Of course, scholars and philosophers rarely find themselves seated at the table when important political decisions are made. And yet, insofar as scholars and philosophers work to define and clarify the critical concepts on which these decisions should rest, it is our duty to uphold our commitment to objectivity and truth, and to the analyses of these problems in global perspective—even if we are not consulted in their resolutions. We no longer live in a world where problems can be limited to a single region, nationality, or country. The challenges of globalization are shared by all. Conflicts that may have, at one time in history, been localized or ignored on the global scale, now pose serious danger to international stability, a fact supported by the growing body of scholarship in transnational, hybrid, and global approaches.[1] By including in our volume the voices of leading names in the field and from a variety of disciplines and professions, we hope to contribute to a culture of cross-cultural and international debate.

As this introduction, and ultimately this volume, intends to show, Russian scholarship on globalization is in some important ways part of the European tradition of global studies; and in other important ways, it has developed according to its own tradition, in the same way that Russia has historically viewed itself as neither East nor West. The importance of including the voices of Russian scholars—meaning both Russian and also from Russia and/or writing in the Russian language—into these conversations is not only a scholarly calculation, but a humanitarian one. First, because this volume will fill a gap for the Western reader in search of material on the directions of global studies in Russia today. Second, because the publication of this book, we hope, will contribute to a better understanding of the similarities and differences between Russian and Western social and political thought in the context of modern globalization. And third, by placing this scholarship in global dialogue, we hope to contribute to the kinds of conversations and decision making that can avoid future humanitarian catastrophes like the ongoing tragedy in Ukraine.

The wealth and diversity of material available on the topic of globalization—and, as we have just seen, the importance of the global perspective for our shared future—has made it a rich subject for multidisciplinary scholarly analysis among philosophers, sociologists, and political scientists alike. What is more, in the second half of the twentieth century, work on globalization merged with research on environmental concerns, meaning that at present, globalization studies often go hand-in-hand with questions of sustainability and ecology. In the West, centers dedicated to problems of globalization include the Vienna Institute for the Future (established in 1965), the international foundation Humanity in the Year 2000 (also established in 1965), and the World Future Society (established in 1966 in Washington, DC). Recently,

---

1 See, for instance: Ino Rossi, ed., *Challenges of Globalization and Prospects for an Intercivilizational World Order* (NYC: St. John's University, 2020); Stephan C. Roh, ed., *G7 & Philosophy: A Philosophical Review of the Political Agenda of the G 7 Summit in Taormina, Italy* (Rome: Link Campus University, 2017); *Human Rights Education in Turkey and in the World* (Ankara: Turkish Philosophical Institution, 2020); *Dialogue Among Civilizations and the Human Future* (Denfeng, China: Songshan Forum, 2019).

PREFACE   XV

we have seen a proliferation of similar organizations and institutes that identify themselves with the discipline of "future studies." However, it was not until the founding of the Club of Rome in 1968 that we could talk about an organized effort in the study of globalization. In fact, the presentation topics at that inaugural session still drive inquiry into many of the most pressing issues of globalization today, and serve as a genesis point for the scholarly pursuit of the problems posed by globalization, as well as for public attention to these problems.[2]

It was around that same mid-century point that Soviet scholars began taking globalization seriously as a subject of scholarly, political, and ideological debate, mostly surrounding the government's broader concern with the pressing global problems of that time. Likewise, work on globalization published in the West was making its way to the Soviet Union, where it was translated into Russian, sparking interest in these problems and in their representations abroad. There were conferences, debates, and publications devoted to globalization; in particular, Vladimir Vernadsky's long-forgotten idea of the *noosphere*, conceptualized in the 1930s, was revived in the new context of the late Soviet period, earning Vernadsky a key role within Russian philosophical analyses of globalization from that point on.[3] The culminating moment of Soviet attention to globalization occurred in 1976, with the establishment of the All-Union Scientific Research Institute for System Studies under the auspices of the Academy of Sciences of the USSR. The Institute's director was the Soviet-Georgian philosopher Dzhermen Gvishiani (1928–2003)—a member of the Club of Rome. Thus, from its very founding, the Institute for System Studies collaborated closely with the Club of Rome's International Institute for Applied Systems Analysis, meaning that Soviet scholars were very much a part of the history of the study of globalization in Europe.[4]

The next transformative moment in the Soviet study of globalization was the founding of the Scholarly Council on Philosophy and the Social Problems of Science and Technics at the Academy of Sciences in 1980. The Council was

---

2   See: Dennis Meadows, Donella Meadows, and Jorgen Randers, *The Limits to Growth* (New York: Universe Books, 1972); Mihajlo Mesarovic and Eduard Pestel, *Mankind at the Turning Point* (New York: Dutton, 1974); Jan Tinbergen et al., *Reshaping the International Order: A Report to the Club of Rome* (New York: Dutton, 1976); Ervin Laszlo and the Club of Rome, *Goals for Mankind* (New York: Dutton, 1977).

3   Vladimir Vernadsky (1863–1945) was a Soviet mineralogist, geochemist, and founding theorist of the *noosphere*—the term of his own coinage referring to the highest stage of biospheric development involving the emergence of human consciousness and reason.

4   Alexander Chumakov, Ilya Ilyin, and Ivan Mazour, eds., *Global Studies Directory: People, Organizations, Publications* (Boston: Brill, 2017), 129, 322–24.

headed by the well-known philosopher Ivan Frolov (1929–1999) and became the leading scholarly center for globalization studies in the country, working to coordinate and unite research efforts across many different disciplines.[5] As part of this initiative, one of the leading climatologists of the twentieth century, Mikhail Budyko (1920–2001), together with a group of climate scholars, developed a mathematical model for the global climate called the Budyko-Sellers model. Budyko was the author of many other pioneering works, including those warning of the dangerous impact that human civilization would have on the Earth's climate. He predicted that human impact would lead to catastrophic results for the environment and to global climate change.[6] At the same time, another group of scholars formed around the prominent mathematician Nikita Moiseyev (1917–2000) and his work to create mathematical models of global processes. Alongside American astrophysicist Charles Sagan, Moiseyev is considered to be the author of the idea of the "nuclear winter." Together with his research group, Moiseyev created a mathematical model of the possible consequences of nuclear war for Earth's biosphere. His model has since served as scientific proof of the catastrophic potential of nuclear war, and had a significant influence on world politics, helping in part to stimulate talks on nuclear disarmament among leading countries.[7]

This and other research into globalization and its processes laid the foundation for a new discipline in the USSR—the so-called "globalistics," or global studies. Since the late-Soviet period, this discipline has developed and expanded, in large part due to scholarly initiatives like the first interdisciplinary *Global Studies Encyclopedia*, published in 2003 in English and Russian.[8] This project included contributions from 445 authors representing twenty-eight countries, investigating globalization in all its depth and diversity. Continuing this work, in 2006, Russian scholars published an even larger project: the *Global Studies Encyclopedic Dictionary*, comprising 2,000 entries by 647 scholars, philosophers, politicians, and cultural figures from fifty-eight countries.[9] The contents of this encyclopedia comprised the entire range of inquiry into globalization, including the humanities, social sciences, and natural sciences. In addition, 2012 saw the publication of the *Global Studies Dictionary*

---

5 Chumakov, Ilyin, and Mazour, *Global Studies Directory*, 100–104, 479–80.
6 See: Mikhail Budyko, *The Heat Balance of the Earth's Surface*, (Washington, DC: Dept. of Commerce, Weather Bureau, 1958); Mikhail Budyko, Alexander Ronov, and Alexander Yanshin, eds., *History of the Earth's Atmosphere* (New York: Springer, 1987); Mikhail Budyko, Georgy Golitsyn, and Yury Izrael, eds., *Global Climatic Catastrophes* (New York: Springer, 1988); Mikhail Budyko and Yury Izrael, eds., *Anthropogenic Climatic Change* (Tucson: University of Arizona Press, 1991).
7 Chumakov, Ilyin, and Mazour, eds., *Global Studies Directory*, 237–39.

(by Brill's Contemporary Russian Philosophy series), which catalogued leading names, organizations, and developments in the field of globalization.

The development of global studies as a discipline in the post-Soviet era was facilitated in large part thanks to the establishment of the Russian Ecological Academy in 1992, which united Russian scholars, philosophers, and ecologists under a single institutional umbrella. The main goal of this organization was to encourage and support theoretical research that might eventually lead to solutions for the problems caused by interactions between society and nature, as well other global problems of the era.[10] The year 1992 also saw the founding of a private university for environmental education—the International Independent Ecological-Political University, which sought to prepare its students to become highly qualified specialists in the areas of ecology, natural resource management, environmental law, eco-politics, and global studies. The university organized many international events and conferences in these fields, further contributing to the development of the discipline in the immediate post-Soviet period.

The year 2005 marked another important step in the development of global studies in Russia: the creation of the Department of Global Processes at the Lomonosov Moscow State University.[11] The department has since become the leading center for global studies in Russia, coordinating projects among multiple disciplines. Every two years the department sponsors an International Global Studies Congress that hosts leading scholars from Russia and abroad, with the participation of organizations like UNESCO, the Club of Rome, the World Academy of Art and Science, the International Academy of Global Research, and the Russian Society for Global Research.[12]

The articles in this collection are representative of the new directions of Russian global studies in the twenty-first century. In introducing readers to the authors and topics presented here, we would like to note two things. First, the publication of this volume continues the longstanding collaboration between Russian philosophers and Brill. Since 2014, the book series in Contemporary Russian Philosophy has published several titles specifically on the philosophy of global studies, and many more on the study of philosophy in Russia

---

8 Alexander Chumakov, William Gay, and Ivan Mazour, eds., *Global Studies Encyclopedia* (Moscow: Raduga, 2003).

9 Alexander Chumakov, Ivan Mazour, and William Gay, eds., *Global Studies Encyclopedic Dictionary*, with a foreword by Mikhail Gorbachev (Boston: Brill, 2014).

10 See: Russian Ecological Academy, http://rosekoakademia.ru/.

11 Chumakov, Ilyin, and Mazour, eds., *Global Studies Directory*, 345–51. See also: Department of Global Processes, Lomonosov Moscow State University, http://fgp.msu.ru/.

12 See: Russian Globalistics, https://www.globalistika.ru/.

more broadly. Second, it is quite rare even today for Russian authors to find an audience in the West and to publish their work in English. There are many reasons for this, but we would like to highlight just one: for much of the twentieth century, the Soviet Union and the West were unable to engage in real dialogue. Be it the "iron curtain" or the Cold War, both are names for the ideological chasm that separated these two civilizations. For a brief time after the collapse of the Soviet Union in 1991, collaboration between Russia and the West appeared to be possible at last. As indeed it was—for a time. Nevertheless, the relationship between Russia and the West has always been fraught; for a variety of historical, political, and economic reasons, that long-awaited dialogue between Russian and Western scholars never quite reached its full potential.

As a result, the Western reader is unlikely to be familiar with Russian thought or with the Russian humanities. The same can be said for philosophy and global studies as practiced in Russia. And yet, in the decades since the collapse of the Soviet Union, the Russian humanities have undergone significant changes. Marxist philosophy has long lost its overarching influence on social thought and philosophy, and is now studied as one approach among many in the history of philosophy. As for the relationship of Marxism to global studies, Marxism is a part of the discipline's past, but today it plays an almost undetectable role in the research and views of contemporary Russian scholars of globalization. The fact that this volume is co-edited by scholars from Russia and the United States is perhaps one small step on the path towards direct engagement between Russian and Western thought.

We have carefully selected the articles in this volume, authored by leaders in their respective fields, to present the Western reader with a rich and accurate picture of the variety and character of global-studies research conducted in Russia today. Some of the approaches contained within will be familiar to the reader; others may perhaps be wholly new and unexpected. Readers may be surprised by the extent to which philosophical thinking and philosophical ideas permeate nearly every level of Russian global studies, making philosophy of globalization a distinct field in its own right. As we noted above, work on the contents of this volume was completed by the summer of 2021, a full half year before the start of the ongoing crisis in Ukraine. And yet, the articles contained within remain relevant. In the work of those scholars writing about globalization in the contemporary world, some of the predictions or worries they expressed have even begun to come true.

In order to guide the reader through this multidisciplinary and multithematic volume, we have arranged the articles in five sections.

Part I, "Globalization in the Focus of Interdisciplinary Research," is devoted to the interdisciplinary character of global research in Russia. The articles in this section address the philosophical and theoretical dimensions of globalization, and the trajectory of its development, from the viewpoints of history, economics, and political science.

Part II, "Philosophical and Sociocultural Aspects of Globalization," includes five contributions that focus on moments of crisis in the contemporary world, including the 2020–2021 COVID-19 pandemic. The works in this section pay particular attention to global political and protest movements, including those advocating the process of counter-globalization.

Part III, "Nature, Society, and Humans in a Global World," looks at the troubled relationship between human beings and the natural world—a topic that has always been, and remains, of particular importance for Russian thinkers. Here we find articles in a variety of sub-disciplines and addressing a wide array of issues, ranging from the harmonization of the biosphere and technosphere to advances in sustainable development and ecological preservation. The final chapter in this section addresses the idea of cosmopolitanism as a substitute for the traditional international system of nation-states.

Part IV, "Russia in the Global World: Philosophy, History, Geopolitics," includes chapters by philosophers, historians, and geopolitical scientists who address Russia's role in the global world. Here we find contributions that take on the most urgent questions of Russian society today: for instance, investigations into Russian civilization's developmental trajectory, the impact of the Russian Revolution on world systems, and the philosophical school of Russian cosmism, which remains one of Russia's distinctive contributions to world philosophy.

Finally, the articles in Part V, "Humanistic Aspects of Global Civilization," address the role of the humanities and humanistic concerns within the broader context of globalization. The authors included in this section investigate a variety of topics, including civilizational values, global security, the theory and practice of sports management at a global level, and religious and ethical concerns in the context of globalization.

We would like to express our profound gratitude to the translators who worked on this volume, to Anna Razumnaya for her editorial expertise, and to the editorial team at Brill, for their support of this complex multidisciplinary project.

We hope that the publication of this volume in English will not only introduce new names and ideas to a Western audience, but will also help facilitate international dialogue on questions of globalization—questions that are critical to us all, inhabitants of a shared, global world.

Alexander N. Chumakov
Alyssa DeBlasio
Ilya V. Ilyin
March 2022

Notes on Contributors

Tatiana Alexandrovna Alekseeva
D.Phil. Professor and Head of the Political Theory Department, School of Governance and Politics, Moscow State Institute of International Relations (MGIMO), Distinguished Scholar of the Russian Federation, author of nineteen monographs. Member of the International Studies Association (ISA) and the Russian International Studies Association (RISA). Laureate of the State Order of Friendship.

Ivan Andreyevich Aleshkovski
Associate Professor, Deputy Dean of the Faculty of Global Studies, Lomonosov Moscow State University. Graduated with honors from the Department of Economics, Lomonosov Moscow State University, in 2006. Received a PhD in Economics in 2007. Research interests focus on population studies, international migration, migration policy, and globalization. Author and coauthor of more than 220 scientific works, including thirty-seven monographs and textbooks.

Aleksandr Vladimirovich Buzgalin
Doctor of Economics, Professor, Director of the Center for Modern Marxist Studies at the Department of Philosophy, Lomonosov Moscow State University. Professor Emeritus of Lomonosov Moscow State University; Visiting Professor at Beijing University and a number of other universities. Editor-in-Chief of the journal *Questions of Political Economy* and member of the editorial boards of six journals in Russia and other countries (*International Critical Thought, Terra Economy*, and others). Author of more than 400 works, including twenty-eight books, a number of which have been translated into English, German, Spanish, and other languages, and of numerous articles in journals in Russia and elsewhere (*Cambridge Journal of Economics, Critical Sociology*, etc.). Has delivered lectures and presented papers at universities and centers of higher learning in more than twenty countries.

Alexander Nikolayevich Chumakov
D.Phil. Professor of the Department of Global Processes, Lomonosov Moscow State University. Editor-in-Chief of *The Age of Globalization*, a scholarly journal. Member of the Presidium of the Russian Ecological Academy. Member of the Board of Association Internationale des Professeurs de Philosophie (AIPPH). Author of more than 700 scholarly works in the areas of social philos-

ophy and philosophy and methodology of global studies, including a number of works translated into foreign languages. Organizer and Co-Chairman of the Organizing Committee of the Russian Philosophical Congress. Regular participant and leader of sections and round tables on global studies at the World Congress of Philosophy (meetings XVIII–XXIV). Project initiator, editor, and contributor in a series of fundamental international reference works in global studies. Gusi Peace Prize Laureate (2015).

Victor Ivanovich Danilov-Danilyan
Doctor of Economics, Professor, Corresponding Member of the Russian Academy of Sciences and Scientific Director of the Academy's Institute of Water Problems. Author and co-author of over 600 scholarly works, including more than thirty monographs in the fields of environmental economics, hydrology, mathematical modelling, and the theory of sustainable development. Laureate of the Russian Federal Government Prize in science and technology.

Edward V. Demenchonok
Professor of Foreign Languages and Philosophy at Fort Valley State University (United States), with research interests in philosophy of culture, political philosophy, and ethics. Author of *The Quest for Change: From Domination to Dialogue* (2016); *A World Beyond Global Disorder: The Courage to Hope* (co-authored with Fred Dallmayr, 2017); *Intercultural Dialogue: In Search of Harmony in Diversity* (2016); *Philosophy after Hiroshima* (2010); *Between Global Violence and Ethics of Peace: Philosophical Perspectives* (2009), and other scholarly works.

Alexander Tengizovich Gasparishvili
Associate Professor at the Department of Global Studies, Lomonosov Moscow State University; Associate Professor of the Faculty of Humanities and Social Sciences, Russian University of Peoples' Friendship; Senior Research Fellow of the Institute of Sociology at the Federal Center for Theoretical and Applied Sociology, Russian Academy of Sciences. Graduated from the Department of Philosophy, Lomonosov Moscow State University, in 1978. In 2004, defended the PhD thesis, *Global Issues in American Sociology*. Author and coauthor of more than 150 scientific works, including twelve monographs and textbooks.

Yury Dmitriyevich Granin
Doctor of Philosophy, Professor, Lead Researcher at the Institute of Philosophy of the Russian Academy of Sciences. Specializes in philosophy of history and in theory and history of globalization, nations, and nationalism. Has proposed

and substantiated a hypothesis concerning the historical forms of globalization. Interprets globalization as a megatrend of unification—civilizational, cultural, economic, political, etc.—of a divided humanity into a planetary community bound by a system of universal values. Author of ten monographs and 200 scholarly articles. Member of the Russian Union of Journalists.

Leonid Efimovich Grinin
D.Phil. Senior Research Professor at the National Research University Higher School of Economics (Moscow); Director of the Eurasian Center for Big History and System Forecasting of the Russian Academy of Sciences; Editor-in-Chief of *Vek globalizatsii* (*The Age of Globalization*), a scholarly journal; Co-Editor of the *Journal of Globalization Studies* and *Social Evolution & History*; Vice-President of the N. D. Kondratiev International Foundation. Author of more than 600 scholarly works in Russian, English, German, Spanish, and Chinese, including more than thirty monographs investigating globalization, the theory of historical process, and of evolutionary and revolutionary transformations in history and contemporaneity. Winner of the 2012 N. D. Kondratiev Gold Medal for contributions to the development of the social sciences.

Alexey Anatolyevich Gromyko
Doctor of Political Science, Professor and Corresponding Member of the Russian Academy of Sciences (RAS), director of the RAS Institute of Europe; President of the Russian Association of European Studies, Chairman of the A. A. Gromyko Association for Foreign Policy Studies. Member of the Academic Council for the Russian Minister of Foreign Affairs. Member of the Academic Board at the Security Council of Russia. Editor-in-Chief of the journal *Contemporary Europe* and Executive Editor of the journal *Social Sciences and Contemporary World*. Specializes in European studies, international relations, international security, and regional integration.

Ilya Vyacheslavovich Ilyin
DHabil. in political science, Professor and Head of the Department of Global Studies, Lomonosov Moscow State University. Active participant in the development of new research areas, including political and evolutionary globalistics, and global ecology. Ilyin's works focus on clarifying the current scientific worldview, emphasizing factors of global development as a set of co-evolving global processes and systems. Author of the classification system for global processes, systems, and problems, and of more than 300 scholarly works, including twenty monographs.

Vladislav Leonidovich Inozemtsev
Professor of Economics and Senior Associate, Center for Strategic and International Studies, Washington, DC.

Aza Davidovna Ioseliani
Doctor of Philosophy, Professor of the Financial University under the Government of the Russian Federation. Author of more than 300 scholarly works in the fields of foreign languages, global studies, philosophy of science and technology, and the problems of interaction between nature, humanity, and the information society, published both in Russia and abroad.

Igor Fyodorovich Kefeli
Doctor of Philosophy, Professor, Director of the Center for Geopolitical Expertise of the Northwestern Institute of Management, Russian Presidential Academy of National Economy and Public Administration (RANEPA), expert of the Russian Academy of Sciences. Author of more than 300 scholarly papers in multiple languages, in the fields of social philosophy, globalism, cultural studies, geopolitics, and history of science and technology.

Anatoliy Grigoryevich Kossichenko
Doctor of Philosophical Sciences, Professor, Chief Researcher at the Institute of Philosophy, Political Science, and Religious Studies of the Ministry of Education and Science of the Republic of Kazakhstan. Author of more than 450 scholarly publications, including a number of individual and collective monographs. He has edited three collective monographs and co-authored more than ten collective monographs devoted to the problems of globalization. His research interests include methodology of science, science as a cultural phenomenon, the spiritual essence of a person, and the role and significance of religion in the modern world. Anatoliy Kossichenko has spent twenty years investigating the problems of globalization, participating in twelve conferences on globalism. The focus of his studies is on the personal aspects of globalization, man in the context of contemporary global processes, and cultural and spiritual issues of globalism.

Victor Borisovich Kuvaldin
Professor and Head of the Department of Social and Political Sciences at Lomonosov Moscow State University's Moscow School of Economics. Entered the field of global studies in the mid-1990s, having previously worked in political science. While heading the Gorbachev Foundation's Center for Political Analysis, edited one of the first Russian collective monographs on the

subject—*Facets of Globalization* (2003)—which advanced the concept of *megasociety* as the initial phase in the emergence of a globalized world. Victor Kuvaldin's two subsequent monographs (published in 2009 and 2017) continued to develop this problematic. The author attends closely to the complex characteristics of globalization and of the globalized world as a qualitatively new and higher stage in the development of civilization, which opens up unprecedented opportunities—and equally unprecedented dangers—for humanity.

Kristina Sergeyevna Leonova
Lecturer, Department of Global Studies, Lomonosov Moscow State University. Specializes in sustainable development and lectures on the fundamentals of globalistics, international relations, sustainable development, and security in the context of global development.

Olga Georgievna Leonova
Doctor of Political Science, Professor of the Department of Globalistics, Faculty of Global Studies, Lomonosov Moscow State University. Author and co-author of approximately 200 scholarly publications on globalization, international relations, and soft power. Teaches courses on the problems of international relations, global development, and global political processes. Member of the editorial boards of *Vestnik Moskovskogo universiteta* (*Bulletin of Moscow University*), Series 27: Globalistics and Geopolitics, and *Studia Humanitatis*, an online scholarly journal.

Igor Konstantinovich Liseyev
D.Phil., Professor, Lead Researcher at the Institute of Philosophy of the Russian Academy of Sciences (RAS), member of the presidium of the Russian Philosophical Society, member of the presidium of the Russian Society for Global Studies, author of more than 300 scholarly publications on philosophical problems of globalism, biology, and ecology; served for more than twenty-five years as Department Head at the RAS Institute of Philosophy; participant of multiple meetings of the World Philosophy Congress, organizer and participant of all eight meetings of the Russian Philosophical Congress.

Ivan Dmitrievich Loshkariov
PhD (Political Science); Senior Lecturer at the Department of Political Theory, School of Governance and Politics, Moscow State Institute of International Relations (MGIMO). Author of four textbooks, two monographs, and more

than forty journal articles. Member of the International Studies Association (ISA) and the Russian International Studies Association (RISA).

Tair Makhamatovich Makhamatov

Doctor of Philosophy, Professor of the Financial University Under the Government of Russian Federation; Professor of the Diplomatic Academy of the Russian Ministry of Foreign Affairs; Professor of Lomonosov Moscow State University's Institute of Asia and Africa. Member of the Russian Ecological Academy. Regular contributor to the journal *Vek Globalizatsii* (*The Age of Globalization*). Author of more than 200 scholarly publications, in Russian and English, on globalization, political philosophy, philosophy of science, existentialism, and linguistics.

Nizami Mustafa oglu Mamedov

Doctor of Philosophy, Professor of the Russian Academy of National Economy and Public Administration, full member of the Russian Academy of Natural Sciences and the Russian Ecological Academy, UNESCO expert. Author and co-author of more than 400 academic papers, monographs, and textbooks, including the standard Russian public school textbooks on ecology. One of the first scholars to pay close attention to philosophical and axiological aspects of the relationship between technology and the biosphere, and to the emergence of fundamentally new methodological problems in technical sciences in connection with the worsening ecological situation. His best-known works include: *The Ecological Problem and Technical Sciences: Philosophical and Methodological Aspects* (1982); *Ecology and Technology: The Problem of Optimal Orientation in the Development of Technology* (1988); *The Fundamentals of Social Ecology* (2003); *Ecology and Sustainable Development* (2013).

Ilham Ramiz-oglu Mamedzade

Doctor of Philosophy, Professor Emeritus of the Faculty of Law and Political Science at the University of Nice Sophia Antipolis (France), Editor-in-Chief of the journal *Nauchnye Trudy* (*Scholarly Research*), Director of the Institute of Philosophy and Sociology of Azerbaijan National Academy of Sciences. Author of nearly 300 research works in several languages, in the fields of ethics, history of philosophy, philosophy of culture, and methodology of political research. Regular leader and participant of panels and roundtables on multiculturalism at the recurrent Baku International Forum of the Humanities.

NOTES ON CONTRIBUTORS

Anastasia Vladimirovna Mitrofanova
Leading Research Fellow at the Institute of Sociology of the Federal Center for Theoretical and Applied Sociology of the Russian Academy of Sciences; Professor of the Financial University under the Government of Russia. Received her M.A. in 1994 and PhD. in 1998, from the Department of Philosophy of the Lomonosov Moscow State University; she completed her habilitation in 2005, at the Diplomatic Academy of the Foreign Affairs Ministry of Russia. Research interests include religious politicization, fundamentalism, Orthodox Christianity and politics, nationalism in post-Soviet states, social movements, late-Soviet and post-Soviet society, and the politics of memory. Author of *The Politicization of Russian Orthodoxy: Actors and Ideas* (2005) and other publications.

Boris Isayevich Pruzhinin
D.Phil. Editor-in-Chief of *Voprosy filosofii* (*Problems of Philosophy*), an academic journal. Head of the Department of Philosophy of Natural Sciences at the Institute of Philosophy of the Russian Academy of Sciences. Professor of the Humanities at the National Research University Higher School of Economics (Moscow). Research Director, Faculty of Social Sciences, Belgorod State University. Research interests include philosophy and methodology of science and history of Russian philosophy. Boris Pruzhinin investigates the relations of theoretical and applied sciences, taking special interest in scientific thought as a matter of intellectual style. Together with Tatiana Shchedrina, he is developing the concept of cultural-historical epistemology. Since 2012, he is Series Editor of *Russian Philosophy of the First Half of the Twentieth Century* (published by RossPEn, Moscow, with thirty-three volumes to date). Author and editor of ten monographs and more than 200 articles and other publications in Russian, English, French, and Chinese.

Sergey Germanovich Seyranov
D.Habil. Academician of the Russian Academy of Education, Professor, Honored Scientist of the Russian Federation, Honorary Worker of Higher Vocational Education of the Russian Federation, Honorary Professor of Kazakh Academy of Sports and Tourism, Honorary Professor of Armenian State Institute of Physical Education, Honorary Doctor of the State University of Physical Education and Sports of the Republic of Moldova, Honorary Doctor of Georgian State Educational University of Physical Culture and Sport. Rector of Moscow State Academy of Physical Education, President of the Russian Student Sport Union. Published more than 200 scientific papers, including

eight monographs. Conferred with numerous state, departmental, and public awards in the Russian Federation and abroad.

Tatiana Gennadiyevna Shchedrina
D.Phil. Executive Secretary of *Voprosy filosofii*. Professor of Philosophy at the Moscow State Pedagogical University and the Far-Eastern Federal University. Specializes in the history of Russian philosophy in the nineteenth and twentieth centuries, and in the methodology of historical and philosophical research. Tatiana Shchedrina develops the methods of historical-philosophical reconstruction of what she terms "the archive of the epoch"—which involve the transcription and interpretation of epistolary manuscripts by Russian and European philosophers. Together with Boris Pruzhinin, she works on the concept of cultural-historical epistemology. Conducted archival research in the Russian Federation, Ukraine, France, Switzerland, Israel, and Germany; recipient of FNRS (National Fund for Scientific Research, Belgium) and CNRS (National Center for Scientific Research, France) grants. Since 2004, edits the *Collected Works* of the Russian philosopher Gustav Shpet (RossPEn, Moscow, twelve volumes to date.) Since 2012, Tatiana Shchedrina is the Archives Editor for *Russian Philosophy of the First Half of the Twentieth Century* and the initiator of *Thought and Word*—a book series addressing the problems of contemporary Russian philosophy (five volumes published to date). She has supervised twelve doctoral dissertations and authored and edited ten monographs and more than 200 articles and other publications in Russian, English, French, and Chinese.

Tatiana Lvovna Shestova
D.Phil. Professor of the Department of Global Processes, Lomonosov Moscow State University. Author of scholarly works in the fields of philosophy of history, social philosophy, global history, and global studies. Member of the Russian Ecological Academy. Member of the editorial board of *Vestnik Moskovskogo universiteta* (*Bulletin of Moscow University*), Series 27: Globalistics and Geopolitics. Member of the organizing committees of the biannual international scientific congress Globalistics and other conferences on globalistics, ecological consciousness, philosophy, and history. Participant of international congresses, including the European Congress on World and Global History and the World Philosophy Congress.

Valery Viktorovich Snakin
Doctor of Biology, Head of the Laboratory of Landscape Ecology at the Institute of Fundamental Problems of Biology of the Russian Academy of Sciences;

Department Head at the Lomonosov Moscow State University Museum of Earth Sciences; Editor of the interdisciplinary scientific journal *Zhizn Zemli* (*Life of the Earth*); member of the Presidium of the Russian Ecological Academy. Author of more than 300 scientific publications, including twenty books and encyclopedic dictionaries. Laureate of the State Prize in Science and Technology (2004).

Alexander Mikhailovich Starostin
Doctor of Political Science, Professor, Director of the Institute for Interdisciplinary Study of Global Processes and Globalization, Rostov State University of Economics.

Vladislav Ivanovich Stolyarov
D.Phil. Professor of the Russian State University of Physical Culture, Sports, Youth, and Tourism; Professor of Federal Scientific Center for Physical Culture and Sports; Professor of the Russian International Olympic University. Author of more than 900 scholarly papers (120 papers presented in foreign languages), including more than seventy monographs concerning the problems of physical education, sports, Olympism, and the logic and methodology of science. Initiated a unique project of integrating sports with art implemented in Russia for over three decades. Winner of the 2014 and 2020 National Prize in physical culture and sports. Laureate of the European Fair Play award.

Arkady Dmitriyevich Ursul
DHabil. in philosophy, full member of the Academy of Sciences of Moldova, the Russian Ecological Academy, and a number of other academies. Director of the Center for Global Studies and Professor at the Department of Global Studies, Lomonosov Moscow State University. Author and co-author of more than 1,000 scholarly publications in the fields of philosophy and the socionatural aspects of globalistics. Key contributions include the monographs *Space Exploration* (1967), *Humanity, Earth, Universe* (1977), *Philosophy and Integrative General Scientific Processes* (1981), *The Path to the Noosphere* (1993), *Security and Sustainable Development* (2001), *Universal Evolutionism* (2007), *Globalization and the Transition to Sustainable Development* (2008), and *Global Evolutionism* (2010).

Tatiana Albertovna Ursul
DHabil. in philosophy, the Russian Federation's Distinguished Worker of Higher Professional Education, Professor and Head of the Department of Social Sciences and Technologies of the National University of Science and

Technology ("MISIS"). Specializes in global studies, global evolutionism, philosophical and methodological problems of science and technology, social ecology, and security and sustainable development.

PART 1

Globalization in the Focus of Interdisciplinary Research

Globalization from the Philosophical Point of View

Alexander N. Chumakov

1   The Global Agenda as a New Philosophical Theme

Over its two-and-a-half thousand years of history, philosophy has developed differentiated fields of inquiry, such as ontology, gnoseology, social philosophy, anthropology, ethics, aesthetics, logic, etc. In one way or another, all of them are rooted in antiquity. Historians of philosophy are right to say that almost every philosophical problem can be found, in its essential form, in the works of Plato and Aristotle. Different aspects of philosophical thought came to the forefront during different historical periods, and for a variety of reasons. And yet, despite the diversity of these aspects of investigation, philosophical cognition has remained fairly consistent with the early directions of thought that emerged in antiquity.

The situation changed with the advent of the twentieth century, when the discipline of philosophy saw the introduction of a fundamentally new domain of investigation—one that had not existed up until that point, and concerns Planet Earth as a single holistic system, and the globe as a distinct cosmic body, where various global processes take place, being generated by social relations. These processes amount to what we call *globalization*.[1] But why should this subject take on not only a scientific but also a philosophical tone? And why did this take place in the twentieth century? The answer should be pursued at the macro-level and in keeping with historical standards, and also in concert with the revolutionary qualitative changes that have taken place on our planet, effected by the objective processes of historical development and by the unprecedented advances in science and technology.

If we consider the history of mankind, even its most recent centuries, each century is known by some name that most accurately reflects its essence. The twentieth century is no exception: it can rightly be called both the Nuclear and the Cosmic Age. Yet its essence is even better expressed in the fact that in its course the world community became literally a *global* phenomenon.

At the dawn of our era, the world human population was around 250 million people, reaching its first billion only by the nineteenth century. The

---

1   Alexander Chumakov, Ivan Mazour, and William Gay, eds., *Global Studies Encyclopedic Dictionary*, with a foreword by Mikhail Gorbachev (Boston: Brill, 2014), 229–42.

world community entered the twentieth century with a population of 1.65 billion people and concluded the century with a population of over six billion.[2] During the first twenty years of the current century, that figure increased by another 1.85 billion, thus reaching 7.85 billion people. It is with good reason that such unprecedented population growth was dubbed a "demographic explosion." We have seen, too, the exponential growth of scientific and technological progress, and the ever-increasing pace of socio-economic development among the world community. This rapid pace of development has qualitatively changed the way of life for increasing numbers of people, affecting the availability of certain technology and hardware, consumption patterns, health care, etc. Due to the finite nature of our planet and its limited resources, this state of affairs could not but affect the relations of nature and society, as well as the nature and the manifestations of planetary-scale social problems.

The essence of these changes is that global problems have arisen together with local and regional problems—problems that had, in fact, accompanied humanity for centuries and even millennia. Was it possible to avoid this state of affairs? Unfortunately, it was not, since, to the extent that the world community was going global, these individual problems became increasingly apparent at the global level. The appearance of these problems is directly related to the development of the global social processes that we call *globalization*.[3] To put it succinctly, globalization can be defined as an *objective historical process of the formation of planetary structures, connections, and relations across all spheres of social life.*

It is important to emphasize that globalization did not happen all at once. It was preceded by an era of fragmentary events and local social relations—an era then succeeded, with the emergence of the state, by an era of regional events and territory-driven international relations. This was followed by an era of global events and universal economic and socio-political dependence. The age of discovery paved the way for this development, as people first learned that they inhabited a globe, and then began to interact on a planetary scale. Since then, globalization has undergone three main stages of development: *actual globalization* (fifteenth to mid-nineteenth centuries); *fundamental globalization* (mid-nineteenth to mid-twentieth centuries); and *multi-aspect glob-*

---

2 Alexander Chumakov and Ivan Mazour, eds., *Global Studies: International Interdisciplinary Encyclopedic Dictionary* (New York: Piter, 2006).
3 Steven Hicks and Daniel Shannon, eds., *The Challenges of Globalization: Rethinking Nature, Culture, and Freedom* (Malden, MA: Blackwell, 2007).

alization (from mid-twentieth century until the present).[4] The cosmic expansion of humans belongs to this last period.

Now that the world community has become a holistic planetary system in terms of the basic parameters of social life, individual problems have also been raised to global proportions. As a result, the world community is facing the kinds of dangers that we first encountered in the twentieth century. Here we speak not only of ever-increasing population growth and its negative impact on the environment; nor are we solely referring to the ongoing extension of the impressive list of world problems, including but not limited to such threats as global terrorism, transnational cybercrime, and global pandemics, not to mention poorly controlled nuclear weapons that pose a real threat of human self-destruction. In recent decades, new risks and challenges have been added to the tangle of the global concerns of our time. The most important of these is the fact that we are witnessing *a dramatically rapid change in the architectonics of world connections and relations, while the global community demonstrates its inability to adequately respond to these changes and new challenges.*

This situation poses potential threats to humanity at large. These threats can, in turn, be evaluated according to two multidirectional tendencies that are becoming increasingly clear: the *integration* and the *differentiation* of the world community. These tendencies have a serious "unbalancing" effect on social development. Integration consists in the fact that, due mostly to objective reasons, humanity is rapidly globalizing and transforming into a holistic system, in which the number of interacting elements is growing, and their interconnectedness and interdependence is constantly increasing. Differentiation, on the other hand, is associated with increasing resistance to integration, by nation-states that do not fit into the global processes, and also into broad public opinion based in traditional culture.[5] As this conflict of interests in the world community deepens, *the global world, faced with fundamentally new challenges, is increasingly drawn into a situation of increasing contradictions and uncertainty.*

By now, we can see quite clearly how, by the end of the twentieth century, the world community has gone completely global, and how relations, communications, and information networks have become transnational. Essentially, all this has turned humanity into a single organism, a single system, at least across the main parameters of social life. At the same time, nation-states (now

---

4 Chumakov, Mazour, and Gay, eds., *Global Studies Encyclopedic Dictionary*, 231–40.
5 Alexander Chumakov and William Gay, eds., *Between Past Orthodoxies and the Future of Globalization: Contemporary Philosophical Problems* (Boston: Brill, 2016).

about 200 in number) are no longer the only subjects of international relations. Multiple transnational corporations and international organizations, including criminal organizations engaged in drug trafficking, international terrorism, and illegal emigration, now act in the same capacity as nation-states. In this manner, the entire world, with its multitude of interdependent and antagonistic subjects, is completely bereft of the management and regulation it so desperately needs. As a result, the entire world has become a battleground for various interests, where the "rule of force," "double standards," "soft power," and all kinds of sanctions are actively deployed, once again placing humanity in a situation of "war of all against all." The only difference between this situation and the one described in Thomas Hobbes's *Leviathan* is that now—unlike in prehistoric times—the opposing parties to this kind of universal war are not individuals, but the multiple subjects of international relations, the most powerful among them being the nation-states that have no Leviathan to subdue them from above.

The situation is further aggravated by the fact that the biosocial nature of human beings is inherently conservative; it cannot keep up with the pace of change dictated by modern life. In particular, this was brought into view by the well-known theorist of globalization Ervin Laszlo, who wrote:

> Culture and society change rapidly, whereas genes change slowly: not more than half a percent of a person's genetically-determined abilities are likely to change over a century. Therefore, most of our genes trace their history back to the Stone Age or even earlier; they might help us live in the primitive jungle, but not in the wilds of civilization.[6]

Indeed, today, just as centuries ago, both good and bad qualities—love and hate, good and evil, peacefulness and aggression—are still present in human beings and can be manifested depending on the circumstances. And although culture, nurture, education, and enlightenment do make people more patient, humane, and tolerant, we still retain what is predetermined by nature: the struggle for survival, aggressiveness, and the desire to dominate and to solve problems from a position of strength. All this is also fully manifest in the behavior of individual communities, as well as the policies of nation-states.

In this vein, the words attributed to Albert Einstein after the nuclear bombings of Hiroshima and Nagasaki are especially relevant: "What mankind needs

---

6 Ervin Laszlo, *Макросдвиг: К устойчивости мира курсом перемен* [*The Macro-Shift: Towards World Stability via a Course of Change*] (Moscow: Taidex, 2004), 199–200.

the most is a bench to sit down and think." This was a message directed to the entire world community, arising from the scientist's profound concern with the unprecedented pace of scientific and technological progress and the threat of nuclear war. In the present context of an ever more complex and tightening knot of contradictions and problems in the modern world, the relevance of this message continues to grow. The global coronavirus pandemic has clearly demonstrated the global community's inability to deal with universal threats in a coordinated and effective manner, further evidence that we find it rather difficult to slow down, stop, look back, and think. Everything around us, from our personal lives to economy and politics, is focused on growth, strengthening, increase, acceleration. Struck by the crisis of the pandemic, confronted with self-isolation—we are reminded "to sit down and think." Let us then look around, analyze, consider, and draw appropriate conclusions.

2   The Awareness of the World's Integrity

In order to effectively address negative phenomena and their causes, it is first of all necessary to understand the objective bases and patterns in the emergence of those phenomena, and the new threats and challenges that they usher in. Moreover, these phenomena are not always obvious, nor are they easy to identify. This is where science and specialized knowledge come to the rescue. And yet, even these are not enough on their own: a philosophical understanding of reality is also necessary. The more complicated a task, the greater the need for philosophy. As the Stoics rightly pointed out, humans cast philosophy aside in times of complacency, and turn to it again when pressed by misfortune. The latter situation is just as we find ourselves at present, and it requires that we take a fresh look at our circumstances.

One must emphasize that the world community has gradually formed into an integral system, in the context of the stage-by-stage evolution of the global world—but our awareness of this fact did not arrive immediately. In essence, intellectuals began to think in universal human categories starting in the late eighteenth and early nineteenth centuries, as we can clearly see in the works of Immanuel Kant, Thomas Malthus, Karl Marx, Friedrich Engels, Nikolay Danilevsky, and Oswald Spengler. However, it was not until the twentieth century that the global world and the world community became the subject of special attention and of analysis in the full sense of the word.[7]

---

7 Helmut Anheier and Mark Juergensmeyer, eds., *Encyclopedia of Global Studies* (Thousand Oaks, CA: SAGE, 2012).

In this regard, it is important to refer to the works of the pioneers of global studies. Here we should single out the following thinkers: Arnold Toynbee, Pierre Teilhard de Chardin, Vladimir Vernadsky, Karl Jaspers, Bertrand Russell, and Albert Einstein.[8] It was these people who, in the first half of the twentieth century, paid special attention to humanity as a whole, and began considering it as an integral component of nature. They accepted as fact the transition from an atomized, disengaged, and fragmented world community to the unity, integrity, and global interdependence of a planetary mankind. Thus, for example, the English historian Arnold Toynbee, who viewed social development as a succession of different civilizations, concluded that universal world history began in the twentieth century. In this way, Toynbee emphasized that radical changes affected not only the foundations of the social fabric, but also the main tendencies of global social processes.

By that time, other thinkers had also begun expressing serious concerns about the dangers posed by these new tendencies. Vladimir Vernadsky played a particularly important role in the emerging philosophical thought about contemporary problems of the relations between society and nature, and of the development of the concept of the *noosphere*, understood as a holistic planetary phenomenon.[9] The French philosopher and theologian Pierre Teilhard de Chardin expressed similar views. In his attempts to substantiate the uniqueness of man as an integral part of the biosphere, he developed the concept of harmonizing man's relations with nature, while advocating the refusal of selfish aspirations, for the sake of the unification of all mankind. The philosopher Karl Jaspers adhered to an even more concrete discourse on the essence of the global world. In 1948, he published *The Origin and Goal of History*, in which he wrote:

> What is historically new and, for the first time in history, decisive about our situation is the real unity of mankind on the earth. The planet has become for man a single whole dominated by the technology of communications; it is "smaller" than the Roman Empire was formerly…. Now the whole world has become the problem and task. With this a total metamorphosis of history has taken place.
>
> The essential fact is: There is no longer anything outside. The world is closed. The unity of the earth has arrived. New perils and new opportuni-

---

8 Alexander Chumakov, Ilya Ilyin, and Ivan Mazour, eds., *Global Studies Directory: People, Organizations, Publications* (Boston: Brill, 2017).

9 Vladimir Vernadsky, *Философские мысли натуралиста* [*The Philosophical Thoughts of a Naturalist*] (Moscow: Nauka, 1988).

ties are revealed. All the crucial problems have become world problems, the situation a situation of mankind.[10]

In this way, in the first half of the twentieth century, philosophers and scientists already understood both that a new era—an era of planetary phenomena—was coming, and that under these new conditions only together people would be able to confront the natural and social forces.

A further stage of the insight into global processes was related to the activities of the Club of Rome and the publication of its well-known reports.[11] Its first report, *The Limits to Growth*, published in 1972, had an "exploding bomb effect," since it showed that mankind was unthinkingly "playing with matches while sitting on a powder keg." Prefacing this study, Aurelio Peccei, the founder and first president of the Club of Rome, noted that no sane person could believe any longer that "good old Mother Earth" could withstand any rate of growth, satisfy any human whims. It was then clear to that there were real limits, but what limits and where exactly they might be, had yet to be established.[12] The publication was followed by a series of later reports, which revealed many aspects of global problems and brought them to the attention not only of scientists and philosophers, but also of politicians, public figures, and the world community at large.

3 Globalization in the Mirror of World Philosophy

The World Congress of Philosophy, which has been held every five years since 1900, demonstrates persuasively that, by the end of the 1980s, the global agenda had been firmly established at the scholarly level, including philosophical consciousness, and had attracted wide public attention. The regular meetings of the Congress also provide insights into the public's responses to the challenges of globalization, and into the potential of philosophy to interpret and address them. In this regard, philosophers' interest in interpreting

---

10   Karl Jaspers, *The Origin and Goal of History* (New York: Routledge, 2011), 126–27.
11   See: Donella Meadows et al., *The Limits to Growth: A Report for the Club of Rome's Project on the Predicament of Mankind* (New York: Universe Books, 2017); Mihajlo Mesarovic and Eduard Pestel, *Mankind at the Turning Point* (New York: Dutton, 1974); Ervin Laszlo et al., *Goals for Mankind: A Report to the Club of Rome on the New Horizons of Global Community* (New York: Dutton, 1977).
12   See: Aurelio Peccei, *Human Quality* (New York: Pergamon, 1977).

the global world deserves special attention, since philosophy is a genuine mirror of public life and thus an indicator of the relevance of socially-significant problems.

Although by the mid-1980s the global agenda was already being actively discussed in scientific and some philosophical circles, it remained mostly outside of the mainstream of philosophical thought. It was only in 1988, at the eighteenth World Congress of Philosophy held in Brighton (United Kingdom) under the title *The Philosophical Understanding of Human Beings*, that the concerns of the world philosophical community about global problems and the future of humanity first became apparent. At this respected international intellectual forum, a global agenda was discussed, particularly in the plenary session focused on "The Present and Future of Mankind," in the two sections on "Global Environmental Challenges and the Future Life of the Earth" and "Global Problems in the Light of System Analysis," and in three round tables, "Philosophy in the Setting of World Problems," "Philosophy and the New Problem of Nuclear Self-Destruction," and "Man and Nature: Issues of Co-Evolution." The Congress also featured the active work of International Philosophers for the Prevention of Nuclear Omnicide, led by its president, John Somerville.[13]

The next, nineteenth congress, which took place in 1993 in Moscow, was entitled *Mankind at a Turning Point: Philosophical Perspectives*. This time, two plenary sessions were devoted to this topic: "The Fate of the Technology-Driven Civilization" and "New Thinking: Traditions and Innovations". A colloquium, "Man and Nature," and a section on "Ecology and the Future of Life on Earth" were complemented by three round tables: "Environmental Ethics and Sustainable Development in the Global Context," "The Third World Future in the Global Era," and "Ethical Issues of Conflict between North and South." Here, one must emphasize that until 1993, world philosophical thought did not yet use the term "globalization," but focused on contemporary global problems, with an explicit emphasis on environmental issues. Nevertheless, *anxiety for the future of life on Earth* was surging, and the widening gap in the socio-economic development of different countries and regions was causing a deepening concern.

At the twentieth congress, held in Boston in 1998 under the title *Paideia: Philosophy Educating Humanity*, there was a noticeable increase in attention paid to global issues, which were discussed both at the opening of the congress, in papers on "Ethics, Religion, and the Future of Humanity," "Philosophy and

---

13   Chumakov, Ilyin, and Mazour, eds., *Global Studies Directory*, 291–92.

the Future of Education," in the symposium "Global Issues in Teaching Philosophy," in the section on "Philosophy and the Environment," at the round tables "Critical Thoughts on the State of Global Consciousness," "Is Global Philosophy Possible?," "Is Global Ethics Possible?," "Philosophy of Nature and Society: Theory and Practice," "Self-Identification in the Intersubjective and Global Relations," and, finally, in field-specific sessions, "Philosophy in the Global Context: India and Tibet," "Philosophy in the Global Context: Japan and China," and "Problems of Democracy in the Age of Globalization." Not only did this congress reveal a significant increase in attention paid to the global agenda on a wide range of issues, from environment to education, ethics, and global consciousness, but it was also the first time when the term "globalization" was officially used in the program.

Nevertheless, it was only at the next, twenty-first World Congress of Philosophy, held in 2003 in Istanbul under the title *Philosophy Facing World Problems*, that philosophers around the world truly turned to *globalization* as such—thirty-five years after the Club of Rome first called upon the international community to unite so as to confront the global problems of the day.[14] Since the congress was entirely devoted to the global agenda, this topic became the subject not only of individual plenary and breakout sessions, round tables, and special sessions, but of many other sessions that discussed philosophy of science, technology, education, social and political life, dialog of cultures, etc., in the context of globalization processes. This approach was realized through plenary sessions, symposia, and special sessions, whose themes spoke for themselves, including "Globalization and Cultural Identity," "Human Rights, the State, and International Order," "Violence, War, and Peace," "Global Federation: Proposal for the Twenty-First Century," etc.

Along with the active use of the term "globalization," many sessions were devoted to topics involving the concepts of "global system," "global responsibility," "world problems," "global institutions," "global justice," "global capitalism," "global century," etc. At the same time, it seems worth noting that, although philosophical analysis (as compared to previous congresses) had shifted to the humanities, its work was significantly based on scientific data. Philosophers actively engaged with empirical material (though to a lesser extent than before), appealing to numbers and facts to support their theoretical positions and conclusions.

---

14   Ioanna Kuçuradi, Stephen Voss, and Cemal Güzel, eds., *The Proceedings of the Twenty-First World Congress of Philosophy: Philosophy Facing World Problems* (Ankara: Philosophical Society of Turkey, 2007).

Five more years went by. Although the main theme of the twenty-second World Congress of Philosophy, held in 2008 in Seoul, was *Rethinking Philosophy Today*, the global agenda clearly predominated at that congress.[15] The title of the congress was chosen deliberately. In his inaugural remarks, the president of the Korean organizing committee, Professor Myung-Hyun Lee said:

> Today, humanity is facing tremendous changes. That is why the congress is held under the title *Rethinking Philosophy Today*, to reflect—on philosophy—and on the state of philosophical thought and its facing global problems and dangers for the future of civilization. The new era demands a new philosophy, a new grammar of thought.[16]

Lee also drew attention to the fact that it was the first time in its history when the World Congress of Philosophy was held in Asia, so that philosophers from Asia and the West were finally able to meet face to face, and to conduct a philosophical forum on an Eastern intellectual platform. (Asian philosophy has not been included in the concept of "world philosophy" until but recently, and the term "philosophy" itself used to be regarded as synonymous with "Western philosophy.") The congress in Seoul demonstrated the possibility for Eastern and Western philosophies to inhabit a single umbrella term of *world philosophy*.

The speakers who followed also pointed to the unprecedented impact of globalization on the world today and emphasized the special role that philosophy played in interpreting the nature of both global processes and the consequences to which they gave rise. However, in our context, the address to the congress by UNESCO's Director General Koichiro Matsuura deserves special attention: "The global problems of our time have approached the humanity's doorstep and require an immediate solution. Philosophers are uniquely placed in a position to see these problems and should try to develop a methodology for solving them. This is not an easy task." "Neither philosophers nor scientists of individual states are able to solve this task separately," he emphasized, expressing a hope that the methodological, theoretical, and practical developments to be worked out at the World Congress of Philosophy in Korea would help shape the development of human civilization for the next five years.[17]

---

15   "К итогам XXII Всемирного философского конгресса" ["On the Results of the XXII World Philosophy Congress"], *Voprosy filosofii*, 2009, No. 1, 3–52.
16   S. Shermuhamedov and N. Shermuhamedova, "Размышляя об итогах конгресса" ["Contemplating the Results of the Congress"], *Vestnik RFO*, 2008 (47), No. 3, 25.
17   Shermuhamedov and Shermuhamedova, "Размышляя об итогах конгресса," 25–26.

Certain speeches set the appropriate tone for the work of the entire congress, where one of the plenary sessions was devoted to the topic of "Rethinking Moral, Social, and Political Philosophy: Democracy, Justice, and Global Responsibility." Two of the four symposia also dealt with the global agenda. One of them was called "Globalization and Cosmopolitanism," the other— "Bioethics, Environmental Ethics, and the Future Generations." By that time, the "Philosophy of Nature" section had already become traditional. As for round tables, the following can be singled out: "Contours of the World: Globalization, Cosmopolitanism, and Global Citizenship," "Values and Faith in Asia in the Globalization Context," "Cultural Dialogue between East and West: Past and Future," "Rawls's Theory and Global Justice," and "Indian Philosophy and Globalization."

In summarizing the results of this congress, one should note that, both in terms of membership and of the problems discussed, it was distinctly different from the previous meetings: this time the ratio of philosophers from the West and the East clearly shifted to the latter; thematically, many sessions were permeated by the idea of the increasing significance of the East and its role. This state of affairs was undoubtedly assisted by the fact that, in addition to numerous Koreans and Chinese, the congress's participants included scholars from India, Japan, and representatives of almost all Asian and many African countries. It was also apparent that, as compared with previous congresses, the conversation about humanity's contemporary problems appealed not so much to specific figures, facts, and data borrowed from the natural and exact sciences, but to their essentially philosophical interpretations in relation to subjects like globalization and cosmopolitanism, civil society and world civilization, national identity, and the global worldview. It was the first time when the problem of cosmopolitanism was formulated so explicitly, and the discussion was so varied and thorough, that one can state with confidence that *starting from this moment, world philosophical thought turned to issues of worldview and ethics in interpreting globalization and its consequences.*[18]

It is therefore quite clear that at the turn of the twentieth and twenty-first centuries, the global agenda had firmly entered the realm of those major issues that had begun to be raised as serious concerns among the world philosophical community. The twenty-third World Congress of Philosophy, entitled *Philosophy as Inquiry and Way of Life*, was held in Athens in 2013—and further confirmed this thesis. Although a historical-philosophical and metaphysical agenda prevailed in its program (understandably, since the forum was held

---

18   See: Alexander Chumakov, "Globalization and Cosmopolitanism in the Context of Modernity," *Journal of Philosophical Research*, 2008, 37.

in the historic homeland of philosophy), nevertheless there was active discussion of the theme of the global world and of the interactions between nature and society. Relevant topics were considered at the symposium on "Technology and Environment," in the sections "Philosophy of Globalization," "Environmental Philosophy," and at several round tables on such topics as "North–South Dialogue," "Culture and Environmental Responsibility in the Global Era," and others. However, what made the discourse on these topics special was that, in addition to the field-specific sessions of the congress that had already become commonplace, the global agenda permeated many contributions not necessarily directly devoted to it.

A characteristic example of this trend was one of the key plenary reports of the congress, delivered by the world-famous German philosopher Jürgen Habermas, who devoted his lecture to the complicated economic and political issues of the European Union, suggesting ways to solve these issues through the transformation of national democracy into its supranational form. In his lecture, Habermas—known for his elaboration of the Kantian project of a cosmopolitan world order as a "realistic utopia"—turned to cosmopolitanism, considering it as the means of civilized management of political power by means of the law. Since cosmopolitanism goes beyond nation-states, Habermas believes that one can speak of a gradual transition from coordination to cooperation among constitutional states. To further Habermas's ideas, several other reports also noted that political solidarity was important not only regionally, but also globally—as an alternative to nationalistic or hegemonic positions. This is the best reminder of the importance of an ethics of joint responsibility—meaning that our actions and their consequences have an impact on the future of humanity within a pluralistic, globally-interdependent world.

Multiple presentations were devoted to environmental protection and to the impact of the latter on the human way of life. Another plenary report presented by the Japanese philosopher Keiichi Noe emphasized that advanced technology is detrimental to civilization. The greater the civilization, the stronger the reverse impact it experiences from nature, the speaker proposed. This idea was connected to a lack of consideration for the laws of nature. Noe qualified Hiroshima and Fukushima as "disasters of civilization," and modern society as a "risk society." Another disaster he chose to include in his discussion was the Chernobyl tragedy, which taught everyone the lesson that worst-case scenarios were both real and possible, that destruction of nuclear weapons had become a political opportunity and a necessity, and that dialogue between state and technology regulation in the nuclear sphere could yield the best outcome.

In the presentation of the American philosopher Kristin Schrader-Frechette, technology certainly helps overcome the limitations of nature and is necessary for survival, but it also destroys people's social environment. The world is experiencing a dramatic increase in anthropogenic toxicity. This causes multiple mutations that result in diseases and impact human embryos, ultimately affecting natural selection. Pollution of the natural environment can take generations to manifest itself, the speaker said, but there is no real control over these processes.

Thus, the leitmotif of the congress became the idea that *there is no escape from global problems in an interdependent world.* Unlike short-sighted politicians and pragmatic business representatives, philosophers called us to pay due attention to globalization and its negative effects. They emphasized that the solution or mitigation of these problems will require a joint effort by the world community as a whole. When discussing these issues, the world philosophical community agreed that *dialogue of cultures and civilizations is the only possible means of resolving the contradictions attending upon the national and global levels of social development.*

Finally, the twenty-fourth World Congress of Philosophy, held in Beijing in 2018, ran under the headline *Learning to Be Human*. As the Chinese themselves have pointed out, the basic mission statement of the meeting was connected with the spirit of Chinese philosophy and intended to set the tone and the focus of all the events held in the course of this international forum. During the opening ceremony, this was also highlighted by Dermot Moran, President of the International Federation of Philosophical Societies, who said that the program of the congress had been carefully designed to incorporate the approaches from the East, West, North, and South. The congress thus aimed to "critically interpret the role of philosophy in relation to world culture, globalization, and the various existential and ecological threats that challenge us, citizens of the world, on our way to implementation of our common humanity."[19]

We find this philosophical approach for interpreting the current situation in the main program of the congress and in the spirit of the problems discussed. In particular, one of the plenary sessions was devoted to "Nature." At the symposium on "Science, Technology, and the Environment," and during the sections on "Philosophy of Globalization," "Cosmopolitanism," "Ecological

---

19 Alexander Chumakov and Andrei Korolyov, "Учиться быть человеком в глобальном мире (К итогам XXIV Всемирного философского конгресса)" ["Learning to be Human in the Global World (On the Results of the XXIV World Congress of Philosophy)"], *Voprosy filosofii*, 2019, No. 3, 15–21.

Philosophy," and a series of round tables with similar agenda, global issues were discussed extensively.

The special session of the congress on "Global Peace: Conflicting Interests" deserves special attention in this regard. Its participants included well-known philosophers from various countries and continents, virtually unanimous in their view that everything was changing rapidly in today's world under the influence of two key factors: the information technology revolution and multifaceted globalization. They also noted that new state-of-the-art technologies, media, and communications were transforming nations and peoples across the planet into a single community, a holistic system. As a result, competition on the world stage is intensifying, aggravating confrontations in the struggle for dominance and for the most advantageous economic, political, cultural, and ideological positions. The participants of this session analyzed the structure and dynamics of changes in the global world in terms of its development as a holistic, spontaneously regulated cultural and civilizational system. While discussing the best ways to solve the problems of our time and offering possible scenarios for further global development, they agreed that such problems could not be solved without theoretical, including philosophical, interpretation of their nature and root causes, or without the joint efforts and cooperation of the critical majority of the Earth's inhabitants.

The social and natural aspects of the contemporary globalization became an object of special attention during sections on "Environmental Philosophy" and "Philosophy of Nature," where the destructive impact of modern architecture on the environmental condition of cities and the health of city dwellers was discussed. Speakers noted that high-rise architecture was especially detrimental to the biosphere and to human health, causing the "sick building" syndrome involving psychological distress, fatigue, and headaches. Particular attention was paid to the design of urban environments in the extreme conditions of the Far North, the most vulnerable area in terms of its biospheric fragility.

In the context of our analysis, the results of the section devoted to "Philosophy of Globalization" are of special interest. Here, globalization became the leitmotif of discussion, treated as an objective natural and historical process of universalization, structural evolution, and increasing connectedness and interrelatedness across the Earth and the various spheres of social life. Presenters argued that major actors in the geopolitical arena must maintain a balance between centrifugal and centripetal tendencies, between national interests and the search for solidarity-based responses to global challenges, between national and universal forms of identity. If the peculiar features of national culture, mentality, ways of life are lost, then, according to the participants of this section, we will lose the orienting values and the criteria for globalization as an objective and generally positive process.

This thirty-year history and the last World Congress of Philosophy clearly demonstrate that the new, rapidly changing world cannot be explained in terms of pre-existing views. Nor can it be described by means of the established concepts formulated under conditions fundamentally different from those arising now in the world of global relations. Today, it is becoming increasingly evident that these new conditions require new guidelines and new values to replace the former social representations and values that have since lost their significance; moreover, that it is virtually impossible to define and form these new values without philosophy. Without philosophy, it is also impossible to develop the strategy and tactics necessary for joint actions among the world community—actions aimed at overcoming global challenges. The need for such actions is becoming increasingly urgent. In this way, the modern era has presented us with a fundamentally new theme: the single destiny of humanity and the preservation of life on Earth, which did not previously figure among the "eternal" philosophical problems of existence, consciousness, the meaning of life, and other familiar questions of philosophy.

4   Philosophy and Its Place and Role in Global Studies

Philosophy has always been interested not only in eternal problems that each generation tried to solve anew, but also in the daily practices of real life, its current concerns, and ways of addressing them. It is for this reason that the mirror of philosophy reflects the features and characteristics of each historical era. The modern world, a completely new reality created by the processes of globalization, is no exception to this. And since science always comes to humanity's rescue in solving certain problems, the very first warnings of the dangers of global processes once again had people turn their eyes to science and scientists.

In general, the interpretation of this new reality constitutes the domain of *global studies*—an interdisciplinary field of scholarly knowledge about global systems, structures, and processes inherent in all planetary spheres (non-living, living, and social), where philosophy plays special methodological, integrative, and axiological roles, to name but a few. As an independent scientific field and a sphere of social practice, global studies began to take shape in the late 1960s, although, as shown above, the preconditions for the discipline's emergence were under formation even much earlier. One must emphasize that global studies is not just a special discipline. New disciplines usually arise as a result of the differentiation of scientific knowledge, or at the junction of related disciplines. In the case of global studies, the opposite is true, since this discipline is generated by the integrative processes typical of modern science, and represents a *special field of research where various scholarly disciplines—including philosophy—analyze all possible aspects of the global world, globalization, and global problems, proposing solutions to them, for the most part in close interaction with one another, but each from the perspective of its own subject.*

While any specific problems can be examined both by a single science or by several sciences together, global processes and the problems they generate are beyond the power of individual sciences, due to their exceptional complexity. That is why, irrespective of the specific tasks solved by any discipline, the philosophical view of the processes and phenomena accompanying them (i.e., of the situation as a whole, including the results ultimately obtained) is a necessary prerequisite. Neither fundamental discoveries, nor the development of science itself can be possible without a broad cross-disciplinary holistic view of its subject matter and the problems faced by the humanity—a view reflective and inclusive of all the latest achievements in other fields of knowledge.

At the same time, philosophy has an undeniable advantage over science. This advantage is closely connected both with science, and with other spheres of social life (economic, political, social, legal, etc.), and is not limited to the realm of details and specific facts. Science easily leaves out the private, fragmentary, and transient, which allows it to focus on the essence of the matter and to highlight its most important elements. These qualities of philosophy have special value under the conditions of the present age, when one is faced with solving the difficult, integral problems pertaining to complex systems. Such systems include, for example, the world community as a whole, or various aspects of the relationship between nature and society, where the global, the universal, and the human interact and give rise to oppositions, and to severe conflict with the national, the local, and the private. In this regard, the techniques and methods of philosophical analysis, such as separating the essential from the non-essential, the substantive from the accidental, distinguishing objective tendencies from the subjective factors of historical development, etc., become crucial not only for a theoretical interpretation of globalization or the practical resolution of the global issues generated by it, but also for finding the best ways forward for social development.

Speaking of the role of philosophy in global studies, we should note the most important features inherent to this form of cognition, and which arise from the basic functions of philosophy as such:

- Philosophy shapes people's worldviews and their ideas about the world and human beings' place in it. However, it does not necessarily and directly influence political, social, or other decisions, although this cannot be completely excluded. Nonetheless, it is apparent that philosophy affects people's worldviews, and thus predetermines, to an extent, their behaviors and approaches to making decisions;
- One serious obstacle to interaction among the disciplines is the lack of a holistic view of complex systems. In this regard, the *methodological function of philosophy*—the generalizing theories it gives rise to—is a crucial contribution to the integration of scientific knowledge;
- Philosophy provides an opportunity to explain social phenomena and processes in a historical context. It formulates the *general laws of the development of society and nature*, and therefore, when studying global processes, aims at understanding them as a naturally determined phenomenon that is organically related to social progress;
- An important methodological function of philosophy is the development of *fundamental categories for global studies*, such as "nature," "society," "globalization," "global problems," "holistic world," "world community," etc. These categories reflect the problems of humanity today and play an important role in interpreting and properly understanding the objective tendencies of world development;
- Philosophy performs *culturological and axiological functions*, since, being connected to cultures and value systems of different peoples, it contributes to the formation of universal human culture, without which no societal problems could be solved;
- Finally, philosophy raises questions about *human life and its purpose*, and about *death and immortality*, which, in the face of globalization and the threat of global problems, is of particular importance and relevance.

5 Philosophical Perspectives on World Development

The theoretical interpretation of globalization processes and the process of overcoming global problems have become a matter of fundamental importance, since they are directly related to the fate and prospects of development of all humankind, as well as for individual countries and peoples. At the same time, we must connect our attempts to overcome global challenges with changes in people's worldviews. This is connected with the inception and the rise of a new ethics in the mass consciousness, and with the development and humanization of culture, since a given person's attitudes and way of thinking largely predetermine the way he or she will act. Such a worldview must be grounded in a new humanism, one that is focused on the development of a *global consciousness* and incorporates at least these three fundamental principles: a sense of the global, an intolerance for violence, and a respect for justice that arises from the recognition of basic human rights.[20]

Experience from history has shown that the rapprochement of different peoples occurs where their interests and levels of civilizational development coincide. The better civilizational interests are realized, the more tangible the results of integration. The greatest difficulties to be overcome on this way are related to ideological conservatism, with its established thought patterns, traditions, and interests. Though such traditions do tend to change, it happens with great difficulty and very slowly, frequently under the pressure of external or internal circumstances.

Hence, we argue that the problem of values and the search for new priorities of social development and other worldview orientations should become the main tasks of the spiritual renewal of society. In this regard, questions of humanism once again come to the forefront in the latest philosophical literature.[21] This includes the urgent need for a radical change in human activities, so as to make science and technology progress in a way that is directly dependent on the moral qualities of both the individual and humanity as a whole. Aurelio Peccei, the outstanding public intellectual and humanist, wrote that only that progress and only those changes that meet human interests and are within their capacity to adapt have the right to exist and to be encouraged.[22]

In connection with contemporary conditions, we should speak of a *new humanism* as a universal unifying principle. The essence of this principle is to establish rules and principles of existence that would reflect the vital interests of all people of the planet, and would be therefore perceived as universal values. Some of these values were first stated in ancient philosophy, and in the form of the universal commandments of the world religions—in particular, Christianity. In later epochs, the individual became the starting point of universal morality and of a common system of values. This was particularly

---

20   See: Ioanna Kuçuradi, *Human Rights: Concepts and Problems* (Berlin: Dr. W. Hopf, 2013); Gregory J. Walters, *Human Rights in an Information Age* (Toronto: University of Toronto Press, 2001).

21   See: Roland Robertson and Didem Buhari-Gulmez, eds., *Global Culture: Consciousness and Connectivity* (London: Routledge, 2016); Edward Demenchonok, ed., *Between Global Violence and the Ethics of Peace: Philosophical Perspectives* (Malden, MA: Blackwell, 2009); Hans Küng, *Global Responsibility: In Search of a New World Ethic* (Munich: R. Piper, 1990).

22   Peccei, *The Human Quality*, 156.

manifest in the ethics of Hobbes, Gassendi, Voltaire, Rousseau, Kant, Herder, and Locke, as well as in the US Declaration of Independence and the principles underpinning the French Revolution. Such values were stated in full in the Universal Declaration of Human Rights adopted by the UN General Assembly in 1948 and ratified in the Helsinki Accords of 1975.

It has not been easy for humanity to arrive at an awareness of individual rights, but the creation of a unified system of universal human values, where human rights are only a part of the larger system, is bound to be an even more difficult task. We must emphasize the complicated interdependence of such a whole and its parts. Thus, the recognition of universal human values by a community does not guarantee unconditional compliance with the fundamental rights of every person, for these rights are interpreted differently in different cultures, where traditions, religions, and the maturity of civil society vary. History abounds in examples of this kind. Today, compliance with the Universal Declaration of Human Rights is the most efficient means of maintaining public morals under the conditions of contemporary globalization.

Like any other self-governing system, the world community struggles for existence and for a better future. The contemporary processes of globalization and the varied problems associated with it leave humanity with no choice but to overcome fragmentation and discord, and to move towards unity, while simultaneously preserving cultural identities, age-old traditions, and other characteristics of individual nations and peoples. Unity, in turn, can only result from the recognition of—and compliance with—universal human values, among which inalienable human rights and the general principles of relations in the globalized world are central. It is the primary purpose of philosophy to develop and support such values.

Of course, philosophy cannot immediately shape the decisions of national governments or the activities of international organizations. Still, as rightly noted by Richard Rorty, philosophers are best positioned to build bridges between peoples and to initiate cosmopolitan initiatives—since, unless philosophers themselves become internationalists, no one else will.[23] Philosophers are the only ones, he reasonably observes, who can formulate and substantiate a clear picture of a cosmopolitan human future: the image of a planetary democracy, of a society where torture or the closure of a univer-

---

23   *Философский прагматизм Ричарда Рорти и российский контекст* [*Richard Rorty's Philosophical Pragmatism and the Russian Context*] (Moscow: Traditsiia, 1997), 110.

sity or a newspaper in a distant corner of the world would provoke the same indignation as if it had happened in one's home country.[24]

Essentially, this is what Derrida talks about, too, when he argues that the individual "does not want philosophy to be an associate judge, but prefers it to become a traveler and wanderer having no place to bow its head, rushing here and there when it hears the other's call to action."[25] This is correct. After all, philosophy is cosmopolitan by nature, simply because it is outside the polis. In this regard, we must also agree with Karl Marx, to whom (as witnessed by the *Theses on Feuerbach*) the task of philosophy is not just to explain the world, but also to transform it. The time has come when, as an important step in this direction, we should engage with all seriousness in the interpretation of the globalization agenda and of cosmopolitan ideas, so as to ultimately transform them into concrete instruments for building a just, sustainable, and more secure global world.

---

24   Richard Rorty, "Philosophy and the Future," translated into Russian by T. N. Blagovaya, *Voprosy filosofii*, 1994, No. 6.
25   John D. Caputo, *Deconstruction in a Nutshell: A Conversation with Jacques Derrida* (New York: Fordham University Press, 1997), 51.

Globalization as a Holistic Process
Philosophical and Methodological Aspects

Boris I. Pruzhinin and Tatiana G. Shchedrina

In analyzing the phenomenon of globalization, the typical approach involves isolating particular processes, in order to investigate their parameters and effects upon the specific aspects of various socio-cultural formations. Without disputing the value of this approach, we would like to draw attention to the applicability and practical advantages of another way of analyzing and assessing the processes of globalization. The central idea of this chapter is that globalization represents a holistic phenomenon, and full-fledged judgments about its constitutive processes (themselves heterogeneous in nature) can only be possible where this fact is taken into account. A holistic approach, then, can afford the modern researcher new avenues for interpreting the phenomenon of globalization, by locating it within new contexts. The necessary condition for realizing such a holistic perspective is constituted, in our view, by a recourse to philosophy—viewed as a source of methodological guarantees and key governing assumptions and principles.

The authors are well aware that this perspective on *globalization* enlarges the usual scope of the term. Since the middle of the past century, studies in globalization have been marked by the prevalence of analysis in economic and geopolitical terms. Meanwhile, the humanistic dimensions of globalization have often been neglected (or else disproportionately linked with its negative effects). In order to emphasize the beneficially humanistic aspects of globalization—related primarily to its encouragement of cross-cultural exchanges—we have previously proposed the term "a different globalization."[1] This coinage reflected our realization that, in the lived actuality of nations, regions, ethnic groups, and even individuals, socio-economic and cultural-historic aspects of globalization can hardly be convincingly separated. Beyond this, we think that the economic, social, cultural, and even psychological contexts of globalization processes are now so deeply intertwined that they can *only* be understood, and assessed in their social effects, within the framework of this unity.

---

1 Boris Pruzhinin and Tatiana Shchedrina, "Международный философский конгресс как феномен 'Другой глобализации'" ["The International Congress of Philosophy as a Phenomenon of 'a Different Globalization'"], *Voprosy filosofii*, 2019, No. 3, 33–39.

Once, globalization studies were indeed predominantly concerned with the economic aspects of the phenomenon; accordingly, its gains and losses were evaluated precisely in terms of production and consumption. There was also an emphasis on its erasure of cultural differences, and on its effect of instilling a hegemony of dominant regions and of their norms and standards in the public life. The "primitivization" of these standards was also frequently observed. In this way, the processes of globalization have heightened the urgency surrounding questions of ethnic identity, for individuals and ethnic groups alike. Similar viewpoints on globalization are occasionally voiced today. And yet, the processes of globalization have a way of changing not only the world, but also, recursively, themselves: even as their effects expand into new spheres of human activity, the trends of globalization themselves adapt to human realities. Humanity is, meanwhile, able to judge the possibilities of neutralizing the losses associated with globalization, while capitalizing on the gains.

For this reason, it is not an outright opposition to globalization, or a wish to return social formations to their isolated state, that chiefly conditions the attitudes in the regions—even as they take measures to preserve their identities, with the aid of their unique cultural heritage. The positive sides of the situation are, in fact, of particular significance for the residents of smaller regions characterized by traditional social norms. It is, for example, digital communication (a feature of the globalized landscape) that enables people, scattered as they are across the world by the same forces of globalization, to rediscover their genetic roots, and to revive the historic relations among families by means of internet-based forums and the social media. (This trend has been greatly aided by the opening of state archives to the public.)[2] Contemporary cultural-historical space suggests an urgent need for comprehensive analysis, which implies, in turn, the necessity of philosophical and methodological inquiry into the phenomenon of globalization as a whole.

In order to substantiate our last statement, we would like to turn to the experience of considering globalization in the context of regions and ethnic groups, where the specificity of cultural life is still primarily founded in the historically established tradition. Any adaptation of the social norms that had, for thousands of years, assured the survival of minority ethnic groups, requires cautious and carefully premeditated steps in the absorption of globalizing trends. Here, philosophical and more broadly humanistic and humane reflec-

---

2 Boris Pruzhinin and Tatiana Shchedrina, "Культурные смыслы образования и медиамир" ["Cultural Meanings of Education and the Mediated World"], *Voprosy filosofii*, 2020, No. 5, 98–102.

tion proves valuable in assessing both the social perceptions and the practical and humanizing adaptations of these large-scale processes.

When unfolding under their own momentum, in isolation from the humanistic dimensions of globalization, its economic and geopolitical aspects act as a direct and exceptionally difficult challenge to cultures founded upon historic tradition. This manifests with particular severity (and particular vividness, to aid our case) in regions characterized by cultural distinctiveness and by an absence of a local philosophical tradition. Such an instance is presented by Abkhazia, where, against the backdrop of thousands of years of tumultuous history, written language emerged quite late (the alphabet itself having been changed five times), and where millennial communal traditions are now facing powerful new globalizing pressures. We turn to the particular situation in Abkhazia in order to demonstrate the necessity of turning to philosophy and what it might involve in relation to questions of globalization and its accompanying processes.

Abkhazia is a region that is quite singular in this regard: its centuries-old, deeply traditional culture coincides with a great openness to globalization. What kind of a balance could be established under these conditions? And how can a minority ethnic group maintain itself, while benefitting from the technological, social, and cultural developments that globalization brings? These questions are of immediate interest to the ordinary Abkhaz people, but also to Abkhazia's intellectual and cultural elites. The latter especially find it evident that what matters is not so much the set of ethnic characteristics particular to the Abkhaz as the discovery of a rational basis for their valuation from a globalized viewpoint. In other words, it is the meaning of ethnic membership for today's Abkhaz individual, and the meaning of her or his ethnically-conditioned feelings, from dignity to the sense of fear or offence, as experienced by a member of the Abkhaz society.[3] In order to respond appropriately to the contemporary challenges of globalization, it is necessary to reflect on the grounds that enable a person to experience her- or himself as a representative of a certain ethnicity. The country's elites in particular need to arrive at an appreciation of that purposeful intellectual work, which can render the ethnic self-consciousness of the entire group vital and current. In this particular applied context, the interest of Abkhazia's elites in philosophy appears to us quite natural.

---

3 K. M. Gozhev and Ivan Tarba, *Сознание и самосознание—этническое и национальное (социально-философский континуум)* [*Consciousness and self-consciousness, ethnic and national (a socio-philosophical continuum)*] (Sukhum: RIO ASU, 2013), 190.

By virtue of what substantive features can an appeal to philosophy, as a holistic type of knowledge, assist us in delineating the relations among disparate globalization factors, or to envision and sketch out some plausible variations of those relations? In our view, philosophy, due to its aspiration towards the universal—and towards universal communication—effectively emphasizes two significant features of globalization as a process. As a type of rational knowledge, philosophy uncovers the real reasons for the ways in which specific aspects of globalization are inevitably, albeit variously, realized at all levels of social life. At the same time, philosophy can substantively demonstrate that the interpenetration of various aspects of globalization opens up possibilities for purposeful intervention and for influencing its ultimate effects on the social life of states, regions, ethnic collectives, and individuals. With its conceptual apparatus, philosophy is able to persuade ethnic intelligentsia that globalization need not be understood solely in terms of a given group's economic and sociopolitical integration into a rigorously standardized global community. Philosophy encompasses, too, a cultural-historical component that inflects the entire character of its influence, in reflecting the varieties of humane communication. By encouraging the appreciation of culture as something more than a passive superstructure of the practical ends of society (for it in fact represents its crucial active component), philosophy has the capacity to alter key understandings of globalization, and therefore practical responses to the latter as well.

Philosophy may be understood in the broad sense, as a worldview or a system of such views, and in the narrow sense of professionalized reflection upon the universals of culture. It is such professional reflection that is necessary to the comprehension of the rapidly-changing culture of today's world. The world we inhabit today is multicultural, and each of us shares, to some degree, the universal values of humanity, while at the same time identifying with particular national or ethnic traditions. In order to address philosophically the contemporary significance of ethnic and national cultures, it will not suffice to distance ourselves by turning culture into an object of our outward reflections, evaluations, and judgments. The philosopher is conscious of being unable to escape the boundaries of traditional culture; still, he or she can discover the limits of her or his own thought. This implies that any professional reflection upon national and ethnic culture must be informed by the tradition of contemplating the universals of humanity. These problems become particularly urgent within the scope of communication, at the boundaries between cultures, states, and ethnically distinct regions. In this way, professional philosophy arrives in places where tradition and intuitive experiencing of the world had previously sufficed, and reigned. This is particularly evident in the sphere of communication.

In Abkhaz culture, the mechanism for solving all social problems is constituted by its distinctive ethical code, the *apsuara*, which prioritizes conscience, family ties, and patriotism. *Apsuara* presupposes a sphere of spirituality, with a contemplative component that "is thought in the ethnic aspect, as relationship with oneself, others, and the natural flow of history."[4] It is on these grounds that professional philosophy can meet and establish a dialogue with traditional Abkhaz wisdom. Such a meeting calls for mutual respect, for the cultivation of a space for conversation, for interpreting universal values into the language of traditional culture and *vice versa*. The translation of key ideas represents the path towards mutual enrichment, for both the cosmopolitan and traditional cultures. What Abkhazia's situation reveals is that a reflective relationship with one's own culture is capable of paving the way towards a given group's survival and continued flourishing in the globalized environment. In today's Abkhazia, a new interest in modern perspectives upon traditional Abkhaz thought as a systematic worldview is evident, and is significant to our discussion. It is this kind of essentially philosophical reference to the traditional Abkhaz thought that assists the Abkhaz in framing globalization not solely as a technological phenomenon, but as a cultural-historic one as well.[5]

When considering the dynamics of intellectual processes taking place in today's Abkhazia, we must note that the Abkhaz intellectual elites are largely aware that philosophical self-consciousness as such is essentially aimed at globality, and suited to the present moment of globalization. This aspect of philosophical self-consciousness is very much foregrounded in global contemporary philosophy as well. Philosophy has always been oriented towards universal values and is universal in its contents. This detail is of principal significance, since the root of philosophical aspiration towards universality is not to be found in the ambitions of hypothetical speculation. It is the experience of concrete, lived historic existence—the experience of maintaining community in all manner of historic circumstances (including the experiences of ethnic groups and nations in preserving their identities), that prove to

---

4 Valery Biguaa, *Апсуара. Структурный метод исследования* [*Apsuara: A Structural Method for Research*] (Sukhum: Proekt, 2009), 8.

5 See: Guram Amkuab, *Средства массовой информации как культурный феномен в контексте глобализации (теоретико-методологический анализ)* [*Mass Media as a Cultural Phenomenon in the Context of Globalization (Theoretical and Methodological Analysis)*] (Moscow: Center for Initiatives in the Humanities, 2016).

be of profound salience to philosophy. These communicative experiences are absorbed into the global humane experience of philosophical thought, itself a global intellectual phenomenon capable of supplying a holistic interpretation of the modern world.

In order to clarify this discussion of the role of philosophy in comprehending globalization as a holistic phenomenon, we think it necessary to make a brief excursus into the history of philosophical thought. The relationship between the regional and the global in philosophy, which we described earlier, did not emerge all at once. Philosophical thought strove towards universality from the outset, endeavoring to develop a language in which the world and humanity could be understood without recourse to outward distinctions and circumstances—in their very essences. Initially, it did not take into account the historic experience and cultural traditions within which its thinkers were creating. Classical philosophy removed itself on principle from such experience. The life experience of the ancient Greeks accumulated and was transmitted from generation to generation by means of a tradition expressed in myth and epic poetry. Philosophy, on the other hand, was characterized by a direct appeal to the universal, in both immediate and mediated communication.

Ancient philosophy was founded upon the Greeks' reflections on genuine existence, spreading beyond the limits of the perceptible. Martin Heidegger thought that the question of being and its solution by Parmenides predetermined the fate of the Western world, for culture thereby received the idea of an intelligible world of absolutes—an eternal, immutable, and self-sufficient source of meanings beyond the scope of the sensible. The attention of ancient philosophy was directed at this eternal world—while everyday life, with its problems and experiences, conditions and norms, which naturally differed widely among the peoples of the vast Mediterranean region, was beyond the scope of its interests. Philosophy instructed on how to live; yet, in order to live up to its imperatives, one had to abstract from the everyday. Medieval philosophy adduced the Bible and patristic writings to its foundations, also enlarging its regional linguistic diversity to include Latin, Byzantine Greek, Arabic, Chinese, and Sanskrit. Nevertheless, the concrete cultural-historical experience of various groups did not enter the philosophical foundations. Biblical texts narrated life situations presented as instances of the eternal truths. Concrete experience entered philosophy only with the twilight of the Middle Ages, when nation-states began to coalesce and national languages started to penetrate the spheres of cultural production and creative intellectual speculation. This took place during the Renaissance, and it is from this time onwards that we are able speak of the English, Scottish, French, German, and other national philosophical traditions. It is also from this time onwards that the question of the relation of national philosophies and philosophy as such takes shape, proving not to be reducible to the Hegelian relation of universals and particulars.

It is only on first glance that the relations of national (and regional) philosophies and philosophy at large (here, conceived as a process of "a different globalization") appear to follow the Hegelian scheme. The philosophical self-consciousness of a nation or an ethnic group is a facet of its identity, developed in the course of that group's real history with all its peculiarities. It preserves the intellectual and cultural traditions recorded in the very language, and embodies the historic experience of the nation, with its reflections upon its destiny, history, and culture in philosophical categories. This engenders a certain set of ideas that may be absorbed into the universal-historic tradition, which generalizes the experience of humanity in its most promising developmental directions. In this, the possibility of communication and mutual influence plays an important role in the way a national philosophy may or may not enter into the cosmopolitan philosophical tradition. In other words, the opportunity to appreciate one's own tradition and one's participation in it, combined with receptiveness to the discoveries of other traditions, forms the core of the cosmopolitan disposition. The main issue that arises at the moment when a national philosophy enters the global philosophical tradition is that of preserving the historic and cultural continuities. While contributing its specificity, a national philosophy must be compatible (even as a critique) with all that constitutes philosophy as a process of developing a common metaphysical language. This necessitates a particular vigilance and receptiveness to views that risk being lost if under-appreciated; that is, the focus on mutual understanding of people belonging to various (and, in particular, differing in the degree of technological availability) traditions.[6]

Having previously invoked Hegel, we might note that Hegel's Germany was not the most developed country in Europe, but it was there that the epoch's philosophical experience was consolidated and expressed. In our view, what this scheme misses is in fact very important for the dynamics of philosophy: that is, its fundamental internal, problematic nature as a cultural phenomenon (that is, as "another globalization," which allows us to see the role of national philosophies in a new perspective). The Russian philosopher Gustav Shpet drew attention to this aspect of the matter, by posing the question:

---

6 "Культурная идентичность малого народа в условиях глобализации. Материалы 'круглого стола'" ["The Cultural Identity of a Small Nation in the Context of Globalization. Materials of the Round Table"], *Voprosy filosofii*, 2015, No. 8, 5–27.

"What *is* a national philosophy?" His own reply was that a national philosophy "depends not on personalities, but upon *problems*, as units and in their coordination."[7] This formula alleviates the difficulty connected with the observation that national philosophies on their way towards merging with the global philosophical tradition have a way of springing up in unexpected places: they often emerge in countries one would think remote from the most intensive transformative activity of their time. A nation may not be the most developed, yet this may be the reason of its subtle alertness to the problems put forward by the dynamic culture of the more advanced regions. In other words, philosophy advances where perspectives of development are presented and understood as the main problems confronting humanity in a given setting.

A national philosophy represents a pursuit of such forms of existence that lend meaning to the lives of concrete individuals. This frames anew the globalization-related problems facing socially underdeveloped regions. Though each epoch presents it in its own way, the problem is forever the same: how to find oneself under the circumstances? In the times of Germany's relative backwardness, finding itself, for Germany, meant definition against the backdrop of the flourishing, exuberant France. German national philosophy solved this problem (with Hegel as one of its pinnacles). Today, philosophical reflection upon globalization processes remains important. This is made evident by the case of Abkhazia and its challenge of preserving a unique identity with the aid of self-reflection. Twentieth-century European philosophers have long perceived that only those ethnic groups that are capable of adopting a reflective stance towards their own cultural origins shall be able to persist in the face of globalization. Jacques Derrida, when considering the problem of hospitality (one of the key principles of traditional societies), advanced the thesis that each people has a right to a philosophy. According to Derrida, philosophy is a phenomenon characterized by antinomies. On the one hand, its roots fathom the depths of a long tradition. (If we were to discuss an indigenous Abkhaz philosophy, its roots would find its substrate in Abkhaz epic poetry, literature, and other native forms of cultural expression.) On the other hand, philosophy appeals to the absolute and the universal—and it is this appeal that affords the opportunity, for the Abkhaz people in this case, to experience oneself as an element at once alien to the globalized world and inscribed into its dynamics.

In the world transformed by globalization, each of us is a foreigner, with respect to both our own culture and also to the culture arriving from abroad.

---

7 Gustav Shpet, *Очерк развития русской философии* [*An Essay on the Development of Russian Philosophy*], ed. Tatiana Shchedrina (Moscow: RossPEn, 2009), 24.

This is felt most keenly by the culture's creators, by the intelligentsia of traditional societies. They must bear in mind this important point, so as to resist the negative trends of globalization and to appreciate the value of its "benefits." They are, after all, at the forefront of adapting new media and technology to the ends of cultural preservation and enrichment, and are charged with responsibility for the new forms of life which they introduce into the life of their own ethnic group. The life of Jacques Derrida is particularly germane to our discussion, since his existential experience revealed to him all the alienation of a culture within which he was born and raised. Here is how Natalia Avtonomova describes his experience. "Derrida was born in a Jewish family in the town of El Biar, in Algeria"; "the desire to speak publicly, in the powerful, brilliant, at once native and alien French tongue, guided the young Derrida in his search of himself."

> He became the philosopher who was able, more than any other, to test new forms of philosophy's existence, to demonstrate, with the aid of a vast body of cultural evidence, the significance of the matter that is language for the construction of philosophical thought. At the heart of his existential and speculative process was the paradox of experiencing language as both *mine* and *not mine*. What he called his only language—the French—was not his language, but an external norm, of which an interiority could be built up, yet deprived of something that constitutes the specificity of a "mother tongue" (denoted in French by the adjective *maternelle*). He grew up deprived of the French of the lullabies and folk ballads, the language in which mothers and wet-nurses had sung to children, comforting and lulling them to sleep at night—the language that can serve as a refuge in anxiety.[8]

The French language had been alien to him from the start. "This is the source," Avtonomova continues,

> of his entire history of refashioning himself. In this, he was adamant: either command the language flawlessly, erasing every remnant of provincialism, or leave the sphere of public expression once and for all. This required work on voice and intonation, gave rise to the fear of giving himself away with his southern accent, and turned vigilance into a vital

---

8 Natalia Avtonomova, *Философский язык Жака Деррида* [*The Philosophical Language of Jacques Derrida*] (Moscow: RossPEn, 2011), 36.

reflex. Inevitably, this became the impetus for seeking asylum in *writing*, where he would not be exposed and denounced: the written text could not be in the "Algerian French."⁹

Engaging the French as inherently foreign allowed Derrida to appreciate its value and singular character. In the same manner, the question of the true foundations of human existence and human norms takes on an ethnic inflection when figuring against the background of diversity. This, in turn, accentuates some aspects of philosophy as a metaphysical construction. The problem of human identity and self-consciousness, and the preservation of the Self, are the present day's unignorable motifs, made all the more so in the era of technological globalization. The experience of ethnic identity matters to the intellectual conversation about the world, humanity, and the meaning of life, which must include questions aimed at the real diversity of concrete social forms of human existence.

Globalization is experienced as a problem of identity loss. Against this backdrop, when faced with the complex and contradictory situation that raises the question of survival in a rapidly changing world, members of ethnic minorities have good grounds for experiencing the process as a possible crisis of identity, and as a fading of the group's distinctive energies and genetic memory. What is felt is the loss of the very qualities and characteristics that once defined the group's particular spirit, mentality, and way of life. If the resulting pursuit of new ways of preserving the increasingly elusive distinctiveness is marked by an appeal to philosophical universality, it is because regional experience itself infuses the global current of philosophy, such as preserving the human identity. That latter experience of preserving an identity in the context of life's various conflicting aspects, is a key moment of philosophical self-reflection— of rational reflection upon the self in the context of reality and of practical problems, many of which are now becoming global in nature. The experience of preserving oneself (and one's selfhood) presupposes consciousness and places new demands on forms of conscious self-preservation, such as literature, language, and philosophy. This conscious element represents a new feature of globalization, apparent against the backdrop of intercultural exchange. By immersing themselves in it, the intellectual elites of minority ethnic groups once again plunge into the "archives" of group consciousness, in order to rediscover the threads that bind ethnic identity and the historical tradition.

When are we most reflective in relation to cultural values? When they are not our own. This is why European philosophers suggest that we treat our

---

9 Avtonomova, *Философский язык Жака Деррида*, 37.

own cultural experience as if it were someone else's. We think that Abkhaz philosophers and scholars of humanities must also consider their own cultural traditions as if they were someone else's experience, in order to address them with reflective detachment. It is necessary to express the spiritual foundations of Abkhaz culture in a modern language. This entails a necessity of isolating the philosophical concepts and terms in which Abkhaz philosophy can address the problems of contemporary Abkhaz society. It is this requirement that we consider the most important for Abkhaz culture and its capacity for self-reflection, and positive examples of such developments already exist.

One such instance is presented by the work of Vitaly Reshevich Bganba, author of *The Fundamentals of Abkhaz Philosophy*—a book which endeavors to translate into Russian philosophical language the entire complex of Abkhaz contemplative experience, presenting Bganba's native culture as a philosophically informed one, with its own religious and ethical foundations, and capable of developing a philosophical conceptual apparatus to address contemporary social problems. "In pursuit of a path towards developing an Abkhaz identity," he writes,

> theorists, scholars, and thinkers of Abkhazia resort increasingly to the long-forgotten historiosophic concepts and theories. The necessity for such a recourse to the past is attributable to the fact that Abkhazia does not yet possess a national idea commensurate with the current social realities and processes, and if such an idea does exist, it is only in the form of a spiritual and political predisposition towards its emergence.[10]

In the experience of Abkhaz philosophers, who are now turning to the roots of the Abkhaz worldview, the chief difficulty is that of translation and of linguistic and cultural exchange. As today's Abkhaz philosophy speaks in the Abkhaz language, it should first of all endeavor to translate its basic concepts— *apsuara* ("Abkhazness"), *auyura* (compassion), *acheidjika* (generosity), *alamys* (conscience), *asasdkylara* (hospitality)—into the language of Russian or European philosophy, and vice versa. In this way, it can self-reflexively enrich itself while enriching the universal experience of philosophy, to which we all share an equal right.

In order to accomplish this, it is necessary to turn to the essentially positive cultural and historic foundations of public life. What we are learning now,

---

[10]   Vitaly Bganba, *Основания абхазской философии (краткий очерк)* [*Fundamentals of Abkhaz Philosophy (A Brief Sketch)*] (Sukhum: Abkhaz Academy of Sciences, 2005).

in conversation with the Abkhaz intelligentsia, suggests that the development of a national language can supply a consolidating impulse for the Abkhaz. It matters, too, that culture in its socially organizing function appears upon an earlier fundamental substrate of meanings, whose emergence was compared by Cicero to the product of agricultural cultivation, though what he meant was the cultivation of the soul. In this manner, the Abkhaz poet Dmitry Gulia engaged in building this soil, with his work on the Abkhaz language. As philologist, author, and intellectual, he succeeded in creating something of lasting significance for the flourishing of his people. This work of cultivation, of tending to the language, has now been duly acknowledged and appreciated by his own people. The continuation of Gulia's work, the emergence of research centers, the ongoing scholarship in the humanities and philosophy all represent, in our view, that intellectual and educational effort which is so crucial to Abkhaz intelligentsia in the consolidation of the Abkhaz identity under the conditions of globalization.

In reflecting upon its native culture, Abkhaz philosophy relies on modern linguistic practices. In the framework of a return to folk traditions and to the native Abkhaz philosophy, globalization can be considered a cultural phenomenon. The contemporary Abkhaz intelligentsia are searching for a new perspective informed by their ethnic identity—and the Abkhaz tradition can assist them in this search. The experiences of traditional community gatherings, of song and storytelling, of oral communication and the responsibility involved in transmitting cultural experience, all matter here. This experience of traditional Abkhaz culture needs to be appreciated concurrently with Abkhaz philosophy, which urgently calls for contemporary realization and expression in its native—yet modern—Abkhaz tongue.

It is apparent that the question of identity makes germane the question of national philosophies, and it does so not solely in terms of regional specificity and uniqueness expressive of an anti-globalist attitude. The theme of national philosophies emerges as a generalization of the experience of formation and preservation of regional identities under various historic conditions. That our theme appears under such an aspect is due to the accentuation of the role of philosophy and its specificity as a type of intellectual activity. This implies the centrality of *communication* and *conversation*, in the course of which local particulars may attain universal significance without being absorbed or dissolved in it. Today, this is vividly demonstrated by philosophical congresses, where professional communication among philosophers plays an important role, paving the way to mutual understanding among national and ethnic schools of philosophy.[11] (This, once again, accentuates the relevance of translation and, more generally, of linguistic work among philosophers.) Globalization, meanwhile, opens up new avenues of communication, not by means of standardization but, on the contrary, by taking stock of unique particulars. Here, too, it is appropriate to speak of "a different globalization," since here we see the processes of globalization yielding new opportunities for intercultural dialogue, which does not preclude the preservation and development of ethno-cultural specificities. Of particular relevance today is the identification and accentuation of essentially global cultural processes combining the impulse towards a common body of meaning with receptiveness to diversity. These are the processes that we have chosen to denote by our term "a different globalization," whose effects are so evident in contemporary philosophical culture, with its altered problematics and contents.

To this end, we must immerse ourselves in "the archives," in order to rediscover the threads that bind us to historic tradition. In today's socio-political system, the intelligentsia—thanks to its fundamental historical, philological, and philosophical work—is creating a stable foundation for cultural independence among the regions brought into close contact by the forces of globalization. Against this background, the 2,500 years of philosophical culture as a positive experience of "a different globalization" present evident advantages, though studies in globalism have not engaged with this side of the story. It is precisely the development of philosophical culture from its traditional roots that contributes today to ethnic self-determination and to the formation of universally meaningful elements of minority languages in an era of technological globalization.

Philosophy thereby opens new opportunities within the scope of globalization—prospects of "a different globalization." Philosophy lifts the rigid and futile opposition between globalization and anti-globalism, inviting a reconsideration (a rational re-visiting) of the experience of human identity and its preservation at all levels, with the concomitant enrichment of the universal. We have found it necessary to emphasize this circumstance, obvious in our own opinion. First of all, this is because not only in the popular media, but even in technical discussions, what is understood by "analysis" of globalization frequently proves to be analysis in the etymological sense—or conceptual dismemberment which leaves the living reality behind. Meanwhile, it is the integrity of multifaceted globalization processes that determines both their real course and the specificity of their consequences. Philosophy, in this

---

11 Pruzhinin and Shchedrina, "The International Congress of Philosophy," 33–39.

respect, represents a conceptual toolkit that permits us to become conscious of this state of affairs, and to transform it into a methodological prerequisite for further analysis of globalization—and for its effective practical implementation.

The Age of Competing Globalizations

Vladislav L. Inozemtsev

It seems an obvious statement that we live in a globalized world. The very term "globalized" presupposes that a certain process, called "globalization," is affecting all nations and peoples in an equal or nearly equal measure. Globalization, as Manfred Steger says, is "a multidimensional set of social processes that create, multiply, and intensify worldwide social interdependencies and exchanges," and is therefore a trend that continues to evolve as different nations and communities participate in it, presumably on equal terms.[1] *Globalization*, I would argue, should not be confused with *westernization*: the former refers to a process whose participants are sovereign actors, while the latter invokes the transformation of the world by the culture commonly referred to as "the West."[2] It would not be an exaggeration to say that the term "westernization" can be used interchangeably with "europeanization."[3] (As Fernand Braudel once put it, "europeanization" itself addresses the process of turning "économie du monde européen" into "économie-monde européenne.")[4]

The twentieth century has been by far the most dramatic in human history, partly because it was a time in which westernization was gradually replaced by globalization. I do not fully agree with Eric Hobsbawm, who divided modernity into periods of empire-building and those defined by "extremes."[5] Rather, the most notable periods of the past two centuries are those marked by moments of transition from a westernized to a globalized world—a process that, I would argue, is far from over. At least four such periods should be mentioned in order to explain how we arrived at the current situation.

---

1   Manfred Steger, *Globalization: A Very Short Introduction* (Oxford: Oxford University Press, 2003), 13.
2   On the origins of the term, see: Roger Scruton, *The West and the Rest: Globalization and the Terrorist Threat* (New York: Continuum, 2002), 7–11.
3   See: Theodore von Laue, *The World Revolution of Westernization: The Twentieth Century in Global Perspective* (Oxford: Oxford University Press, 1987); John Headley, *The Europeanization of the World: On the Origins of Human Rights and Democracy* (Princeton: Princeton University Press, 2008).
4   Fernand Braudel, *Civilisation matérielle, économie et capitalisme, XV–XVIII siècle*, v. 3 (Paris: Armand Colin, 1979), 12–14.
5   The following books by Eric Hobsbawm are representative: *The Age of Empire 1875–1914* (London: Abacus, 1996); *The Age of Extremes 1914–1991* (London: Abacus, 1996); *On the Edge of the New Century*, co-authored with Antonio Polito (New York: The New Press, 2000).

The first of these might be referred to as a period of "true westernization." It began around the 1830s, when European powers resumed their attempts to conquer the world, after their empires had been dismantled by the American War of Independence and by the creation of sovereign states in South America. At that time, the European powers, as well as both the United States (as a European "offshoot" in North America) and Russia (as another European "outskirt") all sought to expand into lands and territories seen as "inferior" to the West.[6] Europeans scrambled for parts of Africa and South Asia; Americans exterminated Indians as they advanced westward, towards the Pacific coast; Russians conquered the Northern Caucasus and Central Asia; and all these powers united during an expedition into China that culminated in the capture and looting of the Forbidden City in August 1900.[7] By the start of the twentieth century, the world that had, as of the late 1820s, consisted almost entirely of independent states or quasi-state entities, was partitioned between the western powers. Quite soon, those powers would face each other in an unparalleled military conflict, immediately named the Great War, which led to the collapse of several great (but also greatly outmoded) empires—Austrian, Ottoman, Russian, and Chinese.

The next period was the most dramatic and complicated in human history. On the one hand, it was marked by a clash of ideologies. In 1917, Communists took power in Russia, and embarked on rebuilding its former empire under the name of the Soviet Union.[8] Fascists, meanwhile, emerged as a leading force in Italy and Spain, followed by the Nazis in Germany. The free world found itself in such trouble that only a conflict between two totalitarian ideologies, both of which had sprung up early in the 1940s, could bring down Fascism in Europe. But the victory of 1945 did not put an end to struggle. The Communists proceeded to install pro-Soviet regimes in many parts of the world, and only the economic demise of the Soviet Union, hastened by Michael Gorbachev's "new thinking," brought the Cold War to an end. I would propose that this period, which started in 1917 and ended in 1989, might also be seen as an instance of westernization. Even as the world came to be divided into two competing blocks, both of those blocks included "natural leaders," who

---

6 Here, "offshoot" is derived from: Angus Maddison, *The World Economy: A Millennial Perspective* (Paris: OECD Publications Service, 2001), 9–11. See, for greater detail on Russia as a European "outskirt": Vladislav Inozemtsev, "Europe as the 'Center' and Its 'Outskirts,'" *Russia in Global Affairs*, 2007(5), No. 1, 148–66.

7 See: Peter Fleming, *The Siege at Peking: The Boxer Rebellion* (New York: Dorset, 1992), 184–89.

8 See: Alexander Abalov and Vladislav Inozemtsev, Бесконечная империя: Россия в поисках себя [*An Endless Empire: Russia In Search of Itself*] (Moscow: Alpina, 2021), 216–272.

projected their particular ideologies, social orders, and production techniques over the parts of the world within their influence. The distinction between the "agents" and their "subjects" was just as obvious here as before. I call this the phase of "competing westernizations." It was, in fact, so brutal and dramatic that the British-American historian Niall Ferguson refers to it as a prolonged "War of the World."[9]

The third period started in the late 1980s and signaled the arrival of globalization in the proper sense of the word—expressed by Francis Fukuyama's phrase "the end of history."[10] The most dramatic change that occurred during that time was the recognition of equal sovereignty among countries within the global community. Democracy and human rights were declared universal values, no longer believed to be possible when installed from abroad. (The humanitarian operations of the 1990s and at the turn of the millennium did not succeed in dispelling this sentiment.) The global economy became more competitive than ever, with new superpowers like China emerging in just a couple of decades.[11] Countering the era of westernization, the new period of globalization altered the direction of commercial investment, and even the flow of migration, uniting the world economically and culturally in a more intensive way than ever seen during the Cold War or in the period of "true westernization." The most striking feature of the new global world was the disappearance of anything that might be thought of as a "periphery," as the First World established itself around the globe, from London to Shenzhen, from Moscow to São Paulo, and from Los Angeles to Dubai. History "ended," in a purely economic sense—but, with the progress of globalization, it became clear that in the field of political competition it went on nevertheless.[12]

I would propose that presently, in the early 2020s, we have finally arrived at the dawn of a new age. This age is in some ways comparable to the 1990s, and to the relation of the "competitive" and the "true" modes of westernization. The world we inhabit—I shall borrow a phrase from Will Hutton's well-known book—looks above all else like a world of "competitive globalizations" led by several nations that, for various reasons, enjoy a kind of global reach.[13] There

---

9   See: Niall Ferguson, *The War of the World: Twentieth-Century Conflict and the Descent of the West* (New York: Penguin, 2006).
10 Francis Fukuyama, "The End of History," *National Interest*, 1989, No. 16, 3–18.
11 See: Zhang Weiwei, *The China Horizon: Glory and Dream of a Civilizational State* (Beijing: World Century, 2016).
12 See: Robert Kagan, *The Return of History and the End of Dreams* (New York: Knopf, 2008); Edward Luttwak, *The Rise of China vs. the Logic of Strategy* (Cambridge, MA: Belknap, 2012).
13 See: Will Hutton, *The World We're In* (London: Little, Brown, 2002).

are many different versions of this disjunction: some say that the dividing line lies between the democratic and liberal worlds led by the United States and China; others believe that we are witnessing a disjunction between the "postmodern polities" of Europe and the modern states (such as the United States, Russia, and China) and the "pre-modern" rest of the world.[14] Some scholars speak of "three empires"—European, American and Chinese—and of the "second World," which seeks to find a place for itself between those giants.[15] But almost everyone agrees that "history is back."[16] I will not dive deeper into what distinctions might be more germane than others, as we more crucial issues to resolve, for we need to uncover what is behind the new global division, how deep run the differences, and in what direction the world is more likely to evolve from here. In order to do this, we should take a moment to assess the age of "competing westernizations," observing both the common grounds upon which both models of society are based, and the main differences that set them apart.

On the one hand, both centers of "competing westernizations" shared common industrial and economic foundations. The European colonial powers arose as undisputed centers of the industrial world. Later, they were surpassed by the United States as the greatest "workshop" on the globe. Both the early Soviet Union and the totalitarian powers of continental Europe—Italy and Germany—appeared as corporate industrial states in the 1920s and 1930s. Later, the United States and the USSR positioned themselves as industrial superpowers, while the 1980s Japan proudly proclaimed itself "the ultimate industrial society."[17] The distinguished French social philosopher Raymond Aron famously observed, back in late 1950s, that Europe was not so much split between two profoundly different worlds, the Soviet world and the West, as constituted by a single, if not wholly homogeneous, reality of the industrial civilization.[18] He appears to have been correct. Moreover, both models took for granted the superiority of the old civilizational centers, as they either championed colonial and neo-colonial policies or restored the former empires

---

14 Robert Cooper, *The Breaking of Nations: Order and Chaos in the Twenty-First Century* (London: Atlantic Books, 2003), 7–9.
15 Parag Khanna, *The Second World: Empires and Influence in the New Global Order* (London: Allen Lane, 2008), xiv–xxiii.
16 Daniel Bell, *The End of Ideology: On the Exhaustion of Political Ideas in the Fifties* (Cambridge, MA: Harvard University Press, 2000), xi–xxviii.
17 Taichi Sakaiya, *What is Japan? Contradictions and Transformations* (New York: Kodansha International, 1995), 233.
18 Raymond Aron, *Eighteen Lectures on Industrial Society* (London: Weidenfeld & Nicholson, 1968), 42.

under the guise of "aiding" their colonies and dependents.[19] (Arguably, the dissolution of both the European empires and the Soviet Union resulted in a rapid drop in the economic performance of their former colonies, compared to that of metropoles.) The age of "competing westernizations" was the natural continuation of "true westernization," the one major difference being that the industrial paradigm now merged with, and was employed by, different ideological doctrines.

This ideological indoctrination determined both the political differences between the systems and their relationships with one another. Internally, the societies governed by the two ideologies were differently organized, one system extolling individual freedom and free-market capitalism, the other opting for strict regulation, supposed to result in economic efficiency. Outwardly, both powers, in one way or another, imposed their agendas onto their allies and projected their power towards different parts of the globe. Military alliances and frameworks of economic cooperation cemented the division between the two and created strong political and economic "guidelines" for nations under their leadership (e.g., the Brezhnev-era doctrine of "limited sovereignty"). Both "the West" and "the East" appeared to be internally unified, so that a barrier ultimately rose between them, as foreseen by Winston Churchill in his "Iron Curtain Speech." Thus, "competing westernizations" developed each in its "own" part of the world, introducing different social and technological patterns to the two parts of the divided Europe. This was so important that it downgraded any internal inconsistencies within the competing blocs that surfaced as the Cold War came to an end. (As noted by Dominique Moisi, after 1989, "a single West and two Europes" were replaced by "a united Europe and two Wests.")[20] What is important here is that the competition between the two models of westernization ended in the collapse of the one that proved less economically efficient and unable to adjust to emerging post-industrial trends.

When turning to the forthcoming era of "competing globalizations," we are confronted with a substantially different picture. The economic divergence greatly exceeds that which existed before. One part of the world is greatly de-industrialized,[21] but champions technological innovation and controls two

---

19 Alexander Abalov and Vladislav Inozemtsev, "Russia: The Everlasting Empire," *The Israel Journal of Foreign Affairs*, 2019(13), No. 3, 329–38.

20 Dominique Moisi, "Reinventing the West", *Foreign Affairs*, 2003(82), No. 6, 70.

21 See: Edward Luttwak, *The Endangered American Dream: How to Stop the United States from Becoming a Third-World Country and How to Win the Geo-Economic Struggle for Industrial Supremacy* (New York: Touchstone, 1993).

crucial elements of contemporary economic power. On the one hand, it is an obvious leader in high-tech innovation, also setting the standards for the developing "network economy." On the other hand, it has created a completely new financial system, which allows it to control the global financial flows and to dig itself out of almost any financial crisis. (No country, other than the United States or the European Union, has the ability to "print" more money in three months than China had amassed in its foreign exchange reserves during the last twenty years, without negative effects for its own economy.) The leading countries (the United States, the European Union, the United Kingdom, and Japan) appear absolutely superior to the rest of the world, which remains engaged mostly in secondary, or even primary, economic activity (i.e., industrial or commodity economy).

At the same time, as economic paths seem to diverge, societal trends evolve in the opposite way. In almost all modern nations, whether they are "free" or "not free," a large number of economic freedoms and opportunities are guaranteed, different political parties are allowed to exist, and people enjoy significant personal liberties.[22] Moreover, there is no longer any such strong guidance from competing powers that their allies would not be able to resist. For instance, the post-Soviet states, though seemingly dependent upon Russia, are able turn their backs on it, just as neither American nor Chinese power can be fully projected upon the nations taken to be their nominal allies. The global system appears much more flexible and versatile than it was just a half of a century ago, when the barriers between the new centers were almost completely demolished. (The trade turnover between the most adverse powers, the United States and China, reached $606 billion on average for the last five years, with more than 700,000 Chinese citizens residing in the United States.[23] To compare this situation to the Cold War is to feel a very real difference.)[24] And so, globalization certainly continues—but the global leaders' paths may begin to diverge.

The age of "competing globalizations" is now fueled by several trends that took hold, I think, in the last ten years, even though they have been evolving for some time. The "true globalization" of 1989–2007 was caused by unparalleled technological advances, the lifting of trade barriers, the decreasing cost

---

22 Vladislav Inozemtsev, "Russie, une société libre sous contrôle authoritaire," *Le Monde diplomatique*, 2010, No. 10, 4–5.
23 "Trade in Goods with China," US Census Bureau, https://www.census.gov/foreign-trade/balance/c5700.html.
24 "USCIS Long-Term Visa Statistics for 2019," US Department of State, https://travel.state.gov/content/dam/visas/Statistics/Non-Immigrant-Statistics/NIVDetailTables/FY19NIVDetailTable.pdf.

of transportation and the spread of the human-rights doctrine and multiculturalist ideas. As a result, the flow of trade became more equally distributed throughout the world; the wellbeing of both industrial and commodity economies went up, as a result of the "flying geese" growth scheme, as additional demand for end-consumer goods from the United States and Europe propelled Asian industrial development, which, in due course, contributed to a hike in resource and energy prices. The formerly "peripheral" countries like China and India turned into the primary source of economic growth, while western nations appeared to be the most indebted, as China's foreign exchange reserves topped $4 trillion in 2014.[25] Even though China did not catch up with the United States in terms of per capita income (actually, the 2019 gap was roughly three times wider than it was in 2000—$10,300 in current US dollars, compared to $960 in 2019, as compared to $65,100 to $36,300 in 2000), it successfully emerged, in 2009, as the world's largest exporter of goods and, in 2014, as the world's largest economy in terms of GDP purchasing power parity.[26] In its new status, China began to be viewed as a challenge, if not as a threat, by the United States, and both nations slipped into a full-scale trade war in 2017. Arguably, from this time on, the world has been living in an age of "competing globalizations."

Many used to describe our "new reality" as a showdown between diverging political and ideological systems, a reality that elicits telling parallels with the previous century. I disagree with this vision. However large the differences may seem, one should bear in mind that we overlook the fact that the world has been globalizing, but not westernizing. Today's major powers have no drive to transform the world according to their model, nor to claim the entire globe as "their own"; instead, they are trying to seduce the rest of the world into accommodating their interests, while responding to the needs of their partners. Today, no one believes that the world, or even significant parts of it, can be managed from a single point. The global "periphery"—and every great power has its own definition for that word—is used as a source of additional wealth, as a market for goods, as a part of the global network of clients and customers. Political goals can be achieved by purely economic means, and with greater success than in any previous era. For instance, the so-called "Third Colonialism" extracts up to one trillion dollars annually from the poorer

---

25 "China Foreign Exchange Reserves," Trading Economics, https://tradingeconomics.com/china/foreign-exchange-reserves.
26 World Bank Open Data, https://data.worldbank.org/indicator/NY.GDP.PCAP.CD?locations=CN (indicator no longer available) and https://data.worldbank.org/indicator/NY.GDP.PCAP.CD?locations=US.

nations, redirecting these funds towards the leading financial centers, practically without political pressure.[27] Both ideological and political goals may be involved here, but gone are the times when these could supersede the economic goals. Arguably, the coming age of "competing globalizations" is likely to be a peaceful age—but the competition will be fierce, and long.

What are, then, the main "assets" of both parties that they hope will allow them to prevail over their opponents? The developed world (to which I shall refer to as "the North," since all of its major members, except Russia, spread up to the latitude 33° north) is now engaged in a "New Economy," based on several major pillars.[28] Technologically, it relies on the production of goods—those being either "goods of status" or "goods of belonging." (The first kind highlight an individual's position in the social hierarchy, like the high-end luxury goods and other elements of prestigious consumption. The latter can be reproduced for an insignificant fraction of the development costs, so that one can buy copies instead of the original product—these include computer operation systems, microchips, and medical drugs.)[29] Many of the world's richest people, such as Bernard Arnault of LVMH or Microsoft's Bill Gates, now own corporations that produce such goods. These corporations create all the newest devices that will later dominate the world, just as Apple or Tesla do. The nations of the global North adhere to the rule of law, a principle that makes life there predictable and secure, and which ensures an ever-growing quality of life, the most attractive factor for millions of aliens who flock to the North every year. Being increasingly attractive, the North expands its influence through the information networks, which unite more people than ever before in almost all countries in the world, the majority of such customers residing outside the nations where these networks were launched.

Last but not least, the North enjoys overwhelming financial power, as its members use all the most traded and valued global currencies (the US dollar, the Euro, the Japanese yen, the British pound, and the Swiss franc nowadays account for 86.2% of central banks' foreign exchange reserves.)[30] As the 2020 pandemic crisis has shown, these nations are able to issue more money in

---

27   Wladislaw Inosemzew and Alexander Lebedew, "Der Dritte Kolonialismus," *Le Monde Diplomatique Deutschland*, November 2016, 3.
28   Vladislav Inozemtsev, "Russia and America Can Reset Relations by Looking North," *Financial Times*, October 9, 2017, 9.
29   Vladislav Inozemtsev, *The Constitution of the Post-Economic State: Post-Industrial Theories and Post-Economic Trends in the Contemporary World* (London: Ashgate, 1998), 213–44.
30   "Currency Composition of Official Foreign Exchange," International Monetary Fund, https://data.imf.org/?sk=E6A5F467-C14B-4AA8-9F6D-5A09EC4E62A4.

a matter of weeks than the rest of the world has accumulated in decades—making their economies stronger than they were at the start of the emergency. All these features—the power of brands, the selling of copies, and control of the financial system—makes the North a source of what Paul Pilzer called the "unlimited wealth," which secures the North's global predominance.[31]

The North's opponent, the developing world, which I shall call "the South," was built upon very different grounds. It emerged in its modern sense as an industrial appendage to the North, and turned into the most important pole of economic growth as the North itself began to de-industrialize.[32] During the age of the "true globalization," the South became North's "Other," as the North capitalized on the South's industrial renaissance and its development into the most promising partner for resource-based economies. As the trajectories of the main centers of global power begin to diverge, China (the South's natural leader) capitalizes mainly off its state-of-the-art industrial production, and supplies the world with hardware, while the North bets on the network economy. In a world where billions of people live in need, cheap and reliable goods might be of great, if not the greatest, importance. Betting on the "globalization of the poor," China may lead an alternative model that emphasizes not liberties, freedoms, and innovation, but instead efficiency, control, and mobilization. The rapid development that China enjoyed during the last forty years, might be highly seductive to the greater part of the world, which does not belong to the "golden billion." The South will need to create its own infrastructure of alternative globalization, with its own operation system and microchip production, and to develop new global communication tools and social networks. (Even today, Chinese social networks are used mostly by the Chinese at home, with limited reach overseas.)[33] In other words, if the famous (thanks to Niall Ferguson) "Chi-merica" connection loosens, China may well become the leader of the alternative global project, gaining a great many loyal supporters,

---

31   See: Paul Pilzer, *Unlimited Wealth: The Theory and Practice of Economic Alchemy* (New York: Crown Business, 1990).

32   Vladislav Inozemtsev, *Les leurres de l'économie de rattrapage. Le fracture postindustrielle* (Paris: L'Harmattan, 2001), 18–23.

33   Among the ten most popular social networks US-based Facebook, YouTube, WhatsApp and Instagram account for 8.12 billion users, while the Chinese or Chinese-oriented QQ, Douyin and Sina Weibo only have 1.67 billion. (As of December 2020.) "Most Popular Social Networks Worldwide," Statista, https://www.statista.com/statistics/272014/global-social-networks-ranked-by-number-of-users/.

not only because of its "anti-American" nature, but also because their model suits the poorer regions of the world better than the US model does.[34]

Still, I would say that any decoupling—be it caused by China's aspirations or by the American will to "put China in its place"—will become very costly. As of 2019, more than half of all desktops and notebook computers in the world were produced in China, yet it can furnish fewer than one-third of this number with locally made microchips, remaining highly dependent on imports, and up to 60% of all global manufacture rely on Intel microchips.[35] In server processors, Intel dominance is even more pronounced, at 98%.[36] Both Intel and AMD lead a new generation of chip development. The mass manufacturing of devices has been relocated to Asia, where many companies, like SK Hynix of South Korea or TSMC and UMC of Taiwan, position themselves as competitors of American firms, while depending on them for the most vital technologies used in production. In 2018, more than 65% of all smartphones produced in the world were manufactured in China, with 78% built by "real" Chinese brands, such as Huawei, Xiaomi, OPPO, and Vivo[37]—but, of these, 97.98% run either on Windows, Android, or IOS.[38] (If all the computers and computer-like devices are to be counted, the combined share of Microsoft, Google, and Apple software comes to an impressive 95.93%.)[39] Where the market for search engines is concerned, Google alone controls 92.82% of the market, compared to 1.02% held by Baidu, China's most popular search engine, and to a mere 0.54% controlled by Yandex, which claims to be the Russian high-tech sector's undisputed leader.[40] The Chinese sit on a huge stockpile of American securities. (As of November 1, 2020, both mainland China and Hong

---

34 Niall Ferguson, "The Trillion Dollar Question: China or America," *The Telegraph*, June 1, 2009, https://www.telegraph.co.uk/comment/5424112/The-trillion-dollar-question-China-or-America.html.

35 Max Smolaks, "China responsible for just, oh, 20% of global semiconductor revenue in 2018, no biggie," *The Register*, https://www.theregister.co.uk/2019/04/10/china_sold_almost_100_billion_worth_of_semiconductors_in_2018/.

36 "Аналитики определили долю Intel на рынке серверных процессоров" ["Experts Established Intel's Share of Server Processors Market"], iXBT, https://www.ixbt.com/news/2018/11/30/analitiki-opredelili-dolju-intel-na-rynke-servernyh-processorov.html.

37 "Global Smartphone Production by Volume," TrendForce, https://press.trendforce.com/node/view/3200.html (page no longer available).

38 As of April 2019. "Mobile Operating System Market Share Worldwide," StatCounter Global Stats, http://gs.statcounter.com/os-market-share/mobile/worldwide.

39 As of April 2019. "Operating System Market Share Worldwide," StatCounter Global Stats, http://gs.statcounter.com/os-market-share.

40 For the period from April 2018 to April 2019. "Browser Market Share Worldwide," StatCounter Global Stats, http://gs.statcounter.com/search-engines-market-share.

Kong held around $1.28 trillion in US Treasury securities[41]—but, if they try to sell them off, no "financial tsunami" will arise, since US banks can easily buy them out and get loans from the Federal Reserve using Treasury securities as a perfect collateral: one might remember that in the wake of the current "corona-crisis" the Federal Reserve's balance sheet grew by $2.1 trillion in several weeks.[42] This can well be repeated at any time in the future, should China wish to engage in a full-scale financial confrontation.)

Such a development—which is quite probable in the coming decades—will not be as dangerous for the world as many experts and policymakers currently believe. To look back upon the history of the world is to realize that the greatest military conflicts to challenge human history developed either before the advent of the "true westernization" or during its peak. The Second World War itself was but a single episode of a protracted global conflict that unfolded during the period of "competing westernizations," with the real competition arising during the Cold War. I would argue that a global military conflict in the age of "competing globalizations" is even more unlikely than it had been during the times of "competing westernizations." On the one hand, the leaders of both camps will be in command of nuclear arsenals and other weapon stockpiles that can easily destroy the entire world without securing any real military victory. A global conflict would therefore be counterproductive. On the other hand, since the foundations of both alliances are bound to be mainly economic in nature, they will not be united by any one ideology. The main reason for an alliance would be to ensure development instead of destruction. I doubt that "competing globalizations" will need as strong alliances as those in the age of "competing westernizations," and for this reason I maintain that the new epoch will be generally peaceful.

Admittedly, even under such circumstances, everyone wants to ask the major question: who can prevail (if not win outright) in a showdown? I would propose that, sooner or later, the West will secure its success—for the same reasons as during the time of "competing westernizations." Economic cooperation and development will eventually improve the standard of living in all the countries involved, since in today's world only autarchy and self-reliance can stop economic growth. As nations develop, the quest for freedom will increase and the importance of pure efficiency will decline. The concept of sovereignty that is now nurtured by many non-Western governments across the world will

---

41 "Major Foreign Holders of Treasury Securities," US Treasury, https://ticdata.treasury.gov/Publish/mfh.txt.

42 US Federal Reserve data: https://fred.stlouisfed.org/series/WALCL.

prevent any kind of unified political structure, or even a deeply integrated community, from emerging in the China-led part of the world. Therefore, the border between two globalizing parts of the world will remain porous and transparent. Further, I would say that the increasing intensity of the flow of information will dramatically change the impact that propaganda has on people. The alternative globalization in this case may have a positive effect on global development, as it brings peripheral nations into the modern economy, resembling the way in which the Soviet Union acted fifty years earlier, but doing it much more efficiently. The end result will nevertheless be the same: both systems will merge, launching another stage of the "end of history," this time even more deserving of its name than the period that began in the late 1980s.

No one knows how stable the system of "competing globalizations" might become, but what looks quite probable is that it will cause a lot of challenges for the nations that might be called "in-betweens": those that do not have the economic capabilities to be involved in any of the blocs as trend-setters. I am talking first of all about those nations relying on commodity economies and possessing no developed technological or industrial sectors.

In conclusion, I would like to summarize my argument with the following key points. The events of the first decades of the twenty-first century suggest that the condition we called "globalization," which developed after the end of the Cold War, led to a dramatic new development that retains its many crucial features, but also differs in several major aspects. As the economic and political tensions between the two major global powers (i.e., the United States and China) worsen, globalization loses its all-embracing nature and comes to be, in one sense or another, oriented towards one of the leading global players. This orientation remains partial and limited, since it is reflected predominantly in the spheres of trade, investment, and finance, while ignoring many other issues—namely, the military and political sphere (China is yet to establish any significant strategic military alliances) and the social sphere (it has not become a destination for international migration and possesses very limited cultural influence on the rest of the world). Nevertheless, I believe that we are witnessing the early stages of what I call "competing globalizations"—a worldwide competition between the two models of economic (and in some sense political) globalization.

I would propose that such an approach runs against a very popular notion, which labels current events as "the end of globalization."[43] As I previously

---

43 See: Alan Rugman, *The End of Globalization: A New and Radical Analysis of Globalization and What it Means for Business* (New York: Random House, 2000); Harold James, *The End*

noted, westernization was a process that preceded globalization and prepared its rise. My aim was chiefly to demonstrate that, in the sense of creating a model for the world based on economic and political foundations inspired by the West, the Cold War era was a natural continuation of nineteenth- and twentieth-century processes of westernization. This view differs dramatically from a more traditional approach, focused on different "waves" of globalization.[44] The latter suggests that the "second" globalization of the late-nineteenth and early twentieth centuries was overturned by the Cold War, and resumed once again in 1990s. In contrast, I propose that the Cold War era was in fact crucial to the adoption of western ideologies and practices around the world. "Westernization" did not stop after the First World War—it successfully continued until the late 1980s. The diverging paths of globalization thus should not be taken for the "end of globalization."

Even under new conditions, the key differences between globalization and westernization remain undisturbed. Current economic and political developments, though in some sense "regionalized," are double-edged, and originate in the global North and South. More and less developed countries affect each other in different ways (through the flow of technological transfers, investment, migration, ideological and religious patterns, etc.), and their influence is mutual. In addition to these interactions and influences, both leaders of the "competing globalizations" are tied one to another in almost every possible sense. Therefore, we cannot speak of regionalization, or, far less, of an encapsulation of the world in several distinct sections: the current disjunctions enrich the globalizing process more than they undermine it. There is no sign of returning to the previous, Europe-centered model, nor do americanization or "chinaization" of the world look like viable perspectives for the remainder of the twenty-first century.

Looking towards the future, the opposition between the two competing paradigms will end in a completely different order, much in the same way that the period of "competing westernizations" ended up in the globalization of the 1990s. No one can be sure about the contours of this new order, but what can be said with some certainty is that advances in technology will completely change the very nature of the global society. For centuries, states and nations remained the major agents of change. Today, not only corporations, but also individuals, groups, and networks may act in the same capacity. We can now

---

of Globalization: Lessons from the Great Depression (Cambridge, MA: Harvard University Press, 2001).

44 See: Robbie Robertson, *The Three Waves of Globalization: A History of a Developing Global Consciousness* (Halifax: Fernwood, 2003).

see that millions of people are starting to work without even creating companies; that innovative financial instruments like cryptocurrencies emerge, bypassing the government; that worldwide information networks are functioning more and more independently from any official institutions. I would say that, in contrast with the process of westernization (which was advanced and governed by nation-states), and in contrast with globalization (propelled as it were by corporations and their commercial interests), the coming globalization will reflect the incredible power of sovereign individuals. This is an opening of a fascinating new topic that nevertheless transcends the scope of the present discussion.

Globalization and Global Processes: The Algorithm of Development

Arkady D. Ursul, Ilya V. Ilyin, and Tatiana A. Ursul

1   Introduction

Research in globalization tends to describe the ongoing processes of globalization, as opposed to pursuing the root causes of this global phenomenon. Current scholarship considers globalization mainly in terms of strengthening the integrative interactions between the various segments of society, primarily in the form of economic, financial, political, socio-cultural, informational, socio-ecological, and other relationships. Yet, globalization is also visibly manifest in the unification and universalization of a number of fields of activity (e.g., engineering and technology) and their products in the social and socio-natural spheres. In addition, globalization expands the scope of these processes, thereby increasing their territorial reach.

The contemporary model of development places its primary focus on the economic causation of the phenomena in question, which becomes a key factor in establishing the "starting date" for the process of globalization itself. That said, the situation of global processes, and especially of globalization, is more complicated than it would seem. It would be too simplistic to explain the unfolding of an entire range of globalization trends or processes by means of economic reasoning alone, since, in addition to the economic direction of globalization, several dozen other globalization processes have already been identified. While these processes are related to the economy, they are far from being directly caused by its factors.

In this context, the methodological approach we might employ determines the way that we interpret the onset and unfolding of globalization and evolutionary processes on our planet (or even in the Universe at large). Globalization is most often treated as a unique phenomenon that has developed quite recently in historical terms—for instance, since the flourishing of maritime exploration. In such cases, globalization is explored without being compared to other phenomena that would share some of its characteristics. This research approach is appropriate at the beginning of the scholarly process, but has already created substantial problems that cannot be solved without comparing globalization with other global phenomena, including those that existed in the past, or even those that we might expect to arise in the future.

A number of different approaches can be applicable to research in globalization, including research on the global phenomena that took place early in human history (with the potential to be "extended" into the future). To this end, it is important to identify a set of characteristics (or properties) common to globalization and to other processes, similar to it in some way, that took place in the past. This would enable us to understand that similar processes have already taken place in the evolution of humankind, and that globalization turns out to be just another "wave" of the universal evolutionary process, unfolding according to certain overarching patterns (or "programs") of social or socio-natural evolution. It is therefore possible to show that global processes have accompanied humanity throughout our entire evolutionary trajectory.

At the same time, this new approach to the study of the very phenomenon of globalization will place this particular global process within an evolutionary series of other processes. In this article, we shall discuss some of these processes. This research method has historical precedents, and involves both extrapolation and comparison. This extrapolative-comparative approach used to be common—for example, when the concepts of information and its processes were applied to all of inanimate nature. This approach is also relevant when considering the application of the basic ideas of biological evolution to the global-universal evolutionary process—a thought put forward by Nikita Moiseyev in his original version of universal evolutionism.[1] The expansion of the biological model of evolution involves "extending" the universals of the Darwinian triad of *variability, heredity,* and *selection* to the lower (inanimate nature) and higher (society) stages of universal evolution. Moiseyev's conception considers the possibility of applying the triad of principles to all of nature, with a common interpretation. The application of these methodological ideas can help discover a number of new global processes never previously examined as such.

2   Culture, Civilization, and Information

When we speak of considering the Earth as a whole, what we have in mind are the civilizational and cultural approaches to understanding human evolution.

---

1   See: Nikita Moiseyev, *Восхождение к разуму: Лекции по универсальному эволюционизму и его приложениям* [*The Ascent Towards Reason: Lectures on Universal Evolutionism and Its Applications*] (Moscow: IzdAT, 1993).

The concept of culture is tied with the concept of civilization, and the two are often equated or placed in opposition.[2] We shall proceed from the fact that civilization expresses the social essence of the human race, which has emerged from primitive beginnings. It embodies the social stage of evolution in its earthly existence. Civilization is principally directed towards a cosmic, even a cosmological, future.

The sphere of culture represents the informational core of civilization: it is a post-biological invariant, and the *raison d'être* of civilization as such. Culture, by virtue of being an informational process and structure, ensures the self-regulation of the civilizational system, its self-reproduction and development, and performs functions aimed at its survival. Culture and civilization exhibit part-whole relationships; in other words, culture is an informational component of civilization, and civilization encompasses both culture and a number of other components both informational and non-informational. In this sense, culture is a part of civilization, such that the whole cannot exist without it, since it determines the "evolutionary meaning" of the emergence and the development of the social stage in the evolution of matter. Acting as the informational content of civilization, culture includes real energy and other material components. Much depends on which "coordinate system," or which conceptual systems, we consider in the relationship between culture and civilization. Further, wherever the concept of civilization "gravitates" towards a tangible, economic, technical, and technological interpretation, while representing at the same time a holistic social stage of evolution, the concept of culture shifts correspondingly to refer chiefly to its spiritual and informational components, expressing the deep essence of the civilizational process.

The material objects of civilization act as phenomena of culture only if they are considered not simply from the informational standpoint, but specifically as systems of the semiosphere created by humankind. These systems are able to store and transmit human-created signs that possess not only value, but also meaning (sense), and that regulate the activity of the humans and society. This broad understanding of the relationship between culture and civilization is methodologically productive and serves as the basis for understanding the development of civilization, both on Earth and beyond it.

The origins of the formation of civilization are associated with the gradual shaping of the economic and cultural mechanisms that contributed to

---

2   See: Vyacheslav Styopin, *Цивилизация и культура* [*Civilization and culture*] (St. Petersburg: SPbGUP, 2011); Alexander Chumakov, *Метафизика глобализации. Культурно-цивилизационный контекст* [*Metaphysics of Globalization: Cultural and Civilizational Context*], second ed. (Moscow: Prospect, 2017).

the displacement of biological evolution by social evolution. The civilizational process demonstrates a way to reproduce the intelligent life of individuals, united by a universal connection and by mechanisms that ensure the survival of society at the social stage of evolution.[3] If we assume the possible existence of extraterrestrial civilizations, then, in this extremely broad sense, civilization can be understood as a specific manifestation of the social stage of the evolution of matter. This is an organized system of intelligent beings possessing the means of supra-individual storage, accumulation, transmission, and transformation of information, and engaging with nature in ways that aim at their survival and the permanent progressive development of this stage of global evolution.

The economy-centered interpretation of globalization is largely associated with the civilizational approach, while the culturological concept is related to the informational approach, which, as we shall endeavor to demonstrate, sheds light on the reasons for the development of global and other processes. The same informational approach is also fruitful in the interpretation of the development of the world by human beings, where the cultural priorities of development come to the fore. It is culture that engenders the "programs," codes, and developmental algorithms that direct human activity along a predictable informational trajectory.

Anthroposociogenesis reveals some general principles and tendencies suggesting that the emergence of globalization (and a number of other social and potentially socio-natural global processes) had been previously "programmed" by the emergence of humanity as a social stage of global evolution. The fact is that anthroposociogenesis appeared at the same time as cultural genesis, and this circumstance gives us an opportunity to consider that range of problems which this article seeks to contextualize. To this end, we should employ the most current conception available—that being the informational conception of culture.[4] In this conception, culture is presented as an extra-genetic and extra-organic informational process that expresses the nature of the social stage of evolution. Humanity, as a social stage of evolution, is characterized by a special extra-organic (extra-corporeal) system of the transformation, accumulation, storage, and transmission from generation to generation, which is essential for the collective unification of individuals and groups that constitute society. Information is considered an attribute of the universe "responsi-

---

3   Pavel Gurevich, *Культурология* [*Culturology*], fifth ed. (Moscow: KNORUS, 2017), 278–79.
4   See: Konstantin Kolin and Arkady Ursul, *Культура и информация. Введение в информационную культурологию* [*Culture and Information: Introduction to Information Culture Studies*] (Moscow: Strategicheskiye prioritety, 2015).

ble" for evolutionary processes. Moreover, we can speak of different forms and methods for storing and transferring information at various stages of global evolutionary unfolding.

At the stage of the formation and development of society, a number of information processes (accumulation, storage, transformation, etc.) are beyond the realm of the main structural element of that stage—the individual. This is a specific and essential characteristic of the social stage of evolution, which expresses its fundamental difference from the previous, biological stage, where the main informational processes occurred at the endogenous-genetic level. The accumulation of information in cultural genesis (anthroposociogenesis) begins to unfold not in the structural unit of the corresponding stage, which narrows the possibilities for its further growth and development, but outside of it. At this stage, the environment is developed and its objects are transformed into artifacts.

3 The Informational Nature of Culture

According to the informational interpretation of cultural genesis, culture arises at a point when the humanity is differentiated from the animal world, resulting in the creation of a sphere "external" to humans, a sphere of accumulation and transformation (flow) of information. It is difficult to define the beginning of this unified process, but only in the sense that there are different viewpoints as to the exact "date" at which this social stage comes forth. This difficulty is quantitative, not qualitative in nature. According to the informational interpretation of culture, the social stage arises together with the humanity itself, when, in informational terms, it comes to be distinct from the biological stage. Here, we meet with the continuation of global evolution and the emergence a fundamentally new, extra-corporeal method of accumulating and processing information, radically different from biological informational-genetic mechanisms.

This qualitative conceptual tendency sheds light on the expansion of spatial territories and the increase in the informational content of progressively evolving social systems. The socio-cultural principle of exogenous accumulation, transmission, and transformation of information is consistent with the principles of synergetics, according to which the growth of information in any progressively-evolving system occurs at the expense of the environment, due to the evacuation of negentropy. This is a specific and essential characteristic of the phenomenon of the social stage of evolution, expressive of its fundamental difference from biological evolution.

Humans (and possibly some supposed extraterrestrial civilizations) expand the sphere of their habitation, first on the planet and later in space, thereby increasing the informational content of the socio-sphere. This occurs not so much for the sake of developing the natural material and energy resources, but for the continuation of the cultural and informational processes, and to enable the accumulation of information in the expanding socio-sphere. The transmission and other forms of cultural information flows also require the development of space and material objects as well as active participation of various forms and levels of intelligence.[5]

For a long time, it seemed that humankind used matter and energy mainly as resources, while information was out of sight. This was due to the fact that information as a concept (as a criterion and resource for development) was "discovered" only quite recently, little more than half-a-century ago. The "responsibility" of information, as a new universal property of matter, for the evolutionary processes was discovered even later, when the attributive concept of information and the informational criterion of development were proposed. However, information is immanently connected with matter and energy, thereby highlighting and emphasizing the leading role of the informational and cultural components. It is important in this context that information, in principle, does not exist without material carriers. In the past, and even now, these carriers were often considered fundamental to the evolutionary processes within society. For this reason, and so as not to "demolish" the prevailing preconceptions, we shall speak not only about information, but also about material and energy resources.

The expansion and development of humans that arose by cultural means from the very moment of their emergence have a fundamentally informational nature and vector—due precisely to the emergence of a special, impersonal system of means of accumulation, storage, and transformation of information, as necessary for organizing any social activity—thereby expanding the environment, developing its resources, and strengthening the integration and informational interactions within society. Globalization "fits" into this informational hypothesis of world development and the evolution of civilization: the vector of globalization is simultaneously the vector of its progressive development. It is also important that not all these processes can become global, due to their inherent respective methods of implementation and their special prerequisites.

---

5 Arkady Ursul, "The Information Nature of Evolution and World Exploration: Conceptual Hypothesis," *Automatic Documentation and Mathematical Linguistics*, 2019(53), No. 1, 9–15, https://doi.org/10.3103/S0005105519010060.

This idea is related to the main tendency and criterion of global evolution—the information criterion, which requires permanent accumulation of information content by systems to ensure their progressive development. Humans accumulate informational content by means of extra-genetic informational mechanisms, creating new spheres and areas of activity at the supra-individual, and now also at supra- and international levels. This entails a further accumulation of social globalization and other global processes. The most fundamental and rapid evolutionary transformations of the future will increasingly occur at the international, or global, level. This should remind us of the evolution of the human race, when social nature was established and biological development passed the baton to social development. In turn, social development began to evolve much faster, compared with the biological development of humans, and to undergo more radical transformations (thanks to the extra-corporeal and extra-genetic way of information accumulation).

In such evolutionary socio-natural processes, three main characteristics can be prioritized: the expansion of the space being developed, the increase in the interactions between the main components, and the emergence of universal forms (results) of further, progressive development. In short, it is about such universals of globalization as spatial spread, integration, and universality, all of which are necessarily present in the global processes considered below, but in different degrees and proportions. This triad of characteristics identifies the main, most general features of globalization as a concept. But this triad also turns out to be characteristic of other, similar processes of human evolution, whose various stages we have addressed in this article, and which thus constitute the global processes of the past and the future.

Still, globalization received its "global" name not so much by virtue of the triad just mentioned, but because of the natural properties of the Earth itself. The global character of this process lies primarily in the fact that it is reflected in the most obvious, spatio-geographical form (covering the territory of the entire globe, from the Latin *globus*, meaning a sphere). The spherical, global shape of the Earth is limited in space and thus forced to direct globalization according to the "developmental algorithm." Nevertheless, with the widespread exploration of space, the dispersion process of a certain part of civilization over extraterrestrial space is bound to occur. Only by focusing on the next spherical space object (e.g., the Moon or Mars) will we see the pattern of "global dispersal" and its subsequent globalization set in once again—this time, in both planetary and cosmic forms.

The "triad of global universals" that we have identified reflects, in concentrated form, a kind of matrix or *developmental algorithm*—that term, coined by Moiseyev, involving the Darwinian triad of heredity, variability, and selection, which Moiseyev also considers in his eponymous book, *Developmental Algorithms*.[6] Later, this algorithm turned out to be the very triad on the basis of which the "bio-model" of universal evolutionism was created.[7]

We should note that concepts like *matrices* and *algorithms* are used here not in a mathematical sense, but in the broader conceptual sense, as a certain set of developmental characteristics (in some cases, rules of activity) that are formed, transmitted, and repeated in each "new wave" of the progressive evolution of humankind. We shall briefly consider a number of these characteristics. Concepts of this sort have been used previously in the study of various global processes—including civilizational processes.[8]

4 The Informational View and the Triad of Global Social Processes

The currently prevalent interpretation of globalization as a concept emphasizes universal transnational and integrative processes in the development of civilization and in its attainment of integration across various aspects.[9] There is also some expansion of the space being developed, but the emphasis on its expansion appeared on a larger scale much earlier, which was pointed out in the name itself, although this was also a developmental process. In order to further connections between different peoples (tribes, races, countries, etc.), different groups of people had to engage in the resettlement path of development. This preceded the "universal integration" stage of globalization and would represent, together with globalization, the earlier global process of human mastery over their environment. Globalization did not start on the proverbial "empty space." It was "programmed" both by the features of the Earth—a cosmic body—and by the objective laws of human development. In this sense, one can say that the genesis of the global process of mastery had not, in principle, only social characteristics, but socio-natural ones as well.

We might address the early resettlement of humans and their ancestors, from Africa to other continents and territories, without which globalization as a process of integration would not have begun. However, that early exodus from Africa and across Eurasia had the form of dispersions in multiple

---

6 See: Nikita Moiseyev, *Алгоритмы развития* [*Developmental Algorithms*] (Moscow: Nauka, 1987).
7 See: Moiseyev, *Ascent Towards Reason*.
8 See: Ilya Ilyin and Olga Leonova, *Политическая глобалистика* [*Political Globalistics*] (Moscow: Yurayt, 2017).
9 See: Alexander Chumakov, *Глобализация. Контуры целостного мира* [*Globalization: The Contours of an Integrated World*], third ed. (Moscow: Prospect, 2017).

directions. It was previously assumed that climatic changes and other "external" factors were the reasons for the development of new territories by ancient people. Now, scholars think that phenomena like innovation and mastery of knowledge and skills (all largely informational in nature) represent likelier reasons for human migration from Africa.[10] According to Alexander Zubov, early migrations enriched the genus *Homo* with new information, made it a prerequisite to actively engage in understanding the world, expanded the range of human adaptability, contributed to its universalization as a biological form that became a unique phenomenon on our planet, and determined the parameters of *Homo sapiens* as a cosmic being.

Our ancestors began to use and to start fires as early as the Paleolithic. A fire was useful for cooking diverse foods, for staving off the cold and predators, and allowed for nighttime activity. Controlled use of fire contributed to the further advancement of *Homo erectus* into colder territories, representing, according to Vladimir Vernadsky, a genuine revolution in human existence and development, furthering the gap between humans and other animals, and acting as one of the most important global processes in the Paleolithic.

About two million years ago, *Homo erectus*—and then, about 80,000 years ago, *Homo sapiens*—began to settle, in several waves, upon different parts of the planet. This led to an increase in their numbers (in the Upper Paleolithic era, the population of Cro-Magnons reached several million people). By the end of the Upper Paleolithic, the growth in the number of people, the destruction of some species (chiefly, the megafauna), and the decline in the numbers of others led our ancestors into the first global socio-natural ecological and economic crisis.

The transition to a manufacturing economy began as a way out of the global crisis of the Upper Paleolithic, characterized by food supply shortage and a decrease in human population. The transition to agriculture and livestock farming led to a significant increase in food resources and population growth during the Neolithic period, to at least tens of millions of people. These and similar global processes were based on certain world-historical and even universal-global laws. At a certain stage, these laws led to the emergence of global problems and to the current stage of globalization. In this context, we can assume that the processes of global resettlement and globalization have a deep informational nature, not unlike the process of space exploration. But, whereas the connection to space exploration has been established for

---

10 See: Alexander Zubov, *Становление и первичное расселение рода* Homo [*The Development and Primary Dispersion of the Genus* Homo] (St. Petersburg: Aletheia, 2011).

a while,[11] the same connection in respect of globalization gained currency but recently.[12] Still, we maintain that the informational essence of the emergence and unfolding of these processes is, in fact, the same.

The first early modern humans entered the Middle East 80,000 years ago. (According to other sources, the first people came there 120–130 thousand years ago). Even the development of America did not first occur by sea: the ancestors of all the indigenous Paleo-Americans moved in a single wave, from the Chukchi Peninsula to Alaska, in the late Pleistocene. Historians have stated that the New World was "discovered" several times by Paleolithic and Mesolithic people, thousands of years before the age of discovery. The entire indigenous population of America, the Paleo-Americans, descended from an ancestral group closest to modern Mongoloids, who arrived 14,000 years ago along the Bering Isthmus—land that connected Asia and America into a coherent geographical whole. The most favorable conditions for the migration of fauna, including humans, occurred during the late Pleistocene, about 14,000 years ago. Later, the Bering isthmus was replaced by the newly-formed Bering Strait, and the inhabitants of North America were isolated—for a long time.

Global resettlement is usually viewed mainly as a demographic process, but not as a process of "primary globalization"—though, when viewed in the context of the current stage of globalization, it displays a number of the same features as globalization: spatial expansion, the initiation of interactions between peoples on conquered territories, and the presence of universal laws and patterns of evolution characteristic of the entire human race. This example shows that there are areas of scientific knowledge that, having previously explored certain Paleolithic global processes, did not use (or would not declare) a global approach. Anthropology, which studies global processes like global human resettlement, the use of fire, the Neolithic Revolution, and the formation of city-states, is a case in point. Another (as we are about to show) is the theory of international relations, where global features and their potentialities have been ignored. In principle, the reconsideration of existing scientific

---

11   See: Arkady Ursul, *Освоение космоса (Философско-методологические и социологические проблемы)* [*Space Exploration: Philosophical, Methodological and Sociological Problems*] (Moscow: Mysl, 1967).

12   Arkady Ursul, "Космоглобалистика в ракурсе информационной гипотезы освоения мира" ["Cosmoglobalistics under the Aspect of the Information Hypothesis of World Development"], in I. I. Abylgaziev and Ilya Ilyin, eds., *Глобалистика как область научных исследований и сфера преподавания* [*Globalistics as a Field of Scientific Research and Teaching*] (Moscow: MAKSPress, 2011), 87–123.

knowledge from the global perspective, and under the aspect of the "globalization triad," is bound to reveal other global processes, whose globality had previously gone unnoticed and lay latent.

Global resettlement was followed by a new global process that arose on its basis—the Neolithic Revolution that unfolded over many millennia. The transition from appropriating to productive economy took place in the Neolithic era (approximately eight to ten millennia BCE), which, on the one hand, led to an increase in the cost-effectiveness of economic activity, and, on the other hand, to local turmoil, and to a global ecological crisis later on. This was the result of the emergence of socio-natural activities, based on a productive economy and on the principles of nature management that originated in the Neolithic—and undermined the environment.

The Agro-Neolithic Revolution, a transition from hunting and gathering to agriculture and animal husbandry, first manifested in Northern Mesopotamia, as early as the eighth millennium BCE. It played a special role not only in the formation of the first civilizations, but also in the emergence of the first city-states. The emergence of a new socio-natural way of interaction (material production) also entailed the formation of new social relations and social processes, of which the development of international ties was one of the most important forms.

The formation of local civilizations began in the course of the Neolithic Revolution, but closer to its middle period. The interactions of nomadic tribes at the stage of barbarism (or even between nomadic and sedentary cultures) are unlikely to be considered the beginning of international relations. Such relations required a number of territorial and demographic preconditions in the form of the emergence of early local civilizations. Unlike specific innovative and technological transformations, spaced hundreds of thousands of years apart in the Paleolithic times, the Neolithic Revolution had an accelerated systemic nature. It took only about 5–6 millennia for this revolution, an example of one of the most important global socio-natural processes, to spread across almost the entire globe. Major transformations in the structure of society took place in the course of the Neolithic Revolution. Many local civilizations arose, as did the phenomenon of statehood.

The earliest state formations (primarily the ancient slave-owning city-states) arose on the basis of different tribes and nationalities, which gained territories of residence and started leading settled life. Such forms appeared with the context of agricultural tribes, who later created small ancient city-states of Egypt and Mesopotamia, which arose about 4,000 years BCE. Beginning in this period, Sumerian city-states began to arise in southern Mesopotamia. This "urban revolution" was completed as early as the first half of the third millennium BCE. Up to several dozen Egyptian and Sumerian city-states appeared on relatively small riverside territories. International relations as a form of interaction between city-states first arose in the Sumerian part of Mesopotamia, where states appeared earlier than elsewhere and entered into mutual relationships, implementing their two major functions of ensuring security and development. Thus, the initial chronological framework for the international relations in the Ancient East can be dated to the end of the fourth millennium BCE.[13]

This was the starting point of international relations within the framework of the Sumerian civilization. The next early form of international relations was the interaction between city-states of different civilizations. Quite possibly, this may have first occurred at the moment of Egypt's encounter with Nubia (some historians represent Nubia as a completely independent and unique ancient civilization); later, about 3,500 years ago, it was represented by the interactions between the Egyptian state and Syria, during the Mesopotamian campaign of Thutmose I. In this instance, international relations have the form of interactions between the individual city-states of one local civilization or another, rather than interactions between the Sumerian and Egyptian civilizations and cultures.

International processes are social in nature, and are among the first integrated directions of globalization. A stronger assumption that the current stage of globalization (in the aggregate of all the above-mentioned interpretations of the "global algorithm") began precisely with the onset of international processes and, to a large extent, continues through them, cannot be excluded—but the reasoning behind this assumption requires more detailed research. Still, when discussing the possibility of establishing the global vector of international relations, we should remember that some international processes will remain beyond the scope of discussion. It is quite obvious that some states will not become actors of global international relations. Some countries (this is especially true for the smaller, unrecognized countries and other special cases) may very well be interested than others in participating in future global international relations. This raises certain questions with regard to the ultimate meaning of globalization in international relations. There are also other circumstances indicating that global trends will affect only some areas of international processes.

---

13   See: Shamansur Shahalilov, *История международных отношений: движущие силы, глобальные тенденции* [*History of International Relations: Driving Forces, Global Trends*] (Moscow: Moscow State University Press, 2015).

5 From Global Development to Space Exploration

The previously mentioned "global triad" will continue, in one form or another, into the future, including its spatial dimension—the outer space. The properties and qualities of global evolution, which are cultural and informational by nature, will give impetus to the human need to expand the scope of the species' transformative activity—first on the planet, and then beyond. All of them are accompanied by other components of the global "developmental algorithm." With respect to our planet, these components include the global human resettlement, the Agro-Neolithic Revolution, etc.; in the future, they will involve globalization and other processes that have an informational orientation from their very inception and transmit the triad we had mentioned earlier. Therefore, in contrast with the previous stages of the evolution of matter, humans (and possibly some supposed extraterrestrial civilizations) expand the sphere of their spread, first on Earth, and then in space. The reason is not so much to obtain raw materials and energy resources, but to continue the cultural and informational processes, and the accumulation of information in the socio-sphere, by expanding across the planet and into the extraterrestrial space.

The informational concept of world exploration was first proposed as early as the 1970s. The discussion was focused on humans leaving planet Earth and joining the superhighway of global evolution. The unfolding of social and socio-natural processes in a global view confirms this hypothesis not only in its "cosmic" version, but also the planetary-terrestrial. Moreover, something similar to global resettlement will occur away from the planet, when mass human resettlement opens up into space, with exoplanet exploration beckoning in the distant future.[14]

In the future, solutions to global problems and the prevention of dangers to the global development of civilization will take place through the emergent process of sustainable development, which is also necessary for the continuation of the main trajectory of continuous self-organization, now in its socio-natural form. "Sustainable development" refers, in this instance, to the controlled, systemically balanced socio-natural development that does not destroy the environment and ensures the survival and safe existence of civilization for an indefinitely long duration. Speaking more generally, it is a non-regressive, safe development, aimed at the preservation and co-evolution of civilization and the surrounding nature. The starting point for this stage of

---

14   See: Ursul, *Space Exploration*.

socio-natural development in the evolutionary "security corridor" is marked by the transition to sustainable development; its continuation is conceived in the form of co-evolution of nature and society as a global system on its way to the emergence of a noosphere—first, on our own planet, and later, beyond it.

The transition to sustainable socio-natural development as the main form of further global development is a demonstrable objective necessity, if viewed from the standpoint of universal evolution and the continuation of its main vector. This transition, both on the planet and under a "sustainable" strategy of space exploration, adapts global socio-natural development to the universal evolutionary process, creating new opportunities for its spatio-temporal continuation. Here, we can draw an analogy involving human beings in relation to planetary and cosmic processes, and with regard to space exploration. By aiming at global sustainability, humanity adapts to the biospheric processes on the planet, so as to become a necessary part of global evolution. Something similar can be expected in space, where it will be necessary to adapt to the self-organizing processes of cosmogenesis. It can be assumed that the transformative human activity in space will also unfold within the ecological carrying capacity of space ecosystems, which will allow the social stage to follow the path of continuing the globally universal evolution off the planet.

The possibility of a transition to the socio-natural process of sustainable development will entail, to some extent, a co-evolutionary development of the global world, and in the future—the creation of a geocosmic socio-natural world. It would be unduly limiting to say that this future development model can guarantee the survival of humans and their indefinite, non-regressive development whilst preserving the environment. This is not just a long-term extension of socio-natural development—but also a positive contribution to the continuation of the main universal-evolutionary highway, which will attain its socio-natural realization in the form of the planetary-cosmic system "Humanity–Earth–Universe."[15]

15 See: Arkady Ursul, Человечество, Земля, Вселенная [*Humanity, Earth, Universe*] (Moscow: Mysl, 1977).

The Historical Logic of Globalization

Tatiana L. Shestova

Even at the early stages of human development, we can observe the formation of a logic of globalization, aimed at establishing the global community as an arena of planetary evolution. We can observe the mechanism behind this process in its global-historical perspective by looking at the development of forms of community interaction, beginning with the local scale, characteristic of the Stone Age, and up to the global scale typical of the modern era. This historical aspect of globalization allows us to see its direction, aim, and logic, and reveals its role in human, societal, and natural development. While it is usually taken for granted that globalization as such appeared no earlier than the middle of the previous millennium, we can uncover its sources much farther back in history.

Studies of globalization have been carried out within the framework of the social sciences—economics, sociology, political science, etc. For this reason, the most significant and studied aspect of globalization as of today is its social modality, with the different approaches attending to the development of humanity's social coherence. That said, contemporary philosophical approaches suggest a broader view of globalization, situating it in the contexts of the "Society–Nature" system and of the Earth's evolutionary perspective. "Globalization is a result of centuries-old quantitative and qualitative transformations, both in social development and in the 'Society–Nature' system," writes Alexander Chumakov, a prominent Russian philosopher and one of the founders of philosophy of globalization as an arena of philosophical analysis.[1] Chumakov suggests analyzing globalization in the contexts of geological, biological, and social interactions ("geo-bio-socio-epo-metamorphosis"), through which the main trajectories of planetary evolution are realized.[2] Based on this approach, we can view globalization as a longstanding objective-historical process of transforming humanity from a biological population into a global

---

1 Alexander Chumakov, "Social aspects of globalization (From a Globalistics Viewpoint)," in *Globalistics and Globalization Studies*, edited by Leonid Grinin, Andrei Korotayev, and Ilya Ilyin (Volgograd: Uchitel, 2012), https://www.sociostudies.org/almanac/articles/social_aspects_of_globalization_-from_a_globalistics_viewpoint/.
2 Alexander Chumakov, "Триосфера, эпометаморфоз и новые задачи глобалистики" ["Triosphere, Epometamorphosis, and the New Tasks of Globalistics"], *Vek globalizatsii*, 2016, No. 3., 3–15.

community. In this sense, we can find the sources of globalization not only in the development of genuinely global interactions (as occurred during the age of discovery), but all the way back at the very beginnings of human history, with the emergence of culture and the inherently human tendency to broaden its reach.

In the process of creating culture, humankind discovered a new path of planetary evolution. Presently, as a result, the face of the Earth is changing, and community interactions are deepening; the scale of human impact on the environment is broadening as the efficacy of technological paradigms increases. "Man is becoming the greatest geological power," wrote Vladimir Vernadsky at the beginning of the twentieth century, highlighting the global and historical role of human culture (and of science in particular, as its major component) in planetary development.[3] Vernadsky's ideas had a significant impact on both Russian and worldwide scientific thought, and the continued relevance of his many insights once again became clear at the turn of the twenty-first century. During the global pandemic, the role of science in the evolution of our planet became particularly evident. The development of scientific knowledge is a crucial factor in a successful battle against the new dangers that threaten the existence of humans as a biological population. Nevertheless, scientific discoveries will be futile if not supported by cultural and philosophical dispositions aimed at preserving the humanity, both as a biological species and as the bearer of planetary culture. Here, philosophy plays a leading role in the development of global attitudes, and the philosophy of globalization has an especially important function.[4]

Much of the work in the theory of globalization has once again turned to Vernadsky's conceptions and ideas. Many researchers now think that the study of the noosphere is one of the most important avenues of intellectual progress, which has, in the final third of the twentieth century, led global social thought to the idea of sustainable development as a universal strategy for managing a range of global processes.[5] In Western scholarship, similar ideas have been expressed by the British naturalist and philosopher James Lovelock of the Gaia

---

3   Vladimir Vernadsky, "Несколько слов о ноосфере" ["A Few Words on the Noosphere"], V. I. Vernadsky Electronic Archive, http://vernadsky.lib.ru/e-texts/archive/noos.html.
4   See: Alexander Chumakov, *Philosophy of Globalization*, third ed. (Moscow: Moscow State University Press, 2020).
5   See: Ilya Ilyin, Arkady Ursul, and Tatiana Ursul, "Ноосферогенез как глобальный процесс (Концепция нооглобалистики)" ["Noospherogenesis as a Global Process (The Concept of Nooglobalistics)"], *Bulletin of Moscow University*, Series 27, 2014, No. 1–2, 33–51; Ilya Ilyin, V. A. Los and Arkady Ursul, *Устойчивое развитие и глобальные процессы* [*Sustainable Development and Global Processes*] (Moscow: MSU, 2015).

hypothesis, who compared the Earth's evolution with the development of a living organism.[6] Like Vernadsky, Lovelock suggested a cosmic worldview that permitted to imagine the Earth from a distance:

> What of large entities, like ecosystems and Gaia? It took the view of the Earth from space either directly through the eyes of an astronaut, or vicariously through the visual media, to let us sense a planet on which living things, the air, the oceans, and the rocks all combine in one as Gaia.[7]

Lovelock provided a philosophical and scientific explanation of the periodization of the Earth's history in his work, *The Ages of Gaia*. In his concept, he highlights the role of human culture in Gaia's development. The emergence of culture as "second nature" is the most significant moment in human and planetary history. Without this notion, it is difficult to see the historical logic of human development in general, and the historical logic of globalization in particular.

Interest in the socio-natural aspects of globalization continues to increase. In contemporary research, questions of how human activity is changing the lithosphere, water, and air, as well as the geochemical balance and biospheric structure are particularly salient. Globalization theory underscores the necessity of new attitudes towards Nature as the natural basis of human existence on Earth. Ecologism is one such ethical current that encourages us to form a global consciousness. Global consciousness is the mental foundation of a humanity fused into an organism—a self-governing and self-reproducing global community. Problems of globalization (including historical aspects of globalization) therefore have an ideological content. Within global history and history of globalization, problems of socio-natural interactions can never be confined to "purely" academic interest, such questions inevitably turning into arenas of confrontation between different political interests.

Due to new developments in technology and mass media, humanity has become a daily witness to events of geo-evolutionary significance. In science and mass media, we see catastrophic changes on the planetary scale. The question of human influence on these processes is one of the most debatable in

---

6   James Lovelock: *The Ages of Gaia: A Biography of Our Living Earth* (Oxford: Oxford University Press, 1995); *The Vanishing Face of Gaia: A Final Warning* (Santa Barbara: Allen Lane, 2009); *Novacene: The Coming Age of Hyperintelligence* (Cambridge, MA: MIT Press, 2019).
7   James Lovelock, *The Ages of Gaia: A Biography of Our Living Earth* (Oxford: Oxford University Press, 1995), 19.

world science. Especially heated are the discussions on the scale of anthropogenic influence on the climate.

In modern science, the term "Anthropocene" refers to a period of the Earth's history where the human species acts as the leading factor of planetary evolution, and this theory is now being actively promoted.[8] Climate problems are likewise at the center of the discourse on the Anthropocene. Such renowned scholars as Paul Crutzen, Joseph McNeill, and others are taking part in the development of the concept of the Anthropocene.[9] In the Russian-language scholarship, another concept has been introduced in the 1920s, by the Soviet naturalist Alexei Pavlov. This is the concept of the *Anthropogene*, which refers to the geological period in which humans emerged (this phase in the Earth's geological history is generally called the Quaternary Period). Neither of these terms, the "Anthropocene" and the "Anthropogene," have yet been acknowledged at the level of international scientific congresses, nor do they appear in the official nomenclature of geological science. Nevertheless, the fact that these terms are showing up more frequently in the academic literature shows the growing influence of the anthropic idea over natural-historical discourse. Naturalistic historicism has penetrated the theory of globalization, and naturalistic criteria are used increasingly in the periodization of the history of globalization.

Periodization is the axial basis of any historical concept. Identifying stages in human history based on this or that criterion is the key instrument of socio-historical analysis. Thus, the periodization of the history of globalization reveals not only the content but also the essence of this process. The question of periodization with respect to the history of globalization is a complex academic problem. Many philosophers, sociologists, and historians have attempted to address this concern. These respected scholars include Immanuel Wallerstein, Andre Gunder Frank, William Thompson, Alexander Chumakov, Vladimir Pantin, Anthony G. Hopkins, David Christian, Andrei Korotayev, Leonid Grinin, Akop Nazaretyan, William Robinson, Christopher Bayly, Nayan Chanda, and many others who have offered original perspectives on the periodization of global history and the history of globalization. Within different paradigms—world-system analysis, global evolutionism, theory of epo-metamorphosis of the trisphere, big history, microhistory, etc.—they have

---

8   Elena Vasilyeva, "Проблема периодизации геологических эпох: Фактор человека" ["The Problem of Periodization of Geological Epochs: The Human Factor"], *Bulletin of Moscow University*, Series 27, 2017, No. 3, 53–58.

9   Will Steffen et al., "The Anthropocene: Conceptual and Historical Perspectives," *Philosophical Transactions*, 2011(369), No. 1938, 842–67, https://doi.org/10.1098/rsta.2010.0327.

created various concepts for understanding and describing the history of globalization.

While scholars of globalization take different approaches to analyzing the beginnings of globalization, and while its periods and stages may be identified according to different criteria, all of these approaches highlight the historicism of the process in question and the presence of objective logic in the formation of global society with its concomitant parts, dynamics, and interactions with nature. Scholars categorize the beginning of globalization according to different historical epochs (Stone and Bronze Ages, the Hellenistic period, the age of discovery, mid-twentieth century, the 1970s, the 1990s, etc.). The academic majority assume that globalization as such began during the age of discovery, with the formation of a unified planetary capitalist marketplace. And yet, despite the complex theoretical justification of this majority opinion, discussion continues to be necessary for deepening and enhancing our understanding of globalization.

One memorable discussion of such beginnings unfolded between Immanuel Wallerstein and Andre Gunder Frank, in the well-known work *The World System: Five Hundred Years or Five Thousand?*[10] Wallenstein follows in the footsteps of Fernand Braudel, who identifies the beginning of world-systemic relations with the formation of capitalism and the development of global economic connections, between the late fifteenth century and the early sixteenth. Frank and his followers see the sources of the world-system in the interactions of Bronze-Age civilizations. The discussion between Alexander Chumakov and Ivan Gobozov played a crucial role in the development of philosophical discourse on globalization, particularly as they raised the question of the beginning of globalization.[11] Gobozov suggested that globalization started in the 1990s, the landmark event being the collapse of the Soviet Union. Chumakov argued that globalization started during the age of discovery and during the formation of first systems of global interactions. One of the most recent insights into the historiography of "the question of the 'age' of globalization" is contained in the monograph *A Big History of Globalization: The Emergence of Global World System*.[12] The authors isolate three approaches to

---

10 Andre G. Frank and Barry K. Gills, eds., *The World System: Five Hundred Years or Five Thousand?* (New York: Routledge, 1996), 320.

11 Alexander Chumakov, "О глобализации с объективной точки зрения" ["On Globalization Objectively"], *Vek globalizatsii*, 2014, No. 2, 39–51; Ivan Gobozov, *Государство и национальная идентичность: Глобализация или интернационалистика?* [*The State and National Identity: Globalization or Internalization?*] Moscow: Librokom, 2013.

12 Julia Zinkina et al., *A Big History of Globalization: The Emergence of Global World System* (New York: Springer, 2019), 13.

the definition of "the age of globalization," proposing their own periodization. The continuance of these discussions emphasizes the theoretical significance of the problem.

In the present paper, I will outline a periodization of global history while also proposing a periodization of the history of globalization. The history of globalization and global history are not equivalent. Global history is the history of humanity taken as a whole: in other words, it is the history of humanity conceived as a "planetary phenomenon," one of the most important aspects of the Earth's evolution. The history of globalization, called "the heart of global history" by the prominent American scholar Bruce Mazlish, is an aspect of global history and one of its central parts.[13] The history of globalization reveals the dynamics of growth and integration of social communities, and aims at forming the global community—a single global social whole.

Assuming that globalization as such began in the middle of the previous millennium, the logic of globalization can be said to have emerged during the early development of humankind, with the onset of rational transformation of nature, and with the emergence of culture. Culture and social skills allowed our species to survive natural catastrophes, climatic shifts, and competition with rival biological species. Along with it, institutions were established and expanded, and communities emerged as a basis for the future process of globalization. One of the key institutions to guarantee the evolutionary stability of our species was the prohibition of in-breeding, which gave rise to the institution of marriage. The regulation of marital relations was one of the first forms of regulating intertribal connections, a practice rooted in the development of social institutions. The institution of family arose from the institution of marriage. Family is the institution that allows humans to preserve themselves as individuals and persons, society, on the other hand, being the institution charged with preserving the species. In this manner, the logic of human community development has become the logic of globalization.

Another factor contributing to our survival was the widespread settlement of the Earth. We are the only hominids living on more than one continent. By settling across the planet, and by competing and clashing in the reclamation of territories and resources, humans tended to be within each other's reach. Models of development emerged from the contacts and connections of human communities, and objectively facilitating the enlargement of social interactions and systems, and the realization of the historical logic of globalization.

---

13   Bruce Mazlish, "An Introduction to Global History," in Bruce Mazlish and Ralph Buultjens, eds., *Conceptualizing Global History* (Boulder, CO: Westview, 1993).

This paper presents the periodization of global history and the history of globalization as constituents of a multi-criterion approach, taking into account the following aspects: the formation of a global community, the interaction between human culture and nature, and "human development." Within this approach, it is possible to reveal the historical logic of globalization and the aims towards which it objectively leads humanity. The periods of global history are at the same time the stages of global socio-natural evolution.

In global history, we can isolate large epochs differing from one another in certain aspects: first, in the nature of self-sufficient communities and the scale of social institutions and systems—local, inter-local, regional, macro-regional, intercontinental, and global; second, in terms of aggregative anthropogenic impact on the planetary ecosystem; and third, in their rates of "human development," including population numbers and average life expectancy—factors that do not necessarily have a scientific value for early historical epochs, but are nevertheless crucial for understanding the logic and aims of global development—since, without consideration of the value of human life, all aspirations for globalization as "the rule of reason" are meaningless. The periodization I propose aims to uncover the axiology of globalization, with its goals and the values of global development. The values of the globalizing world also define the logic of globalization, since they function as strategic landmarks in uniting humanity.[14]

The first stage of global history is the period of local social systems. Local communities take the form of stable, connected, and self-sufficient groups of people who engage with each other directly. Local communities have external relations, yet systemic interrelations are restricted to the inter-local level. From a technological point of view, this would be the extended epoch of the Stone Age (2.5 million–4 thousand years BCE). Among the revolutionary landmarks of this stage are the manufacturing of stone artifacts, the control of fire, Mesolithic Revolution (hunting for small and medium-sized animals, and the emergence of neighboring trade communities), Neolithic Revolution (the beginning of animal and plant domestication, the emergence of ceramics and

---

14   Ivan Aleshkovski, Valentina Bondarenko, and Ilya Ilyin, "Глобальные ценности в контексте понимания будущего России и мира" ["Global Values in the Context of Understanding the Futures of Russia and the World"], *Vek globalizatsii*, 2019, No. 1, 129–36; Ilya Ilyin, Arkady Ursul, and Tatiana Ursul, "Новые глобальные цели устойчивого развития" ["The New Global Goals of Sustainable Development"], *Bulletin of Moscow University*, Series 27, 2015, No. 3–4, 60–84; Ivan Aleshkovski, Valentina Bondarenko, and Ilya Ilyin, "Global Values, Digital Transformation, and Development Strategy for Global Society: Conceptual Framework," *International Journal of Foresight and Innovation Policy*, 2020(14), No. 2–4, 120–34.

weaving, a settled lifestyle—all tantamount to *localization* in the literal sense of the word). With the emergence of agriculture, the impact of humans on nature increased, remaining nevertheless limited until the Metal Age. In that period, agricultural communities were insignificant to the structure of the Earth's population, as the majority lived in hunter-gatherer communities. The Earth's population in the Neolithic epoch constituted around ten million people. According to available estimates, the average life expectancy by the end of the Stone Age (for both men and women) constituted 15–20 years.[15]

The second stage of global history is the period of inter-local systems with contacts extending to the regional level. Here, we come across new uses of fire (e.g., stoves and forges), the formation of metallurgy, and active uses of animal muscle power and air and water energy. The increase in labor productivity allowed for specialization within communities and for rapid advances in technology. Chronologically, this stage comprises the Bronze Age (the third and the second millennia BCE), the epoch of early civilizations, the epoch of the urbanization revolution, and the emergence of first states, literature, legislation, and temple religions. These institutions united local communities into inter-local social systems functioning on the basis of the substitution of direct social contacts for indirect ones. During the Bronze Age, the population in towns was small relative to the Earth's population. Agricultural communities in that period grew significantly but did not dominate over the Mesolithic communities. By the end of this period, a new agricultural belt had formed in Afro-Eurasia, fracturing the ecological integrity, so to speak, of the continents. The Earth's population at that time was between ten and fifty million people, and the average life expectancy was 25–30 years (averaged across bearers of all technological systems).

The third stage is the period in which regional systems with interregional interactions were formed, and when the ancient classical civilizations

---

15 See: Yulia Shchapova and Sergei Grinchenko, *Введение в теорию археологической эпохи: Числовое моделирование и логарифмические шкалы пространственно-временных координат* [*Introduction to the Theory of Archeological Epoch: Numerical Modeling and Logarithmic Scales of Spacio-Temporal Coordinates*] (Moscow: Informatika i upravleniye, 2017); Massimo Livi-Bacci, *A Concise History of World Population* (Oxford: Oxford University Press, 1992); Angus Maddison, *The World Economy* (Paris: OECD, 2006); William H. McNeill and John R. McNeill, *The Human Web: A Bird's-Eye View of World History* (New York: W. W. Norton, 2003); Sergei Malkov, Leonid Grinin, and Andrei Korotayev, eds., *История и математика. Эволюционная историческая макродинамика* [*History and Mathematics: Evolutionary Historical Macrodynamics*] (Moscow: Librokom, 2010); A. P. Buzhilova, *Homo sapiens: История болезни* [*Homo sapiens: A Study in Pathology*] (Moscow: Yazyki slavianskoi kultury, 2005).

emerged. Chronologically, this stage took place from the first millennium BCE to the first centuries CE. Technologically, this was the early Iron Age. Iron tools greatly enhanced the influence on the planetary ecosystem and allowed for demographic growth and massive migrations. Colonization advanced on horseback and by water, hastening the dramatic developments in communication. These developments, in turn, led to the emergence of the institution of money. Anthropogenic deforestation was ushered in through shipbuilding and the clearing of territories for agriculture with iron tools. Livestock breeding and soil manuring changed the atmosphere. Hydraulic technologies appeared, altering the natural geography of freshwater objects. Agriculture began to move north and south from the global civilizational belt. The number of farmers began to approach that of hunter-gatherers. The expansion and new management of territories led to the emergence of a new state system (i.e., empires and their ideological basis), of classical religious teachings, and of what would become world religions. Religion became the spiritual basis of life in the regions, followed by the macro-regional consolidation of communities. Within the framework of systemic ideological teachings, elements of anthropocentric ethics emerged. With the expansion of the agrarian belt, the Earth's population grew to 200 million people, and average life expectancy increased to about 30–35 years.

The fourth stage is the period when mediaeval macro-regional systems were formed—the period of transcontinental civilizations. Technologically, it coincides with the High Iron Age, characterized by the rapid cultural expansion over the Earth and by extensive macro-regional ruralization. Characteristic of this stage are processes like the "great clearing" of territories for agriculture, the widespread use of draught animals for plowing, transcontinental transfer of agriculture, the conquest of the steppe, the semi-desert, the taiga, and the tundra by classical nomads, and the rapid rise in numbers of domestic livestock (horses, deer, sheep, goats, pigs, and camels). This socio-economic structure was dominated by agrarian communities. Macro-regional expansion was accompanied by the feudalization of social relations based on land resources (tillage, pasture), and by the hierarchic estate system. The extended interconnections and the growth in the volume and length of marine and caravan transit created a space for systemic transcontinental interaction. The major parameters of this period were macro-regionalization and the enlargement and centralization of religious cults. The teachings that prevailed in the competitive struggle in this period became world religions, defining the cultural outlook of macro-civilizations. The massive transfer to agriculture affected the overall population (400–500 million) and life expectancy. Given the Earth's total population at the time, life expectancy now constituted about 35–40 years.

From the point of view of globalization, these four stages of global history can be called periods of latent, or covert globalization. Only during the next stage of global history does it become possible to speak of "globalization" as such (i.e., as the spread of certain phenomena and processes around the entire globe).

The fifth stage of global history (and the first large period in the history of globalization) is the period of inter-continental systems. Chronologically, this corresponds to modern history—the period of mechanization, rationalization, industrialization, and urbanization—and to the epoch of nation-states, liberalism, and the emergence and development of capitalist relations. The most significant technological novelties of this period were the extensive use of machines, fossil fuels, steam power, electricity, and combustion engines, and the synthesis of new materials. The modern period is characterized by the rapid increase in anthropogenic impact on the Earth's ecosystems. The extraction and processing of mineral resources now takes place on an industrial scale. Farmlands are cultivated by tractors. Mineral fertilizers have appeared on the market. The composition of livestock has changed with the help of selection. The number of cities and urban populations have grown. Mobility increased sharply with new means of transportation. New means of communication (e.g., telegraph, radio, and the telephone) emerged, radically altering the role of geography in the relations between people. Colonial expansion and capitalization of resources (i.e., the introduction of land, labor, and money into a system of relations that influenced their cost) created the basis for inter-continental systems. Liberalism, a rationalist movement aimed at dismantling social restrictions on economic growth, became the ideological basis of inter-continentalization. In this period, we see a nonlinear relation between rates of population growth and technological development—a consequence of globalization. In the first half of the twentieth century, the planetary population was two billion people, having increased significantly with the aid of agrarian regions. The transition to industrial communities increased average life expectancy: taking into account the non-industrial communities around the world, it came to around 45–50 years.

The sixth stage is the period of global systems, the establishment of the unified social whole. Technologically, this it is the postindustrial epoch, whose beginning was marked by the scientific-technological revolution of the mid-twentieth century. The term "scientific-technological revolution" was introduced in the 1940s by the British Marxist historian John Bernal. A comparable term in modern Western tradition is "the Great Acceleration": the phrase gained currency in the 2010s.[16] This era opened new frontiers of global human history, including space exploration, atomics, and electronics. By the second half of the twentieth century, humanity possessed resources every bit as powerful as the geo-catastrophic factors like asteroids, volcanic eruptions, and tsunamis. To look beyond the atmosphere is to see that humanity in this period also began the age of space expansion. Electronics have led humanity to a new level of social interaction, where spatio-temporal restrictions in communication are all but neutralized. Economic trans-nationalization has led to the formation of global economic institutions. A global market is forming. The centralization of resources has become the basis of a system of global management, whose first institutions emerged in the twentieth century. The establishment of a global society has accelerated. Global culture is in the processes of formation, aiding the unification of human norms and values. The global interdependence of socio-economic development has led to rapid population growth in the countries of "secondary modernization," whose industrialization had not been accomplished by the mid-twentieth century. The Earth's population in 2020 was 7.5 billion people. The most important parameter of this new stage is the increase of the average life expectancy, which now equals 78–83 years.

It is obvious that the next leap in human development will accompany the new technological breakthroughs that will allow humanity not only to pass to the next level of social integration, but also to shift average life expectancy beyond one hundred years. Apart from this parameter, innovations in science, technology, ecology, or sociocultural development will not have the universal value determined by the historical logic of globalization. Considering globalization in its historical dimensions allows us to bring to light its logic and meaning as determined by the unity of humankind as a whole.

16   "Great Acceleration," Welcome to the Anthropocene, http://www.anthropocene.info/great-acceleration.php.

International Cooperation under the Conditions of Globalization: A Holistic Assessment

Tatiana A. Alekseeva and Ivan D. Loshkariov

1   Introductory Remarks

The modern world is experiencing a stage of significant political change. Certain mechanisms that previously acted as sources of influence and sequacity in politics now face increasing resistance from formerly subordinate groups and individuals, as well as challenges posed by new mechanisms of influence and domination. From the point of view of political ontology, modernity is synonymous with a plurality of manifestations of interconnectedness and interdependence. These go by a variety of names, such as cosmopolitanism, hybridization, or trans-nationalization. But globalization is perhaps the broadest term, designating the majority of such examples of interconnectedness and interdependence.

After the collapse of the bipolar system of international relations, a consensus emerged in the social sciences, to the effect that a diversity of forms of political, economic, social, and cultural relationships leads to the emergence of a new quality of social and political life. In other words, it proposed that globalization, among other things, creates a certain type of society with characteristics like "late capitalism," "liquid modernity," and "radical modernity."[1] That consensus did not address values with regard to the new qualities of social and political reality; on the contrary, few scholars actually welcomed the change, most of them remaining skeptical.[2] Indeed, globalization compresses the social space-time, increasing the mobility of ideas, people, and the "infiltration of capital,"[3]—and yet, these phenomena and processes were initially

---

1 See: Zygmunt Bauman, *Liquid Life* (Cambridge: Polity Press, 2005); Fredric Jameson, *Postmodernism, or The Cultural Logic of Late Capitalism* (Durham: Duke University Press, 1991); Anthony Giddens, *The Consequences of Modernity* (Stanford, CA: Stanford University Press, 1990).
2 See: Paul Hirst and Grahame Thompson, *Globalization in Question: The International Economy and the Possibilities of Governance* (Cambridge: Polity Press, 1996); Samuel Huntington, *The Clash of Civilizations and the Remaking of World Order* (New York: Simon & Schuster, 1996).
3 See: James Beckford, *Social Theory and Religion* (Cambridge: Cambridge University Press, 2003); Michael Power, *The Audit Society: Rituals of Verification* (Oxford: Oxford University Press, 1997).

ambiguous, often suggesting mutually exclusive conclusions with respect to the general prospects and to stability in the new era.

It is the political component of globalization that is essentially missing in the current discourse on globalization and its various forms. A great deal of research is devoted to the economic aspects of globalization—the circulation of capital, the relations between states and transnational business, and demand and consumption.[4] The cultural dimension of globalization received even more attention from researchers, especially in reference to issues such as the unification of social meanings, the emergence of new social groups, and the increasing importance of local specificity.[5] When it comes to the political sphere, globalization is presented mainly as a process through which the sovereignty of nation-states comes to be eroded.[6] This process is often associated with the achievements of modern information technologies, the spread of democracy, and the new role of human rights protection groups within the framework of state and society.[7] However, this approach to globalization's political aspects avoids addressing one of the main counterarguments within the social sciences and political philosophy, an argument which focuses on conflict and cooperation.

The conflict potential within a globalized system has gained some attention in academia, seeing a rise of publications on the topic. Although these works contain many valuable and interesting observations, they do not provide a systematic and holistic view of the effects of globalization. A number

---

4 See: David Harvey, *The Condition of Postmodernity: An Enquiry into the Origins of Cultural Change* (Malden, MA: Blackwell, 1989); Paul Virilio, *The Information Bomb* (London: Verso, 2000); Garrett Wallace Brown, "Globalization is What We Make of It: Contemporary Globalization Theory and the Future Construction of Global Interconnection," *Political Studies Review*, 2008, No. 6, 42–53; Kees van der Pilj, *Transnational Classes and International Relations* (London: Routledge, 1998).

5 See: Kenichi Ohmae, *The Invisible Continent: Four Strategic Imperatives of the New Economy* (New York: Harper Business, 2001); Leslie Sklair, "The Transnational Capitalist Class and Global Politics: Deconstructing the Corporate–State Connection," *International Political Science Review*, 2002 (23), No. 2, 159–74; Erik Swyngedouw, "Scaled Geographies: Nature, Place, and the Politics of Scale," in Robert McMaster and Eric Sheppard, eds., *Scale and Geographic Inquiry: Nature, Society and Method* (Oxford: Blackwell, 2004), 129–53.

6 See: Michael Kearney, "The local and the global: The anthropology of globalization," *Annual Review of Anthropology*, 1995, No. 24, 547–65; Michael Mann, "Neither Nation-States Nor Globalism," *Environment and Planning*, 1996, No. 28, 1960–64; John W. Meyer et al., "World Society and the Nation-State," *American Journal of Sociology*, 1997 (103), No. 1, 144–81; Saskia Sassen, *Losing Control? Sovereignty in an Age of Globalization* (New York: Columbia University Press, 1990).

7 See: Margaret Keck and Kathryn Sikkink, *Activists Beyond Borders* (Ithaca: Cornell University Press, 1998).

of authors believe that globalization exacerbates the conflict that existed in the pre-modern social and political space, through the rise of modern and post-modern practices. This conflict erodes trust in the society, spurring the atomization of individuals and the formation of hybrid social identities.[8] This statement is hardly disputable, but it describes the symptoms of current transformations instead of presenting an analysis of globalization's political consequences. Such "symptomatic" studies of globalization have largely emerged from ignoring the antipode of conflict: cooperation.

It is unfortunate that the idea of "cooperation" is not sufficiently defined in the social sciences. Robert Axelrod presented the most well-known definition of cooperation, saying that cooperation implies a certain behavioral strategy that takes into account the fact that its two actors *can meet again*. This definition implies unequal exchange, like any other behavioral strategy, but cooperative behavior leads to the satisfaction of all participants.[9] However, such a definition has almost no heuristic value, since it does not explain why, when, and to what extent the actors might choose to help one another. In practice, actors of similar origin and social background cooperate with like partners and make decisions guided by normative considerations (i.e., "it would be right to do this").[10] Due to these complexities, it is reasonable to assume that part of the responsibility for the incomplete study of the relationship between cooperation and globalization lies in the lack of understanding of cooperation as such.

This chapter aims to fill the relational gap between globalization and cooperation in the political realm. It might seem that the problem rests on something that resembles Talcott Parsons's "ideal types," or similar constructs from the continental philosophical tradition. We assess the nexus between globalization and international cooperation through the lens of practices and recurrences in this realm. In order to strike a balance and investigate both the part and the whole, this study will not attempt to cover all the existing cooperative practices. Instead, we have limited our analysis to international interactions, such as the interactions between social groups and those actors that experienced new forms of globalization earlier than others. Among these actors

---

8 Jeffrey G. Williamson, "Globalization, De-Industrialization and Underdevelopment in the Third World before the Modern Era," *Journal of Iberian and Latin American Economic History*, 2006 (24), No. 1, 9–36; Mayer N. Zald, "Globalizations and Social Movements," in *Culture, Power, and the Transnational Public Sphere*, edited by John Guidry, Michael Kennedy, and Mayer Zald (Ann Arbor: University of Michigan Press, 2009), 1–34.
9 Robert Axelrod, *The Evolution of Cooperation* (New York: Basic Books, 1985), 12–15.
10 Natalie Henrich and Joseph Henrich, *Why Humans Cooperate: A Cultural and Evolutionary Explanation* (Oxford: Oxford University Press, 2007), 35–36.

are states and non-state actors, such as transnational business, network structures, and societal units. We also significantly limited the scope of the study by considering only transformations of international cooperation by globalization, although we admit that the reverse process of the transformation of globalization through cooperation (with regards to its rhythms, contexts, and directions) also exists and deserves to be assessed.

This chapter is divided into five parts: introductory remarks, three problem-oriented sections, and a conclusion. In the first of our problem-oriented sections, we analyze contemporary discussions of cooperation and identify the key characteristics of the concept. We recognize that political discourse exists within a certain frame, and that normative and political concepts reflect desirable practices, as opposed to the actual. We assume that cooperative political practices are of normative and also political nature. Given this, we draw no distinction between a sign and a signifier. With this in mind, we highlight the main characteristics of cooperation, both temporal and spatial. In the second section, we determine what the distinctive features of international cooperation are, and to what extent certain characteristics of cooperation are represented in international cooperation. The third section discusses how the effects of globalization play an essential role in creating new practices of cooperation, and in transforming older patterns of cooperation. While focusing on the norms, principles, and practices of cooperation, we consider the potential for further development of international cooperation in the context of ongoing globalization. The section discusses whether or not the existing conditions favor a further development of international cooperation. Our main aim is to shift the focus from the *institutions* of cooperation (international organizations and regimes, forums, and negotiation platforms) to the *practices* of cooperation and their transformation through the globalization of the modern world.

2   Cooperation as a Political Concept

The groundbreaking field of cooperation studies emerged in recent decades at the intersection of economics and evolutionary biology. Biologists have long noted that the development of life requires either competition (meaning natural selection) or cooperation. In essence, genes work together within the genome, and chromosomes work together within eukaryotic cells. There are also examples of cooperation within the animal world; the mutually beneficial relationships between predatory fish species and the smaller fish species are especially well-studied.[11] (Of course, these represent unconscious behavior, not the results of reflection on purposeful actions, either on one's own or those of one's counterparts.)

Humans' arrival at cooperative practices was also not fully conscious: it seems that the transition from selfish behavior to the first forms of cooperation was caused by the growth of the human population and the struggle for resources. (This is often referred to as the "cultural group selection hypothesis." An alternative approach is the "big mistake hypothesis," following Aristotle's suggestion of the family-based origin of cooperation; this approach is sometimes taken by social psychologists, but has limited appeal to other social disciplines.) Garrett Hardin called this process "the tragedy of the commons": in order to multiply the available resources, people gradually, over the course of many generations, abandoned joint labor and common ownership. Those who opted to use common resources in their various forms simply disappeared as a result of natural selection.[12] Interestingly, this process gradually moved from the interpersonal level to the societal one: starting with the development of the technologies of war during the emerging statehood era, cooperation within groups and societies grew more complex, and increasingly relied on regulatory mechanisms rather than social inertia or intuitive trust.[13] Consequently, due to the duration of this process, an individual would not live long enough to realize its direction, as the formation of cooperative mechanisms was at least partially unconscious.

In European philosophy, Thomas Hobbes was one of the first to focus attention on issues of cooperation in his famous *Leviathan*, which proposed a theory of natural self-interested cooperation. Hobbes argued that human nature's desire for fame may well serve the common good:

> Desire of praise disposeth to laudable actions, such as please them whose judgement they value; for of those men whom we condemn, we condemn also the praises. Desire of fame after death does the same. And though after death there be no sense of the praise given us on earth, as being joys that are either swallowed up in the unspeakable joys of heaven or extinguished in the extreme torments of hell: yet is not such fame vain;

---

11   Lee A. Dugatkin, *Cooperation Among Animals: An Evolutionary Perspective* (Oxford: Oxford University Press, 1997), 59–70; Martin A. Nowak, "Five Rules for the Evolution of Cooperation," *Science*, 2006 (314), No. 5805, 1560–63.
12   Garrett Hardin, "The Tragedy of the Commons," *Science*, 1968 (162), No. 3859, 1243–48.
13   Peter Turchin et al., "War, Space, and the Evolution of Old World Complex Societies," *Proceedings of the National Academy of Sciences*, 2013 (110), No. 41, 16384–89.

because men have a present delight therein, from the foresight of it, and of the benefit that may redound thereby to their posterity.[14]

As more studies on cooperation were conducted, it became prevalent in the social sciences to interpret cooperation as a joint effort to create a public good through selfish interests. This definition also became popular among political economists. The American economist Frank Robotka compiled all existing approaches, highlighting several generally recognized features of cooperation:
1. The creation of a horizontally-integrated entity;
2. Voluntary participation of actors in a horizontally-integrated entity;
3. Only some part of the participants' resources is transferred to the horizontally-integrated entity, and the remaining resources are used independently;
4. The agreements within the horizontally-integrated entity relate to the areas of activity where the actors have previously acted alone;
5. The creation of a horizontally-integrated entity implies the emergence of new functions distributed among the participants.[15]

Thus, cooperation was viewed largely as a result of human behavior—but not as a desirable form of behavior. Further, this line of reasoning focused on cooperation as a positive occurrence rather than as a negative one. In addition, the egoistic approach largely implies that cooperation occurs at the individual level, or is a phenomenon only germane to small groups. Thus, an explanation of collective cooperation was ignored, as combining collective egoism with individual egoism posed a significant theoretical challenge.

Empirical studies of both cooperative group behavior and cooperative individual behavior have allowed us to make several significant observations. First, it is relatively rare for people to disregard teamwork completely. Using game-theory frameworks, economists predicted that the desire to be a "free-rider" (in other words, to enjoy public goods, or the benefits of cooperation, without actually contributing) should be fairly high. Yet, in practice, people are willing to cooperate and to contribute to the common cause, since the expected relative gain outweighs prior individual gains.[16] In other words, even when there is a tangible opportunity to become a "free-rider," people are more likely to take

---

14   Thomas Hobbes, *Leviathan* (New York: Touchstone, 1997), 61–62.
15   Frank Robotka, "A Theory of Cooperation," *Journal of Farm Economics*, 1947 (29), No. 1, 102.
16   Simon P. Anderson, Jacob K. Goeree, and Charles A. Holt, "A Theoretical Analysis of Altruism and Decision Error in Public Goods Games," *Journal of Public Economics*, 1998 (70), No. 2, 297–323.

a risk and cooperate, which suggests that the basis of cooperative behavior lies in egoism of limited nature, rather than absolute.

The second observation is that cooperation is not directly dependent on the number of actors. Thus, cooperation shares the same features at different levels of interaction, be it individual, group, societal, or international. There is no doubt that the number of "free-riders" in a large group may be higher than in a small group, but the number of people willing to cooperate may also be higher.[17] Consequently, cooperation is an umbrella concept (akin to Wittgenstein's "family resemblances") for interactions at various levels of analysis, including the individual and small-group levels.

Third, it has been observed that one of the essential mechanisms for expanding cooperation is reputation-building. People seek approval from others based on their contribution to a common cause. Experiments about anonymity and non-anonymity in the process of producing public goods confirm that the contribution of an individual to common efforts usually increases in conditions of non-anonymity, compared with anonymous contributions.[18] This is probably a remnant of the archaic and partly game-based notions of prestige (as defined by Johan Huizinga): universal approval is associated with the patronage of higher powers, and such approval can be obtained through the practice of distribution and generosity.[19] This corroborates Hobbes's argument that the desire for fame is a source for cooperation.

Fourth, communication between individuals, groups, and states has been observed to facilitate cooperation. Although it seems self-evident, the role of communication in this respect is not limited to the exchange of information. Communication has a specific stabilizing function: cooperators have the opportunity to discuss future interactions, as well as ways of pressuring "free-riders" and those who oppose further cooperation.[20]

Based on these observations, cooperation represents a set of social, cultural, economic, and political practices, all aimed at obtaining benefits for all the participants, even if some of the participants might choose a non-cooperative

---

17   Jeffrey P. Carpenter, "Punishing Free-Riders: How Group Size Affects Mutual Monitoring and the Provision of Public Goods," *Games and Economic Behavior*, 2007 (60), No. 1, 31–51.
18   Manfred Milinski and Bettina Rockenbach, "Spying on Others Evolves," *Science*, 2007 (317), No. 5837, 464–65.
19   See: Juliette Rouchier, Martin O'Connor, and François Bousquet, "The Creation of a Reputation in an Artificial Society Organised by a Gift System," *Journal of Artificial Societies and Social Simulation*, 2001 (4), No. 2; Charles Eisenstein, *Sacred Economics: Money, Gift, and Society in the Age of Transition* (New York: Penguin, 2011).
20   Gary Charness and Martin Dufwenberg, "Promises and Partnership," *Econometrica*, 2006 (74), No. 6, 1579–1601.

course of action. It is noteworthy that cooperative practices, unlike altruism, do not rule out selfish behavior among the participants. Such behavior is based on long-term expectations and non-material benefits (primarily reputational). Moreover, cooperative practices are often unconscious and habitual in nature. In addition to existing as a series of practices, cooperation also exists as a normative ideal—a set of coherent ideas about how to cooperate properly, what actions are considered cooperative, and in what situations cooperation is permissible or even desirable.

As a practice, cooperation has both spatial and temporal characteristics. Individuals, groups, and states can choose from several possible responses and act accordingly. Those decisions about normative actions and the different available options create divisions and alternate decision-making pathways that are the basic elements of the social and political space.[21]

The taxonomy of cooperation as a practice can be determined by the number of participants, the level of interaction, the scope of application, and the unique functions of the participants. In this light, cooperation has its ideal parameters—degree of involvement for the actors, the length or duration of cooperation, and attitudes towards uncooperative actors and actors cooperating within a different group. Some of these characteristics have an explicit temporal (as opposed to spatial) connotation, as seen in long-term cooperation or in the sequences of choices in favor of cooperative behavior.

In other cases, the temporal component appears to be more implicit: for instance, a high degree of specialization (in the distribution of roles) indirectly indicates a situation where it is difficult for participants to exit cooperative relations, and the practice of cooperation is likely to last longer. Similarly, a temporal aspect is attached to an increase in the duration of cooperation after the emergence of new roles that did not previously figure among the roles of separate actors.

This general description of the relationship between temporal and spatial characteristics of cooperation (see Table 1) does not contain a direct indication of cooperation's benefits to the participants, or of possible expectations regarding benefits. However, most of the characteristics are indirectly formed as a result of the participants' expectations about individual and group benefits. For example, the balance between the duration of cooperation and the number of participants directly affects the estimated total benefit: in particular, if there are too many participants, the expected benefit will be small and

---

21   See: Henri Lefebvre, *The Production of Space* (Oxford: Blackwell, 1991); Pierre Bourdieu, *The Logic of Practice* (Cambridge: Polity Press, 1990).

TABLE 1   The features of cooperation

		Cooperation as a practice	
	Dimensions	Spatial	Temporal
Cooperation as an ideal	Spatial	– Number of participants – Level of cooperation – Scope of cooperation – Degree of involvement	– Position towards the Other (for example, the non-participants of cooperation)
	Temporal	– Emergence of new functions – Specialization of participants	– Duration

will negatively impact the duration of cooperation. Similarly, the relationship between specialization and the position towards the Other implies reciprocity: each participant must do his or her part, or else selfish behavior and the desire for egoistic short-term gains would become the dominant pattern. Our analysis of cooperation as a real practice and as an ideal allows us to include both individual and collective features of cooperative behavior in a holistic framework. Consequently, we have presented a framework for assessing the spatial and temporal characteristics of cooperation, as well as the forms and manifestations of cooperation itself.

3   International Cooperation: The Concept and the Practices

As noted in the previous section, cooperation between states and non-state actors at the international level has identical characteristics with other forms of cooperation. At the same time, the international level of interaction implies a narrower framework of analysis with respect to the actors involved, the representation of the Other, and the implications of cooperation.

First, an important distinguishing feature of international cooperation is the overlap in the jurisdictions of various organizational structures and forums of cooperation. In other words, the existence of multiple international-cooperation forums with independent rules of interaction allows participants to significantly minimize their contribution to the production of common goods by choosing the ideal forum for their own needs. Accordingly, the differences between the minimum and maximum degree of involvement among various participants at the international level are much greater than at other levels. Moreover, since the number of cooperative forums tends to increase at this level, it is highly likely that the existing gap in the degree of involvement will become even more apparent.[22]

In some areas, this difference in cooperative interactions among state and non-state actors creates an appearance of a small group of states taking primary responsibility for the implementation of cooperation. For example, cooperation in the 1959 Antarctic Treaty, through which the study and preservation of the natural potential of Antarctica is sheltered in the interests of all humankind, is governed by only twenty-nine states with the status of "contracting parties," maintaining the right "to participate in consultative meetings provided for under Article IX."[23] Similarly, only ninety-two states participate in the UN body on the peaceful uses of outer space, while the Outer Space Treaty stipulates that the study and use of outer space should be carried out "for the benefit and in the interests of all countries."[24] In other words, differentiation in the degree of involvement in international cooperation often results in the participants' unequal status and in the reduction of the number of participants. The only possible exception to this pattern is military affairs, where forums of engagement are numerically insignificant by definition.

Second, the interdependence of actors is a significant feature of international cooperation. Theoretical works on cooperation usually emphasize the importance of contact between participants, but the choices of one actor automatically influence the choices of other actors in the international arena, even if there is no direct contact between them (be it hostile or friendly). This interdependence affects the method of problem-solving within the framework of cooperation. As highlighted in the previous section, cooperation usually implies joint execution of some action or a general prohibition on another action. However, in international cooperation, it is important to harmonize the actors' activities, not merely commit to joint actions. In other words, inter-

---

22   Karen J. Alter and Sophie Meunier, "The Politics of International Regime Complexity," *Perspectives on Politics*, 2009 (1), No. 7, 13–24; Marc Levy, Oran Young, and Michael Zürn, "The Study of International Regimes," *European Journal of International Relations*, 1995 (1), No. 3, 267–330.

23   Olav S. Stokke and Davor Vidas, eds., *Governing the Antarctic: The Effectiveness and Legitimacy of the Antarctic Treaty System* (Cambridge: Cambridge University Press, 1996), 35–47.

24   Yuanyuan Zhao, "An International Space Authority: A Governance Model for a Space Commercialization Regime," *Journal of Air Law and Commerce*, 2004 (30), No. 2, 277–96.

national cooperation emphasizes joint actions and their standardization (as opposed to the principle of "joint actions performed individually").[25]

In cooperative environments where interdependent actors make independent decisions, there is a need for a specific information-exchange system. In other words, it is necessary to accumulate and systematize information in order to ensure the transparency of the actors' behavior. Means of information exchange make shunning obligations at critical moments much more difficult. For example, in the military sphere, the informational function of cooperation is achieved through confidence-building measures (i.e., notifications about military exercises and other activities, invitations to observe military events, and mutual inspections of military facilities and border areas, including airborne), and via communication channels reserved for crisis situations. In the economic realm of cooperation, information exchangeability presents even more tangible evidence, as most transactions are publicly available, which allows actors to instantly respond to possible violations.[26]

Without the interdependence of actors, participants of cooperative interactions would be unlikely to specialize in "narrow" issues, because of severe inequalities in their political, economic, and other potentials. If there were no interdependence between participants in international interactions, the strategy of specialization would be self-defeating for many participants, as there would be no guarantee that the results of specialization would have any relevance for other actors. For example, there is a group of so-called "middle powers" (medium-sized states) that have no opportunities to significantly increase their global influence. They tend to support the current political order, specializing in global threats and challenges like conflict resolution, climate change, and the protection of human rights.[27] In other words, the differences between their potentials predetermine the states' specialization, as states with relatively small potential will come short of intellectual and economic resources for addressing a large-scale agenda or lending political legitimacy to their possible actions in such an arena. Further, the agenda of the middle powers is too limited for relatively large states, because it does not cover many important military and economic issues. Nevertheless, the structural impetus towards

---

25   Duncan Snidal, "Coordination Versus Prisoners' Dilemma: Implications for International Cooperation and Regimes," *American Political Science Review*, 1985 (79), No. 4, 937.

26   Charles Lipson, "International Cooperation in Economic and Security Affairs," *World Politics*, 1984 (37), No. 1, 16–17, 22.

27   Eduard Jordaan, "The Concept of a Middle Power in International Relations: Distinguishing Between Emerging and Traditional Middle Powers," *Politikon*, 2003 (30), No. 1, 166–67.

specialization does not work without conditions of interferences that diminish the actors' ability to avoid at least indirect participation in international affairs.

The dependence of governmental and non-governmental international organizations on financial and personnel circumstances predetermines their focus on certain areas (with the exception of the United Nations). Basically, the main resource of an international organization is its expertise in a narrow sphere of responsibility, as well as its ability to process information in order to create certain interpretations, rules, and norms.[28] Other participants of international interactions place their trust in such specialized international organizations, due precisely to their interdependence and to two other factors: first, their ability to influence the decisions of such organizations in specific situations, and, second, the need to entrust the most important aspects of political cooperation to more neutral entities, rather than the self-interested interdependent players.

Beyond this, international cooperation is not a longstanding set of practices, to look at it from a comparative perspective. In the military sphere, the peak of cooperation is the formation of military alliances, which are based on mutual protection from the other international actors. Empirical studies show that most military alliances are formed with the participation of at least one of the great powers. In turn, according to Jack Levy, the formation of military alliances involving at least one of the great powers led to a probability higher than 56% of wars over the next five years (for some centuries, this figure was close to 100%).[29] This is the main reason for the fragility of military alliances: during and after armed conflicts, the interests of actors and former allies change dramatically, and the old military alliances cannot survive. (One of the most plausible explanations for NATO's more than seven-decade lifespan is its political, rather than purely military, nature, which means that NATO does not conform to the logic of classical military alliances.) Another reason for this fragility lies in the fact that military alliances lack enforcement mechanisms for pressuring actors to fulfill their obligations and for preventing freeloading behaviors. Alan Sabrovsky's shocking calculation revealed that in only slightly more than 20% of all cases over the past two centuries had partic-

---

28   Michael Barnett and Martha Finnemore, *Rules for the World: International Organizations in Global Politics* (Ithaca: Cornell University Press, 2004), 4–8.
29   Jack S. Levy, "Alliance Formation and War Behavior: An Analysis of the Great Powers, 1495–1975," *Journal of Conflict Resolution*, 1981 (25), No. 4, 581–613.

ipants fulfilled a military alliance's primary obligation to wage war alongside their allies.[30]

In non-military spheres of international cooperation, the absence of coercive mechanisms leads strong players to abide by an agreement only when it is profitable, but not in other cases. This results in an uneven distribution of benefits among the participants, which is not conducive to lasting cooperation.[31] Still, there is a relatively viable mechanism for international arbitration and dispute resolution—the World Trade Organization—which partially compensates for the uneven distribution of benefits in the economic sphere. Even where large states act on their own, it is possible to determine who is right in a particular situation, and to construct legitimate means of penalizing violators of agreements. Another important mechanism, at least in cooperative economic formats with a large number of participants, is a certain "crowd effect" afforded by bilateral or "club" agreements that enhance cooperation, and are often viewed by other actors as a loss of some of the benefits of cooperation, which leads to extensions of original compositions of agreeing parties.[32] Accordingly, cooperation can vary greatly (especially with regard to military and non-military interactions), although the international environment creates incentives that impede cooperation instead of facilitating it.

Further, perceptions of participants as actors play an enormous role in international cooperation. If a participant in an international interaction is not perceived by others as real, or "entitative," the interaction simply does not occur, or does not happen in a cooperative format. At other levels of interaction, the problem of recognizing the entitativity of a counterpart also exists, but this issue of perception critically concerns many international-level actors and determines their actions and responses to potential partners. At other levels, where the scale of interactions is reduced to smaller groups and individuals, this characteristic of entitativity becomes one of many factors that

---

30   Alan N. Sabrovsky, "Interstate Alliances: Their Reliability and the Expansion of War," in *The Correlates of War*, vol. 2, edited by J. David Singer (New York: Free Press, 1980), 145–89.
31   Donald J. Puchala and Raymond F. Hopkins, "International Regimes: Lessons from Inductive Analysis," *International Organization*, 1982 (36), No. 2, 250.
32   Tim Büthe and Helen V. Milner, "The Politics of Foreign Direct Investment into Developing Countries: Increasing FDI Through International Trade Agreements?" *American Journal of Political Science*, 2008 (52), No. 4, 741–62; Giovanni Maggi, "The Role of Multilateral Institutions in International Trade Cooperation," *The American Economic Review*, 1999 (89), No. 1, 190–214; G. Richard Shell, "Trade Legalism and International Relations Theory: An Analysis of the World Trade Organization," *Duke Law Journal*, 1994 (44), No. 5, 829–927.

determine social and political behavior, but it does not generally amount to a constitutive function of cooperation.[33]

Additionally, it is important to point out the absence of a common procedure for recognizing actors as entitative. There are different views on *who* decides what socio-political units should be recognized, *what* is considered legitimate, and *how* to determine legitimacy. A typical example compares the situations of South Sudan and Kosovo. South Sudan emerged in 2011 as a result of a referendum resolving the multi-year conflict between the northern and southern regions of Sudan. Most states in the international system (over 130) recognized South Sudan *as a state* (i.e, as an equal entity). The Republic of Kosovo, on the other hand, was declared independent in 2008 by the local parliament, which marked an actual break in the negotiations on the settlement of a multi-year conflict. Kosovo is recognized by only ninety-eight states, and therefore receives less recognition than South Sudan. The paradox of the situation is that Kosovo is *much more of a state* in terms of its formal characteristics (control over its own territory, existence of a single system of government, and self-awareness of the inhabitants). After the independence of South Sudan was declared, a civil war tore apart the newborn country. The explanation for Kosovo's lack of recognition is probably the following: a number of states (like China and Russia) did not accept *how* Kosovo declared itself a state (by breaking talks with Serbia). In other words, Kosovo broke these countries' moral and praxeological expectations about the Other. In contrast, South Sudan met all the expectations about *how* to act in order to gain international recognition. As a result, the example of South Sudan and Kosovo indicates that the recognition of the ontological Other as an actor in international interactions is largely based on subjective factors, including moral and praxeological expectations.[34]

The basic dilemma of actors in international cooperation involves the following state of affairs: some actors, in order to gain recognition, are forced to "pretend" or imitate others according to the expectations of other actors. But no one can pretend forever. In continental philosophy, the very existence of the Other often served as a constitutive element in the formation of the Self, diverting dilemmas from the level of practice to the social-ontological level. Classical definitions reduce social and political identity (or self-categorization,

---

33   Emanuele Castano, Simona Sacchi, and Peter H. Gries, "The Perception of the Other in International Relations: Evidence for the Polarizing Effect of Entitativity," *Political Psychology*, 2003 (24), No. 3, 449–53.

34   Thomas Lindemann and Erik Ringmar, *International Politics of Recognition* (London: Routledge, 2015), 33–46.

in the narrower sense), attributing certain characteristics to the Self and considering the presence of the Other. The most extreme example of this is Carl Schmitt's description of the very essence of the political domain as a permanent distinction between the Self and the non-Self. Nevertheless, transferring conflict to the ontological level has its price: the conflict between different political identities becomes practically insoluble. Still, optimism in the study of international cooperation can be justified, as conflict at the ontological level is noticeably mitigated by the objective needs of international actors. Participants in international interactions need the general predictability of the environment around them and the development of new and more complex benefits, in addition to awareness of themselves and of the rest of the world.[35] Thus, the perception of the Other in international interactions plays a constitutive role in the recognition of other actors; on the other hand, it is not among the fundamental obstacles to cooperation.

In general, the practices of international cooperation are often embodied simultaneously through several negotiation platforms. International cooperation is not only a multi-level exchange of actions but also has tangled interactions at varying levels. In addition, international cooperation implies a relatively high degree of the actors' specialization and a relatively short duration of cooperation. Finally, despite the substantial potential for conflict between "Self" and "Other" in international politics, vagueness in matters of perception with respect to an actor's entitativity and the objective needs of actors serve as a sufficient basis for cooperative behavior.

4   Globalization and Change in International Cooperation

Arjun Appadurai's widely recognized classification identifies "scapes" and "inside" and "in-between flows" as spatial characteristics of globalization. The compression of social time leads to instability in the flows of capital, social ideas, everyday information, and people (tourists and refugees). New flows are likely to emerge, and their scale and density may exceed those of existing flows. This results in new disjunctures between organizational fields because

---

[35]   B. Greenhill, "Recognition and Collective Identity Formation in International Politics," *European Journal of International Relations*, 2008 (14), No. 2, 343–68; Alexander Wendt, "Collective Identity Formation and the International State," *American Political Science Review*, 1994 (88), No. 2, 384–96.

economic processes are developing in connection with cultural ones, and in considerable contradiction with the latter.[36]

Spatial disjuncture in different spheres of activity (politics, economics, communication, and ideas) leads to the emergence of intermediate and hybrid spaces where the principles of several organizational fields operate simultaneously. By the same token, actors can simultaneously employ multiple resources, such as political resources in the economy or cultural resources in the informational realm. Accordingly, the total number of actors involved in international cooperation is increasing; we assume that the proportion of "cooperating" actors will remain at approximately the same level, against the backdrop of a general increase in the total number of actors. The hybridization and interpenetration of actors from various organizational fields can be observed in examples of the new functions of business, described by the expression "social responsibility." Multinational corporations are now engaged either in the production and sale of goods and services, or in such matters as forming cross-industry ethical standards, combating social problems (e.g., homelessness, illiteracy, the spread of HIV), and protecting the environment.[37] Moreover, the struggle against these global challenges does not unfold solely at the national or local levels; more than 9,000 large firms have joined the UN Global Compact in order to coordinate their efforts with those of international institutions.

The trend of simultaneous increase in the numbers of actors and broadening of international cooperation can be traced in the military sphere, too. According to Douglas Gibler's calculations, an increase in the total number of states led to an increase in the number of dyads that could potentially establish military cooperation (from 226 in 1816 to 3,132 by the year 2000). Notably, the number of interstate dyads that participated in military-political alliances was consistently about one-third of the total number of states, with the exception of the period between 1918 and 1946. Moreover, military cooperation and alliances turned from a predominantly European into a global phenomenon, giving rise to global military alliances and regional and trans-

---

36 Arjun Appadurai, "Disjuncture and Difference in the Global Cultural Economy," *Theory, Culture and Society*, 1990 (7), No. 2–3, 295–310.

37 Georg Scherer, Guido Palazzo, and Dorothée Baumann, "Global Rules and Private Actors: Toward a New Role of the Transnational Corporation in Global Governance," *Business Ethics Quarterly*, 2006 (16), No. 4, 505–32; Ole Jacob Sending and Iver B. Neumann, "Governance to Governmentality: Analyzing NGOSs, States, and Power," *International Studies Quarterly*, 2006 (50), No. 3, 651–72.

regional agreements.[38] In addition to interstate forms of military cooperation, there are non-state forms of military cooperation involving actors such as businesses and ethno-cultural groups (e.g., private military companies, insurgents, and terrorist organizations).[39]

Apparently, the transition from the international cooperation among states to international interactions between a variety of actors (both past and current) changes the very essence of cooperation as a practice. In principle, international cooperation is based on rational prerequisites: in many cases, participation in cooperative interactions (though often inconsistent or merely *pro forma*) turns out to be more beneficial than non-participation. On the other hand, the involvement of large numbers of actors hampers rational decision-making, so that only a small part of information about all the interactions can be properly processed and systematized. Therefore, the factor of subjective grounds for the behavior of actors gains additional significance. This means, first and foremost, the collective emotions embedded in particular social contexts and acquiring the character of normative judgments or practical recommendations.[40] It is probably not entirely correct to place all the responsibility for changing the prerequisites of cooperation on globalization, but it is certain that globalization does contribute to the processes of change.

Globalization is also associated with changes in the spheres of interdependence and further specialization of actors. Globalization in the spheres of technology, capital turnover, and ideas is leading to further homogenization as required by globalization structures, and to the production of goods in corresponding organizational fields. Given that international cooperation itself tends to focus on standardizing the actions of actors, globalization actually reinforces the already established trends. For example, Daniel Drezner analyzed the gradual implementation of uniform rules for regulating capital turnover, concluding that globalization has prompted the introduction of banking procedures related to transparency and data security, auditing, and

---

38 Douglas M. Gibler, *International Military Alliances, 1648–2008* (Washingthon, DC: CQ, 2008), 551–53.

39 David E. Cunningham, Kristian S. Gleditsch, and Idean Salehyan, "Non-State Actors in Civil Wars: A New Dataset," *Conflict Management and Peace Science*, 2013 (30), No. 5, 516–31; Jose L. Gómez del Prado, "Impact on Human Rights of a New Non-State Actor: Private Military and Security Companies," *The Brown Journal of World Affairs*, 2011 (18), No. 1, 151–69.

40 Emma Hutchison and Roland Bleiker, "Theorizing Emotions in World Politics," *International Theory*, 2014 (6), No. 3, 491–514; B. E. Sasley, "Theorizing States' Emotions," *International Studies Review*, 2011 (13), No. 3, 452–76.

risk insurance. This process was initially beneficial to developed countries, which sought to reduce the cost of capital turnover on a global scale, to establish forms of liability for regulatory compliance, and to expand opportunities for investment in developing countries. In the medium term, this process brought to developing countries predominantly economic instability and relatively high costs of adaptation to regulatory standards. However, changes in the structure of financial flows have also affected the initial characteristics of financial markets. The most pertinent case is the emergence of a group of offshore countries, which moderated the emerging global financial rules for the developing world.[41] There was also a significant stratification among the developing countries themselves, some of which used unified rules for capital turnover and significantly changed trade flows, offering preferential conditions for investment, localization of production, and technology transfer (this was done, for example, in China, India, and Malaysia). Consequently, the direct losses from financial globalization turned out to be at least partially compensated by the opportunities that have opened up in the markets for goods and services, which have themselves affected the direction of the financial flows.[42]

Another consequence of globalization for international cooperation is the erosion of the image of the Other. As noted above, the basis of international cooperation includes the problem of recognition and the definition of the "Self" and "others." In the process of making such a distinction, the ontological Other is "over there," and the "Self" is somewhere "around." This allows us to stipulate that the Self is a fairly stable set of characteristics with respect to certain criterion (race, ethnicity, gender), just like the Other. However, globalization largely replaces this differentiating function by a function of interdependence and complexity. In other words, the old-fashioned pairs of "friend-foe," "close-far," and "center-periphery" are replaced by multi-level and unstable relationships of inclusion and exclusion, locality and nonlocality.[43] Is it possible to claim that actors in world politics will no longer be able to distinguish each other and will not be able to recognize themselves? This is probably too bold an assumption to make, since the relationship between

---

41   Daniel Drezner, *All Politics is Global: Explaining International Regulatory Regimes* (Princeton: Princeton University Press, 2008), 120–29.
42   Raphael Kaplinsky and Masuma Farooki, *Global Value Chains, the Crisis, and the Shift of Markets from North to South, in Global Value Chains in a Postcrisis World: A Development Perspective* (Washington, DC: The World Bank, 2010), 138–43.
43   Raka Shome and Radha Hegde, "Culture, Communication, and the Challenge of Globalization," *Critical Studies in Media Communication*, 2002 (19), No. 2, 175–77.

actors usually has a long history of conscious existence, which also affects their perceptions of the world. In addition, the specialization of certain actors in certain problems, branches of production, and normative judgments continues to be indicative of the role of the Other in international relations.[44] At the same time, the lines of demarcation are not being hardened, which means that the relationship between "Self" and "Other" will be less determined by the logic of opposition than by the logics of mediation, hybridity, and uncertainty.

The problem of the international "Other" lies in the process of recognizing the Other and becomes as obscure as the Other itself. In Hegel's definition, the opposite of recognition is the ability to assert one's rights and freedoms in situations where the existence of these rights and freedoms is not obvious or natural. An important element of a *claim* to recognition is the presence of an authority to whom such a claim could be addressed. With the dramatic increase in the number of actors, the blurring of semantic differences between them, and certain ontological degradation of the Other, it remains unclear who should act as the authority for such claims. In Hegel's lifetime, this question was supposed to be determined by nation-states, especially in terms of granting legal status to individuals and groups.[45] Currently, the role of granting recognition is carried out in varying degrees either by states or international institutions, human rights organizations, financial groups, and auditing agencies.

A curious consequence of the changes in recognition in international politics is the loss of a clear distinction between the global and the non-global phenomena.[46] As Doreen Massey puts it, spaces in the era of globalization no longer have a clearly defined length and coordinate system, while also facing a higher likelihood of becoming a meeting place for unrelated processes, phenomena, and effects. This means that, in the primary interaction of non-global and global actors, all actors involved become global rather than non-global. This process seems to be enduring, since different phenomena coexist precisely in the state of distinction or difference from each other.[47]

---

44   Iver B. Neumann, "Self and Other in International Relations," *European Journal of International Relations*, 1966 (2), No. 2, 139–74.

45   Gary Browning, *The Recognition of Globalization and the Globalization of Recognition, in Global Justice and the Politics of Recognition* (London: Palgrave Macmillan, 2013), 48–63.

46   J. K. Gibson-Graham, "Beyond Global vs. Local: Economic Politics outside the Binary Frame," in *Geographies of Power: Placing Scale*, edited by Andrew Herod and Melissa Wright (Malden, MA: Blackwell, 2002), 25–60; Saskia Sassen, "Local Actors in Global Politics," *Current Sociology*, 2004 (52), No. 4, 649–70.

47   Doreen Massey, *Imagining Globalization: Power-Geometries of Time-Space, Global Futures* (London: Palgrave Macmillan, 1999), 32–41.

The transformation of the Other and the space of international cooperation itself spur a change in the temporal characteristics of international cooperation. Fredric Jameson notes, in his provocative essay "The End of Temporality," that apparently established phenomena—such as economic cycles (e.g., the so-called Kondratieff waves), ideas about the periodization of the past, and the order of everyday actions—face dramatic alterations. There is no doubt that this statement has some Marxist background, attributing a particular temporality to certain periods of time and modes of production, but it is hard to dispute that the perception of time and its "density" has changed.[48] Going back to Appadurai's thesis on the flows of globalization that form the modern world, the perceived acceleration or movement of those flows acquires an ultimate political meaning, since different actors are required to change their temporal flows. Moreover, the submission of certain actors is ensured through communication technologies and planning tools, at organizational, state, and international levels.[49]

A directed and non-directed change in temporality leads to the emergence of multiple temporalities, making it meaningless to talk about the duration of international cooperative practices: if two actors cooperate, proceeding from different views of time, the duration can be estimated only from the position of one of the actors, in subjective terms. However, there is considerable potential for increasing the relative average duration of international cooperation on specific issues and between specific actors. This is due to the non-simultaneous awareness of the benefits and disadvantages of cooperation, which leaves more room for inertia-like cooperation and multilateral cooperation, largely influenced by the international "crowd effect."

In general, globalization causes "scattering" effects on the practices of international cooperation, because it makes almost all characteristics of cooperation—such as duration, self-identification, and specialization—extremely vague and flexible. In many ways, globalization contributes to the complication of international cooperative practices, which is especially noticeable in the number and qualitative diversity of the actors involved. At the same time, such manifestations of globalization make it impossible to analyze the rationality and non-rationality of the actors' actions, since subjective motives tend to dominate their behavior.

---

48 Fredric Jameson, "The End of Temporality," *Critical Inquiry*, 2003 (29), No. 4, 703–707.
49 Sarah Sharma, *In the Meantime: Temporality and Cultural Politics* (Durham: Duke University Press, 2014), 138–39.

5 Conclusions

The impact of globalization on the practices of international cooperation is rather paradoxical. Globalization enhances the interdependence of actors, standardizes their behavior, and increases the average relative duration of cooperation. And yet, this is achieved because the global and the non-global become more alike, and because many practices fall out of conventional time, giving rise to multiple and multiplying temporalities. Thus, globalization gives a powerful impetus to existing and emergent practices of international cooperation, due to homogenization in one direction, and simultaneously complicates the environment for the implementation of these practices, disorienting the actors of international politics by multiplying entities in other areas.

These processes have an apparent normative dimension. With a certain "blurring" of the ideas of the Other, hybrid forms of international cooperation emerge (including imitational and localized). Under such conditions, disagreements between actors and various forums of international cooperation arise on such matters as what to consider cooperative behavior, what constitutes a sufficient contribution to the fight against global challenges and needs, what is the minimum acceptable threshold for participation in cooperation, and what is the acceptable level of interdependence of actors (given the prospect of partial loss of freedom of choice). We locate a problem not in the disagreements themselves, but in the fact that the accelerated subjectivization of relations (particularly, the growing importance of the emotional component) eliminates the grounds for non-violent cooperative resolution of such differences.

PART 2

Philosophical and Sociocultural Aspects of Globalization

The Role of Global Studies in the Development of a Sustainable Security System

Ilya V. Ilyin and Kristina S. Leonova

1 Vladimir Vernadsky and the Emergence of Global Studies

In the early stages of the development of global studies, scholars identified *global studies* and *globalistics* as two distinct fields, nevertheless believing that the differences between them lay more in their names than in their contents. It was assumed that the term used in western academic literature, "global studies," was equivalent to what was termed "globalistics" in Russian scientific literature. It was also believed that the study of global events and phenomena had begun with the work of the Club of Rome, founded in 1968 by the Italian economist and entrepreneur Aurelio Peccei. Scientists who joined this nongovernmental organization were engaged in the study of global issues that humanity needed to address in order to ensure its own future. The aim of the members of the Club of Rome was not only to study the problems they identified, but also to find ways and means to overcome them, as well as to draw public attention to those issues. The scientific contributions of Jay Wright Forrester (1918–2016) and Dennis Lynn Meadows (born 1942) enabled the use of mathematical modeling in the study of global processes. In the 1970s, the first mathematical models were created to analyze the dynamics of global development and to demonstrate the possible consequences of human activity, both for the humanity and for the environment.

The Club of Rome made a tremendous contribution to the development of global issues. The publication of the Club's reports, which were translated into several dozen languages, led to the spread of information about global phenomena across the globe. Through the Club's efforts, global studies as a field developed its own research methods through mathematical modeling. That said, the origins of global studies predate the creation of nongovernmental organizations such as the Club of Rome. In the first half of the twentieth century, Russian scientist Vladimir Vernadsky (1863–1945), a professor at Moscow University, gave lectures which touched upon various aspects of global processes that still take place today, in the twenty-first century.

Despite the fact that Vernadsky did not use the terminology standard in contemporary studies on global phenomena, he noted the increased interaction between human societies, their unity, and their integration, which are now considered the fundamental features of the process of globalization. In his words, he highlighted that "in the twentieth century, man, for the first time in the history of the Earth, knew and embraced the whole biosphere, completed the geographic map of the planet Earth, and colonized its whole surface. Humanity has become a single whole in the course of its life."[1] In saying this, Vernadsky emphasized that such integrity should not only be present within human society, but it should also extend to the relationship between mankind and nature. He noted the special role that humans play in the biosphere, calling them "a new unprecedented geological force."[2] He stressed that the immense achievements of humankind are based on its intimate connection with the environment.

In the course of its development, human civilization transformed the world around it, changing its structure and properties, as well as the chemical and physical composition of global systems. "Human thought has embraced the biosphere and affects all the processes in a new way, and as a result, the *energy, active energy of the biosphere increases*."[3] Meanwhile, the ongoing natural processes have an impact on human beings and their activities. This belief was also held by representatives of Russian Cosmism—Konstantin Tsiolkovsky, Alexander Chizhevsky, Nikolai Fyodorov, and others. According to Vernadsky, humanity should interact with the environment because of the close interconnectedness and the mutual influences of humanity and nature.

In his work, Vernadsky investigated past and present global processes, and also speculated about future ones. His concept of the *noosphere* involves the human mind's ability to distinguish humans among other species, and to create mechanisms that would reduce the anthropogenic load on the biosphere, contributing to the further co-evolution of humankind and natural systems. Central to the concept of the noosphere is the idea that human civilization must take responsibility for the preservation and further evolution of the biosphere. According to Vernadsky, the main tools that will prompt the transformation of the biosphere into its new stage—which he termed the *noosphere*—are scientific thought and human labor.[4]

---

1 Vladimir Vernadsky, *Философские мысли натуралиста* [*The Philosophical Thoughts of a Naturalist*] (Moscow: Nauka, 1988), 508.
2 Vladimir Vernadsky, *Научная мысль как планетное явление* [*Scientific Thought as a Planetary Phenomenon*] (Moscow: Nauka, 1991), 20–21.
3 *Переписка В. И. Вернадского с Б. Л. Личковым. 1918–1939* [*Correspondence between Vladimir Vernadsky and Boris Lichkov, 1918–1939*], edited by V. S. Neapolitanskaya and Boris Levshin (Moscow: Nauka, 1979), 182.
4 Vernadsky, *Scientific Thought as a Planetary Phenomenon*, 20.

Vernadsky's immense contribution to the formation of global studies is defined not only by the identification of the essence and characteristics of socio-natural processes, but also by the definition of the *planetary* (or global) direction of science and education. In his work *Scientific Thought as a Planetary Phenomenon*, he noted that

> science and the scientific thought that creates it reveal—in this growth of the twentieth century science that we are experiencing, in this profound social phenomenon of human history—its own other, alien, and planetary character.[5]

Vernadsky underscored that

> the scientific thought of a scientist of our time with unprecedented success and force is deepening into new areas of great importance that did not exist before or were the exclusive domain of philosophy and religion. The horizons of scientific knowledge are expanding compared to the nineteenth century—to an unprecedented and unexpected degree.[6]

Based on science's acquisition of a "planetary character," Vernadsky also considered the need to saturate the educational sphere with planetary, global content, given the importance of education in the fields of science.[7]

Further, Vernadsky indicated that new problems (new at that time of his writing, in the twentieth century) require qualitatively new approaches to their study. He described a research method which permits the use of knowledge from various sciences to solve multidimensional problems. This approach is known today as an interdisciplinary approach. Sometimes, when studying a global process, the concepts, methods, and knowledge of a single science do not provide an opportunity for complex understanding or research. Vernadsky revealed that the sciences are densely connected, not only to each other, but also to other areas of human spiritual life, such as philosophy and religion.[8] While conducting research, scientists turn to philosophical ideas and concepts, which subsequently become integral parts of science. Vernadsky put his

---

5 Vernadsky, *Scientific Thought as a Planetary Phenomenon*, 39.
6 Vladimir Vernadsky, Биосфера и ноосфера [*Biosphere and Noosphere*] (Moscow: T8RUGRAM, 2017), 377.
7 See: Vladimir Vernadsky, Задачи высшего образования нашего времени [*The Objectives of Higher Education in Our Time*] (Moscow: Amonashvili, 2001).
8 Vladimir Vernadsky, Труды по всеобщей истории науки [*Works in the General History of Science*] (Moscow: Nauka, 1988), 58.

ideas into practice and developed theoretical foundations. It is thanks to him that a new branch of geochemistry—biogeochemistry—came into being. Biogeochemistry is but one example of an interdisciplinary science that successfully combines three sciences—biology, geology, and chemistry—into one. However, the integration of multiple sciences to successfully solve scientific issues undoubtedly occurred earlier. It is worth mentioning, for instance, the great Russian scientist Mikhail Lomonosov, who had laid the foundations for physical chemistry. Vernadsky repeatedly referred to the works of Lomonosov, noting his significant role in Russian science in several articles. Lomonosov's ideas influenced Vernadsky's own scientific worldview. The examples of disciplines just mentioned indicate that the awareness of the need to integrate the knowledge from the various scientific fields came long before the terms "interdisciplinary" and "global" ever appeared.

Having considered some of Vernadsky's ideas and theories, we can conclude that he is the founder of what we now call "global studies." His concepts and work stimulated the further development of science. Over time, terms and categories were formed to help define those phenomena that were previously identified by Vernadsky. Further, Vernadsky's ideas continue to develop in contemporary global studies. For example, his theory of the noosphere became the basis for the concept of sustainable development, which is currently supported even at the level of the United Nations.

2 The Emergence of Globalistics as the Core of Global Studies

It is becoming increasingly obvious that global studies represent a broader scientific field, covering various global disciplines, including global ecology, global geography, global history, and global economics. Researchers in each of these disciplines must focus on distinct scientific branches created long before the current global focus of studies, which now require a new, global approach correspondent with the features of modern human development. Objects of study of these disciplines do not themselves change, but the approach and the angle from which they are studied do. The scale of research is also changing and becoming more global. The core of the new global studies is globalistics, which combines the knowledge of various sciences in order to produce comprehensive, systematic study of global phenomena that arise not only on the Earth, but also beyond it. Thus, we can argue that the terms "global studies" and "globalistics" are not synonymous. Global studies is a multidisciplinary field of modern science which is represented by individual sciences that study global phenomena in one specific area; globalistics is an interdisciplinary science that integrates knowledge from individual global disciplines to create a more comprehensive and systemic study of global phenomena, identifying relevant relationships and patterns.

Despite the emergence of its own specific categories, terms, theories, and concepts, global studies as a science is only in its initial stages of formation.[9] As is often the case in the formation of a new scientific field, there is a certain sense of chaos in current global studies. Experts note the lack of an ordered system of existing knowledge and various issues and methodological contradictions which need to be addressed. In particular, there is ongoing debate in the scientific world on the legitimacy of globalistics within the system of scientific knowledge. According to a number of scholars, globalistics cannot be considered an independent science, since it does not belong to any of the major classes of disciplines: the natural sciences, mathematics, social sciences, or the humanities. Other scientists are convinced that, despite the use of certain approaches and data-collection methods borrowed from the natural and mathematical sciences, globalistics is more closely related to the social sciences and the humanities. The main aim of globalistics is to find the best ways and means for solving the pre-existing global problems and for preventing the emergence of new global challenges and threats. Globalistics seeks to identify the means for addressing emergent socio-natural contradictions. It is impossible to achieve this goal by applying the knowledge of any one scientific field; therefore, globalistics resorts to the use of tools and mechanisms from a variety of fields at once.

In our opinion, globalistics has all the necessary attributes for qualifying it as a science. First of all, globalistics has three categories that make up its object of study: global systems, global processes, and global problems. Globalistics focuses on those aspects of global phenomena that are associated with human activity. Global natural processes outside of social reality are already the objects of study for other sciences. Given this fact, it is clear that scientific research has a prevailing socio-natural character already operant within the framework of globalistics.

The overarching subject of study for globalistics is global development. This subject of study is the logical product of the formation of globalistics. In both globalistics and global studies in general, there has been a gradual shift from

---

9 Arkady Ursul, "Становление науки о глобальном мире" ["The Formation of the Science of Global World"], *Sotsiodinamika*, 2018, No. 10, 61–67, https://doi.org/10.30884/vglob/2020.04.02.

a focus on global processes to a focus on global development.[10] It is important to understand that, in most cases, human activity is the root cause of global problems, and this understanding has required a revision of the existing model of the spontaneous human development. Because of this, the transition of the world community to sustainable development ("SD") is urgent. The concept of sustainable development aims to overcome existing contradictions in the "society-nature" system by reducing the anthropogenic load on the environment. Although global development is currently considered a subject of globalistics, specifically evolutionary globalistics, development could become a general subject of global studies, given the relationship between global development and global security.

In addition to possessing a specific subject of study, globalistics has the conceptual framework necessary to be considered a science. It uses the specific set of terms, including "global systems," "global processes," "globalization processes," "global problems," "globalization," and "global governance," among others. In addition, globalistics applies research methods such as mathematical modeling and forecasting and analytical approaches such as interdisciplinary, global, systemic, integrative, synergetic, and evolutionary. As noted by one of the first researchers of global processes and problems, Arkady Ursul,

> using a global approach and a set of methods, among which special importance is given to global modeling, globalistics started to turn into a fundamentally new integrative-interdisciplinary phenomenon, acting as the main attractor for studies of many other global processes.[11]

The use of the evolutionary approach in globalistics (and in global studies in general) allows us to analyze global processes not only through their dynamics, change, and movement, but also through development. Unlike the historical approach, the evolutionary approach makes it possible to explore not only the past and the present, but also the future.[12] Evolutionary globalistics emerged

---

10 Arkady Ursul and Kristina Leonova, "От глобальных процессов к глобальному развитию: политическое измерение" ["From Global Processes to Global Development: The Political Dimension"], *Bulletin of Moscow University*, Series 27, 2020, No. 3, 15.
11 Arkady Ursul, "Глобалистика и глобализационные исследования: становление новых интегративных направлений" ["Globalistics and Globalization Studies: The Emergence of New Integrative Directions"], *Filosofskaya mysl*, 2018, No. 4, 17–29, https://doi.org/10.25136/2409-8728.2018.4.24168.
12 Arkady Ursul and Tatiana Ursul, "Глобальное направление науки" ["The Global Direction of Science"], *Filosofskaya mysl*, 2013, No. 10, 58–120, https://doi.org/10.7256/2306-0174.2013.10.8869.

through the evolutionary approach.[13] It identifies the directions that global processes of evolution are taking, and thereby helps ensure effective decision-making and global security.

The formation of globalistics as an independent science can be divided into three stages. Each of these stages is defined by the global issues prevalent at the time. The first stage of globalistics covers the period between the late 1960s to the close of the 1980s, the key global problems being the environmental issues, war and peace, and space exploration. During this period, research methods were developed specifically to study global phenomena. Specifically, mathematical modeling of global dynamics was being developed. The Club of Rome played a special role in the study of global problems. The Club's first report, *The Limits to Growth*, issued in 1972, was based on the results of the study of global processes using mathematical modeling, which proved to the global community that the existing human development model was inefficient and unstable.[14] Global issues are the result of human irresponsibility towards global systems. Because humans cause the issues, it is humanity itself that bears the responsibility for altering its ways, behaviors, and methods.

During the second stage of the development of globalistics, globalization became the main area of concern. Especially during the 1990s, when there was a sudden shift in the balance of power on the international stage, attention turned to the political aspect of globalization, which had not previously been noted. Around the same time, the United Nations officially adopted the concept of sustainable development as a global strategy for human development. The definition of globalistics as the science of globalization probably emerged from this stage, and this is still a widespread definition. However, that definition is not entirely correct. Despite the fact that globalistics is, in part, research of globalization and its characteristics, features, factors, and consequences, the process of globalization is only one of its three subjects of study.

The third stage in the formation of globalistics began around the turn of the millennium and continues to this day. At this stage, globalistics becomes an independent, interdisciplinary social and humanistic science. The object and subject of research were constituted at this stage, the concepts were clarified, and the pool of literature expanded.

---

13 See: Ilya Ilyin and Arkady Ursul, Эволюционная глобалистика (концепция эволюции глобальных процессов) [*Evolutionary Globalistics: The Concept of the Evolution of Global Processes*] (Moscow: Moscow State University Press, 2009).

14 See: Dennis Meadows, Donella Meadows, and Jorgen Randers, *The Limits to Growth* (New York: Universe Books, 1972).

3   The Impact of Globalization on the Development of Global Issues

Undoubtedly, developments in scientific thinking prepared the way for the emergence of global studies, and it was especially thanks to the influence of Vernadsky, whose ideas laid the foundation for global thinking. In addition, the various global processes themselves influenced the formation of this new scientific field. For example, globalization has contributed not only to the spread of knowledge around the world, but also, by penetrating into various scientific areas, to the adoption of global subjects into scientific understanding. The processes of globalization have led to substantial transformations in the spheres of education, information, space, and the environment, among other spheres. As a result of globalization, some disciplines are beginning to view certain issues in the context of global developments or globalization, while other disciplines have become fully global.[15] Science is meant to look for answers to humanity's questions about the phenomena of our world, and this means that science tends to address present-day realities and concerns. The emergence of qualitatively new challenges and threats calls for the formation of new scientific fields that can fully describe and explain developing global processes. In light of this, the development of global studies and of globalistics in particular is an objective, logical, and timely scientific event.

The globalization of science is accompanied by increased interaction between individual disciplines, with the aim of exchanging knowledge in the interests of global security and the consolidation of global knowledge. The development of new scientific concepts, the use of new research tools, and the formation of a new scientific worldview all represent a global scientific revolution which does not displace the post-non-classical revolution, but rather fits into its framework.[16]

In turn, the transformation and globalization of science affect educational processes. Two key trends can be identified: the globalization of education and the formation of global education.[17] The globalization of education is defined as the integration of different educational systems into a structure that preserves national characteristics, introduces innovative technologies and methods, and promotes new forms of education, such as "smart education." At

---

15   Arkady Ursul and Tatiana Ursul, "Наука и образование: Становление глобальных форм" ["Science and Education: The Emergence of Global Forms"] in *Большая Евразия: Развитие, безопасность, сотрудничество* [*The Greater Eurasia: Development, Security, Cooperation*], vol. 2 (Moscow: INION RAN, 2019), 943.

16   Ursul and Ursul, "Наука и образование," 942–44.

17   Ursul and Ursul, "Наука и образование," 942–47.

the same time, this does not mean that a unified education system will be created. Educational globalization is instead about the development of universal standards appropriate to modern needs.

The trend of the formation of global education is connected with the acquisition of new content by individual educational systems. The main focus of current education is on the past and the present processes. This approach, however, no longer meets educational needs. In a postindustrial society, the rate of change is so high that methods are constantly replaced. It is necessary to train specialists who are not only able to describe and analyze past and present events, but also to create hypotheses about the future and to act effectively on the basis of those hypotheses.

Globalization is an objective process of human development, and it is largely aimed at the interactions among people and the formation of relationships within society. The negative consequences of globalization can be overcome by learning how to channel globalization in desirable directions. Therefore, the issues of global governance, its forms, and its mechanisms of implementation become especially relevant in the context of global studies.

4   Global Studies and Global Security

A prime example of the negative consequences of globalization is the growing number of new challenges and threats that undermine security at all levels, be it local, regional, or global. The key threats to global security in the twenty-first century are geopolitical tensions, environmental problems (especially the climate crisis), the growing mistrust among the actors, the risks posed by new technologies, and, of course, public health crises—particularly, the spread of infectious diseases.[18] Global problems are a negative consequence of global processes. The emergence of crises is an objective result of human development. Ongoing processes always have both positive and negative aspects. The security system is intended to prevent the escalation of situations resulting from these negative aspects, as well as prevent the emergence of threats to human life and social development. Unfortunately, the modern security system is not appropriately fitted to maintain peace and stands in urgent need of reform through the introduction of advanced, up-to-date methods.

---

18   António Guterres, "Remarks to the General Assembly on the Secretary-General's priorities for 2020," United Nations, https://www.un.org/sg/en/content/sg/speeches/2020-01-22/remarks-general-assembly-priorities-for-2020.

Science and education have a significant impact on establishing global security, as they are built on the framework of collective knowledge, theoretical conclusions, and empirical data. Both appropriate levels of security and achievements in the fields of science and education are key factors in human development. The scientific and educational spheres should take into account the trends in development during particular periods of time. Today, the nexus between security and development is clearly visible, which means that the future security of humanity depends on the development of an optimal global development model. The failure of the modern development model was recognized back in the 1970s. The concept of sustainable development, adopted by the United Nations in 1992, is meant to replace the previous model of unsustainable, spontaneous development, in order to successfully ensure the progress of humanity. The principles of sustainable development should be fundamental to the field of global security, since they ensure the security of human civilization in harmony with all global systems.

Specialists in the field of global studies are also involved in issues of sustainable development. The Department of Global Studies of Lomonosov Moscow State University are developing a security strategy within the context of sustainable development. The ideas, recommendations, and measures generated in this scientific sphere address present-day realities. The goal of the educational sphere is to contribute to the development of global consciousness through the transmission of this knowledge. For example, education for sustainable development aims to disseminate knowledge on sustainable development issues and to create a more sustainable society. The study of global phenomena, the development of advanced methods and means, and the inclusion of global issues in educational programs are the key factors in the development of a sustainable security system.

5 Conclusion

The modern world is undergoing a number of transformations that affect the interests of all the people, leading to the emergence of new global problems. The processes of globalization lead not only to the integration of the spheres of geography, economics, politics, and information, but also to the emergence of qualitatively new trends in the scientific and educational fields. On the one hand, global processes affect the scientific and educational spheres; on the other hand, science and education set the direction for the development of socio-natural processes by studying, solving, strengthening, or preventing the occurrence of certain phenomena. It is apparent that science and education should follow the prevailing trends in the world, and one of the contemporary trends is the formation of a global world. Undoubtedly, the world has always been global if considered from the point of view of natural processes. However, in the context of our social reality, the modern world is still developing its global features.

The study of global processes began in the first half of the twentieth century, thanks to the great Russian scientist Vladimir Vernadsky. His work laid the foundations for global studies, the core of which is an interdisciplinary study of global systems, processes, and problems called globalistics. Global studies as a scientific field describes global phenomena occurring in the world, investigates their genesis and interconnections—but, beyond this, it also searches for effective methods and measures to ensure global security. The inclusion of disciplines within the spectrum of global studies in educational programs contributes to the development of global consciousness, prepares society for life in a constantly changing world, and forms a responsible attitude towards global systems. All of this has a positive effect on the implementation of the sustainable development strategy designed to overcome socio-natural contradictions and to ensure the security of the humanity and of our environment, in the short and long terms.

The Pandemic and the Crisis of the Global World

Alexey A. Gromyko

"There are decades when nothing happens, and there are weeks that are like compressed decades." This saying rang particularly true in 2020, the year of the pandemic. COVID-19 left a lasting mark on the economy, politics, and people's perception of the world. The expression that came to mind in the spring of 2020 was "the day after"—echoing the title of the famous 1983 film about life after nuclear catastrophe. Today, nevertheless, few people in Europe make apocalyptic predictions because of the pandemic. In most cases, this expression—"the day after"—may be used to imply that life will no longer be the same, not only due to new factors such as COVID-19, but also due to the influence of pre-existing, pre-pandemic factors on these new factors. It is obvious that the world has been thoroughly shaken by the corona-crisis. But the ongoing crisis of global governance and international relations originates in a broad range of causes, whose nature is both political and economic.

1 Some Current Trends

The post-COVID world will be largely a continuation but not a return to our life before the pandemic. Whenever a major historical event happens, eyewitnesses and contemporaries view the mosaic of events as if through a microscope. As the intensity of the drama subsides, the "microscope" is replaced by a "magnifying lens"—and ultimately with a "telescope." When the initial impressions and emotions subside, and when smaller details fade, only then do the changes that are truly profound come to the fore. Bold predictions and expectations of revolutionary changes are replaced by more conservative and moderate forecasts.

At the same time, even the most balanced assessment of the current epidemic does not diminish the scale of its direct and indirect impact. This crisis can be placed in the same category as the Great Depression of the late 1920s and the 1930s, or the Great Recession of 2008–2009. Naturally, we should distinguish between the temporary changes that are necessary at the stage of fighting the disease and those that will remain with us for a long time. Further, some of the changes magnified by the pandemic will not be entirely new; to a large extent, they will bring about a return to ideas and policies that existed before. For example, this concerns the enhanced role of the nation-state and the shift to social market policies.

Today, when people talk about the economy, they often have politics at the back of their minds. In other words, we cannot do without political economy in our analysis. The pandemic intensified competition in various areas— economics, information, technology, etc.—where politics served as the driving force behind it all. This comes as no surprise, since globalization, beginning as a self-regulated economic process, has long turned into a political tool to slow the development of economic rivals. Citing national security interests, a number of countries impose arbitrary restrictions and extraterritorial sanctions, in effect violating the World Trade Organization rules.

The fundamental problems that caused the financial and economic crisis of 2008–2009 have not been resolved. The pandemic further exacerbated the situation. The global economy was hit by two simultaneous shocks, with both supply and demand dropping dramatically. An enormous amount of money is being pumped into the economy to mitigate the impact of the pandemic, ignoring the fact that this leads to mounting public debts and financial bubbles. Geopolitical rivalry between the United States and China is increasing, no matter the occupant of the White House. In 2021, the process of strategic decoupling between the United States and Europe continues. On the whole, systemic and structural changes in international relations and in the mechanisms of global and regional governance and regulation carry on the trends of previous years and even decades.

Some consider this a continuation of deglobalization. In reality, though, it is a continuation of the crisis associated with hyper-globalization, the origins of which appeared some forty years ago. In other words, we are witnessing a crisis of the neoliberal and West-centric model of globalization, a failure of economic and political neoliberalism.[1] The most prominent feature of this new stage of globalization is that global integration is descending from the global to the regional and trans-regional levels. This explains the weakening of most multilateral mechanisms inherited from the twentieth century. Regressive, disintegrative processes happen at a higher level, and at the same time there is an increased demand for integration processes at a lower level. For example, the US–China trade wars or tougher rules for foreign investors in the European Union are elements of disintegration at a global level. The new EU industrial strategy will make the European economy more dirigiste, further distorting market mechanisms and creating new protectionist measures to

---

1 Alexey Gromyko, "Metamorphoses of Political Neoliberalism," *Contemporary Europe*, 2020, No. 2, 6–19, http://www.sov-europe.ru/2020/2-2020/2.pdf.

make the EU's economy more competitive.² Security reasons become a convenient pretext for introducing such measures and criteria of security concerns are mostly dubious and politically driven.

The China strategy review prepared by the European Commission and the High Representative of the Union for Foreign Affairs and Security Policy in March 2019 refers to China as an "economic competitor in the pursuit of technological leadership."³ A year later, Josep Borrell, who has replaced Federica Mogherini as Europe's top diplomat, made the following observation when talking about the coronavirus crisis and how it has affected the European Union's relationship with its key economic opponents: "We should avoid excessive dependence in strategic sectors by building stockpiles of critical materials. We also need to shorten and diversify our supply chains."⁴ In other words, the European Union will use market and non-market tools and methods to reduce its dependence on China in strategic sectors (a non-specific term which can be applied to a very broad range of industries) and to force Beijing to play by the rules that are favorable for the European Single Market.

Additional stimuli favoring greater interdependence within the European Union or the Eurasian Economic Union (EAEU) are elements of further integration at a regional level.⁵ As far as the European Union is concerned, one of the largest "contributions" the coronavirus crisis made to strengthening federalist trends is found in a joint initiative by France and Germany, who proposed to set up a European recovery fund of €750 billion to support EU member states through loans and grants. This financial instrument, which was approved by the European Council in July 2020, is a massive step towards a fiscal union, and signals a major shift in Berlin's position on the issue of a "transfer union" and common EU borrowing. A number of major media out-

---

2 Vladislav Belov, "Новая промышленная стратегия Евросоюза" ["New Industrial Strategy of the European Union"], Whitepaper No. 13, Institute of Europe, Russian Academy of Sciences (2019), http://instituteofeurope.ru/images/uploads/analitika/2020/an196.pdf.

3 "EU–China: A Strategic Outlook," European Union, March 12, 2019, https://ec.europa.eu/commission/sites/beta-political/files/communication-eu-china-a-strategic-outlook.pdf (page no longer available).

4 Josep Borrell, "Trust and Reciprocity: The Necessary Ingredients for EU–China Cooperation," European External Action Service, May 14, 2020, https://eeas.europa.eu/headquarters/headquarters-homepage/79355/trust-and-reciprocity-necessary-ingredients-eu-china-cooperation_en.

5 Natalia Kondratyeva, "Работа институтов ЕАЭС в условиях коронакризиса" ["The Work of EAEU Institutions During the Coronavirus Crisis"], Whitepaper No. 26, Institute of Europe, Russian Academy of Sciences (2020), http://instituteofeurope.ru/images/uploads/analitika/2020/an209.pdf.

lets hailed this decision by Angela Merkel as "historic," saying she has "secured her place in the pantheon of European statesmanship."[6]

It may seem inexplicable (though it makes perfect sense upon in-depth analysis) that the United States and the United Kingdom—two countries that had long constituted the core of the neoliberal model—became the key triggers of the disintegration of hyper-globalization. In recent years, the United States has pulled out of the Trans-Pacific Partnership Agreement, walked away from the talks on the Transatlantic Trade and Investment Partnership with the European Union, undermined the Iran nuclear deal, withdrew from the UNESCO, the UN Human Rights Council, the Paris Climate Agreement, and the Intermediate-Range Nuclear Forces Treaty, effectively blocked the operations of the World Trade Organization, stopped paying its fees to the World Health Organization, and withdrew from the Open Skies Treaty. Some of these decisions have been reversed under Joseph Biden, but the general trend has not been altered and the fragmentation of world politics continues. As for the United Kingdom, Brexit dealt a much heavier blow to the European Union than any mythical threat allegedly posed by Russia or China.

During the pandemic, the role of government regulation, government involvement in various social and market processes, increased dramatically. Nation-states have once again demonstrated that they are indispensable, especially in a situation of *force majeure*. Simultaneously, some natural rights and freedoms proved to be secondary, just like self-regulated market mechanisms. It turned out that, under extreme circumstances, people care more about their basic right to life and their social and economic rights, which at certain points in time may have higher priority than freedom of movement or freedom of assembly.

The practice of relying on profiteering mechanisms, including in health care, has once again demonstrated their dark side. The United States spends 17% of its GDP on health care, but when the pandemic broke out, the system failed, because when it comes to social justice and human capital, what matters is how you spend the money and whom you spend it on. The same holds true for market mechanisms in other areas, like education and fundamental science. After an extended period of unchallenged domination by the theory and practices of political and economic neoliberalism, there are just a handful of countries left where social market economy and welfare state are more than just empty declarations. Most of these countries are in Northern Europe.

---

6 Paul Taylor, "Merkel's Milestone Moment," *Politico*, May 19, 2020, https://www.politico.eu/article/angela-merkel-milestone-moment-europe-coronavirus-response/.

The coronavirus crisis demonstrated the deep-seated features of the nation-states' behavior—namely, the phenomenon of national egoisms. This is normal, since people express solidarity at a national level first, prioritizing their fellow citizens. Then solidarity rises to the next level, where states support one another. And only after that solidarity may rise to the supranational level. There is no contradiction between the central role played by the nation-state and the importance of bilateral and multilateral cooperation. Finally, a comprehensive solution can only be achieved through the efforts of international organizations. "Render unto Caesar the things that are Caesar's, and unto God the things that are God's." Nation-states do their part, and others—e.g., the World Trade Organization, the European Union, the EAEU, and the like—do theirs.

The US–China military tensions represent a major risk. These tensions are not just a single time bomb; there are several time bombs hidden here. For example, there is the possibility of a dramatic escalation over Taiwan. In the spring of 2020, the US Department of State launched a campaign to grant the island observer status in the World Health Organization. These are elements of Washington's long-term policy of putting pressure on Beijing regarding this issue. As always, China protested the move. It would be a mistake to treat this situation as just another "last warning by China"—an expression with an overlay of humor, which became popular in the USSR back in the 1950s and 1960s, due to the extensive coverage of US–China tensions over Taiwan in the Soviet media. At that time, the meaning was that no matter how many times Beijing would protest, Washington would still do what it wanted. In the 2020s, the creeping recognition of Taiwan's sovereignty and provoking China on this issue may become too dangerous.

Since May 2020, there has been a campaign in the United States, including the US judiciary, to strip China of its "sovereign immunity." The principle of sovereign (or state) immunity stems from Roman law: *par in parem non habet imperium*, or "equals have no sovereignty over one another." Yet the US law today allows for numerous caveats and exceptions to this rule, based on the doctrine of limited sovereignty. These loopholes have been used to file several lawsuits against the People's Republic of China, the Communist Party of China, a number of ministries and government agencies, and other Chinese entities, alleging that they had something to do with "infecting US citizens" with the coronavirus. Another idea, mooted in the United States in 2020, is defaulting on the US Treasury bonds acquired by China to the tune of one trillion US dollars (a third of China's international reserves). This would be an unprecedented move in modern history. There was another option under consideration—to punish Beijing for the "Chinese virus" by levying new tariffs on Chinese exports, especially since the US–China Phase One trade deal, made in January 2020, was scrapped as a result of the pandemic.

2   Life after the Pandemic

A pandemic always raises the pressing question of inventing and mass-producing a vaccine. In the case of COVID-19, optimists believed, and they proved to be right, that vaccines would be invented and produced in 2020. But such a quick introduction of various vaccines poses a range of questions about their side effects and the longevity of vaccine-induced immunity response. By the middle of 2021, we knew that several vaccines, including Sputnik V, provide durable protection against coronavirus. At the same time, it is also clear that the duration of this protection will not go beyond a certain period of time—maybe a year or a bit longer. Therefore, the chances are high that COVID-19 might become a constant fixture of life and we will have to immunize ourselves on a regular basis. After all, there are a lot of diseases that are more dangerous than coronavirus, for which there are no vaccines at all. Dengue fever is one example. After more than forty years, we still have no vaccine for HIV.

Unfortunately, there will be more pandemics in the future—especially considering that there are many factors contributing to their genesis. Mankind has to develop resilience in dealing with pandemics, meaning it must learn to adapt to living with COVID-19 and similar diseases. This includes, among other things, an ability to live with lockdowns, self-quarantine, and social distancing. But the solution is not straightforward. Human life is priceless but extensive, and protracted lockdowns paralyzing people's lives, businesses, and economic activities are equally unacceptable from both the economic and political perspectives. A number of countries (Sweden, Belarus, Brazil, the United States, India, etc.) allowed the virus to spread more or less freely, either in hopes of achieving herd immunity as quickly as possible, or for the sake of using the pandemic as a political tool, or simply because of poor governance.

The current pandemic provided a powerful boost to the industries where people can work from home. This helps maintain social distancing and in addition reduces operational costs. But there is the question of who benefits more from this—employees or employers? Because of structural changes on the job market, the cost of office space is bound to go down. Many office buildings will have to shut down or convert to other uses. Software development and telecommunication systems connecting people online are booming. Education, telemedicine, and some other areas are quickly adapting to working remotely.

The pandemic will accelerate the 5G roll-out and the advance of the internet of things. On its part, the restaurant business is under huge pressure, especially in the bar segment, as well as the entertainment industry, including sports—in other words, everything that involves large numbers of people gathered in one place. Just like over the past twenty years, because of the terrorist threat, travelers got used to being strip-searched at airports and train stations, people will now have to get used to wearing face masks in public places and on public transport, taking medical tests on a regular basis, providing additional documents when applying for a visa, etc.

The pandemic spurred a resurgence of the debate about a proper balance between security concerns and civic freedoms. As soon as a number of countries started gradually lifting COVID-19 restrictions in May 2020, protests immediately broke out, reacting either to the restrictions on freedom of association and freedom of movement, or to the worsening standards of living: growing social inequality, unemployment, poverty, and falling incomes. French President Emmanuel Macron saw his approval rating plummet to below 40% in April 2020 (according to Ipsos). The Yellow Vests movement resumed its protests in May. Spanish Prime Minister Pedro Sánchez had to extend the state of emergency until the end of June 2020, because of protests. Germany, too, had a wave of protests roll across the country. The pandemic exacerbated political differences within the United States, as well as its old problems of social inequality, poverty, and racism. In late May and early June 2020, riots throughout the country were triggered by the death of George Floyd, who died of asphyxiation while detained by police officers in Minneapolis. The Black Lives Matter movement was born, with long-ranging implications.

Because of the pandemic, travelers also must cope with a surge in the costs of travel, as airlines and railroads introduce new regulations, which dramatically reduce the number of passengers. Cars once again play a major role in short-distance travel, especially since fuel prices are expected to stay low for the foreseeable future.

The health care sector is going through profound transformations, especially in the countries where the pandemic exposed the weaknesses of the primary care level and the scarcity of hospital beds. The state assumes a bigger role in these matters. Major shifts in urban development are in the pipeline, and the paradigm of megacities may fade in favor of low-rise construction. Sensor technology will be used more widely in order to avoid touching surfaces in public places. This means that we will see more biometric data being collected and stored, including face-recognition technologies, which once again raise the question of privacy and personal data protection.

The pandemic highlighted the problems of poor countries and of migration flows, including those of labor migrants and camps for displaced persons and refugees. The pandemic has dominated the news for more than a year, eclipsing reports about hunger protests in Lebanon, which started in early 2020. At the time, the World Bank estimated that 45% of the Lebanese population were living below the poverty line—although just recently, in 2018, Lebanon had the highest GDP per capita among the Arab world's non-oil producing nations.[7] But in April 2020, the Lebanese government believed that up to 75% of the country needed aid. Across the Mediterranean Sea, in Greece alone, about 100,000 refugees from Africa and the Middle East were waiting for asylum; 40,000 of them—in overcrowded camps on Greek islands. Coronavirus outbreaks were a regular occurrence in these camps.[8]

Another aspect of the problems facing poor countries was revealed in a report released by the UN Conference on Trade and Development (UNCTAD) on April 28, 2020.[9] The report warned of the looming developing country debt crisis. According to the IMF, developing countries needed at least $2.5 trillion in aid, due to the current crisis. The virtual G20 Summit in March 2020 decided only to suspend debt service payments from developing countries until the end of the year. Some of the debts could be written off or restructured. But this entire initiative was only worth $40 billion, an insignificant amount by modern standards. A total of seventy-six countries were in danger of encountering problems with servicing their foreign debts.

3 The European Union: Testing Times

The International Monetary Fund expected the euro area economy to shrink by 7.5% in 2020.[10] The European Commission was even more pessimistic and

---

[7] Tamara Qiblawi and Ghazi Balkiz, "If your child is hungry, you will eat your rulers to feed your children," *CNN*, May 2, 2020, https://www.cnn.com/2020/05/02/middleeast/lebanon-tripoli-hunger-protests-coronavirus-intl/index.html.

[8] Louise Miner, "Greek Migrant Camp is Set Alight as Clashes Shake Chios Island," *Euronews*, April 19, 2020, https://www.euronews.com/2020/04/19/greek-migrant-camp-is-set-alight-as-clashes-shake-chios-island.

[9] "From the Great Lockdown to the Great Meltdown: Developing Country Debt in the Time of COVID-19," United Nations Conference on Trade and Development, April 2020, https://unctad.org/system/files/official-document/gdsinf2020d3_en.pdf.

[10] "World Economic Outlook: The Great Lockdown," International Monetary Fund, April 2020, 7, https://www.imf.org/~/media/Files/Publications/WEO/2020/April/English/Ch1.ashx?la=en.

projected a contraction of 8%.[11] A survey by McKinsey & Company forecasted that the Eurozone GDP would fall in 2020 by a lot more, 10.6%, and that the EU economy would not return to pre-crisis levels until 2024.[12] The European Commission, together with the European Central Bank, expected the overall contraction in EU GDP to be 7.5%.[13] European Central Bank President Christine Lagarde stated that the euro-area economy could shrink by as much as 15% that year.[14] For the sake of comparison, in 2009, which was the worst year of the Great Recession for the European Union, the euro area's GDP shrank by 4.5%.

Looking back from 2021, we know that the global real GDP contracted by 3.3% last year; the US economy—by 3.5%; the euro area's—by 6.6%; Russia's—by 3.1%; China's GDP increased in 2020 by 2.3% (according to the International Monetary Fund). The worst-case scenarios did not materialize. Nevertheless, in general, the world economy is in a dismal state, and the future is highly uncertain.

The EU nation-states were the first line of defense in fighting the pandemic, which is not surprising, as health care remains within national jurisdiction. In order to help the governments of the member states to take effective measures, the European Union agreed to relax its fiscal rules for borrowing and spending. As a result, Spain was able to allocate €200 billion (20% of its GDP) in March 2020 to support its economy.[15] Italy announced a €350 billion aid package for households, and then added another €400 billion to support businesses. Added together, these two packages equaled almost half of the country's gross domestic product.[16] The European Central Bank acted as the second line of

---

11   "Assessment of Public Debt Sustainability and COVID-Related Financing Needs of Euro Area Member States," European Union, https://ec.europa.eu/info/sites/info/files/economy-finance/annex_2_debt_sustainability.pdf.
12   Soeren Kern, "Coronavirus: The Looming Collapse of Europe's Single Currency," Gatestone Institute, International Policy Council, April 7, 2020, https://www.gatestoneinstitute.org/15856/coronavirus-euro-collapse.
13   "European Economic Forecast," European Commission, Institutional Paper 125, May 2020, ix, https://ec.europa.eu/info/sites/info/files/economy-finance/ip125_en.pdf.
14   Viktoria Dendrinou and Boris Groendahl, "Merkel's Stimulus Vow Sets Up EU Battle for Recovery Funds," *Bloomberg*, April 24, 2020, https://www.bloomberg.com/news/articles/2020-04-24/merkel-s-stimulus-vow-sets-up-eu-battle-for-reconstruction-funds-k9dwthfx.
15   "Spain Announces 200 Billion Euro Aid Package for Coronavirus Crisis," *Reuters*, March 17, 2020, https://www.reuters.com/article/uk-health-coronavirus-spain-aid-idUKKBN2142QD.
16   "Coronavirus, via libera a del imprese, Conte: è 'potenza di fuoco,'" *ANSA*, April 7, 2020, https://www.ansa.it/sito/notizie/politica/2020/04/06/governo-consiglio-dei-ministri_482977fb-4ed7-4377-8ec6-01e2c4a0dcb1.html.

defense, announcing that it would buy €750 billion worth of sovereign and corporate bonds.

Experts often use geography to divide EU member states into categories: North and South, East and West. Because of the pandemic, we once again witnessed increased tensions between donors and recipients—i.e., between the North and the South. The Netherlands was the most vocal representative of the former, while Italy was the hardest-hit example of the latter. Disagreements between the West and the East were deteriorating as well. While in the past, starting in 2015, they were primarily due to differences of opinion regarding migration issues, later the rule of law found itself at the heart of the controversy. Hungary and Poland were increasingly viewed as rogue states within the European Union. In May 2020, another crisis was in the making, because of a decision made by Germany's Constitutional Court in Karlsruhe. This key institution questioned the legality of the European Central Bank's sovereign bond-buying program, thus putting national law above the EU legislation.

While European governments have been fighting the pandemic with cash injections, the problem of sovereign debt was looming large. This indicator was going up across the European Union. In April 2020, the debt-to-GDP ratio in the European Union was already over 80%, while in the euro area it exceeded 97%, even though the Stability and Growth Pact sets the limit for public debt at 60% and for budget deficit at 3%.[17] Greece had the worst result: its government debt was at 176% of the GDP in 2019 and was projected to reach 180% in 2021. It is followed by Italy, with 135% in 2019 and a projected 154% in 2021, Portugal with 115% and 120% respectively, France and Belgium with 100% and 110%, then Spain with 95% and 114%. Even Germany exceeded the limit set by the Stability and Growth Pact, piling up 70% of government debt in September 2020. Only smaller economies—the Baltic nations, Luxembourg, and Malta—were expected to stay under the cap.[18]

The third line of EU defense against the pandemic was supranational. The European Union was divided over the question of whether the hardest-hit countries were entitled to receive aid in the form of grants or loans. In other words, will these countries borrow money and pay interest? Or will they receive direct transfers? The most radical solution was to issue "corona bonds" (i.e., to pool together member states' debts). This idea was debated at length at the time of the Great Recession. If the European Union were to issue "corona

---

17 "Fiscal Monitor: Policies to Support People During the COVID-19 Pandemic," International Monetary Fund, April 2020, 6, https://www.imf.org/~/media/Files/Publications/fiscal-monitor/2020/April/English/text.ashx?la=en.

18 "Assessment of Public Debt Sustainability."

bonds" today, it would mean that all member states have the same borrowing terms, thus sharing all the risks, and there is no need to worry about the spreads (the differences between their sovereign bond yields).

The EU Summit on March 26, 2020, instructed the member states' finance ministers to design measures for supporting the European economy. As a result, an emergency fund of €540 billion (about 4% of the EU GDP) was set up. This included about €100 billion earmarked for SURE, a program offering compensations to employers in an effort to stymie unemployment. Another €200 billion were made available through the European Investment Bank in subsidized loans to small and medium-sized businesses. Finally, €240 billion went to the European Stability Mechanism to bail out the EU members in need of urgent aid. On April 23, 2020, the EU Summit supported the idea of creating the fund, and after being ratified by national parliaments, the decision went into effect on June 1. Importantly, this aid was not conditioned on austerity measures, which caused extreme tensions between EU members during and after the Great Recession. As far as "corona bonds" were concerned, the summit decided to postpone the issue in an effort to avoid direct confrontation. EU officials continued debating the risks of sovereign debts and ways to hedge against them, including the idea of a European Redemption Fund, which was first proposed shortly after 2010.[19]

In addition, the European Union continued discussing the need for a new "Marshall Plan"—a long-term recovery and modernization program for the EU economy. It was generally understood that, on top of the financial measures intended to deal with the pandemic and its impact, such a plan should address the broader issue of the European Union's prospects, including the geopolitical dimension. However, unlike the original Marshall Plan, this time Western Europe was left to fend for itself, especially after the pandemic once again demonstrated how little Washington cares about the needs of its European allies. The plan involved the initial steps towards the aforementioned transfer union, massive investment in the European Green Deal, a new industrial strategy, an ambitious seven-year budget for 2021–2027, and so on.

The term "reprioritization" was often used, meaning that resources should be redistributed between various items in the EU budget to allocate a greater share to the southern member states. For instance, the money from the Cohesion Fund that would normally go to Budapest or Warsaw could now go to

---

19   Peter Bofinger et al., "A European Redemption Pact," *VoxEU*, November 9, 2011, https://voxeu.org/article/european-redemption-pact.

Rome or Madrid. Further, in order to cope with the pandemic-induced economic downturn, EU member states contemplated an increase in their contributions. Ursula von der Leyen asked them to raise the ceiling from the current 1.2% to 2% of the GNI for the first two or three years of the new seven-year period.[20]

The European Union was facing several problems at the same time: it was sinking into a deep recession; government debts and deficits were mounting; unemployment was on the rise; and the future of the new seven-year budget was obscure. In addition, Brussels was engaged in difficult talks with London regarding a comprehensive agreement between the two parties after the United Kingdom left the European Union in January 2020.

Due to huge efforts undertaken in July 2020, the next EU budget was approved with elements of the transfer union. In December 2020, against all odds, the post-Brexit agreement between Brussels and London was also signed. Still, it is clear that because of the pandemic, the European Union entered its domestic and international quarrels of 2021 with impaired capabilities. What does it mean for its competitive advantages? The new European Commission, after taking office in December 2019, called itself a geopolitical one. One of its primary objectives was to secure leadership in global trade, regulation, standards, and value chains by implementing the green agenda, digitization, and the new industrial strategy. The Green Deal envisages achieving climate neutrality by 2050. This means overhauling the entire European economy. For this purpose, the European Union intended to introduce a carbon tax on the outer borders of the common market, to create the €1 trillion Just Transition Fund, and to take a number of other ambitious and costly steps.

Today, these plans look questionable because of the pandemic and the resulting financial difficulties. Apart from being costly, the green transformation and digitization will make some jobs redundant—and this in a situation where unemployment is a permanent problem, especially among younger people. Besides, there are parts of the EU economic strategy that may contradict each other. For example, the strategy calls for relocalization of industry (bringing European industrial production back to the EU territory). This goal may come in conflict with the transition to a green economy.

---

20 "Statement by President von der Leyen at the Joint Press Conference with President Michel, Following the EU Leaders' Videoconference on Coronavirus of 23 April," European Commission, April 23, 2020, https://ec.europa.eu/commission/presscorner/detail/en/statement_20_733.

4   Russia: Will the Stagnant Growth Persist?

Russia is facing equally challenging problems because of the pandemic. In May 2018, the Russian president issued an executive order on national goals and strategic objectives for the period until 2024. These included placing Russia among the world's top five economies. The document did not specify which metrics would serve as criteria for attaining this goal. Later, it was clarified that the ranking would be done based on purchasing power parity (PPP). In April 2020, when the IMF released its updated numbers, it turned out that Russia had pulled ahead of Germany by GDP (PPP) and was now ranked fifth.[21] However, assessing the standing and condition of Russia's economy in terms of PPP does not always seem to be a perfect method, since it does not take into account the quality of human capital. Real incomes have dropped by 8% in Russia since 2013, and social inequality increased dramatically over the past few decades. (For instance, the top one percent wealth share in Russia went up from 22% in 1995 to 43% in 2015.)[22] Although the Russian economy shrank less than the Bank of Russia had expected (by 3.1% instead of 4%–6% in 2020), Russia is unlikely to recover to pre-crisis levels before 2022.[23] Obviously, it appears dubious that the national development projects planned for the period through 2024 can be successfully implemented.

Russia's economists have proposed a number of measures to counter the pandemic and its impact and to achieve a new level of economic growth.[24] These include raising the minimum wage and pensions significantly, investing more in human capital, and allowing a moderate budget deficit. Russia also needs a genuine federalist budget structure, a progressive tax system, a radical increase in human capital investment, a fundamental shift in the way the government treats small and medium-sized businesses, and a ban on the cost-trimming programs in science, education, and health care.

---

21   "World Economic Outlook Database," International Monetary Fund, April 2020, https://www.imf.org/en/Publications/WEO/weo-database/2020/April.

22   "World Inequality Report 2018," The World Inequality Lab, https://wir2018.wid.world/files/download/wir2018-full-report-english.pdf.

23   "Банк России принял решение снизить ключевую ставку на 50 б. п., до 5,50% годовых" ["The Bank of Russia Made a Decision to Lower Interest Rates to 5.5%"], Bank of Russia, http://cbr.ru/press/pr/?file=24042020_133000Key.htm.

24   See: "Предложения по мероприятиям в сфере экономической и социальной жизни страны после завершения активной фазы борьбы с коронавирусом" ["Recommendations for Economic and Social Initiatives upon the Completion of the Active Response Phase in Coping with the Coronavirus"], a report of the Institute of Economics, Russian Academy of Sciences, http://inecon.org/docs/2020/publications/Report_IE%20RAS_20200526.pdf.

The changes taking place in connection with the COVID-19 pandemic follow the logic of the general shift towards a polycentric world order. At this point, it is still hard to tell which model of polycentrism will emerge as the dominant one and what the new hierarchy of countries will look like. Rivalries among the world's top nations got even more intense as a result of the pandemic. As tensions between various centers of power rise, Russia should remain geopolitically and otherwise autonomous in global affairs, without getting trapped in the false narrative of the new US–China bipolarity. At the same time, Russia, as a power with global attributes and responsibilities, should be very persistent in handling cleverly its differences with the European Union and the United States, in order to escape an equally false narrative of a new Cold War.

The Globalized World under the Prism of COVID-19

Victor B. Kuvaldin

Three quarters of a century have passed since the end of the Second World War: an equivalent of a human lifetime. This long succession of years has been marked by intermittent periods of upheaval and change that stood in stark contrast with their surroundings and impressed themselves into historic memory. The year 1968 saw a great wave of student protests sweep across the United States and Western Europe, led by the most politically active, educated, and demanding part of the baby-boom generation; 1989 marked the end of the Cold War, the European "Socialist camp" faded away, together with the chasm that had until then divided the old continent. In 2008–2009, an unusually severe financial and economic crisis put an end to the feverish "hyper-globalization" of the preceding two decades.

In terms of its impact on the global community, 2020, the year of the coronavirus pandemic, has surpassed even those memorable milestones of post-war history. COVID-19 disrupted the regular life of countries and populations, broke down the habitual frameworks of private and public life, disorganized economic activity, and disrupted the lives of billions of people on six continents. It forced authorities at all levels to scramble for solutions to urgent situations, confronting the choice between the bad and the worst. The cost of the emergency is enumerated in tens of trillions of dollars of material losses, and in more than three million human lives lost.

The intangible losses inflicted by the pandemic are yet to be assessed, but we can surmise that their magnitude will be comparable. All the fundamental institutions of modern civilization, and humanity itself—with its health, consciousness, and mental stability—have found themselves in direct peril. "It is too early yet to draw up a general assessment of the changes; this calls for more time," reflects Nikolai Neznanov, the director of the Bekhterev National Medical Research Center for Psychiatry and Neurology. "But on the whole, the situation with the COVID-19 pandemic has shown just how vulnerable and fragile our world is: it turned out that no nuclear bombs and no armaments are needed—that an invisible pinch of microorganisms is enough to set everything in motion and to trigger a systemic crisis of economics, politics and psychology."[1]

---

1 Alyona Zhukova, "Измененное состояние" ["An Altered Condition"], *Kommersant*, October 27, 2020 (thematic supplement to the paper), 13.

It is true that today we can firmly conclude that the world has failed the test presented by the coronavirus. The pandemic exposed our globalized world's main flaw: the weakness of global governance and regulatory institutions. The existing mechanisms of addressing global problems via the instruments available to nation-states have proved inadequate. The virus, though limited in its effect, caused mass panic, paralyzed the world economy, and compelled governments to take draconian measures unseen since the end of the Second World War.

In today's world, COVID-19 plays two roles that might seem mutually exclusive. It has simultaneously exposed and masked the crisis of globalization's current model. The shock of the high-tech civilization's utter helplessness in the face of an aggressive alien has made it very difficult to correctly diagnose the real condition of today's world.

This, of course, is not so much about the virus as such, however menacing it might be, but about the state of the world community, about the deep and perhaps irreversible crisis of the neoliberal model of globalization, under whose sign the world has been developing for the past four decades. A critical mass of problems has accumulated, blocking progress and threatening a civilizational breakdown. Whichever way we look—be it human relations with nature, the global economy, political systems, social interactions, cultural patterns and behavioral norms, patterns of identity, international relations—everywhere we see insistent red flags of alarm. These crises intertwine, feed upon, and reinforce one another, amounting to an expressive picture of the general malaise.

The world is suspended in the perilous state of a stalled global project: it is dangerous to remain in the rut, and no sufficiently safe alternative paths are yet discernible. Even the tentative tendencies towards de-globalization aggravate the general situation, instead of defusing it.

This is why what today's world needs the most is a thorough diagnostic of its condition, identifying the fundamental causes of its systemic crisis, and seeking out innovative solutions. Here, the first and foremost problem is that it is not yet clear who might be able to undertake such a complicated task. What is evident is a crisis of global hegemony, of global elites, and the comparative weakness of the opposing counter-elites. A gaping chasm divides the needs of the global order, with their magnitude, from the potential of the socio-political forces supposedly aimed at addressing those needs.

This is most apparent in the case of the Anglo-Saxon elites. Anglo-Saxons have a very special relationship with globalization. Both versions of the globalized world are a product of their doing. In the nineteenth century, Britain was a pioneer of global world-building, and continued to inhabit that Olympus of state power long after the peak of its influence had passed. In the twentieth century, the United States took the baton from Britannia's weakened hands and drew up a new model of the globalized world, surpassing its predecessor both in scope and in effectiveness. The central characteristic of both models of world order, "globalization-1" and "globalization-2," was the key role played, within the system of global regulation, by the nationally limited instruments of the British Crown and the American Presidency. As the largest and most influential constituent of the global elite, the Anglo-Saxons were once uniquely positioned to influence world affairs. But today, they seem incapable even of controlling the situation at home (as evidenced by the Trump phenomenon and Brexit)—let alone what is happening in the rest of the world. It is possible that they find it difficult to reflect critically upon themselves and their own experience, in order to undo the Gordian knots of neoliberal globalization.

The system's other players, meanwhile, simply do not have substantial enough resources for solving problems at that level. Combining and coordinating their efforts is a great effort in itself, and with a limited range of application. Besides, the strongest among them, "the Chinese dragon," is all too accustomed to flying by itself.

This is how we have found ourselves rudderless in the grip of a perfect storm. Today presents us with an urgent need for cooperation among the key players, in coping jointly with failures, blockages, obstacles, bottlenecks, and pitfalls. Will the current turmoil supply enough of an argument in favor of such a fundamental adjustment—or even of a fundamentally new globalization strategy? Will it be possible to consolidate on this basis the most influential segments of the world's elite, on the platforms of the United Nations, the Group of Twenty, the Davos Forum, and other global institutions? Hardly anyone today is in a position to answer such questions, but we should have thought about them yesterday. (Alexander Chumakov rightly foregrounds the key problem of regulation and management of global processes; yet, he is pessimistic about the real possibilities of its solution at the current stage of human development.)[2]

In order to understand the causes of such a large-scale civilizational breakdown in 2020, we have to go back a few decades, when these causes were being set in motion. At the close of the 1970s and the beginning of the 1980s, the capitalist world was looking for an antidote against the stagflation that had stricken it, with an unexpected combination of sluggish economic growth,

---

2   Alexander Chumakov, *Глобальный мир. Столкновение интересов* [*Global Peace: A Clash of Interests*] (Moscow: Prospect, 2018), 154–55, 368, 381, 392, 398, 435, 472.

double-digit unemployment, and inflation. A neoliberal strategy, based on redistributing national income in favor of capital, on folding the social welfare state, and on business and corporate innovation, was offered as a salutary prescription.

And that prescription worked. This much is clear from the experience of countries where the neoliberal program was implemented judiciously. Chile, one of the most advanced countries in Latin America, is one good example. After the restoration of democratic institutions in 1990, the governments of the center-left succeeded in combining economic growth, political stability, and a social orientation in domestic policy. Between the mid-1980s and 2017, the share of the population below the poverty line ($206 per month per person) fell from 45% to 9%.[3] From 1990 to 2020, the share of the middle class rose from 24% to 65%.[4] By this measure, Chile stands equal to the world's highly developed countries. This is why in 2010 it was admitted to the Organization for Economic Cooperation and Development (OECD)—an exclusive club of the world's rich nations.

It would have seemed that everything is for the best in this best of all possible worlds. But alas. In the spring of 2020—even before the coronavirus hit the Latin American continent—a wave of popular anger swept across Chile. Its occasion was minor: a four-cent increase in rush-hour subway fares, but it was enough to cause a massive eruption of discontent. Only at the cost of major concessions, up to and including the election of a Constitutional Assembly, was the government able to pacify the raging passions. Of course, this was not about the price of a subway ticket. It is about the distribution of power and social wealth, which many Chileans consider profoundly unfair. Chile's Gini coefficient—a common indicator of income inequality—stands at 0.45. This is slightly lower than the Latin American average, but much higher than in the OECD countries.[5] In receiving a lion's share of the social pie, the ruling elites were in no hurry to share it with the rest of society. According to the estimates of Rodrigo Valdes, Minister of Finance in Michelle Bachelet's socialist government, the richest one percent of the country pay no more than 15% of their income in taxes.[6] The modesty of the tax contributions by the rich has to be compensated at the expense of the middle class, naturally incurring its resentment and opposition—particularly where this entails the commercialization

---

3   "Can Chile Reinvent Itself?" *The Economist*, March 14, 2020, 36.
4   Chumakov, *Глобальный мир*, 154–55, 368, 381, 392, 398, 435, 472.
5   Chumakov, *Глобальный мир*, 154–55, 368, 381, 392, 398, 435, 472.
6   Chumakov, *Глобальный мир*, 38.

of key segments of the state's social policy (healthcare, education, pensions), which has become the hallmark of neoliberalism.

The Chilean experience minutely reflects the parabolic trajectory of neoliberal strategies. It does not lend itself to unambiguous evaluation. In the time of the preeminence of neoliberal practices, dozens of developing countries took a leap forward, into the more developed world. Hundreds of millions of people escaped poverty and joined the lower strata of the middle class. Average life expectancy increased by ten years, exceeding seventy years in total. These are the substantial achievements of neoliberal globalization, and something that it can confidently take credit for.

Concurrently, the costs of this model of economic growth have also been increasing and compounding. The tipping point occurred in the financial and economic crisis of 2008–2009. In the decade following 2010, the growth rate of the world economy slowed down. The post-crisis debt "overhang" increased instead of diminishing—approximately by a third in developed countries.[7] The key indicators of globalization—the share of world trade in global GDP, foreign-investment dynamics, cross-border migration flows—grew sluggishly or stagnated altogether. The World Trade Organization (WTO) stood in place, customs tariffs were creeping up, protectionist barriers were being raised. There was talk of "slow globalization"—and even of de-globalization.

The deepening crisis of the neoliberal model of expanded reproduction was most visibly manifested in the accelerated growth of global debt. Whereas in 2012–2016 it increased by $6 trillion, by 2021, it grew by an additional $52 trillion and then some. According to expert estimates of the Institute of International Finance (IIF), by the end of 2020, the total amount of global debt should have reached $277 trillion (or 365% of global GDP). Although developed nations lead by these indicators (432% of GDP), the accumulated debt of developing countries (248% of GDP) is no less alarming.[8]

The Russian financial analyst Alexander Losev sounds the alarm:

> The world economy is on the threshold of a systemic crisis: credit has become a palliative therapy for the increasing inequality and widespread reduction of incomes for the larger part of households and businesses; without credit, the model of expanded reproduction no loner works. At the same time, the ability of credit to generate economic growth is diminishing.[9]

---

7 "How to Reform Chile," *The Economist*, April 25, 2020, 14.
8 *Kommersant*, Money, 43 (December 16, 2020), 18.
9 *Kommersant*, Money, 43, 19.

The flip side of the neoliberal model of world economic activity is becoming increasingly obvious. Its first and foremost defect is the progressive inequality. In its most outrageous form, it manifested in the concentration of social wealth (and of the accompanying political influence) at the very top of the social pyramid. In 2014, Credit Suisse estimated that one percent of the world's population owned 48% of its assets—nearly an order of magnitude more than the bottom 80% of the population (with 5.5% of wealth, respectively).[10]

No less significant is the deep division of the Earth's civilization into those who more or less successfully fit into the globalized world and those who are left out. An invisible but palpable line divides communities large and small, territories, countries, and regions into the winners and the losers of globalization. Whether these gains and losses are absolute or relative, they are extremely sensitive.

COVID-19 has once again demonstrated the inequality of living conditions and opportunities for the inhabitants of the globalized world. This blind virus proved to be highly selective in its effects, since its victims are disproportionately the disadvantaged, whether we are talking of macro-groups, societies, or entire regions. For example, the governments of Tropical Africa spent an average of 3% of their GDPs on cushioning the economic shocks of COVID-19, while the developing countries spent 5%, and the developed countries, 7%.[11] Given the vast differences in their per capita GDPs, the absolute gap in spending is tens of times greater.

In this way, COVID-19 has imparted a new, absolute dimension into the division of the global world into winners and losers, by transferring that division onto the plane of life and death. The rich countries, with 14% of the world's population, purchased 53% of the supply of the most effective vaccines, far exceeding their objective needs.[12] The poor are forced to wait for their turn and make do with what is allocated.

Socio-economic processes were forcefully projected onto even the most powerful and ambitious states' domestic and foreign policies. The goddess Clio is known for her willfulness; the irony of History has not spared neoliberal globalization. The beloved brainchild of the West, it has turned in many ways against its parent. Its finest fruits were reaped not by North America and Western Europe, but by East Asia; its foremost beneficiary was not the United States, but China. For four decades, China has been rising like yeast, while

---

10   Deborah Hardoon, "Wealth: Having It All and Wanting More," *Oxfam Issue Briefing*, January 2015, 2.
11   "Africa's Long Covid," *The Economist*, February 6, 2021, 12.
12   *Kommersant*, Money, 3, February 25, 2021, 21.

the godparents of neo-globalism—the United States and Britain—have been plunged into acute domestic crisis, whose consequences will be felt for a long time to come. The year 2020 reaffirmed this constant of twenty-first-century global competition. The Middle Kingdom, the first victim of the coronavirus pandemic, recovered quickly and without great losses, while the United States and Britain, countries with a developed civil society and good medicine, were among those hit hardest.

In today's world, the distinction between economic, political, and cultural processes is fairly arbitrary. The ties between economics and politics are particularly close and durable. The global world can only be engendered by a combination of economic globalization and political centralization. Its distinctive characteristic, its hallmark, is the formation of a *system of global power*, whose main components are the nation-states, the largest and most influential economic entities, interstate global institutions, and, in recent decades, the emergent elements of a global civil society (e.g., Greenpeace, Human Rights Watch, Amnesty International). These agents enter into complex, network-like interactions involving a constant distribution and redistribution of power.

At the highest level of global power, the key role is played by nation-states, especially by the superpowers, great powers, and regional powers. Their special role within the global system of power relations is based on the fact that they, and they alone, possess full-fledged political legitimacy confirmed by popular vote. This role is most distinctly manifest in periods of great upheavals, such as world wars, global economic crises, the most encompassing of natural disasters—and pandemics. Nation-states notably maintain the stability of the world order in times of global crises and during periods of transition from one model of world order to another.

The two historically attested formulas of global power have been quite simple: they amount to the presence of a hegemonic country and its allies. The hegemonic role of the Anglo-Saxons has already been noted: in the first version of the globalized world, it was Great Britain, in the "global world-2"—the United States. Among the allies, the role of European powers was of great importance.

The similarities between the two formulas of global power do not mean that they should be treated as analogous. In the nineteenth century, Britain, which pursued a policy of "splendid isolation," was principally disinclined to bind itself to other powers through durable alliances. Everyone knows the lapidary formula of Britain's then Prime Minister, Lord Palmerston: "We have no eternal allies, and we have no perpetual enemies. Our interests are eternal and perpetual, and those interests it is our duty to follow." Britain's most important military alliance of the day, the 1907 Entente with France and Russia, was only formed in view of the looming prospect of the First World War.

The United States had to act in an entirely different historical context. Its road to global domination lay via the wars of the mid-twentieth century and of its second half: first the Second World War, then the Cold War. The country therefore immediately acquired allies, whose number would but steadily increase.

The two formulas of global power have similar, though not identical, internal dynamics. At first, the power waxes stronger, then it wanes. British power peaked in the mid-nineteenth century, when England was the world's leading industrial nation. At the end of the century, it was confidently overtaken by the United States in all the most important indices of industrial production, and by Germany at the beginning of the next century. Soberly assessing this new balance of power, British politicians embraced an alliance with their longstanding rivals in Europe and in the world—France and Russia.

Britain's global position was definitively undermined by the two world wars and by the great crisis of 1929–1933. These events obliterated the trumps she had in hand early in the twentieth century. Huge foreign assets were replaced by large foreign debts, and the pound lost its place as the world's reserve currency. The British colonial empire, over which the sun never set, entered a period of irreversible decline. The emergence of nuclear weapons made Britain vulnerable as never before.

The American hegemony of the "global world-2" rested on far firmer foundations. In territory and population, the United States belongs to the largest countries in the world. For a century and a half, the United States has been ahead of the whole planet in the world economic system; the almighty dollar controls global financial flows. The United States leads in scientific research and experimental engineering; the country accounts for about half of the best universities in the world. Experts estimate that the United States has the most combat-ready armed forces, with military bases and aircraft carriers covering most of the world space. English has become the recognized language of international communication in the globalized world. The country's far-reaching system of alliances with other states is an effective multiplier of American might.

Still, American hegemony is gradually transforming from absolute to relative. It is undermined not only by objective processes but also by Washington's subjective blunders. A considerable number of centers of power have emerged in the world on the basis of great and regional powers. With all the differences in their objective capabilities, what they have in common is a desire to pursue independent policies guided by their own national interests.[13] American political elites have been slow to appreciate these changes, nor did they give them adequate consideration. Their sobriety was clouded by the euphoria over the "American century" that left the United States as the sole remaining superpower. This created a deceptive sense of omnipotence and of everything being permitted. Only the sobering experiences of the failed Afghan and Iraq campaigns forced the US Establishment to think again about its future prospects.

President Barack Obama's administration (2009–2017) substantively adjusted the country's foreign policy course in two developments of the National Security Strategy (2010 and 2015) and began to implement them. Some of the plans, such as ending the war in Iraq, were realized; some failed, due to the disunity of the political elites (the Trans-Pacific Partnership).

The United States' forty-fifth president, Donald Trump, tried to radically change the American position in the world, essentially abandoning the claims of global leadership and sharply turning the country's foreign policy towards neo-isolationism, grounded in a strong tradition in the US history. This was a questionable strategy for the only remaining superpower in the globalized world, but Trump pursued it with a persistence worthy of a better application.

In this manner, by 2020, "globalization-2" had arrived in its state of profound crisis. Its twin pillars—the neoliberal social and economic policies and American leadership—were both put in question. Instead of a world order, there was more and more talk of global disorder. Then, COVID-19 mixed up all the cards on the table, upheaving along the way the entire system of usual coordinates. The world was plunged deeper into a state of uncertainty, insecurity, confusion, and turmoil.

What are the prospects for globalization and globalized world in the foreseeable future? At present, it is impossible to answer this question with any certainty. First of all, we are not yet in a position to assess all the effects of the pandemic. It could have a very long echo, and, at the time this is being written, we do not even have the statistics for the year 2020 at our disposal yet.

Still, some things can already be stated. COVID-19 has revealed our complete unpreparedness and helplessness in the face of emergencies of this magnitude. This was especially evident at the level of global institutions. The World Health Organization played catch-up with the events, unable to determine anything or even to make sensible recommendations. The United Nations

---

13   See: Victor Kuvaldin, *Западноцентристский миропорядок: вторая проверка на прочность. Страны и регионы в мировой политике* [*West-centric World Order and The Second Test of Its Durability: Countries and Regions in World Politics*], in two vols. (Moscow: Aspect, 2019), vol. 1.

confined itself to dispensing well-meaning advice, good wishes, and sympathies. Nor did the regional organizations prove their mettle. Even within such a tightly knit alliance as the European Union there was no effective coordination among participating countries. Practically the whole burden of fighting the pandemic fell to nation-states. In a world of global interconnections and interrelations, the absence of effective supranational instruments of medical assistance and cooperation drastically reduced the effectiveness of the measures taken.

The cooperation among states was also patently flawed. Everyone looked out for themselves; examples of coordinated actions are few and far in between. On the other hand, solving one's own problems at the expense of others was a common practice. Analyzing this discouraging experience of interstate "cooperation" in solving the most pressing problems facing humanity today, Ralph C. Bryant, a well-known international economist and senior fellow at the Brookings Institution, writes in the foreword to his new book with the telling title *Governance for a Higgledy-Piggledy Planet*: "Nurturing international comity and enhancing cooperation are essential for a safe, sustainable evolution of the planet and its multiple jurisdictions" (nation-states). He continues: "The world community must somehow gradually construct future rules of the road that are stronger, mutually beneficial, and better maintained."[14]

The forced fragmentation of the planetary coronavirus battlefield into separate national campaigns will leave its profound mark. Virtually all commentators agree that the year 2020 will be a milestone in the development of the nation-state and in the expansion of its powers in many spheres of modern society.

Yet another confirmation of the nation-state's primacy in the life of society continues the tradition established in the modern era. For several centuries, the powers-that-be of advanced countries have been increasingly consistent in seeking to control socio-economic processes. Their activity increases sharply in times of crisis, requiring the mobilization of all resources. First of all, we are speaking of continental and world wars, such as the Seven Years' War (1756–1763), the Napoleonic Wars (1803–1815), the First and Second World Wars, and the Cold War. The twentieth century, especially its second half, saw the rise of the fabulously costly geo-strategic, infrastructural, and social megaprojects on a national scale. All attempts to restrain in some way, not to speak of reversing, the expansion of the state into various spheres of public life came

---

14 Ralph C. Bryant, *Governance for a Higgledy-Piggledy Planet* (Washington: Brookings Institution, 2020), 9.

to naught. Provisional measures dictated by an emergency situation surreptitiously acquired permanent status. In real life, it is always easier to increase government spending and budgets than to cut them: this is a one-way street.

An "expensive state" is inconceivable without high taxes, which skyrocket in times of great turmoil, especially for the wealthy. In France in 1914, the top income-tax plank was zero; the year after the First World War ended, it jumped up to 50%. During the Second World War, the US Government turned the income tax from a "class" to a "mass" one; in 1940, it was paid by seven million citizens, in 1945—by forty-two million.[15] In the second half of the century, under the conditions of fierce competition between the two social systems, the creation of the "welfare state" in the leading capitalist countries (the United States, United Kingdom, France, Sweden) was sponsored by an impressive increase in the tax burden.

In the twenty-first century, the nation-state continues to expand its spheres of competence and responsibility. As before, it does so most intensively in difficult times. In response to the financial and economic crisis of 2008–2009, many countries adopted a series of measures, including generous monetary stimuli, to assist the economy. COVID-19 forced the powerful to spend like never before. In the developed world, governments and parliaments spared no expense to support business and households. Businesses were kept afloat with tax breaks, grants, and cheap credit. Where there was great danger of infection in the workplace, workers were paid to self-isolate. Households received deferrals and relief on home loans, other debts, rent, and utilities. There were also lump-sum payments and substantial increases in unemployment benefits.

According to the International Labor Organization (ILO), from February 2020 to January 2021, over 1,600 new social assistance programs were launched. The International Monetary Fund (IMF) estimates that by January 2021, total direct spending in wealthy countries increased by nearly 13% of the GDP. About half of this gargantuan amount went to support working people and households. According to a study by the Boston Consulting Group, in some countries about 60% of recipients had never received social benefit payments previously. Compared to the record indicators of the financial and economic crisis of 2008–2009, emergency financing increased more than four-fold under pandemic conditions.[16] Central banks did not lag behind governments. Usually very conservative and cautious in financial matters, they did all they could to sustain the pulse of economic activity. They reduced interest

---

15   *The Economist*, March 28, 2020, 21–22.
16   *The Economist*, March 6, 2021, 16–17.

rates, increased the money supply, bought government bonds and securities, provided credit guarantees, and easily and willingly lent to economic actors.

Compared with the financial and economic crisis of 2008–2009, the focus of the various efforts has undergone a significant shift. At that time, assistance was provided chiefly to the financial institutions—that is, to the wealthy strata of society. In 2020, coverage was much broader and more democratic, with a lot of state support going to the most disadvantaged and vulnerable categories of the population.

In this way, at the opening of the twenty-first century, the trajectories of globalization and of the nation-states once gain began to diverge. While many global processes have slowed down or simply stalled, nation-states are steeply on the rise and expanding into new spheres of competence. In principle, this creates a dangerous situation. The historical experience of the previous two centuries confirms that the greatest successes of earth's civilization were achieved when state-building was more or less organically inscribed into the formation of the global world.[17]

In today's interconnected and reciprocally vulnerable world, this coordination of the global, macro-regional, and national aspects of public life becomes a categorical imperative. It would have been hard to think of a more persuasive testimony to the commonality of the fate of our civilization then COVID-19 has, in fact, furnished. For humanity, it has been not just a practical challenge, but an existential one. Alexey Gromyko, a corresponding member of the Russian Academy of Sciences, rightly notes:

> The new pandemic not only lays bare the problems of healthcare, but also raises questions about the states' and their people's commitment to solidarity, about their ability to overcome their differences, and about the balance between reciprocal aid and self-interest.[18]

Can neoliberal globalization attain a "human face"? In principle, such a transformation probably cannot be ruled out. Strictly speaking, some signs of movement in this direction have emerged in the conditions of the pandemic,

---

17 Victor Kuvaldin, "Глобализация и национальное государство: вчера, сегодня, завтра" ["Globalization and the Nation-State: Yesterday, Today and Tomorrow"], *Mirovaya ekonomika i mezhdunarodnye otnosheniya*, 2021, No. 1, 5–13.

18 Alexey Gromyko, "Коронавирус как фактор мировой политики" ["Coronavirus as a Factor of World Politics"], *Научно-аналитический вестник Института Европы РАН* [*The Scholarly-Analytical Bulletin of the Europe Institute of the Russian Academy of Sciences*], 2020 (14), No. 2, 11.

especially in European countries. Confronted with the hard dilemma of saving *either* the economy *or* the people, a number of governments in that macro-region chose the latter, notwithstanding the immense material costs and losses. Combined with the intensive stimulation of economic activity, which had a humanitarian aspect, this led to spending unprecedented yet in the history of the world economy. According to the expert estimates of McKinsey & Company, COVID-19 will cost the humankind the exorbitant sum of approximately $30 trillion. That's three times the "price-tag" of the Great Recession of 2009.[19]

Still, this has been more of a firefighting emergency measure than a well-considered correction of the general course. It is difficult to argue with the well-known Russian economist Vladislav Belov when he writes:

> The post-corona world will certainly be changed. But the fundamentals of globalization of the world and of the European economy will remain the same. Here, even the current pandemic is powerless to effect qualitative change. In our opinion, the pandemic would not become a game-changer, a decisive factor of qualitative change to the world's economic mechanisms. It will only accelerate certain trends that have emerged in recent years—the protection of economic sovereignty, comprehensive economic security, protectionism, re-shoring, localization and import substitution, state support for national champions, digital transformation, Industry 4.0, artificial intelligence, online networked business platforms. The fundamentals of the international division of labor will stay the same.[20]

Belov also notes a distinct shift towards the accentuation of national priorities in economic activity.

A certain kind of counterpoint and counterbalance to the growing power of the nation-state is presented by the emerging global civil society, which, too, has become much more active under the influence of the coronavirus pandemic. Along with solutions to the current challenges, it puts on the agenda

---

19   Susan Lund et al., "Risk, Resilience, and Rebalancing in Global Value Chains," a report of McKinsey Global Institute, August 2020, 24, https://www.mckinsey.com/business-functions/operations/our-insights/risk-resilience-and-rebalancing-in-global-value-chains.

20   Vladislav Belov, "COVID-19—Game Changer европейской экономики?" ["COVID-19: A Game-Changer of European Economy?"], *Научно-аналитический вестник Института Европы РАН* [*The Scholarly-Analytical Bulletin of the Europe Institute of the Russian Academy of Sciences*], 2020 (15), No. 3, 9.

deep revision of the present system. Opening a collection of articles devoted to the ambivalent relations between the ruling elites and civil society in many countries of Asia, the Middle East, Europe, Africa, North America, and Latin America under the conditions of the pandemic, its editor Richard Youngs writes:

> The crisis has galvanized global civil society into pushing harder for far-reaching, radical change to social, economic, and political models. The coronavirus crisis has magnified many of the imbalances of countries political and economic systems. As many governments have reacted in restrictive and ineffective ways, civil society has pushed back hard. It has begun to mobilize more proactively and with vibrancy for major reform of social and economic models whose shortcomings the pandemic has cruelly revealed.[21]

In the "welfare states," dissatisfaction with existing social security and insurance systems was evident even before the "corona-crisis." In 2019, among respondents in twenty-six countries, less than one fifth agreed with the statement that the "system" was working for them. Half of the respondents said that it had failed.[22] Even the formerly exotic idea of a universal basic income (UBI), a permanent public payment to the entire adult population, has gained widespread popularity. In 2020, it was approved by more than two thirds of Europeans.[23] In real life, there is still no talk of a practical implementation of the UBI, but the formation of a mass expectation for an enlargement of the states' and businesses' zone of social responsibility is evident.

This new level of civil society's demands on the powerful and the wealthy is sensitively perceived by the global elites. At the very beginning of the pandemic, in January 2020, the World Economic Forum in Davos proposed the concept of "stakeholder capitalism" as an alternative to the neoliberal model. According to its authors, expectations of socially responsible business cannot be confined to its profitability; business can, and should, contribute to the healthy and harmonious development of humankind in every possible way.[24]

---

21 Richard Youngs, ed., *Global Civil Society in the Shadow of Coronavirus* (Washington: Carnegie Endowment for International Peace, 2020), 2.
22 *The Economist*, March 6, 2021, 16.
23 *The Economist*, 9.
24 Klaus Schwab, "Davos Manifesto 2020: The Universal Purpose of a Company in the Fourth Industrial Revolution," World Economic Forum, December 2, 2019, https://www.weforum.org/agenda/2019/12/davos-manifesto-2020-the-universal-purpose-of-a-company-in-the-fourth-industrial-revolution/.

It appears that a serious correction of socio-economic policy is on the developed countries' agenda. Of course, its chances of success in this group of states would be greatly enhanced by its more or less coordinated implementation. And if this deep transformation of the socio-economic dynamics of world leaders can be integrated in some manner into the global context, then "globalization-2" will get a second wind.

It is true that no such concerted action is yet in evidence. As noted earlier, a dampened globalization and the hyperactive nation-state are the reality at the opening of our present century's third decade. Can a common ground be established? A pioneering study by researchers from Gothenburg and Stockholm Universities was devoted to finding an answer to this crucial question.[25] The authors interviewed 860 representatives of elite groups in six countries (Brazil, Germany, Russia, United States, the Philippines, and South Africa). In addition, there was also a "global group" of officials from international organizations.[26] The authors investigate the attitudes towards global governance held by people vested with power within various kinds of national and supranational institutions. According to their assessment, generally, the elites have a keen interest in global institutions and are well informed about their activities. They attach the greatest importance to the democratic nature of the procedures and to the effectiveness of these bodies. They support the globalization of certain areas of political activity (human rights, the environment, international trade).

At the same time, their attitudes towards the development of a broader system of global regulation of world processes can be characterized as *lukewarm and divided*. Summing up their research, the authors write:

> In sum, we may conclude that the often considerable readiness for global governance that elites express in principle (finding 1) is not matched by strong legitimacy beliefs for current global governance in practice (finding 2). Overall levels of confidence in existing GGIs [global governance institutions] are neither so high that we could expect to push for a significant expansion of global governance, nor so low that we could expect elites to obstruct or even dismantle the institutions.
>
> Evidence from this elite survey suggests the future of neither crisis nor boom for global governance, but rather a process of muddling through.

---

25   Jan Aart Scholte, Soetkin Verhaegen, and Jonas Tallberg, "Elite Attitudes and the Future of Global Governance," *International Affairs*, 2021 (97), No. 3, 861–86.
26   Scholte, Verhaegen, and Tallberg, "Elite Attitudes and the Future of Global Governance," 882.

> At the same time, overall medium levels of elite confidence in GGIs could offer reasonably secure ground on which to construct greater global governance as and when future conditions might push for it.[27]

At present, we can only speculate about how the tragic experience of the coronavirus pandemic might further affect the elites' attitudes towards the development of global governance. In most general terms, we can but refer to the suppositions of the study's authors:

> Nor does our evidence about elite confidence in existing GGIs suggest a decline in world-scale governance in the near to medium term. On the contrary, current overall elite attitudes could actually be ripe for an expansion of global governance if GGIs would improve certain aspects of their procedure and performance.[28]

It will take time to answer with some confidence whether the "corona-crisis" has indeed constituted a milestone in the process of "globalization-2."

---

[27] Scholte, Verhaegen, and Tallberg, "Elite Attitudes and the Future of Global Governance," 881.

[28] Scholte, Verhaegen, and Tallberg, "Elite Attitudes and the Future of Global Governance," 886.

The Twilight of Neoliberal Globalization

Alternatives to the Dead-Ends of the Proto-Empire

Aleksandr V. Buzgalin

Only two decades ago, the trend towards globalization appeared to be universal. But after encountering the world crises set in motion in 2007–2008, that trend revealed not only its profound contradictions, but also its limitations. What took place—and what were the contents and contradictions of that process?

1 From Neoliberal Globalization to a New Empire

For all the diverse definitions of globalization, it has increasingly come to be characterized as (1) a non-linear, uneven, and contradictory *process* (the opposite of localization) that develops to the degree to which (2) the world is transformed from a totality of nation-states into a field of struggle between global players that interact on the territories of the nation-states, cities, towns, villages—down to the campus buffet that presents one with a spectacle of the struggle between Coke and Pepsi—while (3) global economic, political and socio-cultural laws become more significant than their national counterparts.

Until recent time, the dominant and unambiguous view in the scholarly community was that globalization was an objectively existing process with a progressive nature. But in the last few years, a conservative trend that regards regionalization and protectionism as the antithesis to globalism has become more and more influential, and has drawn up an anti-globalist agenda.

There is, nevertheless, another way of viewing these questions. It involves searching for a path that does not lead back to a pre-global world, constructed according to the principle of a conservative, regressive restoration of autarchy, but towards a new model of cooperation and integration between peoples and economies on the basis of equal rights. This model rests on a dialogue between cultures—that is, on transcending the contradictions of neoliberal globalization, and on establishing the eco-socio-cultural priorities for future development, instead of an all-encompassing market backed by the geopolitical and economic hegemony of nascent proto-empires. Unlike the globalism that prevailed until recently, this path, which came to be termed *alter-globalism* in the early years of this century, looks and leads forward, and not the other way. It represents a positive alternative not only to the ideology of globalism, but also to the practices of neoliberal globalization.

Contrary to widespread myths, anti-globalists agree that in our new century the world is developing under the conditions of increasing integration of technologies, economies, and cultures. This is a genuine objective process. But the process of integration of technologies, economies, and cultures can proceed differently, with different goals, and employing different means. In a similar fashion, technical progress advanced along diverse paths during the mid-twentieth century—the age that coincided with Stalinism, with enthusiasms about "shining cities" and "Swedish socialism," and with colonial bondage. It can be said, then, that the final decades of the last century witnessed not just a globalization of economic and social life that threatened the sovereignty of peoples and states, but a particular social form of this process, characteristic of late capitalism.[1]

Concealed until now behind the apparent late-twentieth-century market renaissance was a system of relations that one might call, in line with Antonio Gramsci and other Marxists of the last century, the *total hegemony of capital*.[2] It is paradoxical that, while the twenty-first century *market* is ostensibly oriented toward the atomization of producers and towards absolute individualism in the area of human behavior, it is, in reality, *a powerful totalitarian system that oppresses the human individual from every side*. It oppresses us not as some sort of a hierarchical bureaucratic pyramid, but as a diversified and outwardly all but imperceptible field that nevertheless acts upon us in virtually every sphere of our social existence.

This global power of capital presumes, first of all, a total market that penetrates every pore of human life. This is not a market of atomized, freely competing enterprises, but a *total market* constituting the space of struggle among gigantic networks centered upon transnational corporations. All of us—workers, consumers, and residents—fall within this web of diverse forms of dependency upon corporate network structures busily waging war on one another. Second, the hegemony of capital is now constituted mainly by the power of *virtual, fictitious financial capital* that "lives" in the informational

---

1 See: Ernest Mandel, *Late Capitalism* (New York: Verso, 1987); Fredric Jameson, *Postmodernism, or The Cultural Logic of Late Capitalism* (Durham: Duke University Press, 1984), 1–54.
2 The author's interpretation of the nature of the present social system is set out in the book: Aleksandr Buzgalin and Andrei Kolganov, Глобальный капитал [*Global Capital*] (Moscow: URSS, 2018).

space, giving rise to the financialization not just of the economy, but of society as well.[3]

Third, the global hegemony of capital now presupposes not just the exploitation of hired workers through the sale and purchase of labor power, but also the *comprehensive subordination of the individuality of the worker*. In the countries of the "core," the creative potential, talents, education, and indeed the entire existence of skilled people are all appropriated by the modern corporation; the semi-feudal methods of exploitation that are used to lock up workers in ghettos of backwardness are spreading further, not just in the countries of the "periphery" but also in the "semi-periphery," and especially in Russia (in this instance, I am employing the categorical apparatus of the world-systems approach).[4]

Fourth is the widely familiar system of methods used by the capital at the "center" to *monopolize the key resources of development*—that is, the "know-how" and the highly qualified labor power—while devouring the overwhelming bulk of available natural resources, and while engaging in the export of polluting technologies and socio-cultural detritus to the countries of the periphery and semi-periphery. Fifth is the whole complex of *global political and ideological manipulation, and of informational and cultural pressures*.

The appropriate form for such a system—but only a form, and moreover, a mutant form—has been the renaissance of market relations. While presenting a mere appearance of an atomized structure with free competition between constituent elements, it is characterized by the reality of huge corporations that exploit their field of influence, with ample opportunities to manipulate and subjugate economic agents, consumers, and workers. It is in these circumstances that masses of corporate capital, both productive and financial-speculative, are able to escape the sphere of the relatively powerful and restrictive state regulation and the control of strong and effective public organizations. Here, we find the crucial difference between the cur-

---

3 Chang Hun and Zhang Bo, "Трудности экономического развития капиталистической экономики с момента мирового финансового кризиса 2008 г." ["The Difficulties of the Capitalist Economy's Economic Development from the Moment of the Global Financial Crisis of 2008"], *Voprosy politicheskoy ekonomii*, 2019, No. 3, 67–74; Ben Fine, "Financialization through Marxist perspective," *International Journal of Political Economy*, Winter 2013–14 (42), No. 4, 47–66; Catherine Sifakis-Kapitanakis, "Новые факторы глобальных финансов и финансиализация капитализма" ["New Factors of Global Finance and the Financialization of Capitalism"], *Voprosy politicheskoy ekonomii*, 2019, No. 1, 82–93.

4 See: Immanuel Wallerstein, *The Modern World-System*, vol. 1, *Capitalist Agriculture and the Origins of the European World-Economy in the Sixteenth Century* (Berkeley: University of California Press, 2011).

rent system and the earlier system of "socially oriented" capitalism, in which the state, labor unions, and the environmental, municipal, consumer, and other social structures imposed substantial barriers, normative frameworks, and other kinds of restriction upon market relations. In contrast, the illusion that market relations are absolutely free (which is truly an illusion, although an objective illusion) frees the hands of global players, over whom the nominal frameworks of state regulation have little sway. *This model is nevertheless approaching its twilight, and a new system is about to replace it: a system that, in inheriting the totality of its predecessor, will raise that totality to a "new height."*

Twenty years ago, it seemed that the age of globalization would be eternal, and the only change expected was the anticipated transformation of the United States into a new *empire with a claim to the role of the "Big Brother"* (to recall George Orwell) to the rest of the world community. In that empire, all animals would be equal, but some would be "more equal than others." This trend was cut short. On the one hand, this was attributable to China's transformation into a world politico-economic actor of near-equal potential as of 2020.[5] On the other hand, this was due to the general transformation of the world's geopolitical and economic configuration, leading to a gradual separation of the proto-imperial sub-spaces of the global politico-economic system. As one shall soon demonstrate, the proto-empire is characterized by the transformation of democracy into large-scale political, ideological, and spiritual production and manipulation, and also by the danger arising from a pandemic of asymmetrical wars, whose poles are the "missionary wars" of the United States and its allies, and terrorism.

The result is that the world is gradually shifting (and I would like to stress that this process is not yet complete) from an illusion of the restoration of free markets, private property, and open society, from an illusion that grand ideologies are vanishing definitively into the past—to the rule of a proto-empire and to the hegemony of the geopolitical, economic, and ideological concepts corresponding to that world order.[6] This is a shift towards an open acknowledgment of the hegemony of global players with claims to imperial geopolitical and economic functions, once again augmented by an open ideological and political assertion of hegemony, where pluralism capitulates in the face of the conservative great-power propaganda.

---

5 Justin Lin, "China and the global economy," *China Economic Journal*, 2011 (4), No. 1, 1–14; David Shambaugh, *China Goes Global: The Partial Power* (Oxford: Oxford University Press, 2013), 409.
6 Radhika Desai, *Geopolitical Economy: After US Hegemony, Globalization and Empire (The Future of World Capitalism)* (London: Pluto Press, 2013).

All this signifies the onset of a new phase that involves a transition to a system in which—perhaps, for there are still alternatives—numerous predictions made a century ago by creative Marxists will begin to be realized. Here, I should mention the now mostly forgotten idea of *ultra-imperialism* or *re-colonization*. The term "ultra-imperialism" was suggested by Karl Kautsky, and most Russian scholars of the older generation will recall its being criticized by Vladimir Ulyanov.[7] His criticism was bound up with the thesis of the possibility and indeed inevitability of the victory of socialism before the conditions for the rise of ultra-imperialism could take shape; most Marxists did not deny, in principle, that ultra-imperialism was a possibility.

Strange as it might seem, history has confirmed this thesis. The paradox of the twentieth century lay in the fact that the necessity for socialism, a necessity born of global cataclysms on the scale of the First World War and the anti-colonial revolutions, was in fact demonstrated even during the stage of imperialism. The global socialist system arose in a fortuitous fashion, attained a scale encompassing a third of humanity, and lasted for seven decades. It displayed relatively high and stable growth rates, and its rule was marked by impressive achievements in the fields of science, technology, education, social welfare, and culture. At the same time, the seven decades of the global socialist system's existence were burdened with extremely acute contradictions and showed that this system lacked a sufficient basis for its rise. In essence, it was a mutant, a society that had emerged under conditions in which it lacked the necessary objective and subjective prerequisites for proceeding towards constructing a society that would be more economically effective than capitalism, and more socially just and free than the so-called "open society."[8]

This paradox is marked by the fact that "actually existing socialism" not only brought about mighty achievements and breakthroughs in the fields of science, culture, and social welfare, but also witnessed the triumph of an authoritarian political system. The exit from the scene of "mutant socialism" did not signify a breakthrough or inaugurate a new epoch, or a transitional social system preparing the way towards "freedom," but amounted to a reversal of history, one that engendered a trend prefiguring the rise of ultra-imperialism.

---

7 Karl Kautsky, *Ultra-Imperialism*, Marxists Internet Archive, https://www.marxists.org/archive/kautsky/1914/09/ultra-imp.htm; Vladimir Lenin, *Imperialism, the Highest Stage of Capitalism*, Marxists Internet Archive, https://www.marxists.org/archive/lenin/works/1916/imp-hsc/imperialism.pdf.

8 For a more detailed treatment of the dialectic of the contradictions surrounding the rise and collapse of "actually existing socialism," see: Aleksandr Buzgalin et al., *СССР: Оптимистическая трагедия* [*The USSR: An Optimistic Tragedy*] (Moscow: URSS, 2018).

I do not exclude the possibility that this epoch will replace not just the neoliberal "end of history" that has marched triumphant for the past twenty years, but also the whole epoch of imperialism that began around the turn of the twentieth century and that lasted, with a range of variations and modifications, throughout that century. While this ultra-imperialism remains, on the whole, within the framework of antagonistic society, of the world of alienation, of the "realm of necessity," and even of the capitalist socio-economic formation (here, I deliberately employ a "formational" rather than a civilizational approach), it may prove to be the beginning of a new and relatively prolonged epoch characterized by tendencies towards

- an evolution from the semblance of free worldwide competition to the direct dictates of large corporate structures intertwined with proto-imperial states, that is, a sort of "patriotic drift" among transnational corporations;
- replacement of covert political manipulation, aided by various political techniques and public-relations methods, with more or less open authoritarianism and totalitarianism. This may be seen as involving a direct assault on the institutions of democracy, of civil society, and of human rights, both on the "periphery" and in the "center," as well as growth in the popularity of conservative ideology and politics;
- direct use of the "rule of force" and of recolonization methods in geopolitics;
- a shift from hidden ideological manipulation, involving the retention of at least formal ideological pluralism and relative freedom of speech, conscience, and so forth, to the unambiguous dominance of state ("imperial") ideology and pressure on dissidents.

At the same time, the values of "Western civilization" will by increasingly identified with the interests of global players (the "masters" of the empire); anyone who thinks or acts differently, along with their associates, will be characterized either as "antipatriotic" or as "trampling on the values of civilization," with warnings of the threat posed by these new "enemies of the people" (of "civilization," of the empire, and so forth).

For the moment, I will refrain from discussing the danger that these mutations of late capitalism might actually triumph. I will note, all the same, that alternative forces are also present in today's economic, social, political, and spiritual life. I will have more to say about these forces, but must note first that the decline and crisis of the "actually existing socialism," for all the internal contradictions of that system, was not so much a positive factor as a negative one, even though it saw the destruction of the authoritarian system of the past. The *regressive impact of the disintegration of the global socialist system* was expressed not so much in the fact that it created the preconditions for the economic and geopolitical triumph of global capital and for the formation of a monopolar world, as in the fact that in essence, it cleared the way for *a reversal of the course of history, leading to an ultra-imperialist dead-end*. It is, then, no accident that, from a purely methodological point of view, I characterize ultra-imperialism as a reversal of history.

On the socio-philosophical level, the reasons for this may be seen in the tendency by the forces of the "proto-empire" to divert the main trajectory of development into a channel quite incommensurate with free and harmonious development of humanity in dialogue with nature. The priorities of this incipient reversal are in using the growing potential of technology for such purposes as militarism, financial transactions, parasitic over-consumption, and mass culture, while expanding and deepening global problems and conflicts. The arguments supporting these theses are already well known, thanks to Noam Chomsky, Immanuel Wallerstein, Samir Amin, and many others.[9] Let us examine these arguments in more detail.

- The decline of neoliberalism has shown *in practice* its orientation towards increased military spending and towards the use of wars and violence to achieve its goals; imperial geopolitics is practically oriented towards direct recolonization and subordination of poorly developed countries, exacerbating global confrontations.
- Global virtual financial capital (the volume of whose transactions exceeds $500 trillion—not billion—per year) is not simply a major form of capital in the epoch of the decline of neoliberalism, but the hegemonic one. By virtue of its very nature, global virtual financial capital has an interest in ensuring its maximum possible freedom of movement and self-empowerment, and is therefore exceedingly antagonistic to any social or other limitations. In this respect, it differs from productive capital, restricted, at least to some extent, by the need to observe the interests of workers and of the nation-state, to ensure social stability, and so forth.
- The consumer society and the mass culture that corresponds to it are capable of generating only a relatively narrow stratum of specialized professionals, while at the same time, and to an ever-increasing degree, alienating the

---

9 On Chomsky: Noam Chomsky, *Hegemony or Survival?* (London: Hamish Hamilton, 2003), 116. See also: Noam Chomsky et al., *Profit Over People: Neoliberalism and Global Order* (New York: Seven Stories Press, 1999); Noam Chomsky and Edward S. Herman, *Manufacturing Consent: The Political Economy of the Mass Media* (London: Vintage Books, 1994); On Wallerstein: See the following by Immanuel Wallerstein: *The Capitalist World-Economy* (Cambridge: Cambridge University Press, 1979); *Geopolitics and Geoculture: Essays on the Changing World-System* (Cambridge: Cambridge University Press, 1991); *The Politics of the World-Economy: The States, the Movements and the Civilizations* (Cambridge: Cambridge University Press, 1984); On Amin: Samir Amin, *Capitalism in the Age of Globalization* (London: Zed, 2014).

great majority of citizens from free creative activity and compounding their dilemma as conformist consumers and passive objects of manipulation. In pursuing this end, the "empire" (unlike neoliberalism) is not squeamish about using direct methods of politico-ideological pressure.

These trends bear witness to the retrograde nature of this evolution in relation to the line of social progress oriented towards ensuring a scope for the flourishing of human qualities and of genuine culture, and for the protection of nature.[10]

Meanwhile, the question remains open as to whether progress is occurring at all, and whether it can be represented with the use of scientific criteria. Postmodernism answers this question unambiguously and negatively.[11] But for the *practice* of neoliberalism, the criteria of progress and regress exist, and are derived from the actions of the governments of the United States, the European Union, and their allies; the practices of these actors are for all intents and purposes recognized as contributing to the development of civilization.

Hence, we have formulated the thesis that the world is now entering the stage that is seeing the birth of a "proto-empire." The development of the relations of global hegemony of corporate capital characteristic of this phenomenon leads to the formation of a corporate-capitalist nomenclature—the subject of the comprehensive hegemony of capital—and, as the *alter ego* of this process, to the growth of conformism among hired workers (though the latter should and potentially could be the main subject of change in the existing society). This, in turn, creates the preconditions for undermining the most developed, classical forms of socio-political organization in the realm of necessity—civil society and democracy. But at the same time, forces that represent an alternative to this hegemony are also coming into being.

---

10 See: Karen Momdzhian, "О возможности и критериях общественного прогресса" ["On the Possibility and Criteria of Social Progress"], *Bulletin of Moscow University*, Series 7, 2018, No. 5. Lyudmila A. Bulavka-Buzgalina, "Маркс–XXI. Социальный прогресс и его цена: Диалектика отчуждения и разотчуждения" ["Marx–XXI. Social Progress and Its Cost. The Dialectics of Alienation and De-Alienation"], *Bulletin of Moscow University*, Series 7, 2018, No. 5.

11 See: Jean Baudrillard, *Simulacra and Simulation* (Ann Arbor: University of Michigan Press, 1994); Giles Deleuze, *On the Line* (New York: Semiotext(e), 1983); Jacques Derrida, *Margins of Philosophy* (Chicago: University of Chicago Press, 1982); Michel Foucault and Angèle Kremer-Marietti, *L'archéologie du savoir*, vol. 1 (Paris: Gallimard, 1969); Fredric Jameson, *Postmodernism, or The Cultural Logic of Late Capitalism* (Durham: Duke University Press, 1991); Zygmunt Bauman, *Postmodern Ethics* (Oxford: Blackwell, 1993).

2　　The Phenomenology of Alter-Globalism

"A specter is haunting the world, the specter of 'anti-globalism.' Joining in the holy alliance against it are the Bushes and Blairs, liberals and Stalinists, fundamentalists and chauvinists. But our movement is growing and developing, not just from year to year, but from month to month." These lines opened one of my first works on the problems of alter-globalism, at a time when this movement first arose, almost twenty years ago. Originally, that text took the form of a booklet issued in Russian and English on the eve of the second World Social Forum, held in Porto Alegre in January 2002. Incidentally, the author lays claim to having been the first to use the term "alter-globalism," pointing out, at the time, that we were not speaking out *against globalization*, but *in favor of a different globalization, an alternative to the neoliberal variety*. Hence the movement's key slogan: *Another world is possible!* This movement has since grown into one of the most significant oppositional forces of the modern era, recognized by mighty thinkers and social activists like Noam Chomsky, Immanuel Wallerstein, and many others, supported by most of the left opposition parties of Europe, Latin America, Africa, and Asia, and involving tens of thousands of large social organizations and movements.

Answers to questions concerning the nature of this movement and the reasons for its rise should, above all, be sought in the nature of the contemporary world order. It is not by chance that this world order has been described as globalization, nor is it an accident that it is linked increasingly with the genesis of a new empire. (Whereas, in Russia and many other countries of the "periphery" and "semi-periphery," *the empire* is understood as the totality of the power of global players, headed by the United States and arrayed against them, the "center" often interprets it either as a voluntary adherence to the most progressive force of modern times—the neoliberal ideology naturally assigning this role to the United States—or as a sort of new network union of supranational institutions.)[12] It is useful to begin research in this area with a certain systematization of the empirical material. (The author has participated in the alter-globalist movement directly since its very inception, and thus does not distinguish between himself and the movement's other participants. He does not investigate the movement as an observer on the sidelines, but studies it from within, as an active protagonist. This allows him to see a great deal that is not accessible to outside observers, especially the movement's internal problems and contradictions.)

12　　See: Antonio Negri and Michael Hardt, *Empire* (Cambridge: Harvard University Press, 2001).

The alter-globalist movement quickly became popular in many parts of the world. A good deal has been written about it, though a systematic description of the movement is still far from being achieved. It is, nevertheless, already possible to discern a number of phenomena within the movement, and to provide their brief characterizations without venturing descriptions of specific actions and actors.[13] From the ocean of empirical material, I would distinguish the three main spheres of this movement: mass protest actions (from Seattle to Genoa and Barcelona, and to the world-wide days of protest against wars, in Iraq and elsewhere); the constant, day-to-day activity of the organizations that directly associate themselves with the alter-globalist movement—in particular, of the organizations that have endorsed the Social Charter of the World Social Forum (WSF); and social forums—particularly, the twenty meetings of the World Social Forum that have already been held in Porto Alegre, Mumbai, Caracas, and elsewhere, attracting tens of thousands of participants—along with the continental (European, Asian, etc.) and national forums, including the latest Russian Social Forum held in 2019.

The best-known form taken by the anti-globalist movement (though not the most important in terms of its content) has been the form of *protest actions* mounted since 1999 during various kinds of summit meetings held by the agents of globalization (the World Trade Organization, the Davos Forum and others). The empirically verifiable features of these actions, repeated over more than six years in hundreds of the largest protests (literature cited earlier in this article contains descriptions of protest actions in Seattle, Prague, Quebec, Genoa, and elsewhere) include the following:

- massive dimensions (from 50,000 to more than 10 million participants);
- international character (in every case, dozens of countries were represented, with delegations of as many as 10,000 people); a number of actions

---

13   There now exists a fairly broad Russian literature on alter-globalization. Since 2000, the largest selection of Russian-language articles on this topic appeared in the journal *Alternativy*, ranging from the notes by the participants in world, European, and other social forums and protest actions to theoretical reflections by venerable scholars. Other notable coverage of the topic has appeared in *Mezhdunarodnye protsessy* (*International Processes*), *MEiMO* (*World Economy and International Relations*), *Polis, Politicheskiy zhurnal* (*Political Journal*), and *Svobodnaya mysl* (*Free Thought*). The earliest monographs on the subject include: Aleksandr Buzgalin, ed., Альтерглобализм. Теория и практика "антиглобалистического" движения [*Alter-Globalism: The Theory and Practice of the "Anti-globalist" Movement*] (Moscow: URSS, 2003); Christophe Agiton, Альтернативный глобализм. Новые мировые движения протеста [*Alternative Globalism: New World Protest Movements*] (Moscow: Gileya, 2005); and Alex Callinicos, Антипрактический манифест [*An Anti-Capitalist Manifesto*] (Moscow: Praxis, 2005).

were world-wide in scope (sometimes, held on a single day), unfolding across a large number of countries;
- multi-class structure of the participants (from unemployed people and farmers to professionals and members of the petty bourgeoisie); diversity of age groups represented (though with relative dominance of younger people); roughly proportionate representation of men and women;
- principled aims of the initiators, and at the same time, a spontaneous pluralism of ideologies, and of the forms and methods that marked the actions;
- a combination of methods of dialogue with those of civil disobedience, together with engagement with the authorities (during the actions the participants would, as a rule, divide themselves into columns on the basis of whether or not they were prepared to engage in direct clashes with the police, whether they embraced radical left or moderate slogans, and so forth);
- polycentrism and network principles of organization of actions; lack of a single political or other institutional structure to carry out organizational tasks; mobile and temporary nature of the networks coordinating the actions.

Now let us briefly review the organizations taking part in the alter-globalist movement, and their reasons for doing so. Naturally, we are not concerned with drawing up a list of these organizations (at the 2005 World Social Forum alone there were more than 5,000 taking part), but with their primary systematization. The best-known traditional structures include, in the first place, diverse social unions and non-governmental organizations:
- labor unions, including those remote from supporting socialist ideas; in the Seattle protest, for example, there were organizations affiliated with the American Federation of Labor and Congress of Industrial Organizations (AFL–CIO);
- environmental, women's, youth and children's organizations;
- humanitarian and non-government organizations providing aid to developing countries, including those engaged in struggles against poverty, hunger, disease, etc.;
- scientific, educational, and similar organizations; organizations addressing health problems, and many others.

Second, and alongside these bodies, the alter-globalist movement is also supported by a very broad spectrum of traditional left political organizations. Among the most active are a number of communist parties (hence, the Italian Communist Refoundation Party was one of the main organizers of the huge demonstrations in Genoa), as well as Trotskyist and anarchist organizations. A number of these are extremely influential within the Latin-American left and in Western Europe (with deputies in the parliaments of Brazil, Argentina, France, and other countries), and they work very actively in various NGOs and social movements, including labor unions, the French ATTAC, and organizations of women and the unemployed. In Europe, a number of radical left groups organized the bloc "For a Europe without Capitalism, Wars, and Discrimination."

Third, the so-called "new social movements" and alter-globalist organizations in the precise sense are being actively formed in countries around the world. These groups are very diverse in their social makeup, goals, structures, and principles of organization. Here are just two examples. In Brazil, the movement of landless peasants, now with more than two million participants, arose as a grass-roots initiative of the most deprived sector of the peasantry—those who were without either work or land, yet resolved to use joint action to occupy lands that had languished uncultivated for decades. Members of this movement created a network of cooperatives and farmers' collectives with structures of mutual aid and cooperation, social welfare, education, health care, local self-government, and so forth. The French organization ATTAC was initiated by a group of intellectuals from the eminently respectable newspaper *Le Monde Diplomatique*, initially proposing no more than to publicize the idea of introducing a Tobin tax (a tax of 0.1% on funds used in financial speculation). Although this structure has on the whole remained quite moderate, it quickly transformed into one of the world's largest "anti-globalist" networks, with more than 40,000 activists in France, and with organizations sharing its objectives and name in almost all of the countries of Europe, Asia, and Latin America.

Without citing further examples, I would note that *the alter-globalist movement has itself become a so-called new social movement*. It is only in recent times that the phenomenon of such movements has become a topic of study, but the first materials providing a general account of its main traits and comparing it with traditional social organizations have now begun to appear.

Social forums have been among the most interesting objects of study in the area of the alter-globalist movement. Their organizational model presupposes that any social movement or organization that supports the World Social Forum Charter, apart from political parties and organizations, can initiate activities such as conferences and seminars.

It is important that the forums should become a field in which the essentially new social movements (especially the "anti-globalist" movement) would be able to make their existence known. The emergence and rapid growth of such movements, and their practical collaboration with the "old" social movements (above all, labor unions) and left parties is an extremely interesting phenomenon of the new epoch. Moreover, the forums themselves are becoming such a new phenomenon in terms of their principles and organizational methods. They are organized on the basis of numerous initiatives from below, on network principles, and rely on mobilization and joint work. They are pluralist (in terms of the spectrum of "old" ideologies), but at the same time essentially united. Theoretically and in practice, they aim at powerful mobilization actions with huge effects.

3 Technological, Economic, and Social Preconditions for Alter-Globalism

Among the familiar and often-mentioned paradoxes of the alter-globalist movement is the fact that it arose due to one of the best-known phenomena of globalization—the internet. This is a genuine paradox that points to a real contradiction: the very information technologies that had been called into life by the progress of the forces of production around the turn of the century have become one of the most important and practically effective bases for the struggle against neoliberal globalization and the ideology of globalism. Why, and how, did this happen?

The chief reason has been that, at one pole, there was an objective process of the internationalization of technology and culture, while at the other, we could witness global capital as a particular, finished, and historically concrete form of this process. This division goes back to the classical heritage of Karl Marx. (What I have in mind is the well-known opposition and unity of the productive forces and productive relations, one of its most interesting examples being the dialectic of the formal and real subordination of labor to capital, as outlined in Chapters 10–12 of the first volume of *Capital*.) Later, I will address this aspect specifically. For the present, I would stress that it is by no means accidental that alter-globalism should arise, in many respects, as a product of the internet. This is easily to demonstrate empirically. The Zapatistas in Mexico, the landless peasants in Brazil, and the intellectuals from *Le Monde Diplomatique* behind ATTAC all work and are able to act thanks to the internet;[14] the World Social Forums were organized mainly through the internet, and the major actions of the alter-globalists owe their success largely to the internet and to mobile telephones.

---

14   See: Nick Henck, ed., *The Zapatistas' Dignified Rage: Final Public Speeches of Subcommander Marcos* (Baltimore: AK Press, 2018).

The point here is not so much that computers, the internet, and mobile phones are convenient for organizing mass actions. The connection is far more profound. The key fundamental traits of information-network technologies, about which Manuel Castells, Taichi Sakaiya, and others have written at length, are such that make both possible and necessary (and, indeed, optimal) precisely those forms and principles of social organization that are practically embodied by the new social movements—above all, by alter-globalism.[15]

The Marxist socio-philosophical interpretation of the main features of the "network society" is well known, and was analyzed by the present author and his colleagues many years ago.[16] This enables me to make use of the results of this research and to suggest a number of conclusions.

First, the very phenomenon of knowledge indicates the emergence of a resource that is *limitless* in terms of its contents. If we abstract ourselves for a time from market forms and private property as they apply to knowledge (and alter-globalism poses this "abstraction" as a practical demand), then knowledge turns out to be the kind of "product" that enlarges when it is "consumed." In fact, the de-objectification of knowledge and of the phenomena of culture will lead to the growth of this knowledge and to the progress of culture. By "consuming" knowledge, scholars and scientists increase it; by "consuming" the knowledge "produced" by Newton, Einstein did not negate the achievement of his predecessor, but "sublated" it, increasing the sum of knowledge. The same occurs with the use of mathematics and even language—as it happens in art and education.

Second, a network—unlike a hierarchy—is, in terms of its content, *a flexible, mobile, open, and generally accessible formation* (like the sea or an expanse of the atmosphere, it is open to all, so long as it is not controlled by military forces or by pirates). The market, commerce, and private property are all social forms just as incompatible with network technologies and the world of knowledge as serfdom and monarchic forms of class rule were incompatible with industry (the rationale for this conclusion was provided earlier).[17]

---

15 See: Aleksandr Buzgalin, "'Постиндустриальное общество'—тупиковая ветвь социального развития?" ["'Postindustrial Society'—A Dead End of Social Development?"], *Voprosy filosofii*, 2002, No. 5, 26–43.

16 See: Aleksandr Buzgalin and Andrei Kolganov, eds., Критический марксизм. Продолжение дискуссий [*Critical Marxism: Ongoing Discussions*] (Moscow: URSS, 2002), 18–74; Aleksandr Buzgalin, "Общедоступные сети знаний (культурных благ)" ["Accessible Networks of Knowledge and Cultural Goods"], *Alternativy*, 2002, No. 1, 2–14.

17 See: Andrei Kolganov, "Критика частной собственности на знания" ["A Critique of Private Intellectual Property"], *Alternativy*, 2002, No. 1, 14–30.

Third, knowledge and network organization are democratic by nature; this world is essential to us all, and has a place for each and every one of us. At the same time, this world is essential and useful to all of us *in different ways*; it is a world of *general accessibility of unique and individualized "products"* (every item of knowledge is unique, and every work of art is individual). As noted earlier, unemployed people and professionals, peasants and intellectuals can enter this world and do so in practice; meanwhile, everyone is included in it differently, though often they engage in solving common problems. Here, I will provide just one example: at the plenary session of the World Social Forum on the problems of free access to knowledge, participants in the dialog included American computer specialists, campaigning for a system of free software, and peasants from Latin America, fighting against the high monopoly prices charged for high-quality seed and livestock breeds. The costs that the peasants were obliged to pay were largely attributable to "intellectual rents" (the peasants and others stressed that those who received these rents were not the intellectuals involved, but the corporations that had purchased their intellects).

Fourth, the new principles now underlying the organization of activity and communications are spreading to the social sphere, even in places where the new technologies are not yet present. Socially and economically, therefore, the landless Latin-American peasants aspire to construct their productive activity, based on traditional industrial-agrarian technologies, precisely in the form of networks.

In summing up, we might suggest that, of its very nature, the "knowledge society" (or "network society") presumes—abstracting from the market and private property—the realization of such new principles of social organization as:

– The unlimited and at the same time, unique nature of resources;
– The general accessibility, openness and flexibility of networks and their social forms;
– The democratic and inter-structural nature of the organizations, whether the structures involved are professional, regional, or social.

These principles are in fundamental contradiction with those of the modern socio-economic and political-ideological system, which the present author has described, following the traditions of Marx, Lenin, and Gramsci, as the global hegemony of corporate capital. The rise of the alter-globalist movement, however, occurred on an altogether different basis. Paradoxically, the global hegemony of capital acted as a powerful negative premise for alter-globalism.

Let us examine this aspect in more detail. As was noted at the beginning of this text, *the world has encountered not just globalization, but the global hegemony of corporate capital*.[18] This is real hegemony—the total, comprehensive might of capital as a unified economic, social, political, and spiritual force; it is the power of capital, personified above all by a narrow circle of global players, intertwined with the establishments of proto-empires, and representing the power of capital encompassing the entire globe.

This system of world-wide hegemony in the economy (the new quality of the market, of money, and of capital), in politics, and in ideology has also necessitated, as a result of its internal contradictions, the unfolding of a definite totality of *forms and methods of resistance to the global power of corporate capital*, and the emergence of *counter-globalist and counter-hegemonic trends*. The total, all-encompassing power of capital in modern society is creating a negative premise (the basis of negation, of dialectical opposition) for a *sublation, just as complex and many-sided, of this power*.

Simplifying this theoretical model, we are able to say: the all-encompassing power of the global market and capital, penetrating every pore of human life and subjugating us as workers and consumers, as citizens and individuals, cannot fail to call to life an alternative that is just as all-encompassing, and just as massive and resolute. To return once more to theory, this is an alternative to the *global power of capital*, whose negation and sublation it represents. Here, once again, we see the workings of dialectical logic. *In theoretical terms* (for what is involved is solely a theoretical hypothesis that needs yet to be tested by practice), this logic is

- all-round, all-inclusive, but *anti*-total, in being based not on totalitarian unification characteristic of global capital, but on the uniqueness, singularity, and independence of its agents;
- *anti*-hegemonic, sublating the power of capital and the suppression (economic, political, and spiritual) of human beings through its non-alienated forms of equitable dialog);
- *alter*-global, and if you will, post-global—that is, developing the process of internationalization by transcending its present-day corporate-capitalist limitations;
- post-corporate—that is, developing the achievements of corporate structures by transcending their bureaucratic and hierarchical limitations through the development of open associations.

---

18   See: Buzgalin and Kolganov, *Critical Marxism*, 74–127; Vladimir Horos, ed., *Постиндустриальный мир и Россия* [*The Post-Industrial World and Russia*] (Moscow: URSS, 2001), 136–57.

This is a theoretical hypothesis, constructed on the basis of applying the dialectical method to the study of the process through which the global power of corporate capital is being sublated.

4 The Principles and Contradictions of the Alter-Globalist Movement

Before suggesting a number of generalizations to the reader, I would note that *the alter-globalist movement in all its manifestations is intertwined both with traditional forms of opposition, and also with the dominant forces of alienation.* Later, the author will seek to distinguish the genuinely individual features of this new social reality, abstracting from the earlier-mentioned "admixtures" with which it has become combined, and which at times suppress, or at least deform, its new and distinctive quality. At the same time, we shall follow the logic of comparative analysis of the objective preconditions for the rise of the movement and the emergence of its empirically observable traits.

As noted earlier, the alter-globalist movement arose in a legitimate and predictable fashion, during the epoch of the development of network principles of organization. It represented, *in the first instance*, a model of *networked social organization*, even where technological processes in the proper sense (primarily, industrial processes) remained unaffected. In alter-globalism, the *social form* in many cases *"ran ahead,"* coming to pose a still oppositional and extra-systemic, but nevertheless real social challenge to the development of both economic and technological structures. Among *the main features of network organization as one of the principles of alter-globalism*, we may distinguish the following:

- a non-hierarchical character and decentralization, primarily involving horizontal or functional cooperation between the participants;
- flexibility, mobility, and mutability of its forms and configurations; ease and rapidity in the creation and dismantling of its structures;
- openness in terms of entry into and exit from the network; the general availability of the resources (above all informational) of the network;
- the equal rights of all participants in the network regardless of their role, size, or resources; the anti-market, not just anti-commercial, character of their activity;
- the secondary nature of forms and structures compared to the content of activity;
- the uniqueness of the networks.

All of these traits have been abstracted from reality, where they are found in a "mixture" with the traditional features of a partly bureaucratic, partly commercial, partly closed organization. However, this is a genuine abstraction that occurs constantly in practice. Almost every protest action has been organized on the basis of a special, unique network, open to any participant who decides to contribute his or her resources (but with the support of the "stronger" or "wealthier" participants). Every participant has been able to make free use of all the shared resources of the network, of its "brand," and to collaborate with and engage in dialog with any other participant. The configuration of these networks changes constantly, and after an action the relevant network ceases to exist as such, giving rise to new formations. Each of the actions has its organizing committee, but in every case it is open to all, and has neither a president nor a "general secretary."

Second, it is evident that alter-globalism arose as an alternative to capitalist globalization. *As a positive, dialectical negation* of the global hegemony of capital, of the all-encompassing system of subjugation of the individual, the alter-globalist movement has in practice taken on the following features that serve as *principles*, observed in practice despite being unwritten:
– the *internationalism* of the movement;
– its *inter-class* and *inter-ideological* nature;
– its *anti-hegemonic* (and in the most developed forms, anti-capitalist) character; it is no accident that the slogans of the movement include: *The world is not a commodity!*

Third, of its fundamental nature (which is also the content of its *practical actions*), the alter-globalist movement is *constructed as an alternative to alienation* in all its diverse forms and types (the World Social Forum expressed this philosophical theme with a simpler and clearer formula: "Another world is possible"). In this connection, the following firmly enacted and empirically observable principles of the alter-globalist movement should come as no surprise:
– *Solidarity, collaboration, and accountability* as alternatives to alienation (hence the near-constant stress on the "economy of solidarity," "socially responsible organizations," "democracy of participation," and other forms of cooperation in the economy, politics, and social life);
– The organization of the movement on principles extremely similar to the long-familiar theoretical model of alter-alienation—that is, to a *free, voluntary working association*;[19] the movement's practice has shown that it is constructed (if we abstract it from the "admixtures" of the world of alienation) on the basis of openness to all and of an exclusively voluntary and

---

19   Buzgalin and Kolganov, *Critical Marxism*, 159–164.

informal union (the movement does not have a staff or a program, only a few "framework" parameters, set out in the World Social Forum Charter). The basis for membership does not involve finances (dues) or authority (formal adherence to a structure with defined powers, such as a state or a party), but consists of practical participation in activity (the principle of a working association in theory, and the principles of mobilization and participation in practice);

– *Self-organization* and *self-government* as the mechanisms of the movement's vital activity, appearing in the forms of *network democracy, consensus democracy, democracy of participation*, and so forth. Combined with the principle of working association, these mechanisms ensure that everyone has the opportunity for practical participation in decision-making. If you disagree fundamentally with the position taken by an association of which you are part, you simply leave that association, and participate in the work of another where your voice will be heard, and where dialog or desperate argument will lead to agreement. Or, you form your own, new network; the structure that becomes the largest and most active will be the one that is most open, most accepting of dialog, and best suited to the interests of citizens.

In sum, we can draw the conclusion that *the* differentia specifica *of the alter-globalist movement lies in the birth of a qualitatively new, massive, international, and relatively stable (as far as we can currently judge) social phenomenon, extending beyond the bounds of the main vital principles not just of late capitalism and of capitalist globalization, but also of the entire world of alienation.*

I repeat: in practice, the movement is coming to pose an alternative not only to the essence of globalization and capitalism, but also to the "realm of necessity" as a whole. At the same time, the movement lives and develops within the context of the existing world, inheriting many of its features, and is heir to the preceding forces of opposition to capital. It is therefore characterized by profound contradictions, and possesses both internal dialectical contradictions that are fundamental to its essence, and also external contradictions that demonstrate its "otherness" in the contemporary world. These latter are the most obvious, and hence it is with them that we shall begin our investigation.

The counterposition of the world of alienation and the alter-globalist movement cannot fail to be reflected in the latter's very nature. *From the moment of its inception, the alter-globalist movement has been developing in transitional forms* that combine its own new qualities with the qualities of modern global capitalism; without this, the existence of the alter-globalists within today's system would be impossible. Moreover, this coexistence is itself *contradicto in ajecto*, since it is at the same time a real *contradiction between the alter-*

globalist nature of the movement and its inclusion in global capitalism. As such, the movement must necessarily be characterized by the contradictions that flow directly from the latter, and in particular, *between the principles of voluntarily working association, immanent to the movement, on the one hand, and on the other, the need to make use of financial, legal, and political mechanisms and professional activity in our own work.*

The *internal contradictions of alter-globalism* are the very essence of this movement. Here, too, all the above-mentioned principles of the movement are no more than manifestations of its profound contradictions. The author is not ready to put forward a systematic and detailed account of this methodological construct, but it may be stated that among the deep contradictions with a good many empirically observable effects is *the contradictory nature of associated social creativity as the "innate essence" of alter-globalism.*

Above all, there is the *contradiction between social creativity as a dialog between unique individual subjects* (personalities, communities) *and the unified process of jointly agreed activity.* Further, the basis for the joint activity here is not the sameness of the subjects but their uniqueness (while united around a strategy). For alter-globalism this contradiction is more than obvious, and it appears in every aspect of this movement, in its every practical step, where and whenever the constant need appears not simply to agree, but to join together unique combinations of organizations, movements and individuals in a unified process of actions (each time, individual in nature).

5   P. S. The Positive Program of Alter-Globalism

Alternatives to the global power of capital are objectively taking shape; we are obliged to study them, and having studied them, to intensify the positive processes of liberation, while abstaining from crossing the line, beyond which the subjective factor of progress degenerates into subjectivism, leading to regression. To the number of these readily available and well-known alternatives, we should add processes of two kinds.

First, there are attempts at isolationism or "withdrawal" from globalization. Second, there is the creation of new forms of internationalization that represent a practical and theoretical antithesis to globalism. It is this second path to resolving problems that is urged by the alter-globalists, proceeding not from good wishes and moral imperatives (though the latter are certainly not alien to us), but from an analysis of the objectively possible ways of escaping from the dead-ends of the proto-empire. In this case, the escape routes are limited by a sort of *minimum program*, and by the requirements of socializing and democratizing this system. (These requirements, in turn, can and should serve as the prologue for a maximum program.)

In the first place, the alternatives being urged propose that such public goods as natural resources, social infrastructure, cultural goods, knowledge, and the means of acquiring it be removed from private control and handed over to public management. At a minimum, this may be done through the development of international environmental, social, and humanitarian norms, and at a maximum, given the presence of an authentically democratic state, through *nationalization*. The prospect, however, is that the movement will advance the call for the *world-wide socialization* of nature and culture, so that they belong to all on an equal basis. I should note that it is quite possible to implement these measures even while retaining the market-capitalist system. It is simply that knowledge and information will become available free of charge (just as the theorem of Pythagoras or the novels of Tolstoy are available today), while the corporations that extract oil or mineral ores will pay rent not to a private owner, and not to a national state, but to international public structures that finance the development of science, high technology, education, and the arts, as well as helping to solve the problems of the environment and to end poverty.

The question of how to deal with intellectual private property deserves a special comment.[20] The rise of post-industrial technologies means that proposing and realizing new principles for organizing the information space and developing the world of culture has become an especially important field for resisting globalization. The tasks (1) of the free, generally available dissemination of cultural goods (assuming compensation only for expenses, which are extremely small, while the number of users is large), based on the rejection of intellectual private property; (2) of developing the means for the use of these goods (free, generally accessible information networks plus computerization available to all); and (3) of providing free, universally available education, with public support for students from poor families, are becoming crucial for the struggle against the global hegemony of capital in the information era. General access to knowledge and education is becoming the basis for the democratic

---

20   Aleksandr Buzgalin, "Креативная экономика: Почему и как может быть ограничена частная интеллектуальная собственность" ["Creative Economy: Why Private Intellectual Property Should Be Restricted, and How This Can Be Achieved"], *Sotsiologicheskie issledovaniya*, 2017, No. 8, 20–30; Aleksandr Buzgalin, "Креативная экономика: Частная интеллектуальная собственность или собственность каждого на все?" ["Creative Economy: Private Intellectual Property or the Ownership by Each of Everything?"], *Sotsiologicheskiye issledovaniya*, 2017, No. 7, 43–53.

integration of peoples, founded on the progress of the creative sphere. These are just a few of the elements involved in realizing the familiar alter-globalist slogan: *The world is not a commodity!*

Second, and summarizing the various social, environmental, and humanitarian initiatives by participants in this movement, we are able to advance the slogan of creating a sort of *world social economy*, in which the countries admitted to "civilized" integration will not be those that abide by the "Washington consensus," but only those in which

- a socially guaranteed minimum is assured;
- a progressive income tax and a tax on inheritance have been introduced;
- universally available health care and education are guaranteed (even a small limit placed on financial speculation, militarism, and overconsumption by billionaires would suffice to secure funds for these programs);
- labor unions and social organizations are given broad rights to monitor the activities of business;
- democratic structures and the institutions of civil society will possess more power than global players.

This list is now generally familiar, and is being partly realized within the frameworks of particular communities (for example, in the Scandinavian countries). This, too, will not represent resistance to globalization, merely a broader degree of social inclusion, though this time according to different rules—minimally, the rules of international "Swedish capitalism."

On this basis, it will become possible to carry out the task of *evening out the developmental levels among countries on the periphery and at the center*, not through degrading the quality of life in the "core" countries, but through altering the global system of economic relations, redistributing the parasitic spending of the center in order to solve the problems of accelerated modernization (the priority development of the post-industrial sector, education, and so forth), and of overcoming poverty in the countries of the periphery. Most important, however, will be something else—the formation of new social relations, ensuring the orientation of the world economy toward the goals of securing social priorities on a uniform basis, and of doing away with militarism, financial speculation, and so forth. To the proposals, listed above, of the minimum program we would add, in this case, such long-familiar demands as forgiveness of the poorest countries' debts, the introduction of unified international environmental, social, and humanitarian standards, and other measures.

The framework of the alter-globalist minimum program can also accommodate activity aimed at liberating *certain "oases" of economic, social, and cultural life* from the power of corporate capital, and aimed also at applying the tactics of "globalization from below." These "oases," in being integrated from below, could become networks of cooperatives together with organs of local self-government, environmental unions, and so forth, all oriented towards the practical realization of a certain limited range of "rights" corresponding to a new model of integration oriented in a humanitarian, environmental, and social manner. If the new organs establish their own system of international institutions (the basis for this exists: there are international alliances of cooperatives and similar structures), analogous in their role to the "unholy trinity" and oriented precisely towards supranational regulation, these "Lilliputians" (cooperatives and so forth) may come to pose a serious challenge to the global players, despite not yet being able to act as their competitors. In this way, another crucially important slogan of the alter-globalist movement—*Another world is possible!*—may begin to be realized.

The question of who will carry out these tasks is already beginning to be answered. First and foremost, this agency will belong to *the growing forces of international alter-globalism*. Indeed, it will be the *international civil society and the new social movements* that will act as the subject of the new integration from below. And there are a good many other potential participants in this activity.

In conclusion, I shall stress once again: what has been set forward here is no more than a minimum program, whose realization will merely help to reform the present system, and to ensure that it undergoes a significant—though not qualitative—shift in the direction of greater socialization, humanization, and ecologization. But even to win this "peaceful reform," a long and serious fight will be needed.

The Concept of "Political Globalization" and Global Challenges

Olga G. Leonova

1 The Concept of "Political Globalization" in Contemporary Russian Scholarship

Globalization is an objective phenomenon with a multifaceted nature. There are economic, political, sociocultural, ecological, informational, and international-legal aspects of globalization.[1] Globalization is the enforcement of conjugacy and the interdependence of countries in the global world, in which the economic component prevails. Yet the political aspect of globalization also holds power and has begun to influence the development and dynamics of the global economy. Recently, many economic tendencies of modern globalization have become the consequences of political interactions between leaders in the global world and the political decisions that they make.

In their research, Russian scholars have paid special attention to the *political* aspects of globalization. *Political globalization* is viewed as a global dynamic nonlinear process of the enforcement and complication of the interdependence of all the elements in the global political system. These studies of political globalization are closely connected to promising scholarly trends of a broad multi-interdisciplinary character, including synergetics and evolutionism. In addition, they also include the institutional, world-systemic, and system-evolutionary approaches to studying political globalization.[2]

The study of the political aspect of globalization depends on modern complex methods and instruments of systemic analysis of the modern geopolitical situation, which allows for the description of the following: the existent transformation of the international system; the parameters of foreign government

---

1 Ino Rossi, ed., *Challenges of Globalization and Prospects for an Inter-Civilizational World Order* (New York: Springer, 2020).
2 See: Vladimir Pantin and Vladimir Lapkin, Историческое прогнозирование в XXI веке: Циклы Кондратьева, эволюционные циклы и перспективы мирового развития [*Historical Forecasting in the Twenty-First Century: Kondratiev Cycles, Evolutionary Cycles, and the Perspectives of World Development*] (Dubna: Feniks+, 2015); Ilya Ilyin, Arkady Ursul, and Tatiana Ursul, Глобальный эволюционизм: Идеи, проблемы, гипотезы [*Global Evolutionism: Ideas, Problems, Hypotheses*] (Moscow: Moscow State University Press, 2012).

actions in the unstable context of the transforming global world; the interdependencies of foreign government policies; global processes and tendencies; and crucial factors that define the development of the world global community. In monographs, textbooks, and articles, we find the study of the *political* aspect of globalization, including studies of the new contours of the geopolitical space of our planet, analyses of the global world system and its formation, and the exposure of its new geopolitical configuration, structure, architecture, and hierarchy.[3]

The political trend in globalization studies is already an independent trend in modern Russian globalistics. Global political processes and global political problems are the key categories of *political globalistics*—a distinct scholarly discipline being formed in Russia. Political globalistics is an interdisciplinary trend of global studies, a subsection within the more general discipline of globalistics, which looks at global political processes and problems of their mutual influence and interaction, at tendencies of global political development, and at the mechanisms of the formation and evolution of the global political system. The object of research in political globalistics is global political development (i.e., the combination of interconnected and coevolving global political processes and systems). At the end of the twentieth century, many international political processes indeed acquired a global scale. As global processes, they revealed themselves as the universal interdependence of political processes, and the global (planetary) scale of their character and consequences became evident.

Global political processes are those processes that develop in the context of the political aspect of globalization, according to which we can witness the structural transformation of the world system of international relations and the emergence of new global political actors. In addition, here we see the increase of political interconnection and interdependence, as well as the formation of a global political architecture and hierarchy. Within the development of global political processes, we find certain effects connected to their transformation and non-linearity, as well as partial dysfunctions and bifurcations of the political system of the global world. Presently, we can

---

3 See: Ilya Ilyin and Olga Leonova, Политическая глобалистика [*Political Globalistics*] (Moscow: Urait, 2017); Ilya Ilyin, Olga Leonova, and A. S. Rozanov, Теория и практика политической глобалистики [*Theory and Practice of Political Globalistics*] (Moscow: Moscow State University Press, 2013); Alexander Chumakov, Глобализация: Контуры целостного мира [*Globalization: The Contours of an Integral World*], third ed. (Moscow: Prospect, 2017); Leonid Grinin, "The Process of Systematic Integration in the World System," *Journal of Globalization Studies*, 2017 (1), No. 8, 97–118.

identify a clash between the old tendencies of political development from the twentieth-century global world and the new tendencies of the polycentric world. The clash between the old and the new, as well as the transformation of the world political system in its new quality—this is where the global system engenders the new content of globalization political processes.

The modern world is global in its economic, informational, and ecological aspects, but it remains fragmentary in its political and sociocultural relations. Almost two hundred sovereign states interact with one another, together with contradictions in their interests and aims, and they enter into conflicts or, on the contrary, form coalitions and alliances. The whole spectrum of these contradictory relations, from violent resistance to convergence, leads to the acceleration of the dynamics of global political processes. New characteristics in geopolitical space in the twenty-first century has led to the development of new global political processes, resulting in a transition from bipolarity to multi-polarity, and from mono-centrism to polycentrism. These characteristics include the increase in the dynamics of world political processes; reconfiguration, fragmentation, hierarchization, and further change in the global world's architecture; formation of new geopolitical axes; and collusion, competition, and rivalry among the emerging power centers.

In the second decade of the twenty-first century, we began to see, quite unexpectedly, some negative consequences of globalization. Some unforeseen trends arose.[4] It turned out that the interaction and interdependence of countries and regions on the global stage led to the strengthening of asymmetries between them, and thus resulted in deeper disparities in the economic and political development of the governments, especially between the developed West and the global periphery. Instead of the global prosperity that might have been expected, the world has unexpectedly stumbled upon the problem of a new disparity, whose locomotive is globalization, and within which various entities must attempt to find their place in the global process.

Disappointment in this kind of globalization and its unplanned results is evident in the growth of populism and nationalism, and in the new protectionist policies of nearly all the participants of global cooperation.[5] One more unexpected and undesirable consequence of twenty-first-century globalization was the erosion of democracy and its more important principles in many

---

4 See: Jonathan Michie, *Advanced Introduction to Globalisation* (Cheltenham, Northampton: Edward Elgar, 2017).
5 See: Stephen D. King, *Grave New World: The End of Globalization, the Return of History* (New Haven: Yale University Press, 2017); Finbarr Livesey, *From Global to Local: The Making of Things and the End of Globalization* (New York: Pantheon, 2017).

countries with traditionally liberal political systems. This included the part of the population that pins its hopes on improving the situation by means of strict economic measures, and on its nostalgia for strong leaders. Perhaps this is the result of the interesting stage in which the world community currently finds itself: the transformation of the *world* political system into a qualitatively new *global* political system. This, nevertheless, remains a hypothesis, as the phenomenon has not yet been analyzed properly, though it requires a thorough examination.

It is indubitable that in the modern global world, new tendencies are arising, and they allow us to speak of ongoing transformation and of the emergence of a new global phenomenon—the *global political system*. We can enumerate the following *new tendencies and trends of globalization development*:

- The formation of a new structure and architecture of the global world;[6] the formation of new actors and a global political system (poles, power centers, candidates for power centers, global and regional powers), and their alignment into a hierarchical pyramid. This new global structure is quite mobile, and the relations of its hierarchical elements are dynamic, which makes this model quite unstable and unpredictable in its further development.
- Two models of the modernization of global countries begin to be delineated: a western (or Atlantic) liberal model, where the United States and the European Union act as role models, and a Continental model, where China and countries that try to copy its economic strategy are the most vivid examples. Both models have their strong and weak points;[7] they are powerful competitors with a clear civilizational character. That is why the global world of the future can hardly turn out to be an idyllic "global village," nor will it be "a clash of civilizations." It is evident that the future will be a global system, marked by competition between the two models of modernization and development.[8] We are going to see not only competition between models of economic development, but, to a certain extent, between the political systems of the countries under discussion; in fact, this competition will take place between democratic and authoritarian regimes vying to prove their advantages and superior effectiveness, especially under conditions of global

---

6 Vladimir Pantin and Vladimir Lapkin, "Трансформации политических пространств в условиях перехода к полицентрическому миропорядку" ["Transformations of Political Space in the Situation of the Transition to a Polycentric World"] *Polis*, 2018, No. 6, 47–66.
7 Amitav Acharya, *The End of American World Order* (Cambridge: Polity, 2014).
8 Richard J. Heydarian, *The Indo-Pacific: Trump, China, and the New Struggle for Global Mastery* (Singapore: Springer, 2020).

vagueness and instability.⁹ The question of who is going to win (taking into account the latter circumstance) is still open for debate.
- No competition guarantees stability.¹⁰ The winner will be the one who is more dynamic and fit to face external and internal challenges—in this case, the challenges of globalization. We forecast that the growth of instability awaits us on the global level, where there will be no established rules for the economic or political "game," nor firm principles or generally accepted behavioral patterns. We will see a constant reformatting of existing coalitions and blocs, a rapid change of top-priority vectors of countries' foreign policy, etc. Amongst all this ambiguity, a subjective factor will emerge—meaning that the global world will turn into a reflection of the personalities of its leading politicians, leaders of global powers, with their ambitions, hidden complexes, and their beliefs as to what the top-priority values should be.
- Many politicians and analysts are currently confused about the ineffectiveness of global management, which is becoming more evident as we see the complication of the international situation and the growth of global threats to humanity.¹¹ Some global problems have gradually transformed into global risks that threaten life on our planet. We have not yet found any solutions or ways out of this complex situation, and the institutions of global management, which are tasked with solving these problems, have proven to be incompetent and unable to respond promptly and adequately in order to address these new globalization challenges. The acceleration of its dynamics and the scale of globalization call for other approaches and other instruments, corresponding to the new qualities of the global political system.
- We should not forget the conflict of globalization and the national interests of the countries involved, which hampers the globalization processes.¹² This conflict is particularly acute among the countries on the periphery

---

9 See: Ivo Daalder and James Lindsay, "The Committee to Save the World Order. America's Allies Must Step Up as America Steps Down," *Foreign Affairs*, September 30, 2018; Stephen Kotkin, "Realist World. The Players Change, but the Game Remains," *Foreign Affairs*, June 14, 2018.

10 See: G. John Ikenberry, *Liberal Leviathan: The Origins, Crises, and Transformation of the American World Order* (Princeton: Princeton University Press, 2011).

11 G. John Ikenberry, "The End of Liberal International Order?" *International Affairs*, 2018 (94), No. 1, 7–23.

12 See: Robert J. Holton, *Globalization and the Nation State* (London: Palgrave Macmillan, 2011); Bello Taiwo, "Nowhere to Hide: Nation States' Security and Stability in the Age of Globalization," *Journal of Globalization Studies*, 2017 (2), No. 8, 27–41.

of global processes, which, having failed to gain the expected benefits of participation in the global economy, have begun to cast themselves as the victims of that process. As a result, we see the growth of protectionist policy and "responsible nationalism," which gain power even in some western countries that once were the locomotive of globalization. Brexit is but one example of this tendency, and certainly not the only such instance.

- The notion of the "global periphery" is also changing its meaning. It no longer refers solely to those countries that lag behind the globalization process or are unable (or unwilling) to enter it. Now, the geographical periphery of the global world is located mainly within those actively developing Asian countries that have, for some years, been leaders in GDP growth and shown their economic effectiveness and political stability. Their contribution to the global economy grows with each year, and with it they gradually gain political power and acquire a higher rank in the global hierarchy.[13] It seems that in the twenty-first century, these countries will gain a powerful voice and will have courage to articulate their interests, thereby compelling the rest of the world to take them into consideration.

These tendencies in the development of the global political system do not mean that anything like *de*-globalization is underway.[14] They are *the symptoms of a transition from one globalization model to another, the malaise of a transitional period that separates a monocentric world from a polycentric one*, in which there will be several power centers and many poles of economic, political, and military power. Thus, polycentrism and multi-polarity do not guarantee the upcoming global world any political, economic, or military stability. In the twenty-first century it will be more difficult than it had been previously to gain stability and to maintain the balance between the waning power centers and the poles of the global world.

To sum up the tendencies of the global political process, we can conclude that there is room for *variability in global development*. Its trajectory can have many possible directions. Such variability is ensured by the great number of different global actors willing to realize their economic and geopolitical interests on the world stage. In the global world, new vectors of development, as well as new dimensions, problems, and bifurcation points, are constantly emerging. The global world is a constantly changing order, including its structure, hierarchy, and algorithms of the actions of global actors, as

---

[13] Rebecca Friedman Lissner and Mira Rapp-Hooper, "The Liberal Order Is More Than a Myth. But It Must Adapt to the New Balance of Power," *Foreign Affairs*, July 31, 2018.

[14] Hoyoon Jung, "The Trans-Disciplinary Globalization Debates over the Last Two Decades: Small Consensus, Big Controversies," *Journal of Globalization Studies*, 2018 (2), No. 9, 27.

well as their interrelations, values, ideals, aims, and perspectives of development.

2 Global Political Challenges

The conceptual basis of a new complex approach to political globalization should be founded in an analysis of global political space, global processes, and global problems. Globalization engenders certain challenges for the humanity, and the solutions to these problems will either stimulate further development, lead to its degradation, or even threaten its very survival.

Globalization challenges is a popular notion, one that is actively employed by scholars, politicians, and journalists—and yet, there is no clear definition for this phenomenon in the scholarly literature, in contrast with the notion of "global problems," which has been analyzed by many prominent scholars. An important contribution to the study of global problems was published by Vadim Zagladin, Ivan Frolov, and Alexander Chumakov in 2015.[15] It took a long time for scholars to accept the distinction between these two notions, since "problems" and "challenges" are often confused and taken to be synonymous. *Global challenges*, nevertheless, is an expression referring to a problem or a task engendered by globalization and demanding an answer or a solution. There are practically no works in globalistics where global political challenges would be isolated and their nature investigated. That is why, in this paper, we shall try to define the notion of "global political challenges," describe their essence and meaning, and classify them.

Global political challenges are the result of an ambiguous process of political globalization development, and occurrence of any potential bifurcation points should be prevented. It is necessary not only to address global challenges, but to formulate solutions to them promptly, thereby forestalling the development of negative phenomena. Yet, the multifactorial nature of globalization makes it difficult for us to find solutions to its challenges, and demands consideration of many characteristics and indicators that cannot always be

---

15   See: Vadim Zagladin and Ivan Frolov, Глобальные проблемы современности: Научный и социальный аспекты [*Contemporary Global Problems: Scientific and Social Aspects*] (Moscow: Mezhdunarodnye otnosheniya, 1981); Alexander Chumakov and Aza Ioseliani, Философские проблемы глобализации [*Philosophical Problems of Globalization*] (Moscow: Universitetskaya kniga, 2015).

easily examined and analyzed. Global political challenges may have a significant impact on the structure and functioning of the world political system in general, and on certain governments in particular.

Global political challenges in the sphere of international relations and world politics have the power to influence the lives of individuals and, if a timely solution is not found, they may even threaten the lives of future generations. Lately, it has become clear that any progress in global development is increasingly dependent on the world political situation. A complex, critical situation within the system of international relations, including the growth of instability, turbulence, and conflict, may hinder global development and cause a regression, and might even initiate the process of de-globalization.

If we were to leave global political *challenges* without an answer, we would risk letting them grow into acute global political *problems*, and those may in turn evolve into global political *risks*. Thus, global political challenges represent the "embryonic" stage of global political problems. There is a complex multilayer interrelation, interdependency among global political challenges, the international political system, and human activity. Although the future of globalization is unpredictable, we can forecast the negative impact of global political challenges if they are ignored, and if the problems that they pose are not solved. Solutions should be formulated immediately, as the global world is developing at a fast pace, engendering new and graver global political challenges along the way. If economic, cultural, and informational globalizations develop dynamically, political globalization stagnates, or even causes a tendency for political fragmentation in the global world.

Any structural changes in the world political system that occur under the influence of globalization can lead to changes in the nature, directions, and aims of global development at large. The majority of these changes are caused by the process of transition from a unipolar world to the multipolar world of today, and to the polycentric world of the future. Today's humanity realizes that it is necessary to manage the complex system of global political processes, which have many controversial tendencies. As globalization develops and transitions to a qualitatively new level (globalization's "new wave"), it becomes more difficult not only to control it, but also to apprehend it and to answer its new challenges. Global political changes and challenges represent a multilayer interactive complex, and require an interdisciplinary approach in their study.

Although it is impossible to forecast the further development of globalization, it is crucial to define what influence these global political challenges have on our common global future. It is necessary to determine the line at which these global political challenges change into global political problems, and where those latter evolve, in turn, into global political risks. An additional difficulty is that this kind of analysis must take into consideration the situation of global political instability, which we have witnessed but recently. That is why modelling global political challenges and forecasting their possible outcomes demand a complex integral approach and different methods of political analysis should be used.

The diversity and divergence of global challenges, as well as their influence on different aspects of human activity (economics, social, and informational sphere, culture, ecology, etc.), make it necessary to use an *interdisciplinary integrative approach* to their analysis. It helps to choose strategic priorities and effective means for addressing these challenges. This approach also allows us to accentuate those *priorities in values, aims, and ideals* that concern the future of the global community. This approach allows for a choice of actions in response to existing global political challenges, with an orientation towards further perspectives on global development. It also allows us to address a range of global political challenges from the point of view of favorable or unfavorable perspectives of their solution.

This methodological approach allows us to establish the interconnection of political, economic, and sociocultural processes, and to isolate global political challenges arising from global development. This approach is aimed at the analysis of not only static phenomena of global political challenges, but also the study of their development and tendencies (or counter-tendencies), thereby allowing us to see a greater diversity of scenarios for the future.

Thus, our methodology is (1) complex and interdisciplinary, (2) value-oriented, and (3) process-oriented. When choosing among the existing global political challenges to analyze, we have proceeded from two criteria: first, the extent of its influence on the present and future of the global community; and second, the objectivity of their nature and the possibility of analysis. Our analysis of global political challenges is based on the following points:

- The sum of global political challenges is a complex system of interconnected causes and effects, where the human factor plays an important role.
- Global political challenges are closely interconnected with the economic trends of globalization development. They are, on the one hand, their consequence and the result of the global economy. On the other hand, when inefficient political decisions are made, they can become the reasons for economic global problems and challenges.
- There are close interconnections, interdependences, and inter-relations among global political, economic, social, cultural, informational, and ecological challenges.

- Whereas globalization is an objective phenomenon, global political challenges are often the result of the activities of political leaders, political establishment in different countries, and global actors in general, which accounts for their subjective or even artificial character.
- The subjective character of global challenges allows us to formulate satisfactory answers to global political problems, as well as ways of solving them. In contrast to global challenges and problems in the ecological sphere, many of which are irreversible, global political problems have the potential to be solved, assuming that there is political goodwill among the global leaders.
- If left unanswered, global political challenges risk transforming into global political problems. Unsolved global political problems turn into global political risks, which threaten to destroy the world political system.

The variety of discourses of "globalization" can sometimes lead to confusion. The notion of "global political challenges" is often employed in the context of negative changes occurring in the environment, under the influence of human activity. Nowadays, "global political challenges" has become an umbrella term that covers not only political, but also a wide range of economic, social, cultural, informational, and ecological problems of global development in their close interconnection and interdependence. "Challenges" thus become synonymous with "problems," which is not quite correct. We use the term "global political challenges" to denote the sum of changes happening in the process of political globalization, impacting all spheres of human activity, and playing an important role in geopolitics. We examine these "challenges" as an embryonic, incipient stage in the development of global political problems.

Here, we shall single out two closely related types of global political challenges. First, these are local challenges, which originate in a particular place, have a clear geographical linkage, and are most acute at the moment of their emergence. They nevertheless have a great impact on the development of global humanity. The denuclearization of the Korean Peninsula, migration processes in Europe, or the political crisis in Latin America are some of the examples to hand. Second, these global challenges concern the destiny of all of humanity, since they are not connected to a particular geographical point. Among these are the challenges of global instability and growing populism and nationalism, evident in both developing and developed countries, under the conditions of growing inequality between the West and the global South, etc.

Global political challenges are temporal. There are enduring challenges, to which humanity has not found an answer, and new global political challenges will appear with time. At the end of the twentieth century, the following challenges emerged, and remain unsolved at present:

- significant armament buildup in countries that convert military production into civilian production—a costly process;
- the threat of nuclear-weapon spread across the countries of the global periphery;
- the aggravation of political struggle between political alliances of resource-rich countries or those of strategic importance;
- the economic gap between developed and developing countries, including the growth of political distance between the global center and the global periphery.

In the twenty-first century, we see new challenges that demand immediate solutions. These include the following:
- the low efficiency of the global management systems and a lack of control over global political processes;
- a lack of consensus among countries with regard to solving international problems, which aggravates the instability and turbulence of global political processes;
- the growth of populism and nationalism in developing and developed countries;
- the weakening of US leadership;
- the formation of conclaves of transnational terrorism;
- waves of uncontrolled migration in Europe and Latin America.

The classification of existing global political challenges is a relevant problem. We believe that it should not be substituted with existing classifications of global problems, because they have different qualities and degrees of manifestation.

In accordance with our suggested hypothesis, global political challenges can be classified in the following way:

1. From the point of view of the subject:
   - challenges resulting from incorrect political decisions and miscalculations;
   - challenges resulting from irresponsible (i.e., deliberate) decisions and actions.
2. From the point of view of causal relations:
   - challenges representing direct or indirect results of other global processes (economic, social, cultural, informational, or ecological).
3. From the point of view of scale:
   - local global political challenges with an influence on the international situation in the world;
   - global political challenges that encompass all political systems and thus have a truly global scale.

4. From the temporal point of view:
   - temporary and situational global political challenges (the growth of populism and nationalism in different countries, irrespective of their level of development, the weakening of US leadership, the erosion of democracy);
   - long-term global political challenges requiring time and the mutual cooperation of the entire world community (inequality between the developed West and the developing Asian and African countries; increasing instability and turbulence of the global world).
5. By the object of impact:
   - global political challenges that influence the economic sphere in the world and local communities;
   - global political challenges that influence the social sphere in the world and local communities;
   - global political challenges that influence the cultural, religious, and ethical spheres in the world and local communities;
   - global political challenges that influence the ecological sphere in the world and local communities (e.g., the United States' refusal to sign the Paris Agreement);
   - global political challenges that influence the informational sphere of activity in the world and local communities (the so-called "smart power").
6. By the character of the effect produced:
   - global political challenges that have a cumulative effect on the world system (instability, turbulence, lack of civil protection, the widening gap between the developed West and the developing South);
   - global political challenges that have a singular effect, influencing a particular system or sphere of activity (the rise of populism and nationalism, the loss of leadership by the United States, the erosion of democracy).

The dynamics of global political challenges depend on a variety of objective and subjective factors. Among the objective factors, we can single out the following: the pace and character of global economic development, the volume of global trade, the intensity of global financial flows and investment, climate change on the planet, the number of natural disasters, etc.

Among the subjective factors, we can include the following: the activities of political leaders, political elites, international organizations, and other global actors (NGOs and MNCs), and the political decisions that they make. These dynamics also depend on the actions of the subjects of political process at the global, local, and individual levels. Such actions, in turn, are determined by a range of factors—economic (e.g., the living standards, quality of life, accessibility of tangible and social goods, need satisfaction, etc.), political (e.g., security), socio-cultural (e.g., the preservation of cultural and ethnic identities), ecological (e.g., environmental preservation), and informational—as well as their influence on both public and individual consciousness.

All of this highlights the interconnection and interdependence of different kinds of global challenges. Our analysis shows that if we do not find appropriate solutions to existing global challenges, the consequences may be disastrous for humanity. Global political challenges will inevitably grow into global political problems, and in future—into global political risks, which may endanger globalization as such. Global political challenges are closely connected with economic, cultural, ecological, and informational processes of globalization, and have a great impact on them. They may have a negative influence on the processes of economic globalization, and may slow down the processes of economic integration, or even lead to a global economic crisis.

Our hypothesis about the character, essences, and consequences of global political challenges is shown to be true when examined from the viewpoint of an interdisciplinary, integrative, value- and process-oriented approach. As for the fate of the global world political system, we believe that three scenarios are possible:

The first scenario. Global political challenges are ignored, the global world is in political stagnation, and all its negative features are preserved: increased instability, stagnation, turbulence, the gap between the global North and South, etc. Given the decay of American leadership, a gap in global management and global responsibility over world affairs appears, with a risk of leading towards chaos. As time goes by, it will become more and more difficult to seek and find adequate solutions to global political challenges.

The second scenario. Political elites are either unable or unwilling to meet global political challenges. As a result, the latter grow gradually into global political problems. If no solution to these problems is found, they will turn into global political risks that threaten the existence of humanity. Ignoring global political challenges may lead to a situation similar to times of turbulence and chaos faced by the previous generations, particularly the looming threat of nuclear war; there will be harsh competition between global powers for global leadership, and these leaders will use any means available to provoke conflicts or achieve leadership; we shall witness the fragmentation of global political space and closed ethnic societies with visions of national exclusiveness, and the transition of previously democratic regimes to authoritarianism, with the establishment of totalitarian regimes on the world periphery, in reaction to mounting global tendencies.

The third scenario. The world community unites to answer these global challenges with dignity, leading to stability in the world political system and possibly the formation of effective and responsible global management by global actors. Yet, this does not guarantee that no new global political challenges will emerge in the future.

Three different answers are thus possible in relation to global political challenges, but their implementation will not be simple, and will require the consensus and coordination of the world community. Nevertheless, delays in accepting the necessary policy measures may decrease their efficiency, allowing existing challenges to develop into political problems that will be more difficult to solve.

All three scenarios carry potential risks and contain elements of uncertainty, yet they offer perspectives on the future of the global world—perspectives apart from economic or sociocultural globalization. Future investigations into global political challenges must focus on the analysis of those problematic fields that engender these challenges, and of situations that blur their causes and effects. Further investigations must also focus on formulating appropriate methods for solving problems and on developing policies for immediate reaction that would prevent the transformation of global challenges into global political problems and risks. Today, we are faced with an acutely posed question: Will we be able to provide future generations with peace, stability, and development in all spheres of life, among which the political sphere will play a special role?

Existing global challenges include a whole range of questions, from climate change to nuclear disarmament, and must be answered in a thoughtful and effective way. This approach, in turn, must be supported by the collective actions of all countries, based on a collective strategy. Today, we see no such collective action. Instead of constructive discussions, what takes place are ineffectual debates, where political labels are pinned, and sanctions imposed, on some countries, restricting the circle of decision-makers. This leads to increased political tension, such that we find ourselves on the verge of open confrontation and a new arms race. All of this undermines the existing rules of globalization and risks propelling the world into a state of uncontrollable chaos.

3 Conclusion

In Russian scholarship, globalization is treated as a nonlinear phenomenon. Globalization is a complex system with many nonlinear relations. Thus, this system is incapable of calculating and foreseeing the outcomes of its own development, which no methodology or foresight can predict effectively. According to experts, the laws of causation do not apply in the typical sense in the context of globalization. It is evident that numerous factors of globalization, which cannot be taken into account in totality, and whose actions cannot be predicted, can produce a range of nonlinear effects, such that phenomena will differ greatly between the moments of "input" and "output."

It is obvious that "globalization-XXI" has a range of specific characteristics and trends. Even today, some of its new features are quite distinct:
- the rise of the multipolar world;
- the growing number and diversity of global actors, at the expense of non-governmental actors;
- a strengthening of interconnections and interdependences between local (regional) and global systems; as a result, local problems, if not satisfactorily solved, can lead to disastrous global consequences;
- a planetary sense of decay, disintegration, disruption, turbulence, and instability.

All these factors result in the formation of a new essence of the phenomenon in question, which might be called a *non-global globalization*. Studies of new tendencies and consequences of globalization have demonstrated that the world has entered a new stage, characterized by serious changes in all the spheres of life.

By analyzing the peculiarities of the modern state of globalization studies, we have concluded that there is no single concept for explaining the structure, functioning, and evolution of global processes and problems, or for forecasting their trajectories. We must, therefore, create a new concept, through the synthesis of philosophical, political, economic, informational, ecological, and other aspects of globalization.

Today, the relevance of a philosophical understanding of globalization is evident, especially where its political aspect is concerned, and as we seek to form a unified apparatus, to make estimates without ideological distortions, and to forecast possible political scenarios for the development of the global world.

PART 3

Nature, Society, and Humans in a Global World

Sustainable Development of Civilization and the Global Environmental Problem

Victor I. Danilov-Danilyan

1   Introduction

Since ancient times, some of the best minds of our civilization have pondered the dangers of uncontrolled development of human societies. What caused their concern were the effects of development as such, not the external factors that often do not depend on human activities and have no solution—apart from prayer, perhaps. Their concerns were not a result of rigorous scientific analysis, though they had often been presented in philosophic treatises, with the use of rich conceptual frameworks and complex terminology. During the Enlightenment period, concerns about human development abated, despite numerous factors that should have intensified them. Nicolas de Condorset's understanding of the progress of human reason was imbued with social optimism.[1] Scientific analysis of possible futures and of the necessary limitations on development began with the publication of Thomas Malthus's *Essay on the Principle of Population*.[2]

By the late 1960s, two primary threats to the future of humankind emerged, created by humans themselves: these were nuclear war and environmental catastrophe. Awareness of the former was based on the experiments that began in 1945. The latter peril became evident as scientists witnessed the effects of trends in development. In 1969, Aurelio Peccei published the book *The Chasm Ahead*, giving a vivid and convincing argument for the need to alter the developmental patterns of modern society. The publication of this book contributed much to the "greening" of the social conscience.[3] *The Limits to Growth* report, presented to the Club of Rome several years later, was

---

1 This study was carried out under a governmental commission to the Institute of Water Problems of the Russian Academy of Sciences, subject no. 0147-2019-0002. Nicolas de Condorset, *Esquisse d'un tableau historique des progrès de l'esprit humain* (Paris: Masson et fils, 1795).
2 Thomas Malthus, *An Essay on the Principle of Population, as It Affects the Future Improvement of Society, with Remarks on the Speculations of Mr. Godwin, M. Condorcet, and Other Writers* (London: J. Johnson, 1798).
3 Aurelio Peccei, *The Chasm Ahead* (New York: Macmillan, 1969).

also globally successful.[4] It supplied a rationale for Peccei's ideas concerning environmental problems. To support Peccei's argument, the report used simple (too simple, in fact) mathematical models and computerized calculations, whose potential had been previously unknown to the enthusiastic public.

In the second half of the twentieth century, perceptions about global ecology changed significantly, even as many pre-conceived expectations were not met. What had initially seemed more or less understandable, measurable, and computable proved to be so complicated that expected results did not materialize, and the very understanding these immeasurable issues was postponed for the indefinite future. In this article, I will describe the complex concepts that emerged in the twentieth century and their public perception from a modern point of view.

2   The Biosphere and Its Anthropogenic Load

It is a fundamental principle of global ecology that humankind cannot exist beyond the biosphere, and that the biosphere can never be replaced by any technogenic environment and remain a human habitat. To avoid confusion ahead, let me offer two definitions. The first defines *the biota* as *the totality of all living organisms*. The second defines *the biosphere* as *the system that comprises the biota and its habitat* (i.e., the totality of material bodies, physical fields, etc., which affect the biosphere and are affected by it).

Since the Neolithic Revolution (the invention of agriculture, specifically crop growing and cattle breeding, occurring between 10,000 BCE and 12,000 BCE), the biosphere has been suffering ever-increasing anthropogenic pressure, which worsened at the start of the Industrial Revolution (the eighteenth century). This increase in anthropogenic pressure is driven by several factors. The first is the continuous growth of the world population. The second is the ideology of consumer society, which dominates developed economies, while all other countries strive to raise the welfare of their own populations to the level of consumer economies. Third, scientific and technical development is still largely uncontrolled. This development is propelled, primarily, by unregulated markets, becoming even more aggressive towards consumers: producers have realized that the greatest profit can be derived not from meeting rational needs, but instead from what can be forced upon the individual

---

4 Dennis Meadows, Donella Meadows, and Jorgen Randers, *The Limits to Growth* (New York: Universe Books, 1972).

consumer. Additionally, development is directed by military stimuli, which are often irrational. Further, development is propelled by the desire to increase labor capacity and to improve conditions, motives common in technological ideology; in most cases, nevertheless, this is done with no regard for the environmental impact of innovation.

What opposes the increasing anthropogenic pressure on the biosphere is not large-scale actions but rather the hope that such actions will become possible in the future. The only plausible hope is the stabilization of the world population, predicted to reach 9.8 billion.[5] The diminished population growth rate in the late twentieth century is largely the result of the unregulated socioeconomic development of the Third World, though efforts to promote and support family planning also had their effect. The fulfillment of all other hopes is fully dependent on changes that have to take place within mass consciousness. Such changes must lead to the abandonment of over-consumption, war as a method of conflict resolution, and the thoughtless use of scientific and technological advances with no analysis of their possible environmental and social effects. Finally, scientific and technological development has to be reoriented towards the one main goal of current human society: the preservation of the biosphere. It is clear that the spectrum of fundamental and applied education includes an environmental component, though only minimally; moreover, applied studies are mostly focused on marketable rather than environmentally important results. The leading figure in the development of technology has always been the inventor; but times have changed. Today, analysis and forecasting of an invention's expected impact should be more important than the invention itself, and the solution to this problem is to utilize the findings of researchers and experts. This makes the interconnections between fundamental science and interdisciplinary studies extremely valuable.

The anthropogenic load on the biosphere is ever-increasing, and we cannot be sure that this process will stop without special, extraordinary efforts (ordinary efforts can hardly produce the required result). On the other hand, is it necessary to try to stop this process? Could it be that the biosphere has the potential to adapt, of which we do yet not know, and which will allow it to adapt to an anthropogenic pressure of even a larger scale than we are now witnessing? Our knowledge of the biosphere is too limited to give an exact and unambiguous answer to this question. Still, there are many convincing arguments indicating that the answer is No. The most important piece of

---

[5] "World Population Projected to Reach 9.8 Billion in 2050, and 11.2 Billion in 2100," Unites Nations, June 21, 2017, https://www.un.org/development/desa/en/news/population/world-population-prospects-2017.html.

evidence is that the biosphere is clearly failing to cope even with its current load. This can be seen from decreasing biodiversity, non-rehabilitating forests and steppe ecosystems on desertified lands, degrading soils (primarily due to chemical pollution and exorbitant mechanical loads during treatment), and growing concentrations of greenhouse gases in the atmosphere.

The biosphere is an integral system, even though many of its properties still remain unclear to us (for example, the interrelationships between its subsystems, or the role of each subsystem in maintaining the dynamic equilibrium of the system, i.e., the ecological equilibrium). Comparisons are not equal to evidence (*comparaison n'est pas raison*), but, in the absence of rigorous proof, they can serve as an argument. Let us compare the biosphere, an organic system of the highest level, with lower-level living systems, such as an ecosystem, a population, an organism, or a cell. It seems obvious that any such system has an admissible level of adverse impact, above which further impact becomes fatal. There are no observable phenomena to indicate that the biosphere should not obey this rule.

The main factor in the adaptation mechanism of the biosphere is species formation. New ecosystems are formed by new species and biomes, as well as surviving species; these new ecosystems form under conditions altered by negative factors. Changes to the ecosystem ensure the survival of the ecosystem and of the biosphere as a whole. It is clear that the adaptation potential of any ecosystem, and of the biosphere at large, is directly dependent upon biodiversity, which is currently decreasing at an unprecedented rate, due to anthropogenic pressure. Adaptation potential depends not only on biodiversity and the species-formation process, but also on the rate of that process. Present-day evolutionary biology has no estimate of the species formation rate, neither on average nor for limiting cases. There is no estimate of that rate for general biota as a whole, nor for any individual taxa of classification of biological species. One existing opinion argues that a new species requires about six million years to form, a time comparable to the average survival span of a species. If this is the case, the biosphere is not likely to cope with anthropogenic pressure at its current level, and it will cope less and less well, should that pressure increase. To arrive at this conclusion, we must compare the supposed rate of species formation with the rate of a similar process in the techno-sphere: the development of innovations.[6] The innovation process is defined as the time between the generation of an engineering idea (e.g., personal computers, laser video recording, phosphorus-free detergents, etc.) and

---

6 Victor Danilov-Danilyan, "Возможна ли 'коэволюция' природы и общества?" ["Is the 'Co-Evolution' of Nature and Society Possible?"], *Voprosy filosofii*, 1998, No. 8, 15–25.

the start of the product's mass production. This time, observed across all types of innovation over a certain period, is steadily decreasing, and, in the early twenty-first century, it is estimated to be only ten years. Zeno of Elea tried to prove that Achilles would never catch up with the tortoise, and it hardly makes sense to insist that the tortoise will never catch up with Achilles. Even if he runs to death.

3 The Carrying Capacity of the Biosphere

We have sound reasons to suppose that there is an objective limit to the admissible anthropogenic impact on the biosphere (it is referred to as the *carrying capacity* or the sustainable eco-capacity of the biosphere). Exceeding this carrying capacity could lead to an irreversible process of degradation and the creation of an environment unfit for human habitation. Science has not yet fully defined this process. It is no wonder that Martin Holdgate would write, back in 1994, that many ecologists had broken their intellectual teeth on the concept of "carrying capacity," which was an attractive idea in itself, but which is very difficult to apply to real situations.[7] The situation has remained practically unchanged since then.

Now let us return to the comparison of the biosphere to lower-level living systems. The higher the structural level of a system, the more difficult it is to find the limit of admissible impact upon it. That being said, the question is far from simple even for the lowest level—that of a cell. In the case of simple (elementary) impacts, such as a single chemical or a single factor of physical nature (radiation, vibration, noise, temperature, etc.), one can use characteristics such as the *maximal permissible concentrations* (MPC), *maximal permissible doses* (MPD), etc. Yet, strictly speaking, such values are deterministic, as these are essentially random values. A deterministic limit is the exact point (and no earlier) at which all cells of interest will die simultaneously. In reality, the picture is much more complex. For example, in the case of heating, cells of the same type will die at different temperatures within an interval [t_i, t_f], where t_i is the temperature at which the first cells will die, and t_f is the minimal temperature at which all of the cells will be dead. In order to properly analyze such characteristics, we must look at the construction of their distribution functions (an operation which is very rare in such studies). The

---

7 Martin W. Holdgate, "Ecology, Development and Global Policy," *Journal of Applied Ecology*, 1994 (31), No. 2, 201–11.

problem becomes even more complicated, when we deal with the joint effect of several factors, such as a combination of several substances (e.g., a toxicant *and* a change in temperature). In the case of a cell, while the number of known simple effects is large, it is possibly comprehensible, but the combined impacts of multiple factors is inconceivable. This, clearly, does not prevent the identification of typical and common joint impacts. The problem is not the identification of the number of possible combined effects, but the fact that each such effect cannot be reduced to the sum of respective elementary impacts. In addition, the sum of the impact is far from clear.

Such elementary considerations suggest that the search for a precise definition of the maximum permissible impact on a cell has no prospects in classical mathematical constructions (the boundary of some domain in the space of impacts, etc.). Even at the lowest level of life, the complexity of both the lifeforms themselves and their interactions with the environment (especially the anthropogenic environment, due to its foreignness) is so high that even the first attempts to apply conventional mathematical language demonstrated its inadequacy. This language allows some rough simplifications of the problem under consideration. It does not allow for the discovery of the maximal permissible impact in general, but rather in particular cases, like the individual elementary impacts or combined impacts on a system.

MPC, MPD, and other methods are developed not just for the cell level but for more complex organisms, like humans or biological species of the greater economic significance (e.g., commercial fish and their prey). They characterize the margin of safety, or the organism's resistance to some types of change (either elementary or combined). However, the MPCs extend to a higher organizational level of living matter—ecosystems—when the former are used as environmental quality standards (for water, air, and soil). Both the evaluation of such environmental quality characteristics and their extension to the next level of system are prone to many methodological flaws and, in some cases, to unjustified arbitrariness due to the lack of established methodologies. At the same time, these characteristics are obviously related to the carrying capacity of an ecosystem. They can be interpreted as one-dimensional projections of the carrying capacity and variables within the system. Their specific values, even if they have legislative approval, are arbitrary, since such values can be far from rational.

The case of chemical pollutants requires the use of a special term: the *assimilation capacity* of an ecosystem. This is defined as the maximal amount of pollutants that can enter an ecosystem per unit time without disturbance of its normal functioning, specifically while preserving biodiversity and an interval of the natural variations of biological production, considering the composition of the produced biomass. Pollutant flow can be replaced by its concentration. This definition works when only a single pollutant is considered. It becomes weaker with the introduction of a second pollutant. To illustrate this, let us consider a convincing example not of two pollutants but of two characteristics of water, one of which relates to pollution. Fish morbidity and mortality due to pollutants are strongly dependent on the concentration of dissolved oxygen in water (the higher its concentration, the lesser the mortality, even if the toxicant concentration remains the same). In this case, the assimilation capacity for a single pollutant is not a constant but a function of dissolved oxygen content in the water. However, the construction of such functions to analyze a larger number of variables is hardly expedient, because the arbitrary assumptions (e.g., which reference biological species is to be used to evaluate the MPC for humans?), aggravated by considerable measurement errors and other uncontrollable factors, make the results of such construction absolutely uninformative. Clearly, no matter what ecosystem is considered, no scalar characteristic can adequately describe its carrying capacity. However, for want of anything better, such characteristics are used to describe the carrying capacity either for individual ecosystems or for the biosphere as a whole.

The first scalar characteristic chosen to describe the anthropogenic impact on the biosphere seems to be human energy consumption, or the proportion of energy consumption by humans in the total energy cycle of the biosphere. A very similar approach evaluates the carrying capacity of the biosphere through the consumption of the net biota primary production (NBPP) per unit time. The Russian biophysicist Victor Gorshkov developed this idea, and a group of US researchers directed by Peter Vitousek independently followed the same line of study later.[8] In a 1995 study, Gorshkov states that the biosphere will remain stable, provided that humankind does not consume more than 1% of the NBPP, while a long-term exceedance of this threshold will lead to an ecological catastrophe.[9] This conclusion is based on the apparent regularity of biomass distribution between organisms in the biota depending on their size.[10] Whether or not it is appropriate to extend this to establish

---

8 Victor Gorshkov, "Распределение потоков энергии по организмам разных размеров" ["Distribution of Energy Currents Across Organisms of Different Size"], *Zhurnal obshchei biologii*, 1981 (42), No. 3, 417–29; Peter Vitousek et al., "Human Appropriation of the Product of Photosynthesis," *Bioscience*, 1986 (36), No. 5, 368–75.

9 Victor Gorshkov, *Физические и биологические основы устойчивости жизни* [*The Physical and Biological Foundations of Life's Sustainability*] (Moscow: Viniti, 1995), xxiii, 472.

10 Victor Gorshkov, "Структура биосферных потоков энергии" ["The Structure of Biospheric Energy Currents"], *Botanicheskii zhurnal*, 1980 (65), No. 11, 1579–90.

an NBPP consumption standard for humanity has not been substantiated. Gorshkov proposes that the energy consumption in the economy should be equivalent to NBPP consumption per unit time, where the former is easier to express in absolute physical units than NBPP flow is. In Gorshkov's book, *The Physical and Biological Foundations of Life's Sustainability*, energy consumption is calculated at 1–2 terawatt (1 TW = 10^{12} W). Similar results were found in the aforementioned study led by Vitousek. However, the calculations from both studies are based on some challengeable, unreserved assumptions, and the reaction of the results to variations in assumptions (i.e., the appropriate numerical characteristics) has never been examined.

Since Malthus, many attempts have been made to evaluate the number of people that can sustainably live off of what the Earth provides. The authors of many such studies (e.g., Yury Novikov and others) are not even aware of the existing ecological limitations, and that it is *impossible* to calculate the maximum possible area of tillage, assuming that all lands where anything can grow may be plowed.[11] However, considering the ecological limitations on agricultural production growth, the maximum admissible human population can be interpreted as another one-dimensional projection of the biosphere's carrying capacity. Dennis and Donella Meadows, in cooperation with Jorgen Randers, considered one scenario of possible human development, with the main objective of evaluating population size.[12] The authors concluded that limiting population size to 8 billion people would ensure West-European welfare standards for at least the entirety of the twenty-first century. This estimate, as well as the authors' many other estimates, is fully within the framework of their concept of limited growth. In fact, like the maximum human population, any limit to growth, either evaluated or hypothesized, can be understood as a one-dimensional projection of the biosphere's carrying capacity, since it specifies the maximal allowable volume of activity or consumption, or the anthropogenic impact on the biosphere in a specific direction. The construction of one-dimensional projections of the biosphere's carrying capacity includes attempts to evaluate what areas of land could be involved in active use by humankind and what part should be left for unsuppressed natural ecosystems. The first attempt towards this projection appears to have been made by Andrei Sakharov in 1974.[13] According to Sakharov, the proportion

---

11   See: Yury Novikov, *Можно ли накормить человечество?* [*Is It Possible to Feed Humanity?*] (Moscow: Kolos, 1983).
12   Donella Meadows, Dennis Meadows, and Jorgen Randers, *Beyond the Limits: Confronting Global Collapse, Envisioning a Sustainable Future* (Chelsea, VT: Chelsea Green, 1992).
13   Andrei Sakharov, *Мир, прогресс, права человека. Статьи и выступления* [*Peace, Progress, Human Rights: Articles and Talks*] (Leningrad: Sovetsky pisatel, 1990).

between inhabited and undeveloped land should be about 3:8 (the author gave no substantiation to this estimate). It is clear that, however expressed, one-dimensional estimates about the biosphere's carrying capacity will not be able to replace a thorough definition, nor will they create an exhaustive view of the key concept of global ecology. However, each new meaningful projection, provided that their conclusion is comprehensible, expands our understanding about the biosphere's carrying capacity. Note that this research is still far from complete.

4 Sustainable Development in a Consumer Society

The United Nations Conference on the Human Environment (Stockholm, 1972) recognized the existence of a global environmental problem and the need to change the trends in human development in order to prevent an ecological catastrophe. The concept of the biosphere's carrying capacity results in a formula: the development of civilization should proceed in such a way that its impact on the biosphere would not surpass the limits of its carrying capacity. All one-dimensional hypotheses considered in the previous section, if determined with acceptable accuracy, as well as other such projections that have not yet been constructed, will help to precisely define these limits.

Nevertheless, the ecological enthusiasm that followed the Stockholm Conference rapidly faded away. Most actors in the business and political circles across all countries did not feel inclined to solve environmental problems, realizing that the issue is far from their current economic and political interests. It was, however, impossible to ignore the global environmental problem and the need to solve it. There needed to be a way to save face and to intensify efforts to solve the problem so that politicians, public figures, and scientists could still remain champions of environmental ideals. To do this, the United Nations decided to establish the World Commission on Environment and Development in 1983, and the commission was charged with forming a platform for the next UN World Conference, scheduled for 1992. *Our Common Future*, a report prepared by this commission by 1987, introduced a new concept: *sustainable development*.[14] This concept implied the possibility of human development in accordance with an understanding of the global environmental problem.

There seemed to be no obstacle to defining environmentally sustainable development as development that does not disturb the equilibrium of the

---

14 World Commission on Environment and Development, *Our Common Future* (Oxford: Oxford University Press, 1987).

biosphere, or does not have an anthropogenic impact beyond the limits of the biosphere's carrying capacity. This idea might also have been presented in other ways, involving further scientific concepts (at least at the level of *The Limits to Growth*). Still, whatever else might be taking place in consumer society, its principal condition remains that the consumer must be secure in his or her consumer rights. Whether this condition was formulated deliberately, or produced by the collective unconscious of the consumer society, is unclear. In any case, the commission's report defined sustainable development as "development that meets the needs of the present without compromising the ability of future generations to meet their own needs." What are those "needs of the present"? How can they be correlated with the needs of "future generations"? Does "the present" "compromise" their ability to "meet their own needs," by extracting, for example, 75 million barrels of oil per day? Evidently, the authors of the report do not wish to admit these questions. The present generation will not consent to sacrifice "the needs of the present" for the sake of humankind's survival. And yet, such a sacrifice is necessary, and living today at the expense of future generations is precisely unsustainable.

No wonder that, despite hundreds of attempts, no other generally accepted definition of sustainable development has ever been given. As long as the phrase "the needs of the present" remains in the definition, there is no point in trying to improve it, since it contains an ineliminable, unscientific contradiction. Attempts to resolve this problem without compromising with consumer society are doomed. No wonder also that sustainable development strategies, formulated in many countries in accordance with the decisions of the United Nations Conference on Environment and Development (Rio de Janeiro, 1992), are, in most cases, ordinary programs of economic growth, often with little regard not only for the global ecology, but also for the environment in their own country. Environmental terminology is sometimes used to disguise the authors' true intentions—to maintain the consumer society where it already exists, or to ensure its creation in the developing countries.

5   Public Perception of Environmental Problems

The world community's obviously insufficient attention to the problems of the environment and the stability of civilization, and the virtual failure of all four UN World Conferences on Environment and Development, whose goals were not achieved (e.g., the response of nongovernmental organizations to the final draft of "The Future We Don't Want," produced by the 2012 UN Conference on Sustainable Development, Rio+20), are primarily due to the public's inadequate awareness, or else total ignorance, of environmental problems. Mass consciousness is undoubtedly controllable, and its controllability in consumer society increases with the development of mass media (especially the electronic kind), political strategy, advertising, etc., and the steady extension of their tools' scope of application. Nevertheless, this mass consciousness has some inherent features, and the more fully these features are taken into account, the more successfully it can be manipulated. I shall briefly discuss those of them that are most germane to the public perception of environmental problems.

The number of people who work with environmental problems in their professional career (in science, education, state management, and business) is steadily increasing globally (though this growth is not always monotonic). The number of volunteer environmentalists, who devote their free time to these problems, is also increasing. Nevertheless, the majority of the population, even in countries with the highest levels of environmental awareness, show little interest in environmental protection, even though they often adopt and follow elementary rules of environmental behavior, especially simple everyday tidiness. Still, these people never try to explore environmental problems, nor do they bother worrying about the fate of the biosphere. Their stereotypes and reasoning will be the focus of my analysis. These people are not necessarily mediocre; they can represent creative fields (culture or even science), management, or even the business-elite, and, as a rule, they are—consciously or not—members of consumer society who share its ideology.

A characteristic feature of mass environmental consciousness is the underestimation of the specifics of our environmental problems and processes, which are assumed to be commonplace. We consider events to be much more important than processes. Significant events come with a date, which is known in advance (e.g., the dates of parliamentary elections, the release of a new smartphone model, a world championship match, the release of a widely promoted film, the opening of Disneyland), or, otherwise, such events happen unexpectedly (as in the case of catastrophes, accidents, natural disasters, and sudden deaths). Unlike events, processes that unfold slowly (as comprehended by the routine consciousness) have no reference points in time and therefore remain unnoticed. They are neither expected nor recollected. Events attract attention to themselves, while the slowly developing processes are strike neither the eye nor the ear; their understanding requires intellectual effort, observation, and reflection. For a member of the consumer society, this is not easy. Ecological processes that proceed unnoticed usually involve a gradual build-up of small changes, like the slow increase in pollutant concentrations in natural objects, the gradual decrease in the refill of a small river from subsurface water sources, or the advance of the savanna onto the rainforest, of the desert onto the savanna. These changes are imperceptible within short time intervals. Mass consciousness is not forward-thinking and does not foresee the inevitable transformation of quantitative changes into qualitative ones, in the course of a process' long-term development. It is not ready to heed the warnings that the accumulation of pollution will, sooner or later, lead to a decline in biodiversity and to ecological degradation; the small river will grow shallow and then dry out; the recovery of a lost rainforest, although theoretically possible, will be unlikely in reality.

Paradoxical as this might sound, the mass consciousness does not understand the significance of phenomena of mass scale. A person thoughtlessly throws out a plastic bottle, believing that this action cannot have any effect because of its insignificance. But when one billion people each throw away a plastic bottle every day, those bottles form islands in the World Ocean and can be seen even from the bottom of the Mariana Trench. The mass consciousness also does not see such phenomena as time lags and aftereffects, which are very typical for natural systems. A classic example is the extermination of sparrows during the Chinese Great Leap Forward. Sparrows were declared to be the main agricultural pest, blamed for devouring grain crops, and more than two billion birds were killed from spring to December 1958. The 1959 harvest was appreciably higher than the average, and the country celebrated victory. The effect of that event, with a two-year lag, was an outbreak of insects, whose population sparrows would ordinarily keep low, especially when feeding their young. The delayed result was damage to harvests far worse than what had been attributed to sparrows. If not for the lag (i.e., if the number of pests increased concurrently with the decrease in sparrow population), their meaningless extermination would have ceased long before two billion birds had been killed. In the end, a mass import of sparrows became necessary.

The mechanism of delays and long-term impacts is very complicated; their character is sometimes deterministic, but more often stochastic, making them very difficult to forecast. The most convincing examples of this are the cases of infection in an organism (a human, an animal, a plant, or a fungus) or an ecosystem, either of the invasive type or by accumulation of a chemical. Infestation can last for a long time, manifesting itself (and possibly leading to sudden death) under the effect of an initiating impulse (e.g., overcooling, extreme physical load, stress, etc.). The formation of such an impulse is a random event, which may not occur at all should the organism die for some secondary reason. The routine consciousness commonly distrusts warnings regarding such phenomena and underestimates the danger, even of one's own death. This distrust is even more evident with regard to warnings about ecosystems and nature at large.

The mass consciousness is not ready to fully accept ideas about environmental equilibrium and regulation. No doubt, the elimination of two billion sparrows disturbed the equilibrium of an ecosystem in a huge area, if only for a short time. Ecosystem equilibrium can be upset by a seemingly weak variable, such as the invasion of a single organism, as demonstrated by many well-known examples. The equilibrium in an ecosystem is maintained by its regulatory activity, and even a relatively weak change disturbing the functions of the regulator can lead to the degradation of the entire ecosystem. For example, the self-purification capacity of rivers is due to the vital activity of a relatively small number of species of filter feeders, and their community is the biotic regulator of water quality. The filter feeders are very sensitive to some specific types of anthropogenic pollutants (primarily, to polymers). They fail to filter them from the water because polymers do not occur in nature, and they die with the introduction of even relatively small polymer concentrations, resulting in the degradation of the entire ecosystem. The "mass-man" (in the terminology of José Ortega y Gasset) is not prone to delve into such subtleties, and considers insignificant anything that he cannot understand.

One of the myths typical of the mass consciousness—and perhaps the most hazardous—is the belief that we can somehow compensate for the destruction of the environment, or that we can insulate ourselves from it. That is, if we have enough money, we will be able to buy anything we need. For example, a water filter can protect against deteriorating water quality, and air conditioners against global warming. It does not matter that atmospheric air pollution may require one to wear a gas mask; consumers will consent to this, provided that the discomfort is compensated by a high enough subsidy–this will allow one to buy a new, higher-quality car, the latest model of home theater, new shoes, clothes, household appliances, and better food. These little joys will make one's life brighter here and now, and one is disinclined to consider that this is to be paid for by a reduction in life expectancy and an earlier age of disability, which will affect not only oneself but also one's offspring.

6   Generalizations of the Environmental Problematics and the Scope of the Concept of *Sustainable Development*

Environmental ill-being has both a social and an economic background; this has been stated as long ago as the Stockholm Conference. This background came to the forefront in the report *Our Common Future*. In later UN documents and world conferences on sustainable development, environmental problems were pushed aside in favor of fighting hunger, poverty, sanitary problems, etc. These problems proved to be more negotiable for political elites than the tragically complex problems of saving the Earth from destructive anthropogenic impact.

No doubt, the extension of the concept of the *environment* beyond natural structures, an extension which was also occurring in science during this period, and the incorporation of all factors of social and individual life into this concept (as is the case in natural language) was necessary. Interestingly, this extension, highlighted in all UN documents dealing with sustainable development, was not reflected in any way in the definition of sustainable development, even as the United Nations acknowledged it in the policies proposed in *Our Common Future*. At the same time, little attention has been paid to the fact that some other threats to civilization are, in some respects, similar to environmental threats. At least two such hazards must be mentioned: threats to the health of the *Homo sapiens* population and threats to social equilibrium.[15] The population health, or social health, of humankind is subject to powerful and diverse negative anthropogenic impacts. Too many factors in the techno-sphere go against the grain of biological human nature, inviting an obvious analogy with the anthropogenic pressure on the biosphere. Is there an equivalent to the carrying capacity of the biosphere, some limit (a limit far from one-dimensional), beyond which anthropogenic impact on human population health would become destructive, and launch the irreversible biological destruction of *H. sapiens*? Disturbances of the social equilibrium tend to increase in scale, frequency, and depth; in the age of globalization and information society, this in itself threatens the existence of civilization. Social equilibrium is maintained by special social and ideological structures (traditions, religions, justice and the penal system), which are subject to destructive and, therefore, destabilizing pressure from social forces and structures. As often true of ecosystems and organisms, extreme unfavorable conditions can cause dysfunctional transformations in the stabilizing systems, so that they begin to undermine the social system instead of maintaining its equilibrium. The question arises: is there a limit to the pressure that can be applied to the stabilizing social structures, beyond which they will collapse, and society will degrade and perish? Based on these considerations, the following definition

---

15 Victor Danilov-Danilyan, "Устойчивое развитие (теоретико-методологический анализ)" ["Sustainable Development (A Theoretical and Methodological Analysis)"], *Ekonomika i matematicheskiye metody*, 2003 (39), No. 2, 123–135.

has been proposed: *sustainable development is social development that does not disturb its environmental basis, with newly formed living conditions that do not cause human degradation, and which prevents socially destructive processes from developing to a scale hazardous to the safety of society.*[16]

How does mass consciousness perceive the issues of public health and the preservation of the structures that ensure social stabilization? Clearly, its perceptions of these issues are similar to how it looks upon environmental problems. With respect to these new questions, the denial and displacement of information in the mass consciousness are occurring in the same manner and directions as described in this article in relation to environmental problems. Returning to the question of opposing the increasing anthropogenic pressure on the biosphere, I can only reiterate that mass consciousness is in need of undergoing a radical change. Otherwise, sustainable development will remain but a mental construct, while the destructive forces and the processes of degradation will prevail in reality. The needed change can be only achieved through the "greening" of educational policy, by raising the general cultural level of the population, and by the hygiene of the information field within which public consciousness is formed.

---

16   Danilov-Danilyan, "Устойчивое развитие," 132.

Harmonization of the Biosphere and the Technosphere as a Global Problem of Modernity

Nizami M. Mamedov

The rise and development of technology contributed to the formation of a special reality—the technosphere—which has served to determine modern existence, covering the entirety of the biosphere, as well as part of the outer space nearest to Earth. The technosphere is the most important means of deployment for the processes of globalization. The scale of modern technical activity has made necessary the formation of a technosphere compatible with the biosphere, instead of one existing in opposition to it. Factually speaking, the harmonization of socio-economic and environmental development, as well as the sustainable development of society, depends on the solution to this problem.

Until recently, technogenesis, like the interaction of society and nature as a whole, has occurred spontaneously, according to the technical objectification of humanity's goals. Improvement in technologies had led to an increase in the efficiency of human activity, thereby transforming nature. This, in turn, has formed (with some exceptions) a substantially technocratically-oriented human culture.[1]

At present, the technosphere is a collection of technical objects of various levels and quality; given its substantial and functional unity, it takes on the character of a mosaic. Changes in the technosphere are now associated with the objectification of scientific knowledge, and with innovations in the value structure of society, including the nature of human needs and human lifestyles.

Technology obeys the laws of the development of human existence, and is therefore universal; however, this universality is corrected by the intended purpose of technology and, at times, by specific regional demands. The latter is associated with the socio-economic and cultural characteristics of a given region. In our time, the solution to the problems of technology complies with pressing social and environmental requirements and, thus, depends greatly on

---

1 Alexander Chumakov, "Глобалистика в системе современного научного знания" ["Global Studies in the Contemporary System of Scientific Knowledge"], *Voprosy filosofii*, 2012, No. 7, 3–16.

matters like the extent to which outdated technologies are used in developing countries, or the absence of international legal norms aimed at preventing the spread of anti-ecological technology detrimental to the biosphere.

There are, nevertheless, some reasons to believe that in the near future, science-intensive technologies will be among the determining factors in the formation of a new form of civilization. These technologies are associated with the impending transition to a new, higher level of evolution of man and society.[2] This transition promises many benefits, as well as many new risks and uncertainties. It is evident that the implementation of advanced technologies should be preceded by comprehensive anthropological, social, and environmental studies and assessments.

1   The Foundations of Technology

Technology, being a means of adaptation, implements a certain way of practical appropriation of substance, energy, and information, depending on the corresponding needs of society. As a result, natural objects, or some combination of those, acquire a qualitatively new property: they serve as a means of objectifying human goals.

In terms of its content and results, the technical assimilation of reality is objective. It makes use of the laws of nature, as derived empirically or theoretically. By identifying the latter, an individual gains an opportunity to act in accordance with those laws, and to transform the forces, properties, and connections of nature and its "wealth" into ontological forces.

The very possibility of technology is determined by its presence in reality, which includes its numerous invariant relationships—the physical, chemical, biological, and other laws governing organizational relationships among the particular natural phenomena. Humans cannot change the laws of nature. Nevertheless, they are able to change the structure of its organizational ties. This occurs in the creation of necessary additional systems of connections between various phenomena, such as are capable of limiting or directing the action of certain laws in the appropriate way, and which are necessary for the individual and determine the essence of technology.[3] In fact, it is the estab-

---

2 Vladimir Arshinov and Vitaly Gorokhov, "Социальное измерение NBIC-междисциплинарности" ["The Social Dimension of NBIC Interdisciplinarity"], *Filosofskiye nauki*, 2010, No. 6, 22–35.

3 See: Nizami Mamedov, *Экологическая проблема и технические науки (Философско-методологические аспекты)* [*The Ecological Problem and Technical Sciences (Philosophical and Methodological Aspects)*] (Baku, Elm, 1982).

lishment of such a system that comes forward as a technical invention. In his *Philosophy of History*, Hegel observed that objects in nature are powerful and offer a variety of resistance. To subdue them, a person inserts between them other objects that exist in nature, therefore using nature against itself, and inventing tools to achieve that goal.

Technical development has a subjective side, too. This is due to its inclination to set goals, and to the dependence of those goals on the society's particular needs and on value paradigms dominant in the given era. Technical creations stem from the high level of human "bodily organization" achieved as a result of biological evolution. This idea is supported by the fact that rudimental bases of technical activity can also observed in animals. Empirical studies in ethology, archeology, ethnography, and other sciences have shown how rudimentary tool activity, collectivism of production and consumption, and other similar phenomena arose in the animal community—specifically, within the herd.

Still, in animal life, technical creation is one-sided and instinctive, whereas, for humans, it is the chief means of self-affirmation and development, thanks to the production of various tools. And it is by virtue of technical innovation that humans began to create a new reality for themselves, laying the foundation for a new social era. It is precisely the human ability to make a variety of tools and to adapt some forces of nature to counteract others that set our species apart from the animal world.

We can witness significant shifts in the development of technical abilities among prehistoric peoples, especially during difficult geological epochs, when individual branches of our ancestral family were on the verge of extinction. Only by means of the technical assimilation of nature did these peoples manage to escape extinction. If we take a retrospective look at millions of years of human history, a particular picture of human evolution emerges, such that this process can be seen to have taken place at a relatively high rate, usually when difficulties arose in the implementation of predetermined goals. Man changed himself while actively transforming nature, and his mind developed. The emergence of new ideas, methods, and means, which allowed for overcoming obstacles, did not occur immediately, but over the course of prolonged development while confronting the clash between available opportunities and the needs of multiplication and strengthening. This process was necessary for solving new problems.

Technology arose as a result of the struggle between man and nature, altering the character of that struggle in the process. Direct human dependence upon nature has weakened, and the system of links mediating their interactions grew more complex. Because of this, the form and character of the totality of man and nature have also changed, together with the character of their "struggle."

2 Axiological and Philosophical Regulative Principles for the Development of Technology

The fossil records from the Upper Paleolithic show a high level of stone tool-making. An analysis of the tools from those times and of the technological operations used in different regions of our planet reveals their striking uniformity. As noted by the English archaeologist Vir Gordon Childe,

> throughout the vast area where hand-axes are found—in Western Europe, throughout Africa, in Western Asia and on the Indian Subcontinent—during 100 or 200 thousand years of their use, the same four or five types of these axes were repeated with surprising constancy.[4]

Stanislav Lem proceeds from this fact when he tries to uncover the reasons that led to the uneven development of technology on our planet:

> Why is it that this massive tree of technical evolution—a tree whose roots may reach as far back as the last ice age, whose crown stretches to future millennia, and whose growth during the early stages of our civilization, in the Paleolithic and the Neolithic, was more or less the same all over the world—experienced its proper full flourishing in the West?[5]

In our opinion, this historical fact can be explained on the basis of the following assumptions. Human activity is conscious, and people are guided in their acts by the goals derived from their vital needs and from the representations of their consciousness. In the Paleolithic era, at the initial stage of the primitive communal system, the first, naive forms of social consciousness were only just emerging. Their influence on the utilitarian activity of human beings was weak. Subsequently, this uniformity began to break down. As human beings assimilated nature and overcame a one-sided utilitarian attitude to the world, they gradually developed a spiritual-practical attitude to nature, and the value-related foundations of human activity thus arose. Although the

---

4 V. Gordon Childe, *Progress and Archaeology* (Santa Barbara, CA: Greenwood, 1971), 37.
5 Stanislav Lem, *Summa Technologiae* (Minneapolis: University of Minnesota Press, 2013), 51.

internal logic and the laws of technological development were still the same across all regions, their implementations began to diverge.

As early as the Neolithic, humans in different regions of the planet began to form their worldviews. This included distinctive visions of the world within the frameworks of various mythological schemes, which offered, even in their naive form, explanations for natural phenomena, for a person's place in the world, and for other, similar questions. Later on, this circumstance begins to exert an ever-increasing influence on the character and aims of technical activity. Technological processes are often justified and presented in a mystical frame. Technical activity is sometimes turned into a ritual, in which substantive and practical actions are combined with mystical ones. Such was, for example, the ritual of building a boat, in which the technological process of building took the form of alternating religious rites.[6]

We cannot underestimate the influence of the mystical worldview on the definition of the aims of technical activity. The peculiarities of a given worldview would determine the "bifurcation" of technical activity and its purposefulness. The key forces of society focused on the construction of temples and sanctuaries. Only insignificant funds were allocated to "earthly" affairs. The construction of religious buildings, as one of the main forms of sacrifice, has been underway since the Neolithic. Since then, the scale of this activity has increased, reaching close to the maximum possible in the slave-owning society, where it often absorbed the bulk of human and economic resources. In this regard, Karl Marx observed that "in the earliest times, the principal production (for example, the building of temples, etc., in Egypt, India and Mexico) appears to be in the service of the gods, and the product belongs to the gods."[7]

Among these structures, the Egyptian pyramids look especially majestic and strike the imagination with their monumentality and perfection. The role of the mystical worldview that prevailed in Ancient Egypt is expressed here with special clarity. It's easy to agree with the scholar Mikhail Korostovtsev that "for the Egyptians, the requirements of their religion seemed to be of paramount importance, much more important than caring for housing and the daily bread."[8] Nevertheless, even though the mystical orientation of ancient societies caused significant waste of resources, and sometimes even complete depletion, in the course of the implementation of such illusory goals, certain

---

6 Lem, *Summa Technologiae*, 31.
7 Karl Marx and Friedrich Engels, *The Economic and Philosophic Manuscripts of 1844 and the Communist Manifesto* (Amherst: Prometheus Books, 2009), 79.
8 Mikhail Korostovtsev, *Религия древнего Египта* [*Religion of Ancient Egypt*] (Moscow: Nauka, 1976), 266.

technical advances took place all the same. Through the implementation of such goals, even within a mystical frame (e.g., the search for the philosophers' stone, or for the elixir of longevity), random discoveries were made, contributing, to some extent, to the development of the positive side of technical and scientific activity. Experts are still amazed by the accuracy of the calculations evident in the buildings erected during the reign of the pharaohs, especially the pyramids.

Mythological thinking influenced the development of technology until the emergence of the scientific worldview. In this respect, it is interesting to compare the originality of the development of technology in the East and the West. In the countries of ancient civilizations like Babylon, Egypt, China, and India we find the development of various technical inventions like the compass, paper, gunpowder, and original hydraulic engineering devices that later became the property of all mankind. Nevertheless, technical development in these countries appears to have halted, once the possibilities for the empirical assimilation of nature were exhausted. These countries were unable to rise to the level reached by Europe after the Renaissance. Technical knowledge that originated in the East remained a conglomerate of unsystematic rules and descriptions. Abdus Salam, the famous Pakistani physicist and Nobel Prize laureate, considered the reasons for this historical phenomenon, noting that the East supplied no possibility of understanding "the fundamental relationship between science and technology."[9]

3 Science and Technology

The peculiarity of technological development in the West can be explained by the growing influence of scientific thinking and the influence that theoretical knowledge exerts on this process. The emergence of scientific thinking is generally associated with the rise of experimental natural science during Modernity. Yet, the origins of scientific thought can be found in antiquity, specifically in the era of transition from myth to logos. Explicitly or implicitly, it played a significant role in the development of technology. Historical and scientific research has shown that even in the period when scientific data were not directly used in technology, certain scientific ideas and methods could nevertheless be present. Scientific methods have been used in the

---

[9] Abdus Salam, "Ummat ul-ilm: Towards a Commonwealth of Science," *The UNESCO Courier*, 1981 (34), No. 8–9, 53.

development of a number of technical devices. This is confirmed by the work of Archimedes and other outstanding engineers and naturalists, who demonstrated a new attitude towards technology and a combination of scientific and engineering approaches in their work.

Due to economic and socio-cultural circumstances, the union of science and technology did not develop at once; on the contrary, the connection between them arose in a sporadic fashion. Ancient society was not particularly interested in the development of technology. The main reason for this was in the very nature of the slave-owning mode of production, where the slave figured as the main instrument of labor. In such societies, there were no sufficiently strong socio-economic needs or incentives for diversification of technical progress and for the broad application of its achievements. In addition, in the ancient Greece and Rome, theoretical and practical activities were artificially separated: the principle of "knowledge for the sake of knowledge" was at work, bound, as it were, with the opposition of mental and physical labor. For these reasons, technical findings were sometimes used but for diversion, though they would play an important role in the later development of productive forces. Even the water mill, invented in the first century BCE, began to be practically used only in the Middle Ages. Aristotle's words are notable in this respect: "if every instrument at command, or from a preconception of its master's will, could accomplish its work ... the shuttle would then weave, and the lyre play of itself, nor would the architect want servants, or the master slaves."[10] Until the nineteenth century, technology developed largely without scientific methodology, and inventors continued to search for a perpetual-motion machine, while alchemists continued to believe in the mysterious transformation of metals. Even in the seventeenth and eighteenth centuries, as Werner Sombart writes figuratively, the world of technology and invention "was still the same old colorful, violent and eerie world in which people lived until science smashed it to smithereens."[11] Still, beginning with the Renaissance, we find increasingly greater technological advances, due to need and to the corresponding acceleration of scientific mastery. During this period, people realized that the possibilities of technology can increase immeasurably through scientific discovery. It seems that it was Leonardo da Vinci who first wrote about this, when observing that a practical person without science is

---

10   Aristotle, *Politics: A Treatise on Government*, translated by W. Ellis (London: George Routledge and Sons, 1895), 15.
11   Werner Sombart, *Техника эпохи раннего капитализма* [*Technology in the Early Capitalist Epoch*] (Moscow: TsUP VSNKh SSSR, 1925), 9.

like a helmsman entering a ship without a rudder or a compass, and that practice should always be founded upon good theory.

Francis Bacon offered philosophical substantiation for the union of science and technology. He combined the idea that "there are still laid up in the womb of nature many secrets of excellent use, having no affinity or parallelism with anything that is now known, but lying entirely out of the beat of the imagination"[12] with the idea of the unlimited possibilities of an individual capable of turning "knowledge into power." Bacon's philosophical approach found its ideal implementation in the needs of emerging capitalism, and leading naturalists picked up its main principles even during his lifetime. Technology ceased to develop spontaneously, based, as it were, on the intuitions of individual inventors and the technical assimilation of nature; due to the use of scientific methodology, it acquired completely new features.

The influence of science on technology first took the form of methods for increasing the efficiency of the already-known technical inventions: water, wind, and steam engines, improvements in the methods of transferring energy, etc. Later, as research laboratories were created for the needs of production, the flow of scientific ideas into technology increased. By the end of the nineteenth century, the technical assimilation of nature had become organically linked with the successes of natural science.

The use of scientific ideas and discoveries in the process of the technical development of nature is an outstanding phenomenon. We might be able to operate empirically, through trial and error, over mechanical and thermal— and to some extent chemical—forms of movement, and to invent various devices on this basis, but it would be fundamentally impossible to master other forms of movement—or to use electricity or nuclear energy—without science as such.

Natural-scientific development reveals the properties and relationships of real objects outside of direct interaction with the subject. Initially, the characteristics thus revealed are significant as scientific discoveries. Later, the results of these discoveries are employed, either directly or indirectly, in engineering and technology. No matter how strange this might seem, abstract, ideal objects and logical-mathematical methods have yielded results that, in one way or another, contribute to technical development. Suffice it to recall Faraday's, Maxwell's, and Hertz's theoretical pursuits that precipitated the emergence of radio and electrical engineering; research into atomic structure led to the

---

12   J. Spedding, R. L. Ellis, and D. D. Heath, eds., *The Works of Francis Bacon*, in seven volumes, vol. 4 (London, Longmans & Co., 1870), 100.

creation of atomic technology; the field of microelectronics owes its existence to solid-state physics, etc.

Until recent time, it was difficult to imagine the production of durable new materials based in nanotechnology and used in today's mechanical engineering, aviation, and medicine. Nanotechnology is a technology of manipulating a small number of atoms, or even individual atoms, aided by tools and devices that distinguish objects of nanometric scale. Such devices operate on the basis of quantum effects, and enable the creation of the so-called nanoclusters: configurations of atoms with quantum properties. These nanoclusters (i.e, artificially created nanoscale objects) then become the basis for purposeful design of materials with new structural and functional properties. Nanodesign relies on processes of self-organization at the nanoscale level.

Together with nanotechnology, we inevitably enter an era of microcosm process control—the era of high technological integration. Manuel Castells highlights the features of this new technological wave when he names one of its key characteristics: the convergence into a highly integrated system of specific technologies, synergistically linked into a cluster of information technologies, biotechnologies, nanotechnologies, and cognitive sciences. This is the so-called "NBIC convergence" (where "N" stands for "nano," "B" for "bio," "I" for "info," and "C" for "cogno").[13]

I would like to emphasize that the phrase "converging technologies" defines a new strategy for the development of technology and therefore calls for a comprehensive humanitarian, socio-economic, and geopolitical assessment. It is imperative to conduct an examination of the risks and uncertainties associated with the coming "nanotechnological revolution."

It is apparent that scientific knowledge expands the possible paths of technical development, becoming increasingly its necessary condition and basis. The peculiarities of a particular era's technology are largely determined by the characteristics of the current scientific paradigm, and by the predominant methods and research approaches. In this regard, the following fact is noteworthy: until now, technical systems have been considered in isolation, as closed systems (i.e., ignoring their influence on the external environment). This made it possible to significantly simplify their design and to focus on the main goal of increasing technical and economic indicators. Such consideration of a technical system does not require the development of special methods, nor does it require any means of accounting for the consequences of its impact on the

---

13   See: Manuel Castells, *The Information Age, Volumes 1–3: Economy, Society and Culture* (Hoboken, NJ: Blackwell, 1999).

natural environment. The practical awareness of the philosophical idea that "everything is connected with everything" did not arise proactively, but only with the discovery of the negative socio-ecological results of technical activity.

The influence of classical science is significantly reflected in the organization of production and technology. Until now, production has been based on the extraction of the necessary elements from raw materials and on their subsequent synthesis. The unused parts of the raw materials were considered unnecessary and discarded back into the natural environment. Within this framework, "industry" can be understood as the process of separating raw material into the "useful" and the "useless" parts, and of synthesizing the "useful" elements in accordance with predetermined goals. This prevalent technological method of modern production has its moments of similarity with the scientific treatment of the objects of science.

The practical and theoretical relationship of the humanity to nature thus represents an indissoluble unity, one that determines the possibility of the development of technology. Within this unity, theory is interpreted as a derivative, or a reflection, of practical activity. Yet, this reflection is not passive, for it actively enables us to outstrip practice and to overcome the limitations of a direct sensory relationship with nature. Technological progress is closely connected with theoretical scientific knowledge, and, in the course of its development, the latter enables the practical mastery of previously unknown processes and natural phenomena.

At the same time, technical assimilation of nature is the most important link in the dialectical progression of knowledge. Not only does it test the veracity of the theoretical assimilation of nature, but it also reveals the gaps in that assimilation. Properties, connections, and relations revealed in the course of technical activity, those unaccounted for in scientific knowledge, become the subjects of new theoretical research. As the results of those studies find practical application, new aspects of reality are once again disclosed.

4 The Logic of Technological Development

Generally, the logic of technological development can be traced in two main, mutually related directions. The first one concerns the objectification of human functions in various fields of activity, and the transfer of their implementation to various technical systems. The second concerns the humanization of nature. In general, this is a single process in which the objectification of the diverse functions of an individual requires the use of the properties of matter, the forms of its movement, etc.

First of all, the development of technology manifests itself in the objectification of labor and of the technological functions of individuals. The objectification of technological human functions has gradually led to the elimination of the subjective basis of technical devices. For example, prior to mechanization and automation, technological processes were subordinate to a given person's subjective capabilities—his or her strength, manual agility, endurance, eye precision, etc. In this regard, there is no doubt that the transition to automated production is a movement towards the highest phase of objectification of human technological functions. Further, the development of production technology, along with the mastery of new technological methods, types of energy, etc., should steadily increase the efficiency and quality of automated systems, by uncovering and utilizing possibilities that had been previously unknown.

It is impossible to characterize modern technical progress solely in terms of expanding the possibilities of objectifying human production functions. The relationship of humans and technology is much richer and more diverse than that. Technology is a means of objectification in other spheres of human activity: science, art (including film and television), etc. But this is just one aspect of the matter.

When establishing the features of technical development in a particular historical period, one should proceed from the unity and interaction of two main factors determining the character of this process: the characteristics of society's technical needs and the achieved level of theoretical and practical development. The first specifies the social determination of technology, its functional purpose; the second defines the natural, substrate contents of technology.[14] Moreover, the concept of the substrate of technology is integral to characterizing the material basis, or the material carrier, of the social functioning of technology: its social properties, connections, and relations. These include: the substrate of an isolated technical system, of all the aggregate technology available to society at the moment, and of technology in a fundamentally unlimited perspective of its development.

By distinguishing the substrate and the functional contents of technology, we are able to take a differentiated approach to the understanding of technical progress, with its criteria and main directions. Whereas, on a functional basis, the progress of technology is expressed in the degree of substitution of persons by technical systems in various areas of human activity, the substrate

---

14 Valery P. Goryunov, *Техника и природа* [*Technology and Nature*] (Leningrad: LGU, 1989), 25.

manifests itself through change in the natural basis of technical systems that enable functional substitution. The progress of technology can thus, in a certain sense, be traced along the lines of its changing substrate—factoring in its increased organization, the levels and varieties of matter and forms of motion it utilizes.

Technological development also proceeds along the lines of disclosing and deepening the relationship between nature and technology, involving new segments of natural reality in social life. By considering technical development under the aspect of substrate, we can take a concrete historical approach to the question of the relationship between nature and technology, without making a priori judgments about technology's "guilt" in aggravating the ecological situation, but instead revealing the limitations of certain aspects of its real natural contents. The possibility of expanding the natural prerequisites for technical development is of particular importance due to the significantly different environmental consequences of qualitatively different technical systems. In principle, the development of substrate contents of technology comes with many alternatives, and this essential circumstance should be considered when searching for solutions for environmental problems.

5 Green Economy Attitudes and Assessment of Technical Innovations

Environmental problems (e.g., climate change, desertification, decrease in biodiversity, lack of fresh water, environmental pollution, etc.) are associated with the development of technology in the structure of the traditional "brown economy." In effect, this model is aimed at short-term interest, unlimited growth, and consumption.

At the UN Conference on Sustainable Development Rio+20, held in 2012 in Rio de Janeiro, attention was drawn to the fact that the traditional model of economic development has lost its effectiveness, and humanity must enter the era of green economy. According to the United Nations Environment Programme (UNEP), the green economy is designed to reduce environmental risks, to prevent environmental degradation, and to improve the quality of life. The concept of a green economy is amenable to all countries: developed, developing, and emerging. Green-economy-related attitudes are becoming critical factors in the methodologies of technical innovation assessment. This comprehensive assessment of technical innovation involves social, economic, and environmental expertise with regard to the impacts on the natural and social environments.

Under present-day conditions, we face an urgent need for the development and adoption of methodological principles of international-scale technological development. The adoption of such principles would make it possible to manage this process at the global and regional levels. We also find a need for substantiation, and for general legal and organizational norms that would enable purposeful development of the technosphere without destroying the foundations of our planet's natural environment. This comes forward as an objective necessity as we consider the special significance of technological progress and its direction for the humanity and for the future of our civilization.

Our time represents an extraordinary moment in the development of the technosphere. We can witness a tightening of environmental legislation in developed countries, in relation to outdated technologies and to various types of transport, as well as new technical innovations. Environmental and legal actions have swept across the European Union, the United States, Canada, and Japan. Thanks to these actions, a genuine technological revolution is underway in developed countries: alternative technologies have been introduced, the consumption of natural resources has significantly decreased, the state of the environment has improved together with the quality of life.

These positive actions have, nevertheless, intensified the stratification of the world, given the variety of attitudes that countries bring to bear on environmental problems. The disparity of ecological conditions between the global "North" and "South" has worsened. Due to their weak economies, developing countries cannot devise new equipment, and are forced to import outdated equipment and technologies. This situation has consequences, not only at the regional level, but such that affect the state of the biosphere as a whole. It follows that we must universalize environmental legislation, taking into account the unity of the biosphere, the principles of social justice, and the basic human right to a hospitable natural environment. Unfortunately, the socio-economic situation in most developing countries forestalls the solution of this problem.

Globalization enters a variety of spheres of human activity, seeking to eliminate regional disparities in technological development. Technological progress, meanwhile, is not a one-time phenomenon, but a complex historical process, whose spatial-temporal factor has always played, and will continue to play, a significant role in the deployment of the technosphere. Even under the right economic, social, cultural, and political conditions, the dissemination of technical ideas, their development, testing, and replication requires a significant amount of time. Time is also necessary for replacing obsolete technology, as well as for the spread of new technologies. It is vital that we aspire towards a system of global targets for the development of technology, based on the principles of sustainable development, and contextualized by the traditions and capabilities of specific individual countries.

Natural-Historic Aspects of Globalization

Valery V. Snakin

1 Introduction

Studies of the phenomenon of globalization typically involve analyses in terms of the multidimensional processes of global economic, political, and cultural integration—all characteristic of our time. The term "globalization" itself invokes, first and foremost, a rise in economic and social regulation, manifest in the internationalization of capital and in the creation of transnational companies, international governmental organizations and NGOs, and universal databases regulating the activities of every person—all transforming the world into a unified global system. And yet, globalization represents a broader planetary process conditioned by the entire course of the biosphere's development, and by the activity of living matter, which defines, or, at the very least, inflects the natural processes that can be observed in today's world.

From a natural-historical viewpoint, globalization is a product of the imminent increase in the pressures exerted by living matter upon the planet. This effect is most pronounced in the activities of the human population, which has succeeded in eliminating all geographic barriers to its expansion. In turn, globalization inevitably affects the flow of natural processes, altering not solely the speed but sometimes the very direction of evolution. Let us consider the natural preconditions and some of the effects of globalization across nature and human societies.[1]

---

[1] The author has previously explored some of the aspects of this problem. See, for instance, the following works in Russian by Valery Snakin: "Глобализация и социобиология" ["Globalization and Sociobiology"], *Vek Globalizatsii* [*The Age of Globalization*], 2017 (24), No. 4, 23–32; "Глобализация и экология" ["Globalization and Ecology"], *Zhizn Zemli* [*Life on Earth*], 2018 (40), No. 4, 465–72, https://doi.org/10.29003/m223.0514-7468.2018_40_4/379-494; "Глобализация как закономерный этап эволюции биосферы" ["Globalization as a Natural Stage of Biospheric Evolution"], *Zhizn Zemli*, 2019 (41), No. 3, 272–83; https://doi.org/10.29003/m670.0514-7468.2019_41_3/272-283; "Природопользование как главный инструмент глобализации" ["Natural Resource Use as the Main Instrument of Globalization"], *The Use and Protection of Natural Resources of Russia*, 2020 (162), No. 2, 5–13.

2   "The Pressure of Life" as the Main Natural Source of Globalization

Globalization is conditioned by the central law of biospheric evolution—the law concerned with the expansion of living matter and with what Vladimir Vernadsky termed "the pressure of life"—a phenomenon responsible for intensifying the degree of interdependence among biospheric processes. According to Vernadsky and the views he had formulated in his treatise *The Biosphere* (first published in 1926), in the process of biospheric evolution, as life expanded across habitats, living matter came to exert an ever-greater transformative pressure upon its inanimate environments, as well as upon itself. This pressure of life and the concomitant expansion of living matter are limited solely by the availability of resources. Yet this basis of available resources likewise has a tendency towards expansion.

The purpose of globalization can, in this sense, be understood as the expansion of living matter into all the geospheres of the Earth and further, into outer space, with the subsequent utilization of those environments for its own development. This tendency does not at all represent a "top-down" initiative but constitutes every living entity's "bottom-up" natural aspiration. Anthropogenic change, meanwhile, is the most powerful of all biological factors. Of all the biological species that have existed and continue to exist on Earth, humans alone have been able to transform nearly all of its geospheres into their own habitable environment, becoming a powerful geological force that spans across continents, dramatically reducing geographic isolation. This has resulted in the increasing ecological consolidation of the biosphere.

3   Utilization of Nature as the Principal Instrument of Globalization

The transformation of natural environments by biological species according to their own needs is a fundamental principle of biospheric evolution. Not only do living organisms adapt to existing environmental conditions, they also actively transform them, thereby increasing their autonomy and enabling the emergence of new ecological niches. Since the moment of their first appearance in the biosphere, and especially since the Neolithic Revolution, humans have been continuously improving their techniques of natural resource management, making ever-greater resources available, and thereby removing the only limiting factor curtailing "the pressure of life." The Industrial Revolution marked a qualitative leap that paved the way towards the contemporary stage of globalization. (Vernadsky described this phenomenon of the early twentieth century as an "explosion of scientific creativity.")[2] *The utilization of natural resources and the resulting transformation of natural environments constitute the key instruments of globalization.* By continuously increasing its resource base, humanity has altered the face of the Earth, thereby becoming a geological factor of immense power.

Agriculture and various segments of industry, the most powerful among them being the global fuel-and-energy complex, have become the key players behind the acceleration of pressures upon all the constituents of the natural environment. Agricultural land development, mining and other forms of extraction, housing and infrastructure development, the energy industry, and the creation of irrigation systems and reservoirs have all contributed to the mounting pressure.

As a result of agricultural activity, the area of cultivated land (including arable land, orchards, and plantations) now totals 1,507 million hectares, or 11.2% of the total landmass of the planet. Among the subcontinents, Europe has the greatest proportion of arable land (32% of its landmass). Among the largest countries, a particularly high proportion of arable land to total landmass is found in India (54%) and Argentina (40%). Russia's Central Black-Soil Region, with 61.9% of its total area used for growing crops, encompasses regions like Orel, where the share of agricultural land approaches 81%.

The Earth's forest cover (the ratio of its forested area to the total area) is 30.3%, with a tendency to decrease (by 0.4%, between 1990 and 2005 alone).[3] On the Russian territory, forest cover constitutes 45.4%—as compared to 52%, the ratio across the European part of Russia as of three centuries ago. By the 1920s, that ratio had decreased to about 27%, and increased slightly, to 38%, towards the beginning of the twenty-first century, owing mainly to reforestation of abandoned croplands and meadows, transferred thereafter into the category of forested land.[4]

An important part of the infrastructure of any territory is the network of roads that enables the movement of people, transport, and materials. The total length of paved and rutted roads on Earth is approximately 7.3 million kilometers; its greatest shares belong to the United States, India, China, Brazil, and

---

2 Vladimir Vernadsky, Научная мысль как планетное явление [*Scientific Thought as a Planetary Phenomenon*] (Moscow: Nauka, 1991), 38.
3 Food and Agriculture Organization of the United Nations, *The State of the World's Forests* (Rome: FAO, 2009).
4 Национальный атлас России [*National Atlas of Russia*], vol. 11: Природа и экология [*Nature and Ecology*] (Moscow: Roskartografiya, 2007).

Russia (a total of 1.28 million kilometers). By 2050, the total length of the roads around the world is forecasted to increase by 60%.

The development of the fuel-and-energy complex, spurred by the human population's growing demand for energy resources, has essentially connected all the countries of the world into a single energy network, thus becoming the main lever of industrial and agricultural development and a key factor in international policy-making.

The unprecedented degree of redistribution of matter and energy on the planet—aided by roads, railways, oil and gas pipelines, water, sea, and air transportation, and by power grids—all ensure the unity of today's world. This also contributes to both deliberate and accidental migration of living organisms.

Global human activity is accompanied by a number of negative environmental consequences: the generation of vast amounts of production and consumption waste, soil degradation, disruption of the hydrogeological regime, the death of forests, desertification, and profound changes to local climates, landscapes, and biodiversity dynamics.

4   Globalization and Environmental Pollution

Among the ecological consequences of globalization, environmental pollution poses one of the most severe problems for the preservation of biodiversity and for the well-being of human civilization. Not only are the vast expanses of the world's oceans critically polluted (the so-called "garbage islands" floating in the oceans are comparable in area to large countries), but so is outer space, to a degree that can interfere with the functioning of space and ground equipment (especially the radio-technical and astronomical equipment). Air pollution due to the rapid movement of air masses has become universal, causing, in turn, the pollution of other biospheric components. Persistent (i.e., difficult to degrade) organochlorine substances (including DDT) are found in the bodies of animals living in Antarctica, and radiocarbon (^{14}C) from nuclear tests was discovered in the Mariana Trench of the Pacific, at the depth of nearly 11,000 meters.[5]

---

5   Ning Wang et al., "Penetration of Bomb ^{14}C into the Deepest Ocean Trench," *Geophysical Research Letters*, 2019 (46), No. 10, 5413–19, https://doi.org/10.1029/2018GL081514.

5   Globalization and Species Extinction

The extinction of species as a result of natural processes is a normal phenomenon, balanced in geological time by the appearance of new species. In *The Origin of Species*, Charles Darwin attributed the extinction of species and entire groups of species, which has played such a prominent role in the history of the organic world, to the imminent consequences of natural selection. Throughout the long history of the biosphere, the planet's biodiversity has repeatedly undergone periods of abrupt decline, invariably recovering, sometimes to exceed even the pre-crisis abundance. Nevertheless, some species and clusters of species have become extinct, generally due to competitive selection, and others took their place. Of the many hominid species, only one, *Homo sapiens*, secured its place in the biosphere and succeeded in spreading globally. The other members of the genus *Homo* are now extinct.

Globalization has greatly reduced the geographical isolation of species. The active migration of *H. sapiens* has facilitated the hitherto unprecedented frequency of migration among other species of life. (It should be noted that microorganisms have always actively migrated, with the aid of sea and air currents, and of migrating birds.) The frequency of new species' introduction (deliberate migration) and of their unintentional migration (invasion) to previously foreign regions intensifies inter-species competition and leads to the demise of species less adapted to the new conditions. These victims are often the region's aboriginal inhabitants.

Biological pollution—the introduction and reproduction of alien species in new ecosystems—has significant evolutionary implications. The erasure of geographic barriers to species migration and the domestication and dispersal of species through acclimatization and biotechnological activities (including the emergence of laboratory strains of microorganisms, artificial hybrids, and genetically modified organisms) are some of the principal causes of the decline in biodiversity and of the possible advent of the sixth mass extinction of species.[6]

---

6 Gerardo Ceballos et al., "Accelerated Modern Human-Induced Species Losses: Entering the Sixth Mass Extinction," *Science Advances*, June 19, 2015, No. 1, https://doi.org/10.1126/sciadv .1400253. See also: Valery Snakin, "Массовые вымирания видов животных в истории биосферы Земли: Еще одна гипотеза" ["Mass Extinctions in the Biosphere History: Another Hypothesis"], *Izvestiya Rossiiskoi akademii nauk. Seriya Geograficheskaya* [*The Dispatches of the Russian Academy of Sciences, Geographic Series*], 2016, No. 5, 82–90, https://doi.org/10 .15356/0373-2444-2016-5-82-90.

6 Sociobiological Aspects of Globalization

The increasing degree of planetary unity and the growing density of human population not only entail a transition from extensive to intensive use of natural resources, but also herald changes in the *population strategy* of mankind, as well as its behavioral stereotypes.

Population strategies are characterized by elaborate sets of traits and adaptations, including the integral traits of competitiveness, tolerance, and reactivity. In 1938, Leonty Ramensky proposed an original classification of plant populations' life strategies, which isolated the categories of *explerents* (pioneer species with a high rate of reproduction), *violents* (highly competitive "lion-plants") and *patients* (hardy plants, tolerant of unfavorable conditions). Other distinctions isolate the *r*-strategy—characterized by a high reproductive capacity with no regard for the offspring, characteristic of *explerents*, and the *K*-strategy involving a low reproductive rate, with a high degree of care for the offspring, characteristic of the *violents*.[7] *K*-selection favors a more efficient use of resources, including food, while *r*-selection favors a higher population growth rate and productivity; the latter is prevalent in adverse environmental conditions and in developing new territories by pioneer species. These two types of selection have a fundamental difference. At the earliest stages of appropriating a new territory, *explerents* and *r*-selection predominate. Most species inhabiting stable habitats, when reaching the maximum population size, tend to decrease *r*-selection, with a concurrent tendency to promote *K*-selection, in the interests of more subtle adaptation to local conditions. In periods of unfavorable conditions, *r*-selection takes precedence once again, and competitive species (*violents*) give way to *explerents*.[8]

In the period of globalization, it is the *K*-strategy that takes precedence, which explains the observed dynamics of the human population (demographic transition): in developed countries, the number of children per family is steadily decreasing, against the backdrop of intensifying care for the offspring. The replacement of the *r*-strategy by the *K*-strategy explains the recent population decline observed in many countries. The decrease in the number of children per woman, the transition from large families to families with one or two children, later age of childbirth, and greater investment in child-rearing

---

7 Robert MacArthur and Edward O. Wilson, *The Theory of Island Biogeography* (Princeton, New Jersey: Princeton University Press, 1967).

8 Valentin Krasilov, *Охрана природы: принципы, проблемы, приоритеты* [*Nature Conservation: Principles, Problems, Priorities*] (Moscow: VNII Priroda, 1992).

all lead to higher levels of education and increased competitiveness of the offspring in the face of increasing social and industrial complexity.

Yet another socio-biological aspect of contemporary globalization is presented by the phenomenon of *feminization*, noted by many researchers, and accompanied by an increase in the role and influence of women, with the purpose of eliminating gender inequality. The movement for gender equality (feminism) that has intensified in the past century is concerned not solely with feminization, but also with masculinization—meaning a change in the fundamental functions of the male and the female, and a kind of convergence of the masculine and the feminine principles. The concurrent transformation of the norms of sexual behavior, and the emergence of movements like "childfree" (a position of deliberate opting out of childbearing) can also be treated as manifestations of biological mechanisms of population regulation. The increasing complexity of the global economy leads to the diversification of "ecological niches" within it, contributing also to a decrease in competition across society. This is especially important to populations characterized by high density. The value of human life has generally increased (as argued by Steven Pinker in *The Better Angels of Our Nature*), a trend accompanied by a decrease in violence across human societies, due to the concerted efforts of the authorities and lawmakers, as well as the processes of feminization and reduced competition mentioned earlier.[9] (Although we could recall Michelangelo's verses condemning Renaissance-era cruelties, objectivity suggests that we compare modern levels of violence with those of the Middle Ages and the centuries of slave trade.)

The processes of globalization are eliminating geographic, economic, political, and cultural borders. The development of the internet, educational exchanges, and the growth of the international environmental and human-rights movements have led to the emergence of a new geopolitics and a new worldview, inevitably accelerating all types of migration, including active population migration, often provoked by sociopolitical and environmental moments such as poverty, military and ethnic conflicts, natural disasters, etc. Population migration is essentially analogous to animal migration and can compensate for natural population decline (depopulation) in a given country. On the other hand, it creates problems both for the countries experiencing such a mass exodus and for places where migrants might seek refuge. These

---

9 Steven Pinker, *The Better Angels of Our Nature: Why Violence Has Declined* (New York: Viking, 2011).

problems range from the so-called "brain drain" to the difficulties of assimilation in place, with subsequent alterations in the demographic structure, cultural traditions, etc.[10] Population migration is characterized by heterogeneity and represents a vivid illustration of the "pressure of life." Due to the intensification of migration, governments in many countries now pay considerable attention to demographic policy. The purposeful activity of state agencies and other institutions in the arena of reproductive regulation is attributable to the felt need to attain the demographic optimum. Among its various directions are different forms of state assistance to families with children, the creation of optimal conditions for combining professional activities with family responsibilities, improvements to the quality of life, the regulation of population migration, etc. Still, the history of demographic policy shows that it has not always had a noticeable effect on reproduction rates.

Another unignorable aspect of globalization's impact upon demographic processes is represented by the coronavirus pandemic, which has gripped the world for the past two years, as the globally integrated humanity proved to be a highly favorable environment for its spread.[11] This pandemic has once again emphasized that growth cannot go on unimpeded and that periods of unhampered development are inevitably succeeded by crises, called upon to adjust the mechanisms of continued evolution. It appears to be no coincidence that the pandemic began in the most populous country in the world, China, while the most economically developed country, the United States, has suffered the greatest losses. On the one hand, then, the pandemic can be seen as a form of natural global biotic regulation due to humanity's high burden on the rest of nature and the aging of the world's human population.[12] On the other hand, the practice of combating the pandemic will test the effectiveness of various approaches to survival in such crises, from the total mobilization of the Chinese population to the comparatively milder quarantine measures adopted by European democracies.

On the whole, the analysis of the states' attempts to influence demographic processes suggests that *natural evolutionary processes remain the determining*

---

10 Alexander Chumakov, *Глобализация. Контуры целостного мира* [*Globalization: The Contours of a Holistic World*] (Moscow: Prospect, 2017).

11 Alexander Chumakov, "Глобалистика в контексте современности: испытание пандемией" ["Globalistics in the Context of Our Time: The Pandemic Test"], *Vek globalizatsii*, 2020 (35), No. 3, 3–14.

12 Leonid Grinin and Anton Grinin, "Глобальное старение и будущее глобального мира" ["Global Aging and the Future of the Global World"], *Vek globalizatsii*, 2020 (33), No. 1, 3–21, https://doi.org/10.30884/vglob/2020.01.01.

factors in the Earth's population dynamics. The contribution of particular governments to the overall dynamics of population regulation (by stimulating birth rates or vice versa) is estimated to be but 8%–15% of the total population change. A number of such measures (including abortion bans and the so-called "maternity capital," a policy adopted by Russia) do not change the overall situation, but only the population dynamics, by accelerating or delaying childbirth. In this way, the results of the Chinese government's policy to limit the birth rate (its "one family, one child" program, initiated in 1978) are assessed ambiguously. Meanwhile, the dynamics of population growth in China and Russia are similar, even though Russia has taken measures to stimulate the birth rate.[13] To a significant extent, the drop of birth-rates is a consequence of economic progress and of the desire for gender equality.

7 Globalization and the Expansion of Human Population's Resource Base

Another important global problem confronting our civilization is the depletion of natural resources. Despite the availability of global resources, we know that finite resources will inevitably run out. What is to be done? Are we to limit consumption? This is complicated by the continued population growth. The situation is helped, to a degree, by the more efficient use of resources, and per capita energy consumption is falling in developed countries. Still, a reduction of population can only postpone the depletion of exhaustible resources. The solution appears to be in scientific research and technical development of new energy types and sources, such as atmospheric electricity, geothermal energy, solar power, etc.—as well as in the development of nuclear technologies and space resources.

The process of globalization, set in motion largely by the intensive development of natural resource utilization, *transforms and intensifies natural resource use under the influence of new scientific and technological developments*, which spread almost instantaneously around the globe. This is strikingly evident in the accelerated development of the oil-and-gas complex and particularly in the so-called "shale revolution"—the introduction into commercial exploitation of the technology of natural gas and oil extraction from oil shale and tar sands, as well as the development of gigantic deposits of hydrocarbon gas hydrates.

---

13 "Population Pyramids of the World from 1950 to 2100," https://www.populationpyramid.net/.

Globalized science ensures the development of new technologies for the use of natural resources and the prospecting of new energy sources. In the energy industry, the widespread development of alternative, or "green" energy (as opposed to traditional energy sources) has become an important direction. Alternative energy (geothermal, solar, wind, and tidal forms of energy, biotechnological systems, and heat pumps) is more environmentally friendly when compared with traditional energy sources. It is also becoming increasingly economical: for instance, in the course of the 1980s alone, the cost of solar panels was reduced by 95%. In most cases, the need for costly transportation over long distances is also eliminated. Many countries have chosen to stimulate the development of alternative energy sources. In Japan, a grand program to install solar panels on rooftops subsidizes half of the cost of their installation. Brazil's program supporting the production of ethanol from sugar cane has made it possible to replace half of the gasoline consumed by Brazilian cars with that fuel.

8   Globalization in the Noospheric Age

The transition of the biosphere to the *noospheric* state as a result of the rational activity of humanity is representative of yet another aspect of globalization. To what extent, and in what ways, can human rational activity influence the processes of globalization and minimize their negative consequences?

In his treatise on *Scientific Thought as a Planetary Phenomenon*, Vladimir Vernadsky noted that, in acquiring knowledge, the mind does not *observe*, but instead *creates* reality itself. In the *noosphere*, "humanity, for the first time, becomes a major geological force." This new, from the evolutionary perspective, geological force, constituted by the scientific thought of human society, enables an expansion of the humanity's resource base, to an extent unprecedented in the history of biological species. But to what degree can the negative phenomena accompanying this expansion (e.g., environmental pollution; reduction in the diversity of species, soils, and entire landscapes) be mitigated within the framework of modern civilization?

Unlike other biological species, humans are consciously engaged in nature conservation, essentially representing the development of a negative feedback loop in the humanity-biosphere system, aimed at that system's stabilization. By the middle of the twentieth century, the forces of globalization promoted nature conservation to the international level of coordination. International organizations and initiatives (IUCN, WWF, UNEP, UNESCO's Man and the Biosphere Programme (MAB), World Conservation Strategy, and others) have appeared, and numerous international conventions and agreements aimed at developing and coordinating international conservation efforts have been signed. The motives that can induce people towards protecting nature include utilitarianism (the idea that nature conservation is useful to humans), scientific interest (the satisfaction of natural curiosity in the study of wildlife), as well as the actively developing ethico-aesthetic position, which holds that nature matters in itself, possessing intrinsic value.

Modern conservation practices make clear that many ecological problems can be successfully addressed. What remains problematic, however, is finding the balance between necessary and excessively charitable conservation. To what extent can our understanding of evolution safeguard the appropriateness of conservation measures, which essentially represent human interventions in the evolutionary process?

What needs to be emphasized is that the environmental movement must be scientifically informed, rather than driven along by unsubstantiated assumptions. Unfortunately, some international agreements (the Kyoto Protocol, the Paris Agreement) are insufficiently substantiated by science, which reduces their effectiveness, while contributing to the popularization of environmental nihilism.[14] The concept of sustainable development, as put forward by politicians, is little more than a set of good wishes lacking a scientific basis; it has proved itself ineffective and is essentially anti-evolutionary.[15] Regrettably, this idea is being actively popularized through education and across the scientific community, since it cannot be said to belong to the field of scientific knowledge as such. Yet, despite the inconsistencies of international environmental policy, the growing effectiveness of these efforts is evident: the contraband of rare and endangered animals and plants is being suppressed (the effect of the CITES Convention); so is the transboundary movement of hazardous waste (Basel Convention); emissions of sulfur and nitrogen oxides, heavy metals, and persistent organic compounds are limited (by the Convention on Long-Range Transboundary Air Pollution). Still, international conventions can sometimes have a limited effect, due to a lack of clear scientific criteria for monitoring and

---

14   Valery Snakin, "Глобальные изменения климата: прогнозы и реальность" ["Global Climate Change: Forecasts and Reality"], *Zhizn zemli*, 2019 (41), No. 2, 148–64, https://doi.org/10.29003/m649.0514-7468.2019_41_2/121-246. See also: Valery Snakin, *Экология, глобальные природные процессы и эволюция биосферы. Энциклопедический словарь* [*Ecology, Global Environmental Processes and Biospheric Evolution: An Encyclopedic Dictionary*] (Moscow: Moscow University Press, 2020).

15   Valery Snakin, "Путь к устойчивому развитию: мифы и реальность" ["The Path to Sustainable Development: Myths and Reality"], *Vek globalizatsii*, 2016, No. 1–2, 80–86.

evaluating their effectiveness, and also due to the non-involvement of a number of key countries.

It has already been noted that *pollution* has become a global environmental problem with a tendency to escalate. Concurrently, scientific and technological progress combined with the effects of globalization has, for the first time in history, resulted in the reduction of pollution in some of the developed countries.[16] The penetration of leading technologies into developing countries offers hope for a global solution to the problem of environmental pollution. A high efficiency of environmental protection measures can be observed in the framework of the UNECE Convention on Long-Range Transboundary Air Pollution (CLRTAP). Over its forty-year history, the Convention has practically resolved the issue of excessive critical deposition of acid-forming agents (sulfur and nitrogen oxides) on European territory, and emissions of persistent organic compounds and heavy metals have been significantly reduced.[17]

The loss of biodiversity is another difficult problem to solve, but it also has its positive aspects, such as developments in selective breeding and especially in genetic engineering, which lead to the emergence of new plant and animal varietals and subspecies. Human activity itself generates new ecological niches that promote speciation, paving the way to increased biodiversity. This process is assisted by cryopreservation, cryo-banking, and other forms of gene pool conservation, not only for the purposes of preservation, but also for possible future use in restoring populations, genetic engineering, biomedicine, etc.

New habitats created by humans are actively colonized by biological species. According to the *National Atlas of Russia* (2007), of the 311 key ornithological territories identified in the European part of Russia, more than twenty are of anthropogenic origin. A population of cockatoos (*Cacatuidae*) has settled in Sydney, and yellow-headed amazon parrots (*Amazona oratrix*)—in Stuttgart, quite far from their natural habitats; monk parrots (*Myiopsitta monachus*) have settled in Buenos Aires, thanks to the human introduction of the tree species necessary to their nesting; now they are displacing pigeons from their urban environment; the same species has mastered the surroundings of the Sagrada Familia in Barcelona. The population of Burmese tiger pythons in the swamps of Florida has already exceeded their aboriginal population. The largest habitat (80% of the population) of the endangered American manatee (*Trichechus manatus*) has recently been recorded off the coast of Florida, thanks to the heating of water by thermal power plants.

---

16   Alexander Tarko, *О настоящем и будущем России и мира* [*On the Present and Future of Russia and the World*] (Tula: Prom-Pilot, 2016).

17   Center for Meteorological Synthesis EMEP, 2020, http://www.ru.msceast.org.

All this represents the grounds for a positive solution to the ecological problems arising in the course of globalization. Such optimism is consonant with Vladimir Vernadsky's certainty in the irreversible development of science and in the positive role of human rationality in the evolutionary process.

9 Conclusions

1. The natural source of globalization is living organisms' (or living matter's, to put it in Vernadsky's terms) drive to expand their environments. "The pressure of life" is limited only by the availability of natural resources, but this limitation is removed under modern conditions, as the resource base is expanded by means of new methods and technologies for the utilization and transformation of the environment. The pressure of life and the use of natural resources are the two main complementary natural factors of globalization, maximally manifested in the course of the development of human civilization.
2. Globalization is accompanied by an unprecedented degree of transformation of natural ecosystems. In order to expand agricultural and industrial production, extraction and transportation of minerals, and construction of settlements and related infrastructure, natural landscapes are destroyed and defaced, and wild habitats are reduced in scope. The problem of environmental pollution is becoming pervasive.
3. Globalization significantly accelerates the deliberate introduction of—and accidental invasion by—animal and plant species alien to the given area. This entails a diminishment of the role of geographic barriers, accompanied by the displacement of local species, and the consequent acceleration of species extinction and dwindling biodiversity. Globalization is particularly detrimental to island communities.
4. Globalization brings radical change to biosocial processes. The reproductive strategies of populations are changing (fewer children with greater care for the offspring being the trend); feminization and masculinization processes are intensifying, which contributes, in turn, to the reduction of violence and competition within society, and to changes in the demographic situation. Undoubtedly, these significant social processes trigger further changes in social behavior (the subject of eco-psychology), particularly in aspects responsible for the adaptation of individuals to changing environmental conditions. This takes the form of increased altruism, cooperation, reciprocity, tolerance, increased value of human

life, etc. Identifying these changes is an important task of socio-biological research.
5. The ecological and biosocial problems of globalization trigger societal responses. Humans have emerged as the sole species concerned with the intrinsic value of nature and its conservation. An increasingly comprehensive global system of protected natural territories is being created. Globalization provides an unprecedented opportunity for cooperation in environmental protection policy. Effective international agreements covering entire continents are being created. Active migration and increasing population density lead to a further integration of human society and the continued evolution of humans as they adapt to life under the conditions of globalization.
6. In addition to supplying a growing resource base, human rationality and the pursuit of knowledge have come to play an augmented role in the evolutionary process. Scientific thought, considered by Vernadsky to be the most powerful of geological forces, is capable of solving the problems arising in the course of globalization. It is important, though, that environmental measures, international conventions, and agreements be based on reliable results of scientific research.
7. Globalization is a natural stage in the development of human society, which has fundamentally changed the course of many natural processes in an effort to transform its environment in its own interests. Anthropogenic globalization has a significant impact on all aspects of natural ecosystem functioning and on human society itself. It is evident, too, that globalization represents an important new stage in biospheric development, in which the anthropogenic factor serves as the main accelerator of evolution.

Global Digital Society and the Problems of Social Adaptation

Aza D. Ioseliani

1 Introduction

One of the outstanding characteristics of development in modern civilization is the digitalization of being: that is, the conversion of being into the language of numbers and the accelerated and widespread development of advanced technologies, including remote technologies. We cannot forget that global civilizational changes can cause dangerous challenges and contradictions. At the heart of these contradictions in the societal interaction of the global technogenic world and nature is the discrepancy between practical human needs and the ecological capacities of the biosphere. It is important, then, that we address the question of priorities with regard to social development: namely, the question of the unconditional escalation of needs that ultimately casts doubt on the conservation of conditions for human existence, and of optimal self-restraint that could enable progress while maintaining the fragile balance within the anthropo-socio-techno-natural complex.

The most significant features of the global digital society are constituted by the following phenomena: the development of infrastructure that makes the internet more accessible, and the data transfer speeds higher; the improvement of information systems; and the growth of human involvement in these systems. Digitalization affects all spheres of life: the economic sphere, industry, business, education, healthcare, and social life in general. Information society is characterized by the heightened role of information and by the growing technicalization and informatization of society, including the use of the telephone, radio, television, the internet, and the media, both traditional and electronic. These technological processes, which have permeated all areas of life, have changed the way we communicate and organize our work, and the way we are educated and spend our leisure time. The main vector of further human development should incorporate a principle of social and natural correspondence, according to which human activity is determined by the environmental imperative, environmental education, and environmental safety.

In these circumstances, a new phenomenon has emerged in modern society, and was soon embraced as necessary for the humankind. What I have in mind is the remote banking service called "innovative banking," whose features are about to be discussed. The banking sector, as well as other spheres of global society, is undergoing development alongside the latest scientific and technological breakthroughs.

2 The Priorities of the Ecological Imperative and Ecological Humanism

As of the close of the twentieth century, humanism was understood via the concepts of "non-violence," "dialogue," and "education." The new civilizational consciousness, as a new form of ecological consciousness and humanism, has effected changes in the pivotal conceptual core of humanism, in which the point of intensity is not no longer man, but the living environment. The indeterminacy and fragility of our civilization's existence can be explained by the collision of the natural and the artificial in the human environment. Nature has been dismantled and disintegrated by the sciences and technology: technology has become an integral living environment, within which a person lives, feels, thinks, and gains experience. New technological structures must become a specialized organ of that whole living organism, not some alien "splinter" within it. Yet, the implementation of such an approach to technical human activity calls for a new worldview, a new paradigm—and for a soberly humane attitude towards nature as a complex organism, an attitude that would not invite imbalances between consumption and the restoration of nature, nor violate the basic functional ties within it.

The problem of this new humanism is genetically related to environmental safety. Ecological humanism and environmental safety can be viewed in relation to interdependence and determination. Modern versions of humanism appear to be associated with ecology, with the formation of ecological thinking. Ecology entered the European consciousness at the end of the nineteenth century, but only by the end of the twentieth century did it become clear that ecology, and safe ecology, had become a form of the civilization's self-determination. The ecological approach constitutes a new type of monistic thinking, whose essence is that an object of research should be taken in its wholeness, as a hierarchically organized system in all its main manifestations. Moreover, thinking itself can be understood as a product of phylo- and ontogenesis, and as a natural biosocial development.

In the context of civilizational development, it is important to identify the significance and interdependences of the development of industrial and humanitarian intelligences, while maintaining the law of technohumanitarian balance: the higher the potential of production technologies, the more perfect the means of influencing nature, and the less aggressive the struggle for the survival of mankind. As Akop Nazaretyan rightly notes,

> a planetary civilization that has mastered unparalleled technological potential will be able to avoid self-destruction at the next abrupt turn of evolution only if, this time, people do succeed in improving their system of basic values, norms, and mechanisms of self-organization, in accordance with the new historic requirements.[1]

Such an opportunity is attributed to the widespread use of electronic networks that "free human contacts from spatial dependencies."

This new attitude, leading to new paradigms, is distinctive in several ways. First, the attitude towards nature has changed, nature no longer being understood as an inexhaustible storehouse set up for the satisfaction of human needs. Second, the attitude towards the person is also shifting: the essence of morality is under revision, and the question is no longer how morality should proceed, but how it can meet the specific needs of our time. Third, humanity as a whole is globalizing, the value and interdependence of individual countries and regions is increasing, and the ideals of the priority of universal human values and non-violence are becoming the basis of politics. Fourth, the opposition between subject and object has disappeared. Finally, let us emphasize that the basis for a new understanding of humanism, and of the new ecological paradigm, should be based on the three principles enunciated by Aurelio Peccei, the founder of the Club of Rome: global sensibility, love of justice, and intolerance of violence.[2]

3   The Features and Possibilities of Internet Banking

Experts call remote banking services "electronic banking," and the terms "internet banking" and "innovative banking" have also emerged. These concepts reflect the features, essence, and nature of the modern banking sector. Here, we can see the distinct dependence of the banking sector on the level of development of high technologies and technical innovations, enabling cus-

---

1   Akop P. Nazaretyan, "Синергетика в гуманитарном знании: предварительные итоги," ["Synergetics in Humanistic Scholarship: Preliminary Results"] *Obshchestvennye nauki i sovremennost*, 1997, No. 2, 96.
2   See: Aurelio Peccei, *Human Quality* (New York: Pergamon, 1977).

tomers to carry out transactions online.[3] The fundamental principle of remote banking is the remote exchange of information between the bank and the client, enabling the execution of transactions. Ensuring a high level of security and confidentiality in communication is of particular importance in this context.[4] In the modern technogenic world, the main forms of remote banking services are online banking via mobile communications, the internet, and the special self-service devices (i.e., terminals and ATMs).

The client has vast opportunities for such operations, such as remote access to accounts, transfers, payments, deposit management, as well as the opportunity to receive information about exchange rates or the location of the nearest ATMs, etc.[5] To use the amenities of remote banking, the client must have access to mobile and internet communications, as well as a technical device with appropriate software and further specialized software provided by the bank.

4 The Advantages and Disadvantages of Internet Banking

Many studies conducted by analytical companies indicate a rapid increase in the number of online transactions, which are becoming a dominant trend in modern society. In addition, today's online banking is transforming from a popular add-on into an integral component of retail banks and people's lives. The range of functions and the increasing ease of use have led to a rise in customer interest. One of the purposes of internet banking is to improve the quality of customer service. Innovative banking is characterized by many advantages, including efficiency, time savings, the possibility of tracking ongoing procedures and payments made in any city or country of the world,

---

3 L. P. Kirichenko and O. A. Bulavenko, "Система интернет-банкинга в России" ["The System of Internet Banking in Russia"], *Fundamentalnye issledovaniya*, 2013, No. 11 (Part 5), 991–95; Dmitry A. Trifonov and S. V. Korshunova, "Современные проблемы банковского корпоративного кредитования в России", *Ekonomika i biznes*, 2016, No. 12, 48–52.

4 See: L. A. Taymasov, E. M. Mikhailova, and N. A. Podkina, eds., *Феномен глобализации и проблемы социокультурного многообразия в современном мире* [*The Phenomenon of Globalization and the Problems of Socio-Cultural Diversity in the Contemporary World*] (Cheboksary: ChKI RUK, 2017).

5 I. Eryomin, "Исламский банкинг: экономика и духовность" ["Islamic Banking: Economics and Spirituality"], in *Актуальные вопросы экономики и управления в условиях модернизации* [*Current Questions of Economics and Management in the Conditions of Modernization*], edited by V. D. Golichev (Smolensk: Financial University, 2018), 156–60.

round-the-clock control of personal accounts, and many other options. Modern internet banking is also convenient for clients, since it eliminates the need to carry cash.

Internet banking is likewise very attractive to cyber criminals. Therefore, the modern system of internet banking services should provide for reliable protection of clients' financial assets. Like any other complex social phenomenon, internet banking has both advantages and negative sides engendering certain risks. The disadvantages of remote banking include, for example, insufficient protective mechanisms of the client base and of their funds from cyber fraud, a lack of competent guidance on using the internet banking system, psychological difficulties that cause fear and distrust among customers, problems in using digital signatures, etc.

5 The Socio-Philosophical Foundations of the Transformation of Public Life

In the modern technogenic world, the problems that determine the qualitative change of human beings and their everyday lives have deep socio-philosophical roots. Humanity is globalizing, while the importance and interdependence of individual regions and countries are increasing. The basis of socio-political development is the priority of universal human values, and violence is being rejected.[6]

In a social environment, people communicate, experience feelings, think, and acquire a selfhood. In this process, the mode of human existence emerges, and undergoes a complex and significant transformation. The boundaries of reality begins to blur, since human existence has passed onto the plane of socio-communicative spaces, supported by various technologies and technical equipment. In modern life, people are inseparable from technology, and are merging with technology right before our eyes.[7] Today, people actively use technology in the study of reality. This technology proffers enormous opportunities, but it enslaves us at the same time. It is no longer interesting to observe the natural world; we prefer to be riveted to the screen and immersed in the social networks. Communication utilizing computer technology has led to the

---

[6] See: Alexander Chumakov, *Глобальный мир: столкновение интересов* [*The Global World: A Collision of Interests*] (Moscow: Prospect, 2019).

[7] Aza Ioseliani, "Искусственный интеллект vs. человеческий разум" ["Artificial vs. Human Intelligence"], *Manuscript*, 2019, No. 4, 102–106.

emergence of a large number of communities that exist exclusively in the virtual world. A complex process of modernization of the entirety of social life is taking place, requiring appropriate adaptation mechanisms. Modernization is not limited to economic and political changes, and does not end with them, either. The internal content of the process of modernization is the change in the individual's value priorities. The new society emerging as part of the transformation is both capitalist and informational. In different states, this new society comes in an abundance of characteristic variations, according to the specifics of national institutions, national culture, and history, and in accordance with the level of development of information technologies.

One current definition of human beings is *Homo faber*—a creature that makes tools to facilitate its work and life. Technology is the means of achieving the greatest result with the minimal application of power. In this way, the problems of our era are connected with the fact that the *ends* (i.e., goals) of life are often displaced by its *means*. These means can dominate to such an extent that the ends eventually come to be erased from human consciousness. When life has no technical goal, its goals will be found in other spheres, such as the spheres of spirituality, art, and culture.

The new picture of the modern global society presented by scholars and futurologists is gradually acquiring certain features. First of all, it is the formation of a single computer-based and informational community of people who live in dwellings equipped with electronic and other "intelligent" devices. Second, it is the development of new industries that are formed via the use of information technologies and knowledge-intensive industries. Third, the cultural content of social development is changing: family priorities are changing, virtual museums are emerging, and forms of interaction between people at different levels are changing. Finally, the organization of people's daily life is based on the use of innovative principles and means of production (e.g., electronic money, internet banking, mobile banking, and WAP banking via the phone network, SMS, and other channels). These changes, having a complex impact on all of society as a whole, lead to significant transformations in the individual's productive and spiritual life.

Technological innovations and the wide availability of information serve to increase the adaptive properties of individuals and the volume of their knowledge, but the strength of a person's nature decreases due to the "rationalization" of working conditions and the creation of a more comfortable living environment. This was anticipated by Nikolai Berdyaev, who wrote of technology as "the culprit of terrible failures in intellectual life, and above all in the life of emotion and human feeling." In modern civilization, he wrote, human thought and feeling are extinguished, and the human heart struggles to withstand the cold metallic touch of its environment.[8] The widespread use of computers provides access to information, relieves people from routine work, accelerates the adoption of optimal decisions, and automates the processing of information. As a result, the driving force behind the development of society is production of not material but information product. As for the material product, it becomes more "information-intensive," and largely depends on the volume of innovations applied to its structure. Human activities are focused mainly on information processing, while production of energy and material products is assigned to machines.

In philosophical teachings, a person is a complex being with a broad set of multidimensional universal qualities. In the process of the formation of informational objects by an individual, the individual has a need to comprehend the phenomenon of his original transformation of nature, giving rise to many questions, including existential ones, the answers to which constitute the essence of the problems of modern philosophy. Historically, the path of human existence can be characterized by the interrelationships of humanity, tools, and technology. Over the centuries, the collection and systematization of information concerning a person's surroundings helped our species survive in difficult circumstances: the ability to make tools and hunting equipment was passed down from generation to generation, and the traditions of producing clothes, food, and medicinal products were preserved. New information was constantly assimilated—each analyzed phenomenon providing an opportunity to switch to something new with an increasingly complex structure. With the passage of time, the abundance of information about the world around us began to contribute to scientific and technological progress. Society was constantly progressing: people learned to manage various types of energy and matter. Today, it is information that has become a powerful tool of influence, shaping everything around us, including individuals and the society at large.

As a historical result of human practical activity, the modern world has become an informational and technological space. Crucially, it was the human presence that technologized nature, so that today we exist in a space conditioned by technical means. On the one hand, humanity realizes itself on the basis of the laws of nature; on the other, it does so on the basis of the laws of technology. Under these conditions, one of the decisive factors in the formation of a technically conditioned environment, and in human existence itself, is the transfer of information data, to the effect that information as a product

---

8 Nikolai Berdyaev, Философия творчества, культуры и искусства [*Philosophy of Creativity, Culture, and Art*], edited by R. A. Galtseva, vol. 1 (Moscow: Iskusstvo, 1994), 500–501.

becomes more and more important in people's lives. It becomes then necessary to investigate not only the natural laws, but also the values and concepts of a society transformed by universal informatization. In this context, some negative consequences of the computer revolution need to be pointed out. These include, for example, the fact that the importance of writing as it had been previously known wanes, compared to the flows of information over the internet and other channels.

The emergence of new forms of communication and the transformation of social values take place so rapidly that many experts see the computer revolution as nothing less than a cultural crisis. Whereas, in the past, cultural adaptation to innovative phenomena tended to unfold over time (since rapid transmission, assimilation, and dissemination of large amounts of information was technically impossible), at present, we see a dramatic increase in the pace of adopting the benefits of world culture. Its growth turned out to be so rapid that many theorists became concerned with the resultant problems of human psychology in its capacity to adapt to such volumes of information, and with the degree of change in the mass consciousness.

The cultural genesis of the twenty-first century cannot be imagined without personal gadgets, computers, information technology, the internet and the television. These presences affect the human perception of the world, and not always positively. The temporal speed of our social lives is significantly accelerated by them, and the human psyche is absorbed into an ever-tightening framework. Appliances and applications are becoming more sophisticated; software is becoming smarter. In view of the fact that society is becoming more and more informatized, the importance of authoritarian tendencies is increasing, too. Computer networks provide tremendous opportunities both for the manipulation of mass consciousness and for obtaining detailed information about each individual member of society. It has become possible to imagine a situation in which the elites know everything about everything, while the rest remain in the dark.

Trends in the development of the informational sphere indicate a potential for change in society and politics. For instance, such political power as can be obtained by a majority, due to the concentration of information data, will reduce the importance of elections and the influence of real power. The ruling circles formed in this way may turn into an infocracy, with the dominant role assigned to information. This is a source of power that has no authority over people. Its only potential is the application of information data. This is exemplified by the struggle for the media among the oligarchs, who strive to acquire television channels, newspapers, and radio stations. The super-rich see this as a guarantee of their political power, which is based on their possession of large quantities of information data—which permits them to manipulate information, and thereby mass consciousness.

Due to the fact that electronic systems permeate all spheres of human existence, we need new ways of organizing human relationships. In order to work with advanced technologies, you need a high level of preparedness, spiritual maturity, and personal integrity. When harmony is sacrificed for the sake of technology, and when technology develops faster than the society's moral attitudes, various aspects of existence come to be dehumanized. Moreover, computers are responsible not solely for alienated production, but also for alienated communication (since, instead of our interlocutor, what we see is the computer screen). A new virtual reality based on computerization is taking on distinct forms. This is an artificially created pseudo-environment for communication. From the moment of its inception, computer technology entered modern life, gradually replacing the theater, books, and finally friends, and reducing the intensity of traditional communication. Computers form a reality that can be taken more seriously if compared to the world outside of its bounds. This environment is distinguished by its powerful influence on the human psyche (an influence that cannot be predicted), as, for instance, in the case of gaming, when imitations of human activity have real people fully immersed in a virtual existence.

Whereas anthropogenic civilization is based on the postulate that the human being is of paramount value, both in human society and its individual subsystems, information society dictates new rules in this regard. First among these is the requirement for readiness to change one's activities, to maintain a high level of mobility, and to retrain and master new professions. In the past, the importance of these skills was not obvious. It appears that the future will bring further negative consequences of technicalization and robotization, which will actively shape people and society. So far, humanity remains responsible for the decisions that concern the transformation of its environment. The infosphere, nevertheless, alters this state of affairs.[9]

Intelligent systems do not just store information data, but also exploit it for the purpose of making decisions and answering existing questions. They cooperate with other systems and receive information from them. Even today, the decisions concerning machines are often made by non-human agents, primarily because people do not understand their basic principles. The deeper the introduction of technologies that can be used to carry out complex computational processes, the higher the risk that people will not be able to understand

---

9   Aza Ioseliani, "Формирование инфосферы: социально-философский ракурс" ["The Formation of Infosphere: A Socio-Philosophical Perspective"], *Manuscript*, 2016, No. 3–1, 65.

the essence of machine decisions, nor the logical framework on which these decisions are based. We cannot expect computers to give us adequate explanations for all their actions. This is one of the most significant challenges facing artificial-intelligence professionals. If unsolved, this problem presents a real risk of disasters, accidents, and chaos.[10] It is, therefore, imperative to find ways of effective control over such "intelligent assistants."

It is possible that, in the future, machines will become so reliable that the need for human intervention will disappear. Yet, there is also the danger of devaluating human labor, and of losing the ability to respond to external changes or to make management decisions in cases of serious failure.[11]

Another problem associated with intellectualization concerns the educational level of society's members (since the requirements for their qualification and competence will rise). The demand for unskilled labor is bound to drop, yet it is important to answer the question: does everyone have the abilities needed to use high technologies? People lacking this ability may well find themselves unemployed. As a result, they will rely on the society for support. Further, some experts believe that the massive integration of information systems may lead to the emergence of varieties of parasitism.

It is not yet clear whether these suppositions should be taken seriously, but they cannot be ruled out. The drive to computerize human existence cannot be stopped. But will humanity become overly dependent on soulless machines? Are we destined to be enslaved by our computers? What will be the physical, psychological, and social impact of rapid computerization on humanity? How can we shelter ourselves from being overwhelmed by torrents of information? And can modern advertising be considered a kind of violence against human consciousness?

Some experts have already argued that the process of computerization has a negative impact on individuals and society. It has been proposed, for instance, that computers have a negative effect on the human psyche and creative abilities, causing serious psycho-physical disturbances, and eroding both creativity and vitality.[12] Other scholars believe that these concerns have a right

---

10 Aza Ioseliani, "Man as a Subject of Internet Communication" in *Ubiquitous Computing and the Internet of Things: Prerequisites for the Development of ICT* (New York: Springer, 2018), 449–53.

11 Alexander Chumakov, "Особенности образования в области глобалистики: актуальные проблемы" ["Specifics of an Education in Globalistics: Current Problems"], *Vek globalizatsii*, 2019, No. 3, 38–48.

12 W. Volpert, "Macht die Arbeit am Computer Stumpf?" *Bild der Wissenschaft*, 1984, No. 11, 21–37.

to be articulated, but the problems themselves can be solved. For example, Klaus Haefner has advanced the idea of a humanely computerized society, and of humane and carefully designed relationship between people and computers.[13]

At the end of the twentieth century, humanity entered a new stage of information development. Humanity has not yet witnessed the full extent of the formation of high-tech information society, of the information economy, and of mass personal computerization. Future development should be based on the preservation of the treasures afforded to the humanity by the long process of evolution. This does not entail an abandonment of scientific research and innovation, only a necessity of a new approach.

6   Conclusions

First, the conceptual core of civilizational consciousness has changed in the present era. Second, ecology posits itself as a new form of humanism. The point of intensity in this new humanism is no longer the human being, but its living environment. Third, the uncertainty of the existence of civilization proceeds from the collision of the natural and the artificial in the human environment. Fourth, the strategy for environmental safety should determine the priorities of environmental policy. It should lead towards the establishment of clear principles, means, and methods for ensuring environmental safety and sustainable development, through investigating all the determinants of environmental development that might contribute to a new environmental outlook.

The transformation and digitalization of public life and the introduction of remote technologies do not amount solely to economic and political change. Intelligent systems can influence or radically change the everyday social life. This gives rise to questions: What kind of influence is this going to be? How well is it going to protect human beings? Technical civilization dictates its values and priorities. Deep and ambiguous changes are occurring in all spheres of life, including interpersonal communication. The most significant changes are, nevertheless, taking place in the value orientation of the individual, this process being at the core of modernization.

One of the main priorities of the information society should be the formation of a new social space, with new types of communication determining the

---

13   Klaus Haefner, *Mensch und Computer im Jahre 2000* (Birkhäuser: Boston, 1984), 396.

values of awareness, competence, competition, and profit. The new society emerges within the framework of such transformations, in accordance with the characteristic features of national culture and history that do not negate the importance of digital technologies. In this manner, the collision of the natural and the artificial in the human environment can radically change the priorities of social development and the very conditions of human existence, risking the fragile balance of the anthropogenic and technological spheres, and potentially inviting change to human nature itself.

Globalization Aporia: The Hegemonic "World State" versus Cosmopolitanism to Come

Edward V. Demenchonok

In the biblical story of the tower of Babel, "the whole earth" after the great flood "was of one language, and of one speech." The people said to each other, "let us build us a city and a tower, whose top *may reach* unto heaven; and let us make us a name, lest we be scattered abroad upon the face of the whole earth." Apparently, this was a blasphemous endeavor: "And the Lord said, Behold, the people *is* one, and they have all one language; and this they begin to do"; "let us go down, and there confound their language, that they may not understand one another's speech." Finally, "the Lord scattered them abroad from thence upon the face of all the earth."[1]

This story is especially salient in our age of globalization, and several lessons can be learned from it. First, "after Babel" (that is, after the scattering of languages and peoples), the world's population remained irrevocably diverse, linguistically and in terms of cultural traditions, this becoming a bulwark against the homogenizing tendencies of globalization. Second, this account cautions us against Promethean anthropocentric ambitions of relying on our engineering capabilities whilst disregarding ethical and spiritual values. In our time, this is manifest in the abuses of human reason and in its scientific-technological "progress" (e.g., nuclear weapons, cloning, and the massive destruction of natural resources). Third, it warns us against lust for dominance, epitomized by the military superpowers' attempts to create a homogeneous global empire. This geopolitical ambition of forcible integration of diverse nations into an imperial "world state," and of acquiring an almost god-like power over humanity, is as futile as the building of the tower of Babel, because of the resistance of nations that do not wish to be dominated. But the persuasiveness of this goal escalates confrontation and the nuclear arms race, increasing the risk of pushing humanity toward the precipice of an apocalypse.

The crux of the problem is how to reconcile the socio-cultural diversity of nations on this small planet, each of them having their own interests, with their peaceful coexistence and collaborative unity within the interdependent

---

1 *King James Bible*, Gen. 11:1–9.

globalized world. This requires abandoning self-destructive wars and establishing peaceful coexistence and collaboration as *sine qua non* conditions for mitigating social and global problems and ensuring the survival of humanity.

Two main approaches to globalization and the prospects of humanity can be observed. One is hegemonic and views globalization as the spread of American economic, political, and cultural patterns and the homogenizing "integration" of diverse nations into a hegemon-centric world system, with the United States as the world's "sheriff." The opposite approach is the cosmopolitan project, at the center of which are the humanity and human individuals, the recognition of socio-cultural diversity, and the voluntary collaboration of free nations. Cosmopolitanism represents a positive alternative to both the conflict-ridden state-centric Westphalian system and to the hegemon-centric system; it offers a new type of relationship oriented towards peace, justice, and mutually beneficial collaboration.

In this article, I will review the conceptual opposition of *hegemony* and *cosmopolitanism* in discussions of globalization, for this opposition stands at the forefront of the struggle for the future of humanity. I will start with the emergence of hegemonic geopolitics during the Cold War and its escalation. Then, as a contrast, I will analyze the renaissance of cosmopolitan ideals in the 1990s, as well as challenges posed to it by hegemonic policy in the twenty-first century, before describing the main characteristics of a new cosmopolitanism as being reflexive, rooted, dialogical, critical, democratic, and transformative. Philosophers view it in perspective as "cosmopolitanism to come."

1 Existential Choice for Globalized Humanity: To Survive or to Perish Together

Thinkers from many philosophical traditions have expressed grave concern about human lust for war and domination. In the western philosophical tradition, during modernity, the theme of war and peace was addressed by Erasmus of Rotterdam, Thomas Hobbes, Charles Irénée Castel Saint-Pierre, and Jean-Jacques Rousseau, and was more completely developed by Immanuel Kant in "Toward Perpetual Peace" (1775). To the violent "state of nature," Kant opposed a law-governed social organization based on reason: a society of free citizens with a republican constitution, lawful relations between states that enter into a peaceful federation, and cosmopolitan right.

Kant abandoned his earlier advocacy of a "world republic," modeled after a state, for fear that the hegemony of a powerful state would be like a despotic "universal monarchy" and would therefore pose a danger to human freedom, and also for fear that in a "world state" each person's rights would be limited to those of citizens of a state, and thus there would be no cosmopolitan rights of world citizenship. He therefore proposed a peaceful "federation of free states" (*foedus pacificum*). Kant addressed the traditional problems of international law that stem from the dualism of its normative orientations: its primary objective of preserving peace and its concern for human rights. (This dualism is still reflected in the UN Charter. On the one hand, international law has a primary orientation towards the preservation of peace through prohibiting violation of the individual states' sovereignty. On the other hand, it is concerned with human rights and, in the event of their violation, with their enforcement via a mandate from the UN Security Council—a provision that limits state sovereignty.) As a solution to this dualism, Kant proposed a basic shift from international to cosmopolitan order. He affirmed the idea of cosmopolitan right that would transform the political and international right into "a universal right of humanity": "Cosmopolitan right shall be limited to conditions of universal *hospitality*." Kant also stressed that "it is not a question of philanthropy but of *right*." He grounds this *ius cosmopoliticum* in the principle of universal hospitality. He hopes that the expansion of hospitality as the "use of the right to the earth's surface which belongs to the human race in common" would "finally bring the human race ever closer to a cosmopolitan constitution."[2]

Nevertheless, it was neither the voice of reason, nor the citizens' votes in constitutional democracies that determined the policies of war and peace, but the capitalist lust for profit and imperial expansionism. The clash of empires over the repartition of the world led to the First World War, which signaled the advent of globalized warfare. The aftermath of the war and the establishment of the League of Nations in 1920 was the first concrete attempt to implement the Kantian project of a peaceful federation of free states. And yet, opportunistic attachment to self-interested power politics and expansionism eventually resulted in the Second World War.

The solution to this globalization of warfare required a global approach, and the formation of the United Nations in 1945 was the second attempt to establish a peaceful federation of free states. The United Nations, as stated in its Charter, aims to maintain international peace and security, to develop friendly relations among nations based on respect for the principles of equal rights and self-determination of peoples and nations, to achieve international

---

2 Immanuel Kant, "Toward Perpetual Peace," in *Immanuel Kant, Practical Philosophy*, ed. and trans. Mary J. Gregor (New York: Cambridge University Press, 1996), 327–29.

cooperation in solving international problems, to promote respect for human rights and fundamental freedoms for all, and to be a locus for harmonizing the actions of various nations in the attainment of these common ends.[3]

The United Nations was founded on the principle of collective security. Force can only be used in self-defense, and only when authorized by the Security Council. The goal of promoting and encouraging respect for human rights represents the United Nations' cosmopolitan aspect and was formalized in the Universal Declaration of Human Rights (1948). The morality of individual rights, crystallized in international law, thus became an alternative to politically organized violence.

At that crucial moment, world politics was derailed towards a new war, the so-called Cold War. In reality, it began with the atomic bombing of Hiroshima and Nagasaki, on August 6 and 9, 1945. Most researchers agree that there was no justification for dropping the bomb on Hiroshima, three months after Germany's capitulation, when Japan itself was on the verge of surrender. They argue that Truman's decision to drop an atomic bomb was motivated by the geopolitical interests of an emerging superpower—one in possession of a powerful weapon that could be used as a political instrument—and that its use was a demonstration of force to the Soviet Union and to the rest of the world.[4] This links the super-weapon to the superpower, to the Cold War, and to hegemonic geopolitics. The United States created the NATO military-political alliance in 1949; in response, the Soviet Union formed the Warsaw Pact in 1955.

Some scholars consider the Cold War as the beginning of full-fledged globalization, but also, in its most negative form, as the confrontation of two political blocs. Missiles capable of aiming nuclear warheads at any target on Earth and of destroying human civilization made globalized warfare a global problem.

In the twentieth century, the invention of atomic weapons and their potential use for hegemonic geopolitics created a new existential situation. Now as never before, we live under the threat of humankind's total annihilation. Jean-Paul Sartre pointed out that human history is made by human beings, and thus no one will be around to close the dead eyes of the human race.[5] Albert Camus, John Dewey, and Bertrand Russell all realized the existential threat posed by

---

3 "United Nations Charter," United Nations, https://www.un.org/en/about-us/un-charter/full-text.
4 Gar Alperovitz, *Atomic Diplomacy: Hiroshima and Potsdam; The Use of the Atomic Bomb and the American Confrontation with Soviet Power*, rev. ed. (New York: Penguin, 1985), 290. See also: Tsuyoshi Hasegawa, *Racing the Enemy: Stalin, Truman, and Japan's Surrender in the Pacific War* (Cambridge: Harvard University Press, 2005).
5 Jean-Paul Sartre, *Vérité et Existence* (Paris: Gallimard, 1989), 132.

the atomic weapon. The Russell–Einstein Manifesto of July 9, 1955, stated: "We have to learn to think in a new way." This meant considering human life and the survival of humankind to be the supreme unconditional values. "We appeal as human beings to human beings: Remember your humanity, and forget the rest."[6]

The "extinction" thesis (also termed "nuclear winter," "second death," or "omnicide") was broadly discussed in numerous publications during the 1970s and 1980s, by John Somerville, Carl Sagan, Jonathan Schell, Douglas Lackey, Gregory Kavka, Steven Lee, Russell Hardin, William C. Gay, and Andrei D. Sakharov, among others.

Diplomatic overtures led to a period of détente. The Soviet Union took the initiative by proposing a program of "new political thinking": recognizing the priority of universal human values over all others (ideological, class, national, and state); abandoning the idea of the irreconcilable split of the modern world into two opposite socio-political systems; and recognizing the world as singular and interdependent, with sovereign equality, peaceful coexistence, and constructive mutual cooperation.

The rise of global consciousness, which sprung up new movements for peace and democratization, and encouraged prudence in political leaders, brought an end to the Cold War. But the task was a much broader one, to remove the root cause of wars in a nuclear age. The peace movements were underpinned by an understanding of the necessity of a pluralistic world order, with peaceful, collaborative relationships among the nations. The escalating global problems of the ecological crisis and economic underdevelopment likewise require such relationships as a condition of their possible solution, and even of their mitigation.

The end of the Cold War was a turning point. That historic crossroads presented opportunities for a positive transformation of society and international relations, and for removing the causes of war and injustice and creating the conditions for lasting peace. Many hoped that "they shall beat their swords into plowshares" and that humanity would at last embrace its opportunities for peaceful international cooperation. Since the early 1990s, numerous philosophers and political scientists, including Karl-Otto Apel, Jürgen Habermas, Seyla Benhabib, James Bohman Daniele Archibugi, Ulrich Beck, Richard Falk, David Held, and Mary Kaldor expressed innovative ideas of democratiz-

---

6 "Statement: The Russell-Einstein Manifesto," July 9, 1955, Pugwash Conferences on Science and World Affairs, *pugwash.org*, https://pugwash.org/1955/07/09/statement-manifesto/.

THE HEGEMONIC "WORLD STATE" VERSUS COSMOPOLITANISM TO COME   241

ing the relationships among nations in a multi-centric world, and the possibility of cosmopolitan democracy.[7]

2   The Dystopia of the Hegemon-Centric Unipolar World

Unfortunately, the political forces interested in the preservation of the status quo and the vested interests of power, and the neoconservative "revolution," shifted world politics toward the extreme right, militarism, and world hegemony. This was in diametric opposition to the prospects of lasting peace once envisioned by Kant.

It takes two to tango. The Russians, for their part, voluntarily agreed to peace, by taking the moral imperative of the survival of humankind and the aversion of the nuclear arms race at face value. They dissolved the Warsaw Pact and drastically reduced their arsenal. They also agreed to dissolve the Soviet Union and allowed the former Soviet Republics to become independent states. In 1993, the Russian Federation adopted a new democratic constitution. Regrettably, these peaceful gestures were not reciprocated by the United States, which preferred to become the sole military superpower. The United States declared its military preponderance, expanded NATO towards the Russian borders, withdrew from arms-control treaties, and modernized its nuclear arsenal.

Part of the ideological justification for this political shift was the revisionist interpretation of the end of the Cold War. One neoconservative ideologue, Francis Fukuyama, declared the "end of history." Russia had its difficulties with economic and political reforms, but in military terms it had not been defeated; instead, it had voluntarily entered into an agreement with the United States to establish a relationship of peaceful coexistence and collaboration and to avert a global nuclear catastrophe. The United States' interpretation of the mutually-agreed peaceful end of the Cold War as a "victory" over its former rival was a disingenuous breach of its promises and written agreements.

It is from this perspective that Keith Gessen draws a contrast between the Russians' "new political thinking"—entailing a new world, defined not by hostility but by shared humanity—and the power politics of the western leaders' "realism." West German Chancellor Helmut Kohl, Gessen writes,

---

7   Daniele Archibugi and David Held, eds., *Cosmopolitan Democracy: An Agenda for a New World Order* (Cambridge: Polity Press, 1995).

had assured Gorbachev that the reunification of Germany would be a gradual process, and he also suggested that Germany might stay out of NATO. But reunification took place almost overnight, with full NATO membership attached. Likewise, James Baker, Bush's Secretary of State, unquestionably indicated to Gorbachev that NATO would not expand eastward, a promise that the United States soon reneged on. "To hell with that," Bush said. "We prevailed. They didn't."[8]

The initially promising process of nuclear disarmament was thus stolen and reversed. But it was a Pyrrhic victory over international law and its underpinning moral principles, the aspirations of humanity, trust, and peace. These actions by the West were a prelude to a new Cold War. With this historical memory and loss of trust (and given the current state of world affairs), it is unlikely that the second Cold War will have a peaceful, happy ending.

In the globalized world, security can be achieved through the collective security of sovereign nations, as laid out in the UN Charter. The United States broke the agreements secured to end the Cold War, and took, instead of the moral high ground, the low road of pursuing an illusory dream to achieve security unilaterally, through military preponderance.

To make matters even worse, the arms-control regime was further undermined by the US withdrawal from prior agreements, such George W. Bush's decision to pull the United States out of the Anti-Ballistic Missile Treaty that banned weapons designed to counter ballistic nuclear missiles. The development of the Ballistic Missile Defense System would make it possible for the United States to launch a first strike while hoping to shield itself from a retaliatory response. Donald Trump withdrew from the 1987 Intermediate-Range Nuclear Forces (INF) Treaty and from the Open Sky agreement with Russia, and created the new Space Force. In Trump's first National Security Strategy, unveiled on December 18, 2017, a "layered missile defense system" was mentioned, and "the revisionist powers of China and Russia" were named as "challengers," "rivals," and "adversaries."[9] This, quite obviously, violated the strategic balance and was viewed by both Russia and China as a threat to their national

---

8   Keith Gessen, "The New Thinking: Mikhail Gorbachev Set out to Transform the Soviet Union from Within. What Happened?" *The Nation*, November 13, 2017, https://www.thenation.com/article/archive/mikhail-gorbachevs-new-thinking/.
9   "National Security Strategy of the United States of America," Trump White House, December 2017, https://trumpwhitehouse.archives.gov/wp-content/uploads/2017/12/NSS-Final-12-18-2017-0905.pdf.

security. In response to the US deployment of a strategic missile defense system, Russia developed hypersonic missiles immune to any current system of missile defense.

Neither "Star Wars" nor the Ballistic Missile Defense System can shield America from retaliation. Instead, they increased the risk that the United States might become the target of a retaliatory strike. This triggered a new arms race, as China is now also boosting its strategic potential. Moreover, technical mistakes in the highly complex automated systems can trigger an unintended launch of nuclear missiles. All this increases the already high risk of a nuclear catastrophe for the world.

The following question arises: Why did the United States, the most powerful player both militarily and economically after the Cold War, start a new Cold War and a new arms race? This cannot be explained by security concerns alone. The answer is in the strategic goal of global hegemony. Not many nations would agree to be the vassals of an empire, and either the threat or the actual use of military force is the one means of coercing them into subjection, and of pressuring or destroying those who will not be dominated. The United States' aspiration to become a global empire, or to create a *con-dominium* with its allies, and with this to achieve absolute security and dominance, is a dangerous illusion. What is likely to happen in reality is that attempts to pursue this goal will destroy the world's stability and plunge it into a nuclear holocaust.

The hegemonic superpower is trying to dismantle legal and institutional foundations serving as bulwarks against the domination of powerful states over those less powerful. International law and institutions are thus subject to hegemonic "capture," and have become mere tools for the superpower. There is also the tendency towards a "hegemonic international law," which establishes patron-client relationships in which loyal clients seek the hegemon's security or economic support.[10] The real alternative to the hegemon-centric order is not for power to change hands but a world to be set free from *any* hegemonic domination.

Despite the United States' failure in its role as the self-proclaimed "world leader," it did not abandon its hegemonic ambitions, changing instead only its rhetoric—from attracting other nations with the benefits of a paternalistic "benevolent hegemony" to the necessity of hegemonic rule, even by force, as the only alternative to anarchy. President Trump proclaimed the principle of

---

10   Detlev F. Vagts, "Hegemonic International Law," *American Journal of International Law*, 2001 (95), 843–48.

"America First"—meaning, among other things, that America's national egoism is above the interests of humankind.

Hegemonic ambitions and militarism are a very dangerous combination. As Richard Falk writes, "the prospect of moving toward global democracy, unless, perhaps, in the altered atmosphere of a post-catastrophe global setting, seems currently inconceivable."[11] However, in a nuclear age, a catastrophe may leave nothing to change—because the end of civilization will already have occurred. Does this mean that the only choice left is what type of catastrophe will ensue?

3   The New Cosmopolitanism

Globalization in its homogenizing and hegemonic form has many negative consequences, and its continuation threatens the future of humankind. In search of alternatives, philosophers and political theorists turn to cosmopolitanism. Going beyond the moral ideal, they have developed the cosmopolitan *project* as an alternative to both the state-centered international system and the hegemon-centered "world state." New cosmopolitanism is change in theory, but it has a broader meaning as a new type of relationship. It is also a new view of globalization: not americanization and hegemon-centrism but "globalization with a human face," the globalization of lawful and peaceful international relations and of cosmopolitan values as a transition towards a cosmopolitan order.

Since the 1990s, cosmopolitanism has become one of the key concepts in social science. In taking into account the theoretical criticism of traditional cosmopolitanism and the challenges of hegemonic globalization, the new cosmopolitanism has evolved significantly, and its distinctive characteristics include being (1) reflexive, (2) rooted, (3) dialogic, (4) critical, (5) democratic, and (6) transformative. This innovative evolution is important in response, on the one hand, to relativism, nationalism, and ethno-cultural compartmentalization, and, on the other, to homogenizing globalization, which uses universalistic terms to justify its policy of forcible integration.

(1) The *reflexive* dimension of cosmopolitanism refers to its self-reflection on its philosophical and methodological assumptions and its own conditions of possibility. "Reflexive cosmopolitanism is a universality plus difference that

---

11   Richard Falk, "The Promise and Perils of Global Democracy," in *Global Democracy: Normative and Empirical Perspectives*, edited by Daniele Archibugi, Mathias Koenig-Archibugi, and Raffaele Marchetti (Cambridge: Cambridge University Press, 2012), 282.

reflects on its own conditioned claims. It is thus ... diversality plus reflexivity of historical contingency."[12] To the "imperial cosmopolitanism," these philosophers oppose critical and dialogic cosmopolitanism.

(2) New cosmopolitanism is *rooted*, or embedded, in a specific history, nation, or people, bridging the global and the local. Cosmopolitanism examines its material basis and its rootedness in social institutions and sociopolitical systems. It is supposed to reflect on the point of view of the "Other," to emerge from those at the bottom of the socio-economic pyramid who most suffer the negative consequences of hegemonic globalization.

(3) The *dialogic* dimension of cosmopolitanism articulates cultural diversity harmonized through dialogical relationships within the bounds of cosmopolitan unity. In the world "after Babel," it envisions unifying relationships among people with different cultural or religious backgrounds through dialogical communication and interaction on the common ground of tolerance and mutual interests. It embraces a recognition of and the normativity of dialogical relationships with the "Other," with individuals, social groups, nations, cultures, and religions engaging in dialogue. It values dialogism as a normative principle for its own theorizing and as the best method for conducting sociopolitical relationships, both domestic and international. In contrast to the monologic image of the hegemon-centered order and pseudo-universalistic ethnocentrism, cosmopolitan theorists elaborate on the concept of contextual and "concrete universality." This is "the universalism of the other," which can be a participant of a worldwide "polilogue."[13]

(4) The *critical* dimension of cosmopolitanism plays an important role in critiques of the status quo and of hegemonic globalization. Ulrich Beck has called this approach "methodological cosmopolitanism."[14] Gerard Delanty asserts that "the idea of a critical cosmopolitanism is relevant to the renewal of critical theory in its traditional concern with the critique of social reality and the search for immanent transcendence, a concept that lies at the core of critical theory."[15]

(5) The *democratic* dimension of cosmopolitanism asserts democratic principles and values within society and in international relations. A number of

---

12   Eduardo Mendieta, "From Imperial to Dialogical Cosmopolitanism?" *Ethics & Global Politics*, 2009 (2), No. 3, 252.
13   Walter D. Mignolo, "The Many Faces of Cosmo-Polis: Border Thinking and Critical Cosmopolitanism," in *Cosmopolitanism*, ed. Carol Appadurai Breckenridge (Durham, NC: Duke University Press, 2002), 173, 179.
14   Ulrich Beck, *The Cosmopolitan Vision*, trans. Ciaran Cronin (Cambridge: Polity, 2006), 17.
15   Gerard Delanty, *The Cosmopolitan Imagination: The Renewal of Critical Social Theory* (Cambridge: Cambridge University Press, 2009), 2.

philosophers and political scientists have contributed to the theory of democratic cosmopolitanism.[16] This opposes the authoritarianism of global hegemony, which Kant called "world monarchy."

(6) The crucial characteristic of new cosmopolitanism is its *transformative* orientation—an ideal that is guiding political practices towards the transformation of the social world, with which, importantly, it attempts to connect. Cosmopolitanism as a political philosophy is oriented towards an ideal of a possible future world order as an alternative to both the existing conflicted state-based international system and hegemonic domination. It could become the regulative principle for understanding the interaction between universalistic, national, and cosmopolitan principles in contemporary society. It also emphasizes that there are processes within culture and the public consciousness, and political movements around the world that manifest cosmopolitan views and practices of social transformation representing alternatives to neoliberal hegemonism. World disclosure is one of the central mechanisms of cosmopolitan transformation, which occurs on both macro- and micro- scales.

4   Cosmopolitanism to Come

Unipolar militarized hegemonism, clashing with resistance and with those who struggle for a polycentric world, came to the forefront in our twenty-first century. The anti-hegemonic agenda, however, should not overshadow the long-range vision of the post-hegemonic world order and of the possible cosmopolitan future. Moreover, the articulation of a pluriversal and dialogical cosmopolitanism as a viable alternative provides us with a vision of the path towards the post-hegemonic world order of international collaboration. It also helps in the twofold struggle "against" imperial domination and, positively, "for" a cosmopolitan world order of freedom, justice, and peace.

The struggle between the two main tendencies of globalization—hegemonic totalization versus cosmopolitan peace—will shape the configuration of the world and perhaps the very future of humanity. Within this general context, discussions about the themes of political theory—such as democracy, law, human rights, statehood, sovereignty, international relations, etc.—obtain new meanings and require further rethinking. Two interrelated issues are hotly debated: human rights and state sovereignty.

---

16   Daniele Archibugi, Mathias Koenig-Archibugi, and Raffaele Marchetti, eds., *Global Democracy: Normative and Empirical Perspectives* (Cambridge: Cambridge University Press, 2012).

The United States appeals to universal notions of "human rights" and "democracy," claiming epistemological privilege in interpreting and implementing them. But an obvious tension has arisen between the superpower's self-proclaimed commitment to promoting universally accepted values (e.g., human rights) and its self-interested politics. The human-rights discourse has attained a new function—that of the justification of sanctions and "humanitarian" military invasions. "Human rights," newly redefined in the pursuit of regime change, paradoxically became one of the main factors in the crisis of international law. The abuse of noble humanistic ideas for the ignoble purpose of domination discredits these ideas themselves.

In contrast, theorists of new cosmopolitanism are rethinking the issues of human rights and sovereignty. Discourse ethics seeks to promote a discursive and dialogical approach to human rights, as shown in the works of Karl-Otto Apel, Jürgen Habermas, and, more recently, Rainer Forst, Seyla Benhabib, and James Bohman. Some theorists develop a "political conception" of human rights, that is, special rights that individuals possess in virtue of the specific associative relations in which they stand, and that are conceived as international norms aimed at securing the opportunity for individuals to be included and to participate as members of a political society.[17]

Globalization has led to more transparent borders and cultural-economic interaction among the states, to the increased importance of human rights law, and to the emergence of an "international community." These phenomena are, nevertheless, interpreted differently in the conceptual dispute between hegemonist ideologues and cosmopolitan theorists. The former interpret this as evidence of "the end" of both history and sovereign territorial states. This ideology justifies the *divide et impera* policy of the global hegemon, interested in weakening sovereign states and controlling them as vassals. The "democratic peace" theories claim that sovereignty and the sovereign state are anachronisms and the last resort of autocratic regimes avoiding accountability for human rights violations, and that non-liberal states have no real sovereignty and "do not acquire the right to be free from foreign intervention."[18]

In contrast, cosmopolitan theorists perceive the objective need and possible conditions for structural changes in society and international relations, oriented towards cosmopolitan ideals of global justice and peace, in some

---

17 Kenneth Baynes, "Toward a Political Conception of Human Rights," *Philosophy & Social Criticism*, 2009 (35), No. 4, 371–90.
18 Michael W. Doyle, "Kant, Liberal Legacies, and Foreign Affairs," in *Debating the Democratic Peace*, edited by Michael E. Brown, Sean M. Lynn-Jones, and Steven Miller (Cambridge: MIT Press, 1996), 31–32.

grass-roots cross-cultural and international processes of "glocalization" and in the desire of all good-willed people to live in peace. These theorists are critical of the simplistic, dichotomous, and naive evolutionary thinking of those who believe that globalization has already led to the end of sovereign territorial states and to their substitution by an idealized "world government" (as exemplified by the proponents of "liberal internationalism").[19]

The theorists of the new cosmopolitanism are critical of both extremes: on the one hand, the ideas of a statist international legal order, which prioritize state sovereignty and underestimate human rights, and on the other, the so-called "anti-statist" or "liberal cosmopolitanism" as opposed to political and legal institutions and sovereign equality.[20]

It may at first sound paradoxical that cosmopolitans are defending state sovereignty, international law, and the United Nations. But after the neoliberal corporate robber barons and the neoconservative "revolution" had paved the way to neo-totalitarian tendencies and to militarized ethnocentric hegemonism, cosmopolitans are among those who warn about the danger of perpetuating the status quo, and who try to think beyond the existing institutional structures and political-ideological dogmas. They prioritize the interests of individuals and of the humanity as a whole, beyond the narrow self-interests of particular states, in our globally interrelated world, in which nations can survive or perish—together. They conceptualize the new cosmopolitanism as a political *project* while remaining faithful to its ideals, which are viewed in perspective, and show imaginative realism. This responds to current political realities and to the threats to liberties, democratic principles, and the lawful international order coming from neo-totalitarianism and militarized hegemonism. Counter-hegemonic struggles for restoring the genuine meaning of universal humanistic ideas like freedom, human rights, and democracy, and for achieving true democracy domestically and in international relations, is the starting point of their agenda. The next step in a post-hegemonic environment would be to create favorable conditions for the maturation of genuinely democratic and dialogical relationships, wherein the states would be interested in voluntarily delegating some of their sovereign prerogatives to a supranational body accountable to them. This would open a path to "cosmopolitan

---

19   Anne-Marie Slaughter, *A New World Order* (Princeton: Princeton University Press, 2004), 12. See also: John Ikenberry, *A World Safe for Democracy: Liberal Internationalism and the Crisis of Global Order* (New Haven: Yale University Press, 2020), 12.
20   Allen Buchanan and Robert O. Keohane, "The Preventive Use of Force: A Cosmopolitan Institutional Proposal," *Ethics and International Affairs*, March 2004 (18), No. 1, 20.

democracy" and to a gradual transition from an international to a cosmopolitan order.

The anti-statists assume, prematurely, that nation-states are already withering and being replaced by universalistic supra-national structures. But their critics point out that the changes brought by globalization do not amount to the end of sovereign territorial states. According to Jean Cohen,

> If we assume that a constitutional cosmopolitan legal order already exists which has or should replace international law and its core principles of sovereign equality, territorial integrity, non-intervention, and domestic jurisdiction with "global (cosmopolitan) right" we risk becoming apologists for neoimperial projects.[21]

Instead, in the current situation, international law and institutions should be defended from erosion and their full-functioning role in the international system according to the UN Charter restored. Cohen argues that sovereign equality and human rights are two interrelated legal principles of the dualistic international system, and that both are needed in order to make it more just.

Philosophers view cosmopolitanism in perspective. They refer to the "cosmopolitanism to come" as the yet unrealized but realizable future potential of transformation—of democratic political arrangements within sovereign states and in international relations, in conformity with international law, gradually evolving from an international to a cosmopolitan order. Seyla Benhabib, for example, reflects upon political transformations and makes a case for a "cosmopolitanism without illusions." In contrast to some premature declarations of an age of cosmopolitanism, she argues that we are currently living "in an age of cosmopolitization," in anticipation of its realization:

> The interlocking of democratic iteration struggles within a global civil society and the creation of solidarities beyond borders, including a universal right of hospitality that recognizes the other as a potential co-citizen, anticipate another cosmopolitanism—a cosmopolitanism to come.[22]

---

21 Jean L. Cohen, *Globalization and Sovereignty: Rethinking Legality, Legitimacy and Constitutionalism* (New York: Cambridge University Press, 2012), 27.

22 Seyla Benhabib et al., *Another Cosmopolitanism* (New York: Oxford University Press, 2006), 177.

An original approach to the problems of democracy, cosmopolitanism, and world citizenship was offered by Jacques Derrida. He generally favors the cosmopolitan ideal. However, in order to cultivate the spirit of cosmopolitan tradition,

> we must also try to adjust the limits of this tradition to our own time by questioning the ways in which they have been defined and determined by the ontotheological, philosophical, and religious discourses in which this cosmopolitical ideal was formulated.[23]

According to Derrida, we should think beyond nation-states, citizenship, the state-centric international system, and the traditional "cosmopolitical ideal." "Beyond" is his signature word in trying to broaden the horizon of philosophical thinking about a future world order. The anguished question of how to "live together" underpinned his writings on cosmopolitan law and hospitality in relation to the contemporary problem of refugee immigration.

Derrida highlights the image of cities of refuge as a model for the transformation of societies worldwide, as an approximation of a cosmopolitan ideal. He writes:

> I also imagine the experience of cities of refuge as giving rise to a place (*lieu*) for reflection—for reflection on the questions of asylum and hospitality—and for a new order of law and democracy to come to be put to the test (*experimentation*).

He also refers to the Levinasian figure of the door at the threshold of the home, hospitably opened as a manner of relating oneself to the other: "Being on the threshold of these cities, of these new cities that would be something other than "*new* cities," a certain idea of cosmopolitanism, *an other*, has not yet arrived, *perhaps*."[24]

Derrida also suggests broadening the horizon of our views of cosmopolitanism: "Progress of cosmopolitanism, yes. We can celebrate it, as we do any access to citizenship, in this case, to world citizenship." He stresses that beyond the traditional cosmopolitical ideal, we should see "the coming of a universal

---

[23] Jacques Derrida, "Autoimmunity: Real and Symbolic Suicides. A Dialogue with Jacques Derrida," in *Philosophy in a Time of Terror: Dialogues with Jürgen Habermas and Jacques Derrida*, ed. Giovanna Borradori (Chicago: University of Chicago Press, 2003), 85–136.

[24] Jacques Derrida, *On Cosmopolitanism and Forgiveness* (New York: Routledge, 2001), 23.

alliance or solidarity that extends beyond the internationality of nation states and thus beyond citizenship."[25]

Fred Dallmayr, reflecting on an emerging global city or community, views it as the humanity's historical journey toward the "cosmopolis." This journey opposes the attempts to lock peoples within a homogenizing "world state," and the erection of "a global state or super-state—a modern "tower of Babel"—endowed with the power of centralized management and control."[26] Such a global empire would be a dystopic prison.

The viable collaboration and unity of diverse peoples should be based on freedom and equality, voluntary, and mutually beneficial. Dallmayr reminds us that "we need to remember our condition 'after Babel.'" In this situation, cosmopolis "can only mean a shared aspiration nurtured and negotiated among local or national differences." In contrast to chauvinistic ethnocentrism, he argues for "a layered or 'multiple' citizenship where people might be citizens both in a particular city (or cities) *and* in the cosmopolis."[27] Here, he develops the ideas of "cosmopolitan democracy," that is, "a cosmopolis making room for national or local forms of democratic self-government."[28]

Dallmayr's thought strives for an ideal of a domination-free, cross-cultural, dialogical world order of peace and justice. He examines the conditions for progressing in the direction of cosmopolitan order. He points to gross material disparities, domination, and violence as problems to be solved on the way to this goal. Equally important are regaining social ethics, cultivating co-responsibility and shared well-being, and the role of education: "Hence, any move or journey in the direction of cosmopolis today can only occur in the mode of sustained dialogue, the mode of cross-cultural and inter-religious interaction," he writes.

> Going beyond the narrow confines of anthropocentrism, the journey has to make ample room for dialogue and listening, for the humanizing demands of education, ethics, and spiritual insight. Differently put: *homo faber* has to yield pride of place to *homo loquens, homo quaerens,* and *homo symbolicus*.[29]

---

25   Derrida, *On Cosmopolitanism*, 123–24.
26   Fred Dallmayr, "After Babel: Journeying toward Cosmopolis," in *Intercultural Dialogue: In Search for Harmony in Diversity*, ed. Edward Demenchonok (Newcastle upon Tyne: Cambridge Scholars, 2016), 374–75.
27   Dallmayr, "After Babel," 373.
28   Dallmayr, "After Babel," 374.
29   Dallmayr, "After Babel," 366.

In contrast to the prospect of an imperial super-state dominating the world, cosmopolis "after Babel" means a shared aspiration negotiated among local or national differences. Ultimately, Dallmayr argues for harmony in diversity. This conception strengthens the hope for a "cosmopolis to come," governed by the spirit of equality and mutual respect and promising freedom, justice, and peace.

The ongoing discussions of globalization show the philosophers' concern with its negative consequences and with the escalation of global problems. Especially worrisome are the globalization of warfare and militarized hegemony. The new Cold War precludes the collaboration of nations in mitigating global problems like the nuclear arms race, climate change, underdevelopment, and pandemics, all of which threaten the future of humanity. Far from diminishing the gravity of these problems and the shortcomings of the currently dominant social and political theory, philosophers are striving for possible solutions and positive alternatives. They are developing ideas of a new cosmopolitanism as an alternative to both the war-prone, anarchic, state-centered international system and the hegemon-centered "world state." In response to the challenges of hegemonic globalization, the new cosmopolitanism has evolved significantly, developing the distinctive characteristics of being reflexive, rooted, dialogic, critical, democratic, and transformative.

Philosophers view cosmopolitanism as a "cosmopolitanism to come," as the yet-unrealized but realizable future potential for transformation, for evolving from an international to a cosmopolitan order. Nevertheless, such a transformation of societies and of international relations will not occur automatically, and its attainment depends to a large degree on the present and future actions of the social forces interested in and capable of pursuing this goal. But the ideas of this "cosmopolitanism to come" can serve as a guiding and mobilizing force for social and global transformation, for a more peaceful, just, and humane world. This possibility gives us hope.

PART 4

*Russia in the Global World:
Philosophy, History, Geopolitics*

Russia in the Projects of the Coming World Order

Yury D. Granin

Having transcended the epoch of bipolar world order, humanity has entered a period of transformation in the direction of new emergent centers of global dynamics, with a gradual shift towards Asia. This observable change in the geopolitical and geo-economic configuration of the world stimulates Russia's own turn to the East. But what is it that awaits Russia "around the bend"?—and will it not find itself in a "junior" position within the large geopolitical projects it had itself initiated? Should it, together with China, spearhead the tendency, established earlier, towards a unipolar globalization of the world, within whose framework these two countries had reaped considerable economic benefits? After all, many well-known experts consider it the best possible form of humanity's future development.

∴

The position just described is maintained most vigorously and consistently by Vladislav Inozemtsev. Concurring with scholars who believe that there is but one dominant power in today's world—such an "indispensable nation" being the United States, which seeks to maintain its geopolitical status—and two major "revisionist countries," represented by China and Russia, Inozemtsev writes that

> the leadership of both China and Russia must understand that both the Chinese economic growth and Russia's economic revival are caused exclusively by the rising trend of the world economy, initiated by the unipolar globalization encouraged by the United States. It was American demand and American investment that triggered China's so-called "economic miracle" in the 1990s; the development of a new center of industrial production in China then stimulated the demand for resources

and, together with it, the prices that enabled the Russian economic boom in the decade that followed.[1]

Of course. One could even augment this thesis by echoing the Prime Minister of Singapore in stating that "Asia had prospered thanks to the period of *Pax Americana*, which had lasted since the end of the Second World War, ensuring a favorable strategic context."[2] Yet, this observation does not cancel out the periodic variability of human history. The latter had never been a "one-way street"; meanwhile, the poles and centers of global development changed repeatedly over the past millennium, shifting gradually from Asia to Europe. After the Second World War, they moved to the United States—yet who could possibly guarantee that by mid-twenty-first century they will not be, once again, found in Asia? Given the pace of China's and India's development in recent years, no such guarantee could be offered.

Having emerged from the epoch of bipolar organization, humanity has entered a period of the transformation of the former international order, based on the dominant influence of the Euro-Atlantic civilization, which has set the rules of "the big game" ever since the second half of the twentieth century. That game was played according to the rules set by the United States and the "Greater Europe" controlled by the United States. In recent years, though, these rules have begun to change. The power potential of nation-states is now treated as the cornerstone of their foreign policy, whereas the functions of international institutions have receded into the background. According to some influential analysts, "the world is now governed by 'the law of the jungle' of which the Russians had been warning, to cries of outrage."

> In this struggle without rules, we, the Russians—with our history, resourcefulness, ideological openness, and readiness to take risks—have a competitive advantage. We only need part with the folly of following other rules and institutions, which our partners are meanwhile uncere-

---

1 Vladislav Inozemtsev, "Экономика и политика глобализации: уроки прошлого для настоящего и будущего" ["Economics and Politics of Globalization: Lessons of the Past for the Present and the Future"], *Vek Globalizatsii*, 2019, No. 2, 9.
2 Li Xian Lung, "Америка, Китай и угрозы конфронтации" ["America, China and the Threats of Confrontation"], *Rossiya v globalnoy politike*, July—August 2020, https://globalaffairs.ru/articles/aziatskij-vek-v-opasnosti/.

moniously discarding. If what the world is being offered is "the law of the jungle," one should play by "the law of the taiga."³

This is, of course, an emotionally inflected metaphor; but it is true that West-centrism in politics and thought is outdated and can only be seen as "a sign of intellectual laziness and backwardness." This means that in the foreseeable future, our country has far better prospects in the direction of the "Greater Eurasia"—that new conceptual space of

> geopolitical, geo-economic, and geo-ideological thinking that sets the vector of international relations on that continent. The latter must be aimed at the joint economic, political, and cultural revival, the development of dozens of formerly backward or oppressed Eurasian countries, and at Eurasia's transformation into the center of world economy and global politics.⁴

According to the project's authors, apart from Russia and China, it is going to encompass the countries of the East, the Southeast, and the South Asia, where all the participants will be able to negotiate and establish cooperative ties.⁵ This is possible but problematic, due to the likelihood of competition between China and Russia (which I shall yet touch upon). At the same time, the idea's attractiveness stems from its socio-cultural character: in countering the earlier project of the "Greater Europe" (spanning from the Atlantic to Vladivostok), the "Greater Eurasia" is a *macro-regional project of concerted civilizational development, which, according to its initiators, will encompass some of the European countries.* "If we are to speak about the future picture of the world," predicts the well-known Russian political scientist Sergei Karaganov,

> that picture will contain a divided Europe, split into parts: one of them will belong to the "America +" system, which includes the United States, the other—to Eurasia. It is already generally clear where the border will

---

3   Sergei Karaganov, "Каким будет мир?" ["What will become of the world?"], *Rossiyskaya gazeta*, February 14, 2019, No. 34 (7792), https://rg.ru/2019/02/14/karaganov-mir-nesmotria-na-ego-haotichnost-vpolne-predskazuem.html.
4   *К Великому океану: хроника поворота на Восток. Сборник докладов Валдайского клуба* [*Towards the Great Ocean: Chronicle of the Turn to the East. Collected Reports of the Valdai Club*] (Moscow: Foundation for the Development and Support of the Valdai International Discussion Club, 2019), 275.
5   *К Великому океану*, 276–77.

be drawn. The only question is which way Germany might decide to go. I think it is most likely to be Eurasia.[6]

It would be very good if this were the case. Yet, like all large projects, this particular project of the coming world order is marked by an ineliminable methodological difficulty: it is premised on the principle of extrapolation from the "present" to the "future" and on the assumptions of rational behavior by all participants and of the knowability of the entire spectrum of the political subjects' motives—those motives being actually unknowable in full measure. The project thus represents a geopolitical utopia, whose realization is beyond the horizons of certainty: it may or may not come to fruition. For our present purposes, it is going to be assumed that all the participants of such a large-scale "regional game" will set aside the priority of their national interests and opt for a strategy of cooperation, while the game itself will not be zero-sum. Apart from this, there are epistemological difficulties to consider: to use the well-known "chessboard" metaphor, all geopolitical projects resemble a game in which the same player makes alternate moves both for the white (e.g., Russia) and the black (Europe), with the white designated in advance to be the winner, in virtue of the implicit geopolitical preferences.

Nevertheless, the reality inevitably proves richer than any theory or project. More than a year has passed since the publication of the forecasts just quoted, but the western countries' eagerness to integrate into the project of "Greater Eurasia" is yet to be observed. They prefer the zero-sum game and have so far ignored the invariant of this project proposed by Vladimir Putin: the formation of a Greater Eurasian Partnership, which would unite all-continental efforts with the participation of the EAEU, SCO and ASEAN countries, and would be open to EU countries. Indirectly, this has been confirmed by Sergei Lavrov, the head of the Russian Ministry of Foreign Affairs, who spoke at the twenty-eighth SWOP assembly on December 10, 2020. Nor is there any evidence of the Asian countries' eagerness to form a new continental mega-structure jointly with Russia. Politics is a pragmatic thing, and our partners are more interested in the possibility of using Russia as a transit corridor, as a supplier of raw materials, modern weapons, and space services (whose volume is shrinking steadily), and, of course, as a "battering-ram" for inclusion among the non-permanent members of the UN Security Council. In this matter, Russia is ready

---

6 "Сергей Караганов рассказал о роли России в образовании Евразии" ["Sergei Karaganov Spoke of Russia's Role in the Formation of Eurasia"], *Rossiyskaya gazeta*, January 10, 2019, https://rg.ru/2019/10/01/sergej-karaganov-rasskazal-o-roli-rossii-v-obrazovanii-evrazii.html.

to accommodate them, as well as Brazil and the Republic of South Africa, both of which inquired into this possibility at the last BRICS summit. But its foreign policy options are limited, and its economic situation, especially after the imposition of the sanctions, leaves much to be desired. The only thing that truly brings Russia closer to its main partners in Eurasia (i.e, India and China) is their *objective value-and-meaning-driven opposition to the West* as special "civilization-states," compelled to implement policies of compensatory development while protecting their civilizational identity.

This confrontation has intensified after the United States' attempts to dampen the development of new world centers and its declaration of a "Cold War" with China in 2020, which naturally brought it closer to Russia and increased the chances of the realization of another macro-regional project: the creation of the "Russia–India–China" triangle as a tactical diplomatic alliance of three multi-ethnic and multi-confessional civilizations, whose state interests are not guaranteed by the Euro-Atlantic version of globalization. As diplomatic coalitions, alliances have repeatedly confirmed their effectiveness. Although President Vladimir Putin has not ruled out even a military-political alliance with China (under certain conditions), long-term strategic cooperation between the three great powers is unlikely, due to the prevalence of "national egoism." Although China and India do not feature two-headed eagles on their coats-of-arms, they resemble Russia in looking vigilantly eastward and westward, in search of short- and long-term benefits.

The latter are quite easy to discern under the conditions of a stable world order. Yet, in the current, increasingly chaotic global environment, there is little use in looking too far ahead. It is therefore preferable to bet on a tactical partnership. Yet here, too, the coordination of common objectives of the allies' foreign policy is essential, as the latter serves, always and everywhere, as a means of the countries' domestic development. In turn, the successes of their internal development guarantee the attractiveness of their common foreign-policy course to states that have not yet joined it. The most promising course within the constraints of this dialectic of "within" and "without" is to coordinate the interests of parties to a possible alliance, while taking into account the inequalities of the initial conditions and the objective membership of all three states among the "second-world" countries, which compels them to participate in often unfair economic, scientific-technological, military, and other forms of global competition.

Weathering that competition calls for *coordinated strategies of national development*—strategies that involve a refusal to blindly obey the recommendations of the IMF, WTO, and other institutions of international neoliberalism. What is proposed instead is to recognize the priority of national interests and to reform the economy, not solely on the basis of economic and political models borrowed from the West, but mainly based of the country's own socio-cultural and political traditions and resources. One key feature of such national strategies is the *proportion of western and native forms of modernization.* This allows for a whole range of variations: from a very high degree of westernization in several spheres of the state's life, to a very insignificant degree attendant mainly upon the economic sphere—a variant exemplified by Japan and by the "new industrial countries" of Southeast Asia. The long-term results of their development are not as significant as China's, whose success has been particularly impressive. Let us therefore take a closer look at its example.

Let us note, first of all, the factors that bring China and Russia together: the absence of wars between the two countries, their comparable military potentials, the significant state-owned sectors of their respective economies, centralized governance, the presence of a rigid power vertical, multi-ethnicity (with a significant predominance of the "core peoples" of each civilization—the Russians and the Chinese), and the associated cultural heterogeneity. Together with the presence of the so-called "Soviet syndrome" (a complex of memories about the largely idealized past), these features of the Russian and the Chinese respective populations and authorities are responsible for the objective preconditions for their cooperation. In all their other civilizational parameters—religion, the prevalent worldview, attitudes to family and work, the character of social structures, power, etc.—these two countries differ. This circumstance had a significant influence on how the problem of modernization was formulated and addressed in Russia, India, and China in the late twentieth and early twenty-first centuries.

The Chinese leadership, as well as Chinese scholars and scientists, interpreted modern liberal globalization as a historically inevitable but transient centuries-long trend for the humanity's integration into a relatively unified whole, consequently assessing their country's place in this process quite pragmatically—that is, from the perspective of deriving maximal benefits for China while limiting any potential negative effects tied to this process. To this end, from 2001 to 2010, the Center for Modernization Research, the China Modernization Strategies Research Group, and specialists at the Chinese Academy of Sciences prepared ten annual reports on modernization. Each of them analyzed one of the key aspects of modernization, contextualized by its general outlook around the world and in China for the given year.[7]

The reader is struck not only by the scale of systemic work here, but also by the objectivity of the studies, which divide modernization into "primary" and "secondary" types, elaborating "development indices" and analyzing 131 countries accordingly, with the result of China's inclusion among the merely "pre-developed" countries, projected to reach "mid-level development" (characteristic of states like Russia) only by 2040. Given its growth rate, the famous Chinese pragmatism, and China's longstanding, carefully deliberated foreign and domestic policies, these projections may well have to be significantly adjusted.

The Chinese leadership insistently sought admission to the WTO, and yet showed equal tenacity in maintaining its own interests during the discussions of the conditions of China's admission. Some concessions (such as the reduction of tariffs on US high-tech products, etc.) were made but verbally, so as to secure the results of negotiation. On the strategic side, the policy of protectionism persists, especially with regard to agriculture and the new industries. On the other hand, the Chinese have discovered that some WTO measures (such as the anti-dumping laws, increased quality control over imported goods, etc.) can be made an instrument of self-defense.

In 2010, the US National Science Foundation published a detailed statistical survey of global development in science and technology between 1995 and 2009. China was identified as the country with the fastest-growing science, as it already had the same number of researchers as the United States. Since then, the situation has not changed. The Western Europe and the United States continue to see a moderate growth, while in Russia the main indicators of scientific and technological development are declining. As the authors point out, the Chinese leadership recognized the need for deeper integration with the international economy, and sought to manage this process according to its own rules, in order to maximize the profits and minimize the vulnerabilities. As a result of this nationally-oriented stance, foreign direct investment (FDI) flowed into the country with such a force that China now ranks second in FDI, following the United States.

China's secret of success lies in the role of the state in the economy, which is especially important in the current environment, characterized by the instability of financial capital and fluctuations in the world markets. It is telling

---

7 Chuanqi He and N. I. Lapin, eds., *Обзорный доклад о модернизации в мире и Китае (2001–2010)* [*A Survey Report on Modernization in the World and China (2001–2010)*] (Moscow: Ves mir, 2011).

that the Asian crisis of 1997–1998 did not affect China, although the country is economically linked with Southeast Asia: their financial sector was liberalized, while China's wasn't. As a result, the leaders of modernization—the so-called "Asian tigers"—became less attractive as partners for multinational corporations (MNCs), while China became more interesting, due to its being less encumbered in the globalization of finance. Since the global MNCs' goal when entering China was not to "establish democracy" but to make quick profits, they were interested in a stable government that would enable their production to become "even more Chinese," ensuring, in turn, better sales and higher profits. As a result, the Chinese branches of various MNCs are becoming "patriotic" in their strategy, which is something that other semi-peripheral countries can hardly boast of.

China has the further advantage in that a third of the foreign capital that flows into the country is invested by the Chinese who live abroad. In Russia, as we know, the situation is just the opposite: we have been exporting capital abroad, year after year, against the background lack of long-term development strategies. In the 1990s, we blindly followed the International Monetary Fund's recommendations, succumbing to liberal dogmatism, while the success of Chinese reforms is tied to their gradual character, combined with a secure control over the economy. The latest illustration to this is the antitrust investigation of the Alibaba Group, an immense private company that has become a symbol of China's success and prosperity and was preparing one of its divisions for a major IPO in the fall of 2020. This fact, as far as one can tell, has not affected any major foreign MNCs' intentions to continue operating in China.

In addition to attracting global MNCs, China's transnational economic tools include state-owned MNCs and significant capital exports to Africa, Asia, and Europe, all of which have contributed to a sharp increase in China's activity in the international arena.

Another advantage of China's modernization strategy, to which Russia has no analog, is that with the successful development of market economy, market values cannot overwhelm other areas of life, especially the social and cultural spheres. The result is a successful and forward-looking balance that encourages stable development. As An Wei writes, "civil law guarantees the efficiency of the market, and state administrative law guarantees social justice."[8] This, one should add, is not premised on artificially razing social inequalities, but on the ideas of *social process management*.

---

8 An Wei, "Глобализация и право" ["Globalization and the Law"], *Voprosy filosofii*, 2005, No. 2, 169.

On that basis, as early as 2014, China had developed a system of social credit for its citizens, piloting it for the past six years in Shanghai, Fujian, Jiangsu, Guangdong and Shandong provinces. The western media instantly assessed the concept of "social credit" as a practical implementation of Orwell's dystopia—a system of total surveillance—not bothering to distinguish between state and commercial forms of social credit (e.g., Sesame Credit and Tencent Credit). The latter have long been used effectively by commercial entities, especially banks, in many countries: all the lending institutions and many service providers keep their clients' credit histories, including the information from the law enforcement and other government agencies. In China, commercial social lending is based on scoring that factors, among other things, a publicly available "blacklist" of people who have committed offenses and have been rebuked by Chinese justice. Appearing on this registry can drastically lower a user's rating, depriving him or her of a number of privileges—for example, when renting cars and bicycles or booking hotels.

Matters are more complicated with the state-sponsored social credit, planned to be introduced across the country from 2020 onwards (but never in fact implemented). With the high (in contrast to Russia) level of digitalization of the economy and other spheres of life, social credit can indeed be used as a means of total state control over the citizens in multimillion cities—and, to a degree, even in rural areas (where cashless payments for goods have been implemented for several years). It is possible that the Chinese leadership might harbor such plans. But it would not be alone in that case, for any state is "by definition" oriented towards restricting freedom and controlling the population to some degree. In any case, technology as such, including social technology, is ethically neutral: "it is not guns that kill people, but people with guns," and whether a surgeon or a criminal is wielding the scalpel can make all the difference. Either way, the vast majority of the Chinese assess the system of scoring their compatriots via the social networks positively, as a system of social trust aimed at harmonious development and at building socialism with a Chinese profile.

China, as it isn't difficult to see, distances itself from the idea of equality. Still, despite the presence of dissidents and separatists, China's political and social systems are stable, thanks to being grounded in Confucian ethics and in the innate Han notions of hierarchy. Thus, together with the Chinese Communist Party Central Committee's policy of patriotism and national dignity, the idea of social design and governance is reinforced by the country's increasingly apparent success in improving its people's well-being, and is proving to be an important factor in China's successful socio-economic development.

India represents another country capable of creating an alternative model of modernization on its own civilizational basis. Upon independence, the Indian National Congress (INC) government declared a course for accelerated economic growth with minimal foreign aid. Yet, the influence of consumerist attitudes led, in the 1980s, to the forfeiture of import regulation and of restrictions on the activities of the MNCs, and to an influx of foreign capital. As a result, India's level of economic development has changed little in the 1980s and the 1990s.

Nevertheless, the global economic crisis of 1997–1998 did not inflict the same shocks on India as occurred in Southeast Asia and Latin America. This was a consequence of the fact that Indian society did not view its entry into the global economy as equivalent to obligatory "westernization": it was believed, instead, that the country could choose its own development strategy. This tendency continued even with the rise of the nationalist-oriented Bharatiya Janata Party (BJP), which set some ambitious objectives: not only to establish a "Hindu nation" and a new national identity founded in religion, but also to reform the country, transforming it into the third largest world economy. Despite significant disagreements with the Indian National Congress, oriented towards a western, civic version of nationalism, India's key political forces remain in concurrence on the main issues of development and participation in globalization. India's reforms have not changed its orientation toward the protection of its domestic markets. As a result, the position of national capital has continued to strengthen. Reforms have proceeded gradually, without destructive leaps, which distinguished them favorably from reforms in Russia.

It is no accident that in the first decade of the twenty-first century, the Indian economy grew at a rate comparable to China's rate of growth. After reaching China's 9.1% growth rate for a short while in 2009, India has clearly slowed its development since—to 8.8% in 2010, to 7.1% in 2011, and 6.9% in 2012. Not only has India failed to overtake China in this indicator, it has consistently lagged behind it by 1%–2%. It is true, though, that the collapse of global stock markets and the drop in hydrocarbon prices in January 2016, which had a particularly negative impact on China's economy, barely affected India. A study done by Moody's, an international rating agency, had projected that, in 2015–2016, the growth rate of India's economy would constitute about 7%–7.5%, amounting to the highest rate among the G20.[9] This is indeed what

---

9 "Moody's 2015: Индия покажет самый высокий рост экономики среди G20" ["Moody's 2015: India Will Show the Highest Economic Growth among the G20"], http://www.gigamir.net/money/pub2172021 (page no longer available).

has happened. In 2019, India's rate of economic growth was 7.4%. Its economy was slated to catch up with Britain's by 2020, and to become the fifth largest economy in the world with a nominal GDP of $2.9 trillion. China's rate of economic growth in 2019 was but 6.3%, and was expected to decline to 6.1% in 2020.[10] The pandemic, of course, made its adjustments, dampening all the economies around the world—yet, even against this background, China remained the sole zone of economic growth. The documents of the Fifteenth Five-Year Plan, which commences in 2021, emphasize the development of the domestic market (by expanding the middle class with an annual income exceeding $10,000), as well as further development of infrastructure and support for innovation.

Evidently, the emergence of the "Russia–India–China" geopolitical triangle as a partnership zone of three multi-ethnic and multi-religious civilizations, whose state interests are not sufficiently addressed by the Euro-Atlantic version of globalization, is quite real. All three countries stand for the democratization of the international order, for strengthening the role of the United Nations, and against NATO expansion; in the face of Islamic fundamentalism and extremism they have a common adversary. Nevertheless, Russia is not likely to become the leader of this triad (nor of BRICS or the SCO) in the foreseeable future. And here is why.

First, let us note that the US sanctions against China were not merely a whim or an extravagance of Trump's, but a sound calculation aimed at protecting US interests in the domestic and foreign markets. It has been noted that China is entering a phase of neo-industrialization, with the intention of moving away from export economy (which depends heavily on the West) to a new type of economy, focused on the domestic market and on the production of high-value-added goods, the latter to be marketed partly westward, but mostly to territories that have been, for centuries, treated as the "backyard" to Europe and the United States. The latter's exports to and influence in Southeast Asia—and indeed in Europe, where China has been intensively acquiring assets of strategic enterprises in recent years—could be seriously weakened. Yet something different matters yet for Russia.

Given that the Chinese economy exceeds Russia's nearly five-fold; given the low volume of trade between these countries (1.67% of all Chinese trade) and the high level of higher education in China (in the rankings of 200 universities across countries with developing economies, Russia takes but the fourth

---

10 "Рейтинг экономик мира 2019, таблица ВВП стран мира" ["World Economy Rankings 2019, World GDP table"], Basetop, February 3, 2020, https://basetop.ru/rejting-ekonomik-mira-2019-tablitsa-vvp-stran-mira/ (page no longer available).

place, giving way not only to China, but also to India, with thirty-nine and sixteen universities respectively, against Russia's fifteen); given China's immense (over $4 trillion) gold and foreign-exchange reserves, and the indications of the Human Development Index and of Portland Communications' "Soft Power 30" rankings (in which, after dropping by two points since 2017, Russia is now in the twenty-eighth place, just behind China and ahead of Brazil)[11]—we can assume that BRICS is gradually arranging itself around China and will soon become a Chinese project, in which Russia can occupy only the position of a "younger brother," unless it opts to conduct a systematic modernization of the country.

Unlike China, which had developed its modernization strategy ten years ago, Russia still does not have a state strategy of comprehensive modernization. Its Commission on Modernization was created only in 2010, under President Dmitry Medvedev. Even at that time, it was often remarked that modernization as such was interpreted by the government not systematically but spottily, as a miscellany of reforms in different spheres of life—economy, science, education, healthcare, etc.—and primarily in a technological key, as utilization of technologies that had been tested abroad, though originally developed for wholly other purposes. It was clear to many experts and specialists that what we needed was neither the Bologna standard nor the academic reform that began slightly down the road. But, without regard to their opinions, officials bravely embarked upon "optimizing" scholarship and education, while telling the public tall tales: that one would be able take a Russian university diploma to the European Union, because a Russian bachelor's would be the same as a bachelor's from Sorbonne. What happened in the end? In the end, we introduced none of the academic mobility and teaching freedom required under the Bologna Convention. Universities contented themselves with switching from a specialized model to the baccalaureate, increasing the teaching loads, and lowering the quality of education. Meanwhile, the academic reform, in the shape of "merging the academies" and tied to the introduction of new metrics (the Hirsch index, publications in journals indexed by SCOPUS, WOS, etc.)—the reform that only the lazy did not criticize—resulted only in the manifold increase in reporting to the ministries in charge of research and education, and in the reduction of funding for academic institutions.

The very same happened in the secondary schools. Whereas the Chinese investment in science and education increased by around 20% annually in

---

11   Olga G. Leonova, "Динамика рейтинга "мягкой силы" России" ["Dynamics of Russia's 'Soft Power' Rating"], *Vek Globalizatsii*, 2020, No. 2, 104–18.

recent years, allowing them to equal the United States in the number of researchers (about 1.5 million people), Russia, on the other hand, presented a negative trend: in 1995, it had about 600,000 scientists; now, there remain just over 400,000. In the same period, the number of researchers in China grew by about 9% per year; in 2018, the number of Chinese invention patents was 4.9 times greater than the number of US patents in the same year. In addition, according to some calculations, China outperforms the Russian Federation in research and development funding by a factor of forty-eight; others, perhaps more realistically, make this a factor of ten. This was reported by Alexander Sergeyev, President of the Russian Academy of Sciences, on December 23, 2019. "The country's development strategy suggests that, by 2035, China should become the world leader in most scientific and research areas," the academician added.[12]

Of course, quantitative assessment alone would not be sufficient. It is much more important to understand the basic reasons for what is happening. When discussing them, opposition politicians usually cite the authoritarianism of the political regime and the "absence of democracy." But democracy has never been a significant factor in technical and economic progress, or in the well-being of societies. Rather, the contrary. History shows that authoritarian forms of governance can foster development just as well as stagnation. Of course, no one is immune to error and to hasty decisions—but it is necessary to be able to give them up at the right time. This ability is hampered by the uneven "quality" of our ruling elites and of their attending apparatus: some of them have the capacity for critical reflection and a broad acumen based on the understanding of history's complex dialectics; others think stereotypically, spellbound by theoretical clichés grounded in the paradigm of linear (and westward) progress, and will not listen to expert opinions. Hence the heterogeneity and methodological pluralism of Russian politics. The country's domestic policy is still influenced by the long-out-of-date western theoretical standards for socio-economic and political development, while its foreign and security policy is more balanced, realistic, and varied. It is built, in my opinion, on the theoretical basis of modern social constructivism, which interprets human history not as a space in which impersonal "forces" or "systems" exert their power, but as a *process of joint, socially organized activity of people who*

---

12 Anatoly Kubarev, "Китай вкладывает в научное место в 10 раз больше денег, чем РФ" ["China Invests in the Scientific Location 10 Times More Money than the Russian Federation"], *Politika Segodnia*, December 23, 2019, https://polit.info/481103-kitai-vkladyvaet-v-nauchnoe-mesto-v-desyat-raz-bolshe-deneg-chem-rf.

design their Being not solely from "positive" positions, but also from a normative perspective. This is the philosophical basis of the "Greater Eurasia" project and what makes it a realizable geopolitical utopia. But this megaproject, in my opinion, can (and should) be complemented by the project of civilizational evolution of Russia.

As noted earlier, the "Greater Eurasia" is a macro-regional project of a space of different civilizations' joint development. According to its designers, it is going to include some of the European countries. But it is not enough to propose it. It is necessary to cultivate an attractive image of a common future by demonstrating the successes of one's own *civilizational model* and *long-term development strategy*. Russia has no such model and no such strategy as of yet; what it does have is a host of problems. Many of them are conditioned by our country's civilizational specificity that has grown out of the "Soviet civilization." The fate of this civilization, whose influence spread far beyond the USSR's former borders, with its pan-idea of global superiority and with its meta-ideology of building communism, is well known, and modern Russia inherits after it without a doubt. Yet, not only does it have no political and religious meta-ideology to unite its people, it also has no claims to global dominance, such as the claims of the United States. Instead, as in the early twentieth century, it represents a pseudo-morphosis—a kind of civilizational centaur, combining, in whimsical, sometimes grotesque ways, the elements of archaism, the Soviet past, and western "modernity."[13]

It would seem that China, too, has the same characteristics—yet their civilizational core of values and meanings is not eclectic, but holistic. It has a closed contour, circumscribed by the Confucian religious-philosophical worldview going back to the ideas of the Tao ("the way"), with the key idea of correspondence of the "heavenly" and the "earthly" as an ordered unity, and with an attendant "rationalism." Based not on substantive but on procedural logic determined by the specificity of the language, this Confucian rationalism arises not from a basic contradiction between transcendental and secular currents characteristic of Europe (as delineated by Shmuel N. Eisenstadt), but from an idea of their *harmonious correspondence*.[14] Hence the specifically Chinese *strategy of life as evolution*, presupposing a pursuit of the paths of least resistance, of compromises, and of indirection as a fundamental principle

---

13 Yury D. Granin, "'Цивилизация' и цивилизационная эволюция России" ["'Civilization' and Russia's Civilizational Evolution"], *Voprosy filosofii*, 2020, No. 12, 34–44.
14 Andrei V. Smirnov and Vladimir K. Solondaev, *Процессуальная логика* [*Procedural logic*] (Moscow: Sadra, 2019).

of political activity and diplomacy.[15] This strategy is tied to the ideas of the Chinese people as a "great family" (which likens Chinese attitudes to those in Northern Europe) and of the state as a "celestial empire"—not accidentally proclaimed, after 1949, as the "flourishing country of universal harmony among people." This is why China's socialist period is seen by the elites and by the majority of the population as a continuation of the "great way," and its one-party system as a historical form of the social order's inherent hierarchism.

These views, in their totality, supply the basis of the Han national identity, long since established upon the foundations of cultural (as opposed to civil and political) unity. Meanwhile, we continue to indulge republican ethno-nationalists (who have repeatedly launched the idea of a "Russian nation"), while relying solely upon civic nationalism, without paying due attention to fostering Russia's socio-cultural unity or to actively designing its future.

Within the horizon of such planning are the proposals of the Russian Center for Strategic Research (run by Alexei Kudrin) to abandon the "comprehensive program of modernization," accentuating instead the creation of *new institutions* of development—the so-called "transitional institutions," designed to ensure the transformation of the "natural state" into a state of "open access" to political and economic resources.[16] This plan is based on the theoretical constructs of Douglas North and his colleagues.[17] Theoretically, it could be implemented, provided there were support for it in the Kremlin. It appears to have such support. Yet, the principal difficulty in implementing the reforms entailed by such a project is that power is not concentrated in a single point, or in any one subject, be it the president, his administration, the prime minister, or the government with its apparatus; it is instead dispersed through the entirety of Russian space, with its "subjects" and "municipalities," encompassing the powers and authorities of the multiplicity of elites. It is these elites that must put the "transitional institutions," and the new "system of rules" for reforming the country, into practice. That system's cornerstone is the principle of the "depersonalization of the activities of organizations and institutions." This is just what the president and the government are doing now, in introducing all manner of electronic "government services," in order to limit the

---

15 François Jullien, *Detour and Access: Strategies of Meaning in China and Greece* (Cambridge, MA: MIT Press, 2004).
16 Alexander A. Auzan, Marina A. Avdiyenkova, et al., Социокультурные факторы инновационного развития и имплементации реформ [*Socio-Cultural Factors in Innovation Development and the Implementation of Reforms*] (Moscow: CRC, 2017).
17 Douglas North et al., *Violence and Social Orders: A Conceptual Framework for Interpreting Recorded Human History* (Cambridge: Cambridge University Press, 2013).

collection of bureaucratic rents. But will these measures suffice to transform the "natural" Russian state and society into an "open-access" state and society? Of course not. And the authors of this initiative are well aware of this, relying on a *system of sanctions and compensations* to various groups, in seeking to neutralize their resistance to the new rules.

Will this work? It is hard to tell. It appears that, as before, we must hope for the enlightenment of the ruling elites, as a consequence of which they might voluntarily curtail their egoism and appetites in the name of the country. The history of tsarist Russia knew its "enlightened bureaucrats," "enlightened landowners," and altruistic capitalists. But they did not make weather, due to a variety of concrete historical circumstances. A different set of circumstances, or a different combination of circumstances, could have placed Russia among the states with "open access" to political and economic resources. Time and historic luck both ran short for Russia, as they do now. Many of the political, economic, and other "elites" and the upper echelons of power see this problem. But they rarely realize its geopolitical aspect: in the conditions of aggravated confrontation with the West and inevitable struggle (with the West, but not only with it) for the resources concentrated on our own territory, the problem of modernizing the country flares into a problem of preserving it as an independent sovereign state.

This is why, apart from establishing the new principles and institutions of social and public administration—which presuppose technological development, decent life for citizens, and investments in human capital—major cultural and ideological work is needed, in order to bring to date the meaning-and-value scaffolding of Russian society. Currently, it is oriented towards the past: there, among its past great victories, Russia now seeks (and, moreover, *finds*) the justifications of its current position, its "sovereign democracy," and its other "civilizational specificities." But that gilded carriage of the past will not take the country very far. What is needed is a futuristic, ideologically articulated breakthrough into the future that can mobilize the population towards the realization of a social utopia, towards the building of a social state of a new type: a state of national prosperity, solidarity, justice, and genuine humanism. Such a state does not exist anywhere—but this does not mean that we should not aspire towards it.

Ways for Evolving Russia's Current Civilizational Choice in the Context of Globalization

Igor K. Liseyev

1   Historical Background

The young Russian state that emerged at the turn of the twenty-first century is in the process of clarifying and shaping the basis of its own civilizational choice. As in the past, Russia remains one of the largest countries in the world, in terms of both area and population. It is a multinational, social, secular state, in which representatives of different secular and confessional views coexist inconsistently. This state is united by strong social and cultural traditions and by a shared legacy. At the same time, Russia is comprehensively engaged in contemporary worldwide processes led by globalization. This raises the question: how can Russia's civilizational choice combine this country's historic traditions with the currently dominant, technology-driven trends of the globalizing world? When discussing and considering this matter, it is important to refer to the historical memory of the Russians themselves, to their knowledge and understanding of the ideas and aspirations of their ancestors. Often, the past considerations of scholars who were ahead of their own time become, once again, acutely relevant, and can in fact contribute to the emergence of new approaches in the search for modern civilizational ideas.

The ideas of our outstanding predecessor, Pyotr Kropotkin, are a case in point. Kropotkin (1842–1921) is known as a revolutionary, a well-rounded scholar—geographer, geomorphologist, biologist, historian, and philosopher—and a publicist. He is, nevertheless, best known as a scholar who created his own version of the evolutionary theory. It is his approach that made it possible to offer a new civilizational perspective on the world, on the history of its development, and on the formation of the principles of human activity. Contrary to the Darwinian interpretation of the struggle for existence as competition, in which the strongest and the fittest survive, Kropotkin proposed the idea of mutual aid and cooperation as the main driver and engine of evolutionary progress.[1] Kropotkin's work relied on extensive historical mater-

---

1   See: Pyotr A. Kropotkin, *Взаимная помощь среди животных и людей как фактор эволюции и двигатель прогресса* [*Cooperation Among Animals and Humans as an Evolutionary Factor and an Engine of Progress*] (St. Petersburg: Znaniye, 1907).

ial concerning wildlife and human society, and supplied convincing facts and evidence that demonstrated the superiority of cooperation-based approaches and highlighted the important role of mutual aid in evolutionary development, in contrast with the individualistic competition of "all against all."

From today's perspective, it is quite clear that competition and cooperation represent the two necessary drivers of evolutionary development, and that both offer insights into the evolutionary progress. It is impossible to overestimate Kropotkin's contribution, as he was among the first to draw attention to the phenomenon of cooperation as an evolutionary driver. It is important to consider the complicated, non-linear interactions of these factors when developing ways and directions of modern state-building, and when searching for the prerequisites that shape contemporary Russia's civilizational choice.

An equally important contribution to the development of a new understanding of evolution can be found in the work of another outstanding Russian thinker, Vladimir Vernadsky (1863–1945).[2] Vernadsky, as well as his predecessor Kropotkin, was a scholar of encyclopedic breadth. His scope of interests covered a wide variety of natural sciences and humanities: biogeochemistry, biospherology, crystallography, geology, soil science, radiology, history of science, Russian history, philosophy, etc. It was this breadth of interests that contributed to his views based in the broad synthesis and deep integration of scientific knowledge from diverse fields. "Vernadskian thought"—an intellectual style that crosses disciplinary boundaries—has become one of the most salient trends shaping modern civilizational ideas. In order to analyze and understand the powerful globalization processes taking place in the world, we need an equally powerful model of integrated thinking, based on a holistic view of the world's diversity.

Proceeding from just such a view, Vernadsky was among the first thinkers to demonstrate the profound unity of society and nature, and to substantiate the thesis of the need for their holistic integrated study, in all the richness of their interrelations. In his works, he traced the evolution of our planet as a unified geological, biogenic, and anthropogenic process. Going even further, he showed these factors' connections with the cosmic processes. In this manner, he discovered and substantiated the fact of the co-evolution of interrelated, interdependent, and mutually necessary concurrent lines of development. We find this process of interconnected co-evolution of the Earth, nature, society, humanity, and the cosmos in his doctrine of "noospherogenesis."

---

2 See: Vladimir Vernadsky, *Философские мысли натуралиста* [*Philosophical Thoughts of a Naturalist*] (Moscow: Nauka, 1988).

The idea of the *noosphere* suggests a deep and limitless civilization potential, engendered by human scientific thought and leading to the synthesis of scientific and philosophical concepts. This concept is yet to be fully developed, and its potential is to open up a new world landscape, a new understanding of the possibilities of human activity in the world, and, in turn, a new technology, as well as environmentally-grounded regulative principles, and the unification of nature and culture under a modern civilizational approach.

The methodological regulator of evolutionism was undoubtedly one of the leading imperatives of the twentieth century and has transitioned seamlessly into the current century. The outstanding contributions of scholars like Kropotkin and Vernadsky aid in a new understanding of evolutionism. And yet, we find ourselves in a historical moment when these contributions are in urgent need of interpretation from the perspective of the present and of engaging these ideas in the representations of Russia's contemporary civilizational choice.

The organizational regulator, which brought innovative achievements to its era, was another extremely important methodological regulative principle of the twentieth century. In this field, too, Russia has an outstanding representative, Alexander Bogdanov (1873–1928)—the creator of the first consistent universal organizational science, which he himself called *tectology*. The first volume of his three-volume *The Universal Science of Organization (Tectology)* was published in St. Petersburg in 1913, and the second came out in 1917 in Moscow.[3] This new science was based on the understanding that the laws of organization were the same for all organized objects, regardless of the substrates they consist of. Following this general premise, Bogdanov developed the conception uniting the disparate and establishing a common organizational method, whose applications included all the real and theoretical varieties of selection. Regrettably, both objective and subjective circumstances conspired in keeping Bogdanov's ideas obscure, even though many of his considerations (albeit under different names) were developed by cybernetics, systems theory, synergetics, pedagogical theory, and social development theory.

In particular, the first volume of Bogdanov's *Tectology* offered a clue to the antithesis of the centralism and individualism that had previously appeared unresolvable. Bogdanov considered all possible types and forms of organization and singled out two dominant ones: centralistic and polycentric. Having

---

3 See: Alexander Bogdanov, *Всеобщая организационная наука (Тектология)* [*The Universal Science of Organization (Tectology)*] (St. Petersburg: M. I. Semyonov, 1913).

shown their widespread distribution both in nature and in society, he highlighted each one's advantages and disadvantages. The advantages of centralistic organization are the possibilities of rapid mobilization of all the elements in the system, of setting common goals, and of effective control over the system's capabilities. Its disadvantage is the lack of independence in the development of its parts. The advantages of polycentrism are the high independence of the parts and their freedom of self-development. Its disadvantages include a lack of coordination among the coexisting centers and the impossibility of setting common goals and objectives.

Having analyzed these forms of organization, Bogdanov wondered if there could be an organizational type that had the advantages of both organizational principles without any of their disadvantages. As it turned out, this was the so-called "skeletal" type of organization, discovered by Bogdanov both in nature and in society. In this type, the center integrates free and independent systemic elements, and is, as a center, quite different from its analog in the centralist type of organization. The center of a skeletal organization integrates independent structures without suppressing their autonomy or imposing its will, integrating them within the bounds of authority granted by these independent structures. This is the rationale for the formation of a new civilizational structure of society, an idea now widely discussed and applied as a new principle of statecraft and interstate organization.

An investigation into Russia's contemporary civilizational choice is, above all, determined by an analysis of the current stage of world development, taking into account the globalization tendencies and regularities characteristic of our epoch. At the same time, in the course of its formation, it is necessary to take into account the historical insights gleaned by Russian thinkers who were ahead of their time.

2   Developmental Tendencies

The history of scientific development has revealed the emergence and operation of various regulative principles underpinning the organization of scientific knowledge and the corresponding world landscape. Among them are the regulative principles of integrity, development, and consistency. In the second half of the twentieth century, the organization regulative comes to the forefront. This leads us to the ever-increasing interdependence and interconnection of the economies of different countries of the world, the study of a unified system of global economic relations of the planetary scale, and the geopolitical and confessional manifestations of globalization. In addition, the globalizing world imposes requirements for understanding of the growth and accumulation of scientific knowledge, the emergence of new scientific fields, and the expansion of the traditional understanding of the existing scientific areas.

The most striking example of such a regulative principle is the globalization of the discipline of ecology, which took place literally before the eyes of the current generation. As an integral branch of the biological sciences, ecology is a relatively young field that appeared just over 150 years ago. In 1866, Ernst Haeckel coined the term "ecology" to define the science that studied the comprehensive relations of animals, both in their organic and inorganic environments.[4] Since that time, the purpose of ecology as a science has been to formulate the principles, laws, and regularities of the co-existence of organisms within their habitat. We can say that ecology acts primarily as a science of organization. Danilo J. Markovich defines ecology as a science whose subject is the relation of living beings to their environment, their interrelationships within the environment, and the impact of the environment on living beings.[5] In his foundational monograph, *Fundamentals of Ecology*, Eugene Odum specifies our understanding of ecology by dividing it into autecology and synecology.

Autecology studies individual organisms or individual species. Here, the focus is placed on life-cycles and behavior as ways of adapting to the environment. Synecology studies groups of organisms that make up certain unities.[6] Further research led to an understanding of ecology as a biological science featuring a three-part structure. Our understanding of autecology and synecology was improved, in turn, by the understanding of ecology as bio-geo-cenology, which acted as the study of ecosystems: biocenoses and geocenoses in their unity and relationships.[7]

Thus, bio-ecology became its own discipline and method of analysis; it established a nomenclature and began to successfully develop its field of wildlife research. But, from the very first steps of this scientific branch's development, it was clear that bioecology was no ordinary natural science, but a synthetic science, which cannot exist without uniting natural science and

---

4 See: Erich Haackel, Generelle Morphologie der Organismen (Berlin: Reimer, 1866).
5 Danilo J. Markovich, Социальная экология [*Social Ecology*] (Moscow.: Prosvescheniye, 1991), 6.
6 See: Eugene P. Odum and Gary W. Barrett, *Fundamentals of Ecology* (Philadelphia: Saunders, 2006).
7 See: Nikolay F. Reimers, Концептуальная экология [*Conceptual Ecology*] (Moscow: Rossiya Molodaya, 1992).

the humanities. This is because the objects of its study are closely related both to patterns of wildlife development and to the social patterns of anthropogenic pressure exerted by economic agents. It has become increasingly clear that the subject of ecology must be expanded to include patterns of interaction between nature and society. American sociologists from the Chicago School of Sociology (Ernest Burgess, Robert Park, and others) were among the first to speak of this kind of expansion, in the second decade of the twentieth century. This was accounted for by the need to understand the impact of the anthropogenic urbanized human environment on human life and society.

In the Soviet Union, Eduard Girusov was a consistent supporter of the idea of social ecology. From his point of view, the subject of social ecology is, in fact, the study of society's interaction with the global natural environment, in all the diversity of its anthropogenic transformations. Social ecology thus developed as a theory of optimizing this interaction and preventing the destruction of the biosphere, which would be dangerous for society. One of the main tasks of social ecology is the development of natural resource management standards of what is maximally permissible for the biosphere, including questions concerning emissions of pollutants and outgoing heat, as well as the proportion of resources withdrawn from nature.[8]

Social ecology studies the impact of human production activities on the composition and properties of the environment. Here, the environment includes both natural and social components: cities, factories, and the entire infrastructure of economic activity. One of the most important tasks of ecology is the discovery of patterns and laws of industrial society and its development, and the way they affect the natural and social environment.

Reflecting on the question of identifying the interrelations of nature and society, another Russian proponent of social ecology, Victor Kobylyansky, thought that the relationships between nature and society contributed to the formation of a new, special field of knowledge, whose main task should be to create a detailed theoretical landscape of the interaction between nature and society, and to use this landscape as the basis for developing scientifically sound recommendations for optimizing this interaction.[9] In his works devoted

---

8   See: Eduard V. Girusov, "Экология социальная" ["Social Ecology"], in Alexander Chumakov, Ivan Mazour, and William Gay, eds., *Global Studies Encyclopedic Dictionary*, with a foreword by Mikhail Gorbachev (Boston: Brill, 2014).

9   Victor A. Kobylansky, *К проблеме разграничения и выявления взаимной связи природы и общества* [*On the Problem of Distinguishing and Identifying the Reciprocal Relations of Nature and Society*] (Moscow: Nauka, 1983).

to research of this issue, Kobylyansky analyzes the complex natural socio-ecosystem as an interactive unity of nature and society. He considers each aspect of this system both separately and in their unity. He reveals the character of nature's operation as belonging to the domain of blind, unconscious forces, and the specific features of humanized nature. He shows how humanized natural processes depend on the spontaneous action of natural forces. In the context of examining the natural socio-ecosystem, he emphasizes the fundamentally non-natural character of social relations and considers issues like the development and harmonization of social life. With this accumulated analytical background, we are now able to proceed to the next step: to an examination of the unity, interpenetration, and co-subordination of nature and society, and to a demonstration of the integrity of this process.

The actual need for social ecology as a special "socio-natural" science arises only when the very interaction between nature and society carried out through human activities becomes the object of research. Social ecology must simultaneously serve as a "natural" science of humans and a "social" science of nature (i.e. it must become a borderline science, occupying a space between the "purely" natural and social sciences). It must function as a single science, reflecting the natural and the social in an immediate unity, in coalescence, as a specific phenomenon, which has an isomorphic natural and social character.[10]

Russian scholars have continued to develop the ideas of social ecology, paying increasing attention to the need to move away from purely empirical material, and towards the general theoretical foundations for developing this new branch of science. Yury Trusov concludes that ecological interaction is the interaction between the central object of the system and its environment. The ecological approach is not a specific science, but a kind of method of orientation in the real world that can be applied to any system. In addition, ecology must have certain philosophical and methodological foundations, a nomenclature of general ecological concepts and laws.

Let us identify the basic philosophical and methodological foundations of the general ecological theory. From the thermodynamic point of view, any "central" object in an ecosystem is an essentially open subsystem capable of progressive development. The ecological approach invites the study of specific features and values of the ecological interaction in various spheres and manifestations of the material world. All the components of the environment, with

---

[10] Victor A. Kobylansky, *Философия социоэкологии* [*Philosophy of Socio-Ecology*] (Novosibirsk: RIF, 2004).

which the central object interacts, are considered to be ecological factors and condition the existence of this central object. Thus, the basic principle of ecology is that the existence, actual possibilities, and forms of manifestation of the "central" object depend on a whole set of ecological factors, and qualitative and quantitative characteristics.[11]

As we embark on discussing the concerns of social ecology, what we have in mind is the totality of interrelations between human society and its environment (including the social institutions). Therefore, it is imperative to pay attention to those particular aspects of social production that are aimed at the development of global ecological strategy. It was Evgeny Fadeyev who turned the discussion to the matter of ecological production, arguing that society cannot abandon material production. It makes no sense to return society to its former, pre-industrial stages. The development of production is instrumental in humanity's own development. The idea of abandoning the development of material production is utopian and anti-humane. The continued production growth is logical. As the production sphere grows, we find a need for new forms and methods for organizing it, and we must invent new tools and means to create, reproduce, and deploy these forms and methods. The growth and expansion of production extends the boundary of human contact with nature, which in turn stimulates the creation of new technologies, industries, and types of labor activities.

The ecologization of production is defined as the subordination of production to a series of specific ecological restrictions: waste-free technological cycles, environmentally-friendly machinery, rational use of resources, etc. Here the author offers some outlines of ecological production as a branch of production designed to create unprecedented means of human life and work, different from those given by nature and meeting the new needs of a progressive society. This approach is somewhat contrary to ecologization, which is aimed at adapting the production sphere to certain ecological requirements. According to Fadeyev, ecological production is the transformation of complete natural systems that act as environments and vary from the macro- to mega- levels.[12] Naturally, such projects currently appear to be utopian. The highest current achievement in this area can be found in the harmonization of

---

11 Yury P. Trusov, "О предмете и основных идеях экологии" ["On the Subject and the Fundamental Ideas of Ecology"], in *Философские проблемы глобальной экологии* [*Philosophical Problems of Global Ecology*], ed. Evgeny T. Fadeyev (Moscow: Nauka, 1983).
12 Evgeny T. Fadeyev, "Проблемы экологического производства" ["Problems of Ecological Production"], in *Philosophical Problems of Global Ecology*.

relations between the developing industrial society and the nature it changes, relations which are promising for the future.

Research into the issues of socio-natural history conducted by Eduard Kulpin-Gubaidullin offers an interesting view of the development of socio-ecological ideas. Since 1992, Kulpin has organized the annual international conference, Man and Nature: Problems of Socio-Natural History. At these conferences, humanity was considered as part of a system encompassing inanimate nature, wildlife, and society. Kulpin views this system as unified, and his associates have searched for its underlying principles and the resulting laws that determine the character of its operation.[13] Finally, the third component of this emerging ecology is human ecology, whose subject is the interaction of the human species and its environment. Human ecology acts as a complex interdisciplinary area that studies the ways and patterns of human exposure to the environment and the forms of human adaptation to environmental effects.

In Russian scholarship, pilot developments in this area have been carried out by Vlail Kaznacheyev at the Academy of Medical Sciences. According to Kaznacheyev, human ecology is an interdisciplinary science designed to study the patterns of human interaction with the environment, issues of human population development, conservation and development of human health, and improvements of the physical and mental abilities of man.[14] Human ecology is increasingly becoming the center, around which fundamental and practical research issues of both global and regional ecologies are grouped. Kaznacheyev made a valuable observation about Vernadsky's doctrine of biospheric transition, that the noosphere is acquiring the status of a theoretical natural-scientific foundation for both human ecology and space anthropology.[15] The biosphere and technosphere systems, which protect people from exposure to cosmic factors, suggest a qualitatively new development of human ecology as it reaches the cosmic level and comes forward as the most important segment of interdisciplinary science, called *cosmic anthropo-ecology*. The subject of human ecology, too, is globalized, including areas that study the regularities of human adaptation to environmental conditions, human exposure to natural constants (e.g., climate, temperature, atmosphere, altitude, etc.),

---

13   Eduard S. Kulpin, "Социоестественная история—ответ на вызовы времени" ["Socio-Natural History: A Response to the Challenges of the Time"], *Istoricheskaya psikhologiya i sotsiologiya istorii*, 2008, No. 1, 196–207.

14   See: Vlail Kaznacheyev, ed., Проблемы экологии человека [*Problems of Human Ecology*] (Moscow: Nauka, 1986).

15   See: Vlail Kaznacheyev, Учение о биосфере [*The Doctrine of the Biosphere*] (Moscow: Znaniye, 1985).

and the impact of genetic, psychological, and cultural peculiarities on human development. In recent years, the restructuring of the human mind effected by computer and communication technologies has been actively incorporated into the human ecology agenda. According to Ekaterina Petrova, mankind must learn to develop new adaptation mechanisms or try to modify existing ones in order to adapt successfully in an environment permeated by new technologies. She means both social and natural adaptation, as these processes are inextricably related. The process of adaptation is an integral process, with distiguishable natural and social aspects; although we can analyze the relationships between them, we cannot and need think of them as distinct.[16]

I could continue with the analysis of emerging regional ecologies: for instance, the ecology of culture, the ecology of creativity, the ecology of spirit, etc. This, however, would not offer us much conceptually. All of these lineaments of thought are, in fact, concerned with the interaction between the central object of study and the environment of its existence. And while these are all necessary and useful areas of research, they are not sufficient to fully reveal the universal organizational principles of interaction between the object and its environment within the universal concept of the globalizing world.

The history of science offers numerous examples of similar generalizing concepts: Bogdanov's tectology, Norbert Wiener's cybernetics, elaborated by his followers, Ludwig von Bertalanffy's general systems theory, Hermann Haken's synergetics, and Sergei V. Meyen's diatropics. Today's globalized ecology is influenced by the demands of our time and requires an awareness of modern organizational theory. Scholars in Russia and abroad are attempting to make similar theoretical generalizations, as confirmed by the material discussed earlier. So far, these approaches seek to create a new organizational theory that will lead to our understanding of the emergence and operation of the innovative generative mechanisms of the modern organizational structure of the world.

And yet, this raises the question: What do all these discoveries of the globalizing world offer us for a new understanding of human beings? All of us know very well that a human is a biosocial being. As a matter of fact, our knowledge of them is attained through both the natural sciences and the humanities.

---

16   See: Ekaterina V. Petrova, "Человек как социоприродное существо в эпоху конвергентных технологий" ["Man as a Socio-Natural Being in the Age of Convergent Technologies"], in *Философия социоприродного взаимодействия в век конвергентных технологий* [*Philosophy of Socio-Natural Interaction in the Age of Convergent Technologies*], ed. Igor K. Liseyev (St. Petersburg: Nestor–Istoriya, 2018).

Each of these sciences provides a different view of human beings, and these views vary greatly.

The natural sciences study the natural world, and the humanities study the social world, and yet these two are a single world. The greater the complexity with which natural and social objects are organized, the more they depend on the whole, as they are connected to this whole with biological, genetic, energetic, informational, and social links. Many of our distinguished predecessors—and, above all, Vernadsky, who insisted that humanity be viewed as spontaneously inseparable from society and the biosphere—were well aware of this fact. Mankind, Vernadsky believed, was becoming a powerful geological force through its intelligence. His work thus raised the question of reshaping the biosphere in the interest of a free-thinking humanity as a whole. Vernadsky called this new state of the biosphere transformed by humans "the noosphere." Being a great humanist and in the spirit of the best ideals of his time, Vernadsky believed that the good of the humanity, as mediated by scientific intelligence, could only lead to positive outcomes delivered by rational intelligence. His idea of transforming the biosphere into the noosphere pursued just such a goal.

Our Russian contemporaries also discuss this matter. Co-authors Vlail Kaznacheyev and Evgeny Spirin write of

> the high involvement of human society in such scientific and technological, spiritual and cultural development, when human technological capabilities will allow for a radical transformation of the material and informational organization of the intelligent living substance known as the humanity.[17]

The new trend of transhumanism is of a piece with these ideas. Its proponents argue that, for the sake of humanity's "bright future," it must be freed from all of its problems, such as aging, diseases, physical and mental disabilities, etc., making humans immortal and deploying all possibilities to this purpose, including the replacement of the natural human mind with artificial intelligence.[18] Here, human rights and opportunities are seen as limitless.

---

17 See: Vlail Kaznacheev, Evgeny A. Spirin, *Космопланетарный феномен человека* [*The Cosmo-Planetary Phenomenon of Humanity*] (Novosibirsk: Nauka, 1991).

18 See: Vadim M. Maslov, *Высокие технологии и феномен постчеловеческого в современном обществе* [*The High-Tech and the Phenomenon of the Posthuman in Modern Society*] (doctoral diss., Lobachevsky N. Novgorod University, 2014).

In contrast with this approach, the work of Eduard Girusov is devoted to the rights of nature. Girusov writes that the period of the spontaneous development of the biosphere has come to an end:

> The task of conserving it requires a transition to a planned and consciously regulated development in accordance with scientifically sound and harmonized international regulations. As utopian as it may seem, these are the "requirements" coming from the biosphere that humans must comply with, if they are to remain on the planet. It is hard to get used to these kinds of demands of nature, but one has to understand that nature doesn't recognize our whims. It always acts seriously and thoroughly. This becomes clear when we think of the increasing number of natural disasters observed recently.[19]

In today's context, when a terrible viral pandemic has struck nearly the entire planet, this sounds frighteningly prognostic. In supporting of Girusov's position, I would like to add that it is high time to abandon the progressive illusions of the past and to move towards an understanding of the specific features of sustainable civilizational development.[20]

In connection with what has been said, the question arises: What are the reasons for such contradictory understandings of our being? The variety of factors that contribute to this explanation include the important view of our world from the opposing positions of the naturalistic and socio-humanistic learning. This opposition was described by the English physicist and writer Charles Percy Snow, in his 1959 Cambridge lecture "Two Cultures." Snow described the paradoxical situation that developed in the mid-twentieth century and led to a dramatic split of the formerly unified European culture into the cultures of natural science and of the humanities. This split is determined by a cultural system using two languages, one dominated by the logic of rational scientific knowledge, the other by a different logic of explanation, understanding, interpretation. This amounts to two kinds of worldview, with two distinct modes of argumentation. Unfortunately, despite repeated attempts of consolidation, the gap between these cultures continues to increase over time,

---

19 See: Eduard Girusov, "Социоприродные системы и законы их саморегуляции" ["Socio-Natural Systems and the Laws of their Self-Regulation"], in Liseyev., ed., *Philosophy of Socio-Natural Interaction*.

20 See: Regina S. Karpinskaya, Igor K. Liseev and Alexander P. Ogurtsov, *Философия природы: коэволюционная стратегия* [*Philosophy of Nature: A Co-Evolutionary Strategy*] (Moscow: Interprax, 1995).

and gives rise to negative effects in any society that adheres to these positions. Moreover, this situation is connected with the fact that the possible synthesis of these two areas of culture is inconspicuous. But from our point of view, such opportunities are already available. We are talking about the emergence of synthetic branches of scientific knowledge—for instance, global ecology, which is currently gaining momentum.

All of this demonstrates that today's "big ecology," which has rapidly expanded its subject matter and research methods, poses its reasoned challenges to existing cultural standards, perceptions, and foci. It calls for new ways of organizing scientific knowledge—indeed, for a reformed scientific landscape of the world—and this challenge is attracting attention. In this vein, Mihail C. Roco and William Sims Bainbridge have identified an emerging trend in the unification of knowledge by combining the natural and social sciences with the humanities, following a model of causal explanation.[21]

In his work on Vyacheslav Styopin's theoretical *oeuvre*, Boris Pruzhinin notes that the essence of Styopin's approach consisted in emphasizing the humanistic dimension of science, in considering the variety of questions engendered by this emphasis, and even in "introducing" humanistic parameters into the natural and technical sciences as immanent characteristics of scientific cognitive activity.[22] The emergence of "big ecology" was an objective internalistic process, which developed in response to the demands of emergent scientific research. But having taken the form of a science of regularities in the interactions between a system's core and its environment, it now claims the status of yet another universal theory (along with cybernetics, general systems theory, synergetics, etc.).[23] In the future, this path may lead to a modern universal organizational science (following the lineaments of Bogdanov's tectology). This has yet to happen, but, even at present, this rejuvenated ecology has much to offer in Russia's quest for its modern civilizational path, in virtue of clarifying the organization of scientific knowledge and the outlines of the

---

21 Mihail C. Roco and William S. Bainbridge, *Converging Technologies for Improving Human Performance* (Boston: Cluwer, 2003).

22 Boris I. Pruzhinin, "Техногенная цивилизация и наука как культурный феномен" ["Anthropogenic Civilization and Science as a Cultural Phenomenon"], First Styopin Reading Series (Moscow, 2019).

23 Yury V. Egorov and Natalia N. Kolyasnikova, "Экология человека и социальная экология: термины и смыслы" ["Human and Social Ecology: Terms and Meanings"], *Analitika i control*, 2010 (14), No. 4, 260–66; Yury S. Chuykov, "Социальная экология и экология человека: объекты и направления исследования" ["Social and Human Ecology: Objects and Directions of Research"], *Astrakhan Bulletin of Environmental Education*, 2017 (39), No. 1, 91–109.

modern scientific landscape. Global ecology can also supply a new vision for the scientific and technological revolution currently underway.

3   Specifics Manifesting in the Context of the Modern Techno-Industrial Revolution

The modern industrial and technological revolution, identified by Klaus Schwab as "the fourth industrial revolution," is characterized chiefly by the following: the digitalization of all spheres of life, the development of artificial intelligence, extensive robotization of various areas of activity, the use of the internet as a means of human communication and data exchange, and the creation of cyberspace as the "home for all data." According to Schwab, the globalization of the world will not diminish; on the contrary, it will continue to enlarge. Whereas in the past, global integration advanced as trade barriers fell, it will now rely on the connections of national digital and virtual systems, as well as the flow of ideas and services associated with it.[24] At the same time, global digitalization brings not only unlimited opportunities for future human development, but also serious risks. It is now increasingly clear that the modern digital information revolution has created a significant gap between technological progress and the human capacity to grasp its consequences.

In this context, it is necessary to find the means of controlling the development of modern technology. Gerd Leonhard, the renowned contemporary European futurologist, has identified five new human rights in the digital age. These rights are aimed at freeing people from the bondage of digitalization, and form a part of the future digital ethics manifesto.[25] According to Leonhard, they include the right to remain natural, that is, biological. In the current context of the rapid expansion of transhumanist ideas insisting on the possibility of radical and fundamental transformation of human structure and its organization through technological components, Leonhard believes it necessary to preserve the possibility for humans to function in society without the need to embed additional devices in their organs.

Another human right advocated by Leonhard is the right to be low-efficient, where low efficiency is determined by our physiological limitations. According to Leonhard, the human right to be slower than technology must be an

---

[24]   Klaus Schwab, "Globalization 4.0. A New Architecture for the Fourth Industrial Revolution," *Foreign Affairs*, January 16, 2019, https://www.foreignaffairs.com/articles/world/2019-01-16/globalization-40.

[25]   See: Gerd Leonhard, *Technology vs Humanity* (England: Fast Future, 2016).

undeniable human right. In today's setting of universal control over a person's location and action, Leonhard considers the "offline" situation to be a basic human right. The right to be able to be disconnected for a while should become a fundamental right of every person. Since anonymity and privacy are human attributes that we have no right to eliminate through technology, the right to be anonymous remains fundamental to any civilizational domain. Last but not least is the fifth right, which has emerged unexpectedly but is rapidly expanding its practical domain: the right to engage in work without having to use machines. According to Leonhard, productivity should not be placed above humanity.

When considering these new rules for living in the context of total digitalization, it becomes clear that each of the theses put forward by Leonhard may have its antithesis, and that the discussion has only just begun. Still, as Leonhard has rightly pointed out, the question is not whether technology can do something, but whether it should do something and why. This is why we can say that the main question of our age is in what direction, and to what purpose, are we progressing in the era of the modern techno-industrial revolution. What are the current civilizational benchmarks for humankind? What is in store for us? The modern civilizational choice is impacted by a wide range of matters with national, economic, political, cultural, geopolitical, confessional, and other important civilizational aspects. In recent years, the environmental aspects have gained increasingly fervent support.

Nikita Moiseyev, an outstanding Russian scientist, has made an extraordinary contribution to the development of the modern civilization agenda, with his argument that the concept of civilization should be defined to entail a certain commonality among people united not only by similar lifestyles and characteristic cultural features, but also by common spiritual worlds, proximity of worldviews, recognition of a certain structure of fundamental values, and ultimately, by a generally common mentality.[26] Based on this understanding of civilization, Moiseyev introduced the idea of the *ecological imperative* as a set of environmental properties that depend on the peculiarities of the civilization and cannot be changed under any circumstances.[27] But what discipline should accommodate the activities of such an environmental imperative? Traditionally, it has been viewed as a field of interaction between the developing society and the nature that it alters. This is extremely important in the context

---

26 Nikita N. Moiseyev, Быть или не быть… человечеству [*Humanity: To Be or Not to Be*] (Moscow: Ulyanovsk House of Print, 1999), 214.

27 See: Nikita N. Moiseyev, Современный рационализм [*Contemporary Rationalism*] (Moscow: MGVP KOKS, 1995).

of the dynamic development of the scientific, technical, and technological revolution. Yet, in today's society, we must do more.

Contemporary scientists increasingly define our era as the Anthropocene, a period when human activity becomes responsible for the fate of the planet. Man has long become a global mono-species, whose functioning transforms many a fundamental law of being.[28] In his book *Autopoiesis*, Yury Chaikovsky writes that a new process of evolution, in which the human realm plays a major role, is now being shaped. As the author puts it, it is not clear whether the biosphere can be sustainable in the presence of a kingdom consisting of a single species. As a species, he argues, man dictates the evolution of other species. Moreover, man intentionally shapes some of them. Humans have created a new ecology, which must be linked with politics and economics.

As mentioned earlier, since the second half of the twentieth century, bio-ecology no longer stands as a lone discipline. It has rapidly expanded its scope of research, and has been supplemented with social ecology, human ecology, and other scientific fields that study the interactions between the central object and its environment. Momentum is building to formulate a new approach that would consolidate all the emerging areas under the aegis of global ecology.[29] Thus far, its scope has only just been outlined. There is much to be done in developing the contents and theoretical justifications of this new organizational approach arising from the synthesis of all areas of environmental research. Since the beginning of the twentieth century—the time of Bogdanov and his universal organizational science of tectology—no new statements of such a comprehensive organizational science have been developed. Cybernetics, the systems approach, synergetics, and diatropics all had other goals.

It is a critical need of our time that we establish a modern organizational science based on today's "big ecology." This system must be integral, synthetic, and comprehensive, and it must consider the possibilities, restrictions, and prohibitions already present and rapidly developing in the areas of social and human ecology. And yet, the intricacy of the situation is such that no single research area can resolve the problems it faces outside of an alliance with all the other areas of "big ecology." Only integral thinking—as realized by the authors of the report on the fiftieth anniversary of the Club of Rome—is

---

28 See: Yury V. Chaikovsky, *Автопоэз* [*Autopoiesis*] (St. Petersburg: Piter, 2018).
29 Igor K. Liseyev, "Глобальная экология как объединяющее начало становления глобализирующегося мира" ["Global Ecology as the Unifying Foundation of a Globalizing World"], *Philosophy, Psychology: A Journal of Belarus State University*, 2018, No. 1, 7–13.

capable of perceiving, organizing, coordinating, and reuniting individual fragments, and of achieving a genuine understanding of the underlying reality.[30] The findings developed in the course of such thinking can constitute the basis of a scientifically conscious and informed civilizational choice.

The ecological imperatives of bio-ecology require a systemic equilibrium between living organisms and their environment. It is necessary to study and adjust the anthropogenic changes introduced by humans into the system of natural patterns. When we consider the position of human ecology, we see that ecological imperatives follow a bidirectional process within a unified whole, one direction determined by the protection of the natural environment of the human habitat, and the other—by the protection of humans from harmful natural and industrial factors. Compliance with these ecological imperatives provides humans with an opportunity to see themselves as an organic, holistic, inseparable unity in their natural and social characteristics. As a science that studies direct and indirect impact of industrial activities on the composition and properties of the natural, anthropogenic, and technogenic environment, social ecology, too, can be a source of ecological imperatives.

One such critical ecological imperative is to follow the co-evolutionary patterns of development of the industrial society and of the natural environment it transforms. To follow these patterns, it is necessary, first of all, to recognize, formulate, and create the conditions of their realization. This proposition is likewise true for all the previously discussed ecological imperatives from other areas of ecology. Thus, if we are to follow the Kantian understanding of the relation of constitutive and regulative principles, ecological imperatives will act as the regulative principles underlying Russia's modern civilizational choice. This provides an opportunity to put into practice certain prescriptive functions in relation to human activities, to create new foundations for shaping ecological culture across society, to specify the meaning and significance of the contemporary understanding of the problems of humanism, and to gain insight into the social function of science.

Our contemporary world is in trouble. The successive waves of the COVID-19 pandemic have resulted in the illness and death of millions of people, and in the destruction of social, economic, and cultural ties. What is the root cause of this disaster? Opinions vary. Some people believe that the human factor had something to do with it: that the malignant virus was the product of

---

30   See: Ernst U. von Weizsäcker and Anders Wijkman, *Come On! Capitalism, Short-termism, Population and the Destruction of the Planet: A Report to the Club of Rome* (New York: Springer, 2018).

human activity carried out for military, research, or other purposes. Others believe that the rapid replication of this virus is a natural process and beyond human control. Still others are convinced that the situation reflects the mindless, unregulated socio-natural development of mankind. This is the point of view I, too, adhere to, and have written about it on more than one occasion, along with many other ecologists.

Russian philosophical thought in the second half of the twentieth century comprises a large scientific school of bio-socio-ecological analysis of patterns of social development, centered around the work of Eduard Girusov. Its main representatives include Ivan Frolov, Regina Karpinskaya, Arkady Ursul, Alexander Subetto, Eduard Kulpin-Gubaidullin, Victor Kobylyansky, and Evgeny Fadeyev. Each of these scholars, each from his or her own position, proposed a multi-tiered approach to the analysis of contemporary aspects of interaction of humans, society, and nature in the context of anthropogenic civilization. One could say that the task of describing the new socially significant function of science in modern conditions—of bringing scientific ideas to practical use—has been accomplished via the reflexive philosophical analysis of the achievements of contemporary biology and ecology. The main goal here was to uncover how contemporary life sciences, which explore the foundations of human existence, contribute to the transition from a technology-oriented culture characteristic of the anthropogenic civilization to a bio- and eco-oriented culture of restoring the unity of humans, society, and nature.

If we look at the core characteristics and activities of the anthropogenic civilization, they differ significantly from those underpinning the new, ecogenically oriented civilization that is presently gaining momentum. And yet, both are equally important for the future of human existence. We must take into account the conclusions drawn by contemporary life scientists and the inconsistencies in translating scientific ideas into practice that have so recently led to tragic consequences.

As the St. Petersburg-based scientist Igor Kefeli stated rightly in his new book, *Asphatronics*,

> The goal of man and society is not the transition to the noosphere, understood as an ideal model of the future, as a certain result (a kind of ecological utopianism), but in acting upon the real factors and driving forces of the evolutionary process, and in research aiming to maximize the optimization of the society–nature interaction on the principle of "manage-and-obey." Society and reason must fit into the objective laws

of the biological cycle of the biosphere. Here, we engage not with natural bodies, but with human activity.[31]

The technological horizons of scientific and industrial revolution's era are fascinating, and sometimes frightening, but the question persists: Do we have the right to implement anything that state-of-the-art technology can offer? Once again, we are in need of humanities-derived expertise. Science pinpoints the forthcoming developmental pressure-points; there is no doubt that some of them will become increasingly sensitive. These include the future pandemics, transformations of the human body and spirit, the impending environmental crisis, the climate collapse in the near future, etc. Only sound and consistent analysis of the social and ethical implications of these issues will make it possible to raise the question of how to approach them in practice.

In summary, both the historic pre-requisites and the trends of global anthropogenic development affect Russia's contemporary civilizational choice in the context of the globalized world. The phrase "Russia's civilizational choice" refers to Kropotkin's ideas concerning cooperation as an evolutionary factor and an engine of progress, and to Vernadsky's idea of the noosphere as a transformation of the biosphere towards the harmonization of nature and society. We are also indebted to Bogdanov's ideas about overcoming the antitheses of centralism and individualism, and of uniting natural science and socio-humanistic knowledge within a single organizational concept. We can also trace the achievements of a large group of Russian philosophers, biologists, and ecologists who have advanced the methods of a new "big ecology" as a prerequisite for a consistent new organizational concept. These scholars consider the peculiarities of the contemporary stage of human civilization, with a dual focus on their positive opportunities and the risks involved.

In this light, civilizational choice is viewed as the compatibility of today's technological development with the ecogenic principles of interaction between nature and society. As Vernadsky has taught us, humanity is inseparable from the biosphere—and, as stated by Nikita Moiseyev, "only a thriving biosphere can house a thriving humanity."[32] Man, nature, and society are three inseparable components of one integral system. Each has its own laws of development, but, when included in a single system, each is subject to the systemic laws of functioning and development. Therefore, one of the main tasks

---

31   Igor F. Kefeli, *Асфатроника. На пути к теории глобальной безопасности* [*Asphatronics: Towards a Theory of Global Security*] (St. Petersburg, 2020), 103.
32   See: Nikita Moiseyev, *Человек и ноосфера* [*Man and the Noosphere*] (Moscow: Molodaya Gvardiya, 1990).

of contemporary civilizational development is to ensure the co-development of humans, society, and nature, such that all the components of this unified system do not act in opposition, but can organically accommodate one another in their joint, aligned, and harmonious development.

Globalization, the Great Russian Revolution of 1917, and the Transformation of the World System

A Historical and Philosophical Perspective

Leonid E. Grinin

There are certain events to which the minds of historians and the larger thinking public return involuntarily, again and again. More often than not, these are the events that not only "shook the world" (in John Reed's memorable phrase) at the time of their occurrence, but those that have altered it profoundly, sometimes radically, with the effects of change persisting or even compounding over the succeeding decades.[1] It is in this category that we must consider the Russian Revolution of 1917.

The Socialist Revolution in Russia had a powerful resonance throughout the world and was the impetus of significant change in the development of many societies. It can therefore be considered one of the few great revolutions in global history. (Of those, there have been but three: the French Revolution, in the eighteenth-century; the Russian; the Chinese, completed in 1949;[2] or four, with the English revolution in the seventeenth century.) In Soviet times, it was a common proposition that the October Revolution had been the principal event of the century. That assessment is significant, though not in the sense originally intended by the communists. The October Revolution did not occasion the transition of the world to a new socio-economic (communist) order. Nevertheless, as an event, it altered dramatically both the world-historical process and the World System. The revolution spurred development along new political, economic and social vectors, including state planning, social insurance programs and welfare in capitalist countries. It opened up new avenues for the modernization of underdeveloped countries and contributed substantially to the decolonization of the world. This chapter will examine some aspects of its broad influence.

---

1 John Reed, *Ten Days that Shook the World* (New York: Boni and Liveright, 1919).
2 Theda Skocpol, *States and Social Revolutions: A Comparative Analysis of France, Russia, and China* (Cambridge: Cambridge University Press, 1979).

1 Great Revolutions and the Philosophy of History

The old philosophy of history, concerned as it were with the meaning or goal of history and permeated by eschatology, is hopelessly outdated; yet its principal problematics, involving the analysis of major historical events' influence over the course of history and the appearance of the world, will always remain relevant. In the same way that our perception of an object depends on its distance from us, judgments of great events temporally far and near, and of their direct and indirect results, will vary. This is why every generation of philosophers and historians can assess anew the major, singular historic events.

Every revolution brings about profound change. The *great revolutions*, meanwhile, have drastically changed the world and historical processes, including globalization, which is the very reason why we refer to them as "great." Unsurprisingly, great revolutions have constituted one of the principal themes in the philosophy of history since the seventeenth century. Many studies have been devoted to historical, moral, and political assessments of the problems of the English, American, and French revolutions, their causes—progressive or negative, depending on the political position of the author—and their historical role. (Among them were the writings of Thomas Jefferson, Hume's *The History of England*, first published in 1773, de Mably's *Des droits et des devoirs du citoyen* (written in 1758 and published in 1789), Burke's *Reflections on the Revolution in France* (1790) and Barnave's *Introduction to the French Revolution* (written in 1792 and published in 1843).[3] Without intending to analyze those philosophical and political views of revolution, we might still recall Marxist conception of revolutions as "locomotives of history" and as the culmination of class struggle.[4] (Their views, of course, drew heavily on the ideas of Saint-Simon and French historians of the Bourbon Restoration, who formulated the doctrine of class struggle in the first decades of the nineteenth

---

3 Notable editions include: Gabriel Bonnot de Mably, *Des droits et des devoirs du citoyen*, a critical edition by Jean-Louis Lecercle (Paris: Didier, 1972); *Power, Property, and History: Barnave's Introduction to the French Revolution and Other Writings*, translated by Eamnuel Chill (New York: Harper & Row, 1971).
4 Karl Marx, *The Class Struggles in France* (first published 1850), in *Selected Writings*, edited by David McLellan (Oxford: Oxford University Press, 2000), 313–25; Karl Marx, *Eighteenth Brumaire of Louis Bonaparte* (first published 1851–1852), in *Selected Writings*, 329–55; Friedrich Engels, *Revolution and Counter-Revolution in Germany* (first published 1851–1852), in *The Collected Works of Marx and Engels* (Moscow: Progress, 1979), Vol. 11, 3–96.

century. Among them were Thierry, Guizot and Mignet.)[5] Over the century-and-a-half that followed Marx, much has been said about great revolutions and their leading figures—but the subject is vast, and still far from being exhausted. In particular, one would like to draw attention to a few ideas that matter to our understanding of historical process.

Great revolutions maximally exacerbate socio-political struggles, effecting radical changes that, sooner or later, reverse the revolutionary impulse. Philosophers mark the up-swing and the down-swing stages of revolution.[6] "Every revolution ends in reaction," wrote the Russian philosopher Nikolay Berdyaev; "this is inevitable, this is the law."[7] This is consonant with the idea of a "Thermidor stage" of revolution—after the month of the Jacobins' overthrow by the more moderate revolutionaries (which took place on the ninth day of Thermidor by the French revolutionary calendar, corresponding to July 27, 1794), who replaced them in power—sometimes framed as the "law of Thermidor," according to which, at a certain point in its development, revolution must retreat from its radical manifestations, and henceforth begin a gradual return to pre-revolutionary relations.[8] The "law of Thermidor" and the notion of the "Thermidor stage" was frequently discussed and written about after the Bolshevik Revolution in Russia.[9]

In the author's opinion, as a result of the great revolutions and their radicalism, historical process outpaced the actual degree of social development. Alternative lines of historical development thus emerge—enriching the social evolution, on the one hand, while, on the other hand, manifesting themselves, to a greater or lesser degree, as dead ends. The seventeenth-century English Revolution sprouted a republican line of development unusual for a major power (until then, republics, with the exception of the Roman Republic, were usually small countries). Shortly, though, the idea of an English republic was dismissed, following the Stuart Restoration of 1660 and the Glorious Revo-

---

5   See: L. E. Grinin, "Первая половина XIX в." ["The First Half of the Nineteenth Century"] in *Теория, методология и философия истории: очерки развития исторической мысли от древности до середины XIX века* [*Theory, Methodology, and Philosophy of History: Essays on the Development of Historical Thought from Antiquity to the Middle of the Nineteenth Century*], *Filosofiya i obshchestvo*, 2010, No. 4, 145–97.
6   Pitirim Sorokin, *The Sociology of Revolution* (Philadelphia: J. B. Lippincott, 1925); Samuel Huntington, *Political Order in Changing Societies* (New Haven: Yale University Press, 1968).
7   Nikolai Berdyaev, *Философия неравенства* [*Philosophy of Inequality*, first published 1923] (Moscow: Ima-Press, 1990), 29.
8   Crane Brinton, *The Anatomy of Revolution* (New York: Vintage, 1965; first published 1938), 90.
9   See: Nikolay Ustryalov, *Patriotica* (Prague: 1921); Leon Trotsky, "The Workers' State, Thermidor and Bonapartism," *International Socialist Review*, 1956 (17), No. 3, 93–101, 105.

lution of 1688. The French Revolution likewise failed to prove the viability of either a republican rule or a complete abolition of the estates. The Russian Revolution opened the way to a restructuring of society on the basis of egalitarian socialism and the abolition of private property. Ultimately (and far from immediately), this line of historical development, too, found its dead end.

Nevertheless, from the point of view of world-historical development, the influence of great revolutions is undeniable. By the Hegelian law of double negation, their ideas and practices are widely implemented—but later than expected, and in a different context, and in such a way that this implementation can only be successful if radical extremes can be forfeited in practice, sooner or later. We can see that the republican principle laid down by the English Revolution and continued by the French experience took root, in due course, in many countries. The ideas of the abolition of the estates and of equality before the law, introduced by the French Revolution, became the basis of many a state constitution. Finally, the ideas and principles of social equality (and of gender equality in particular), as raised in Russia in 1917, have gained a foothold in most of the world, and are presently being realized in novel ways across developed countries.

In this manner, great revolutions realize (albeit in ideologically distorted forms) the demands of historical development for change and transformation. At the same time, the societies that gave rise to these revolutions may actually "lose," while other societies may gain by implementing appropriate changes under the influence of revolutionary events, without major social losses of their own. In other words, *great revolutions are a means of developing the historical process, where progress in some societies can be achieved at the cost of others and their failures.* By opening up unprecedented new horizons of socio-political breakdown and reformation, of violence and destruction, such revolutions are not merely destructive, for they appear to delineate the scope of possible social change for a long time ahead. At least some of the revolutionary ideas and principles will spread, sooner or later, not just within the revolutionary society that produced them, but also beyond its limits. In doing so, great revolutions continue to exert their influence on the fates of the world—sometimes centuries after they have taken place.

2 The Socialist Revolution in Russia, the Deceleration of Globalization, and the Changing World Order Prior to 1945

2.1 Revolutions and the Process of Globalization

Since the advent of the Modern period, revolutions have come to play an exceptionally important role in historical progress.[10] Given that globalization, too, has constituted an essential part of the historical process since the start of the Modern Age, revolutions have been historically closely related to the processes of globalization.[11] Globalization is not simply intertwined with the unfolding of the historical process: it enlarges its scope, determining both its unity and its variability. In turn, the processes that take place in particular regions and societies affect the course of globalization. The link between revolutions and globalization has become particularly evident since the late eighteenth century (as marked by the formation of the United States in the aftermath of the War of Independence). With regard to the nineteenth and twentieth centuries, one can speak of several revolutionary waves, some of which significantly affected the processes of globalization.[12] In this way, the revolutions spanning from 1809 into the 1820s in Spain, Portugal and Latin America opened up the latter to the rest of world, though it had largely been closed to foreign trade and economic influence before that time, because of Spain's monopoly. Likewise notable is the early-twentieth-century wave of revolutions (1905–1911). Beginning in Russia, it swept up a number of Eurasian countries—Turkey, Persia and China—as well as Mexico, significantly altering those countries' fates and the relations between them and the rest of the world.

Not every revolutionary wave and not all revolutions facilitated globalization. This has to do with the fact that the process of globalization, which was already underway in the nineteenth century, had split Europe into two opposing factions (the Entente and the Central Empires), whose conflict ultimately led to the First World War. Among the chief results of the wave of post-war revolutions of 1917–1923 was the crash and disintegration of the four

---

10 Leonid Grinin, "Revolutions in the Light of Historical Process," *Social Evolution & History*, 2019 (18), No. 2, 260–85.
11 Leonid Grinin, "Революции, исторический процесс и глобализация" ["Revolutions, Historical Process and Globalization"], *Vek globalizatsii*, 2018, No. 4, 16–29; Leonid Grinin, "Revolutions and Historical Process," *Journal of Globalization Studies*, 2019 (9), No. 2, 126–41.
12 Leonid Grinin, Anton Grinin, "Революции XX века: теоретический и количественный анализ" ["Revolutions in the Twentieth Century: Theoretical and Quantitative Analysis"], *Polis*, 2020, No. 5, 130–47, https://doi.org/10.17976/jpps/2020.05.10.

empires (German, Austro-Hungarian, Russian and Ottoman), which broke up the existing global ties, complicating subsequent globalization. Yet the October Revolution had perhaps the greatest effect of hampering globalization, since it split the world into two opposing camps. This fracture was reinforced by the communist revolutions of the 1940s, so that the world was effectively divided by the Iron Curtain. A wave of national liberation revolutions in the post-war period inaugurated a wave of decolonization, which, too, had an ambiguous effect on globalization. Until then, the vast colonial empires had in some ways lent cohesiveness to the world. The emergence of many more independent countries meant that each of them now had its distinct interests. Still, this would only accelerate the globalization process in the future.

Finally, the last wave of twentieth-century revolutions—namely, the anti-communist revolutions of the late 1980s—eliminated the rigid polarization of the world into two camps, facilitating globalization.

2.2 *Globalization and the Transformation of the World System*

Globalization is generally understood as the increase in the density of the connections within the World System. In turn, the transformation of the World System entails significant changes in the further development of globalization. What we are witnessing in our time is just such a process of transformation, or reconfiguration, of the World System.[13] This is attributable to the crumbling of that world order which emerged after the collapse of the USSR, and to the inception of a new world order.[14]

The outbreak of the First World War resulted in the bankruptcy of the old world order with the dramatic shift of the balance of power in the world.[15] Globalization was considerably dampened by this shift. This found expression in a whole array of phenomena, including the growth of customs tariffs and barriers to trade. But, as has already been mentioned, a special role was played

---

13 See: L. E. Grinin, A. V. Korotayev, "Does "Arab Spring" Mean the Beginning Of World System Reconfiguration?," *World Futures: The Journal of Global Education*, 68(7), 2012, 471–505; L. E. Grinin, A. V. Korotayev, 'Seven Weaknesses of the US, Donald Trump, and the Future of American Hegemony," *World Futures: The Journal of New Paradigm Research* (2020), https://doi.org/10.1080/02604027.2020.1801309.

14 See: Leonid Grinin, "The New World Order and Philosophy: Between Past Orthodoxies and the Future of Globalization," in *Contemporary Philosophical Problems*, edited by Alexander Chumakov and William Gay (Boston: Brill, 2016), 143–56; L. E. Grinin, I. V. Ilyin, A. I. Andreev, "World Order in the Past, Present, and Future," *Social Evolution and History*, 15(1), 2016, 58–84.

15 No lasting world order is possible without a balance of power and its constitutive alliances. See: Henry Kissinger, *World Order* (New York: Penguin, 2014).

by the division of the world into two camps, whose relationship was that of total and continuous confrontation. Against this backdrop, the Soviet Union closed itself off from the world in order to exclude any influence from Western democracies upon its own population, while at the same time trying its best to spread the fire of revolution to countries abroad. Beyond this, the Russian Revolution had an early effect on international relations, especially in popularizing new principles. First, consequent to the policies of the Soviet state, one of the most influential of European political ideas—that of the right of nations to self-determination—was tested in practice. It is true that in the first stage of the revolution the Bolshevik government not only did not stand in their way, but quite sincerely expressed its willingness to recognize the autonomy of national provinces, resulting in the Baltic states' and Finland's appearance on the map. Second, the practice of building national relations within the USSR was also very important. The construction of a new national-federal model in a multinational state (formally based on a voluntary and equal union of nation-states) could not but influence the ideology of various national liberation movements (including those in the colonies), as well as the principles of state-building in a significant number of new states (including India).

The Russian revolution also advanced a number of new principles, all of them absurd from the point of view of the old world order: peace without annexations and reparations, renunciation of war as a means of solving international conflicts, forfeiture of secret diplomacy, etc. Some of these principles—not without the influence of the Bolshevik revolution—came to be included in the arsenal of international relations, as reflected in the Charter of the League of Nations and later in the principles embraced by the United Nations.

2.3 *Political Regime Change in the World and in the USSR*

The very existence of the USSR as a revolutionary state was a kind of oxymoron, simply because the very purpose of a socialist revolution was the destruction of the state as an institution. Not surprisingly, the foreign policy of this new state was replete with inconsistencies. The contradictions ran the range from advocating pacifism while actively preparing for war to declaring the peaceful coexistence of different ideological regimes while instigating revolutions in Western countries; to insistences that Soviet democracy is the highest form of democracy, combined with a rapid movement towards totalitarianism; to unprecedented proclamations of labor rights, combined with the expropriation of the peasantry, etc. This contradictory politics, in its various manifestations, significantly affected the global situation: on the one hand, it attracted the poor or oppressed countries and social strata; on the other hand, it caused grave apprehensions among the cultured, wealthy states.

Let us note the deep changes in Europe's as well as the world's political culture at that time. European empires were being replaced by democratic states. Concurrently, a certain paradox surfaced, in that, while the base of democratic regimes appeared to expand, autocratic and leader-driven regimes of varying degrees of severity (in Italy, Poland, Hungary, Finland, Portugal and Lithuania) began to rise as early as the 1920s, and triumphed afterwards. Various authoritarian and totalitarian regimes, including the Soviet regime, belonged among the mechanisms of state-building and new forms of modernization, yet, after the establishment of the Nazi dictatorship in Germany, they also propelled the world towards war. The rapid economic growth of the USSR, the modernization of the armed forces, and the well-known political events in Europe in 1938–1939 allowed the USSR to increase its influence in the pre-war period. As a result of the Second World War and the subsequent postwar division of Europe and Asia, the USSR was able to emerge as a major geopolitical player.

3 The October Revolution and the Postwar Transformation of the World System

3.1 *The Formation of the World Socialist System and the Two-Bloc World Order*

Though, in 1944–1945, the victors of the Second World War continued to shape the future world order as a system of great powers (the UN Charter, with the five permanent members of the Security Council, furnishing the most obvious proof of this), even by 1945 it had become clear that the post-war world had but two great powers. (These would later be dubbed "superpowers.") Accordingly, the influence of the Russian Socialist Revolution was now amplified into the influence of a superpower, with significant support from a number of allies and cooperative countries. In this way, in the aftermath of Second World War, a new political and economic order began to take shape, differing substantially from the previous versions of the world order, since now there were but two great powers—the United States and the Soviet Union. As a result, shortly after the war the world became *bipolar*, assuming, shortly afterwards, a two-bloc structure (with the NATO and the Warsaw Pact Organization constituting the two major blocs).

It matters that this new world order was formed, for the first time since the religious wars of the sixteenth and the seventeenth centuries, on ideological grounds. Meanwhile, the creation of stable ideological blocs on the world stage was historically unprecedented. All this entailed further features of the postwar world order: (a) the division, not solely on the basis of ideological and political predilections, but also by the conceptions of *property* underpinning the economic systems; (b) the struggles that took place not only in the spheres of ideology, foreign policy and mobilization in the arms race, but in all other spheres of society: culture, sports, propaganda, organization of subversive and opposition movements in enemy countries, etc. In short, *confrontation became total, at the level of literally every person and every action.* Undoubtedly, it was the revolutionary practice of the Soviet leadership that supplied the basis for the unfolding of a propagandistic influence on the population unprecedented in scale, having an immense impact on this variety of foreign confrontation. Geopolitical rivals sought to use any country, any movement and any event for the purposes of strengthening their positions.

All this undoubtedly restrained the processes of globalization, while at the same time placing on the global agenda the leading problem of the time—the elimination of the threat of a thermonuclear war. This rivalry, nevertheless, facilitated the nationalization of a number of economic sectors, as well as the development of anti-poverty programs, social insurance, pension systems, healthcare, etc.—in capitalist and developing countries alike.

It would have seemed that victory in the war had confirmed the strength of the socialist system and the rightfulness of the assertions that the future belongs to communism. The emergence of a number of ruling communist regimes, coupled with military and scientific successes, served as a powerful argument in favor of the idea that the victory of global socialism was but inevitable in the near future. To many political forces in colonial and developing countries this was a persuasive message. It appears that, as of the 1950s and 1960s, the leadership of the USSR and other socialist countries also believed this quite sincerely.

3.2 Soviet Influence on the Anti-colonial Movement, the Third World, and the Processes of Globalization

Since its very inception, the Soviet government supported anti-imperialist and anti-colonial causes abroad. Following the Second World War, the USSR actively supported both combat forms of the struggle for independence (e.g., Indochina's war against France) and other forms, including the possibilities of revolution. The idea that revolutionary victory requires major social transformations with inevitable purges and repressions was reinforced by the authority of the Russian Revolution and the subsequent successes of the USSR, and had a huge impact on the political life of many countries. The Soviet Union's influence over the emerging Third World grew particularly strong in the mid-

1950s. This was perhaps most pronounced in the Middle East and in the confrontation between the Arab countries and Israel, where the USSR assumed an anti-Israeli position.

As a result of the cooperation between the socialist states and the Third World, developing countries underwent substantial industrial modernization, accompanied by technological transfer and the development of heavy industry. The USSR and other members of the Socialist bloc gave assistance to various states, many of which (including India, Egypt, and others), though not open to Soviet-type socialism, nevertheless embraced state-level industrialism. For various reasons, both the West and the USSR faced increasing pressure to ally themselves with developing countries; this resulted in the great powers' struggle for influence in the Third World.[16] Developing countries were in particular needed so that they could be included in the orbit of military-political confrontation, but by no means for this purpose alone. A number of countries joined the so-called the Non-Aligned Movement; the USSR, in turn, positioning itself as a champion of peace, sought to influence this forum with the participation of dozens of other countries. The significance of developing countries as a function of their multiplicity was particularly clear in the operations of international organizations, foremost of these being the United Nations. Overall, the ends of buttressing one's own ideological platform, enabling foreign economic strategies, and numerous other aims required cooperation with developing countries and made it essential.

The collapse of colonial empires essentially completed the processes of globalization that had been underway since the eighteenth and nineteenth centuries. Whereas colonial conquests opened up opportunities for the progression of globalization, the isolation of East-Asian countries in the seventeenth and eighteenth centuries can be interpreted as a moment of anti-globalization. The world had fewer states than are in existence today, and globalization unfolded quite effortlessly for some time. The collapse of colonial empires created dozens of new states, each of which was free to pursue its own policies. Unsurprisingly, this hampered globalization for a while, as did the ideologically charged two-bloc world order. This explains why globalization processes ramped up in the 1990s, when the Socialist bloc collapsed and its former members joined various world organizations.

---

16   Leonid Grinin and Andrei Korotayev, *Great Divergence and Great Convergence: A Global Perspective* (New York: Springer, 2015).

3.3 Soviet Influence on Social Processes

One cannot ignore the influence of Soviet social policy (and the attraction of revolution) as social-policy factors in the West, where social insurance laws, including unemployment insurance and job placement assistance, began to be adopted. Of course, all these ideas had arisen long before the First World War, but their practical implementation was undoubtedly encouraged by the USSR's example. In addition, public opinion in capitalist countries themselves grew increasingly critical of capitalism and exploitation; taxation in Western countries was correspondingly adapted, in order to, among other things, reduce inequality; progressive taxation and estate taxes were introduced to this end. Generally, in the 1920s and 1930s, the Western political spectrum shifted visibly towards the left, as in European democracies, so even in the United States, while totalitarian and fascist states drew upon Soviet policy experience. The powerful rise of global socialism forced capitalist countries to ramp up their social policy, much of which had already been established before the Second World War. As a result, the developed countries embarked upon establishing a welfare state, within which a powerful middle class and social insurance and welfare institutions were established.

3.4 The Soviet Union and the Rise of the State's Societal Role in the Twentieth Century

The Socialist Revolution, which had set out to demolish the state, paradoxically led to a dramatic increase in its importance in the USSR. Another paradox was that, despite the constant the western criticism of the governmentalization of everything in the USSR and other socialist countries, the growing role of the state in the social and economic policy, and the increase of its share of public and industrial property, began to spread to countries where the role of the state had been traditionally weak—including Great Britain, the Unites States, as well as, to a degree, France. This tendency had already been greatly encouraged by the Great Depression of 1929–1933. The USSR's example, with its unprecedented rate of industrialization and economic growth at a time when most of the world's economies were suffering severely, could not but elicit admiration. The fact that the USSR was enjoying total employment at a time when unemployment had reached unprecedented proportions in the United States, Germany, and other countries, as well as a number of other facts, could not but bolster the credibility of Communist ideology. Incidentally, the USSR's economic successes also contributed, at that time and especially in the postwar period, to the strengthening of the role of economic planning on a national scale, not only in socialist states, but also in capitalist and developing countries. (At present, the two largest and most rapidly developing countries, China and India, rely on five-year plans in their development. Nearly thirty countries, not counting the socialist states, have used five-year plans to varying degrees—including, for example, South Korea from 1960 to 1996. Historically, Nazi Germany's idea of a four-year plan (1936–1940) was clearly a borrowing from the Soviet practice.) Most generally, the Soviet Union's influence bolstered the role of the state in a number of countries, where it became increasingly involved in the economy and the redistribution of goods and resources. The global rise of totalitarianism was, in fact, one of the means of strengthening the role of the state under conditions of socio-economic instability. Western countries would eventually succeed in reconciling the augmented role of the state with democracy—but this would not happen immediately. The war, followed by the popularization of Keynesian economics, accelerated the state's interference in all spheres of life. Undoubtedly, the leftward shift of an array of political parties and leaders, and the demands for the nationalization of major enterprises in England, France and other countries, sounded after the war, drew heavily on the Soviet experience. Capitalist states were now actively pursuing the welfare-state path, with higher taxation rates, sometimes as high as 50%–70% tax on profits and personal income. On the other hand, the standard of living was rising rapidly in the USSR and other socialist countries, and the government now had to invest considerable effort in maintaining it. The citizens' proprietary ambitions—to own apartments, cars, dachas, etc.—were also rising. All this entailed a convergence of regimes. It is not surprising that the 1950s and the 1960s saw the rise of theories of the convergence of socialism and capitalism, developed particularly on the basis of the theories of the industrial society (Pitirim Sorokin, Raymond Aron, John Galbraith, Walt Whitman Rostow, Jean Fourastié, and others). A certain convergence was indeed observed. And the more noticeable it became, the less momentum was left for the further influence of the Russian Revolution over the world. This influence was "exhaled," and the economy and the overall development of the USSR and other socialist countries slowed down. The era of socialism was coming to a close.

4   Revolutions as Geopolitical Weapons

As geopolitical weapons and as instruments of either overt or covert state policy, revolutions entered into systematic use in the twentieth century. (They had been deployed but occasionally until then, since the French Revolution.) The Japanese resorted to the aid of revolutionaries (particularly Polish) during the Russo-Japanese War. During the First World War, England and France (via their embassies in Russia) supported the Russian Constitutional Democratic Party, which opposed the monarchy and effectively incited revolution. Germany also made effective use of revolutionaries, who advocated an immediate end to the war; these were chiefly Bolsheviks headed by Lenin. Still, as a continuous line of state foreign policy, support for revolutionary movements and parties with systematic assistance in organizing revolutions was first adopted by the Bolsheviks, almost immediately after the October Revolution. This line would be extended through the entire Soviet period. Western countries, on the other hand, feared revolutions, and therefore resorted to preparing them far less frequently. (Historically, the United States has staged military coups, though it is true that the differences between different types of regime overthrow, especially in Latin America, are not always easy to delineate.) Still, the United States and its allies were usually happy to inspire anti-government sentiments in socialist countries.

The decline of the Socialist camp led to the rise in the United States' and other Western countries' deployment of revolutions as geopolitical weapons. With the elimination of the threat of the emergence of Communist regimes as a result of revolution, beginning in the late 1980s, revolutions came to be seen as useful and advantageous to the West. Once again, they were largely identified with democracy, democracy being itself regarded as an unconditionally positive form of governance. That this is not the case is, nevertheless, becoming increasingly apparent, as "democracy" typically serves as an ideological cover for expansionism, conducted under the banners of democracy, free markets, and of fighting corruption, authoritarianism and violations of human rights.[17]

The late twentieth and early twenty-first centuries saw the emergence of a new type of revolution, marked by a greater share of external interference and instigation, and by the increased use of artificial, non-spontaneous revolutions for the overthrow of undesirable regimes. A succession of so-called "colored" revolutions swept across a number of countries. For this purpose, opposition was actively cultivated, and sometimes trained by special instructors in the targeted states; non-profit organizations and diplomatic missions, as well as revolutionary organizations like the Serbian Otpor, were also used as

---

17   Leonid Grinin, "Новый мировой порядок и эпоха глобализации. Американская гегемония: апогей и ослабление. Что дальше?" ["The New World Order and the Era of Globalization. American Hegemony: Apogee and Weakening. What Comes Next?"], *Vek globalizatsii*, 2015, No. 2, 2–17; Alexander Chumakov, "Культурно-цивилизационные разломы глобального мира" ["Cultural-Civilizational Fractures of the Global World"], *Vek globalizatsii*, 2015, No. 2, 35–47.

coordinators and headquarters of all sorts. Unfortunately, the positive effects of such revolutions are usually minimal, while the resulting losses are often devastating. According to Jack Goldstone, most countries that have undergone "color revolutions" have not seen a quick and reliable transition to democracy, while the revolutions in their aftermath have created new difficulties, struggles for power and high likelihoods of sliding back into authoritarianism.[18] As a result, the role of revolutions as a means of transition to a higher and more progressive social organization is increasingly voided of historical meaning, while the price of revolutions remains high, since, as a mode of change in modern social life, they are too destructive.

5 Conclusion: The Russian Revolution's Historical and Present Influence on the World System

From the very beginning, the Bolsheviks had regarded the October Revolution as the onset of the World Revolution. In the early years of its existence, the very presence of the revolutionary, Socialist Russia, its influence on revolutionary events in Europe and Asia, and the very possibility of a Bolshevik victory in the civil war, etc., had enormous ideological, propagandistic and other kinds of influence (as seen in the social reforms embraced by capitalist countries). This was, in conventional terms, its *revolutionary* phase of influence upon the world.

A mere ten years later, after a fierce inner-party struggle between the supporters of Stalin and Trotsky, the doctrine of socialism in one country, concomitant with a long period of coexistence with capitalism, was embraced by the party. This marked a new phase of the Revolution's influence on change in the rest of the world, which is referred to as the *state phase*.

The third phase was inaugurated in 1939, when the USSR entered the active geopolitical struggle for world influence, at first as part of the pre-war activity, and then directly in the theaters of World War II. This propelled the Soviet Union to the pinnacle of its power, and this phase of influence may be called *geopolitical*.

The final, *superpower* phase of influence was entered in the late 1940s and the early 1950s, and can be divided into two major periods. The first period,

---

18   See: Jack Goldstone, *Revolutions: A Very Short Introduction* (Oxford: Oxford University Press, 2014).

marking the zenith of influence, spans approximately from 1945 to the mid-1960s, when the dynamics of the USSR's and the socialist countries' development, as well as revolutionary activity coinciding with the rise of the national liberation and anti-colonial movement, was still on the upswing. USSR and its example had considerable influence in that period over the state's involvement in the economy and in the redistribution of goods and benefits. The social changes in the wake of the October Revolution were the immediate source of social policy in most of the world in the twentieth century. The second, twilight stage of this phrase, spanning from the 1960s to the 1990s, witnessed the symptoms of the system's crisis, as the loss of its momentum became increasingly apparent. The rise of the standards of living finally extinguished the revolutionary impulse, while increasing the public's dissatisfied expectations from the government. Socialism appeared less and less attractive when compared with capitalism. The USSR's desire to strengthen its role as a superpower came into conflict with its economic capabilities, eventually resulting in its collapse. Having spent the 1930s and the early 1950s on the ideological defensive, the capitalist countries now forged ahead, gradually advancing powerful propaganda campaigns via the radio and other media, and actively nurturing the dissident movement as a "fifth column." This had considerable influence on the views of the Soviet population.

For some time following the collapse of the USSR, perceptions of the October Revolution became negative, as the former socialist countries, and many of the developing ones, were increasingly eager to deny its achievements. This was accompanied by powerful developments in globalization, which engulfed most of the world. Still, the Russian Revolution's achievement was evident in the growth of social policies, especially with regard to the elderly in the developed countries. In Europe, and particularly in Northern Europe, the Social-Democratic and socialist parties played a formative role by successfully combining the principles of socialism and capitalism, which enabled them to attain a high standard of living in their countries. In this, the Social-Democrats were greatly influenced by the Soviet policy, even if they would not avow this influence. The role of social democracy in post-war Germany cannot be overestimated, any more than can Germany's own role at the core of the European Union. In this manner, the influence of the October Revolution in Europe has been, and continues to be, significant.

Further, and more persuasive, evidence of this influence has to do with the fact that the most successful economic development of recent decades has been achieved by a country undeniably affected by the Socialist Revolution in Russia. The People's Republic of China was able to combine the advantages of socialist state economic planning and of the capitalist free markets and competition. In its own way, China perpetuates policies of assistance to developing countries, especially in Africa. As the model of the last great revolution—the Chinese revolution—the Russian Revolution continues to shape the processes of globalization, in competition with the Western model of development, and with the involvement of developing countries in multiple initiatives. The recession of 2008–2009 has put an end to the negative phase of its influence and reception in the world. Shortly after 2010, state policies of developed countries shifted towards some socialist and state-planning ideas (especially in the monetary sphere).

Today, the effects of the Russian Revolution are indirect but noticeable, as socialist ideas are enjoying a revival, even in the United States. One has reason to think that we are yet to see some unexpected aspects of its influence in the coming decades.

The Structures of Social Solidarity in Contemporary Russia

Evolution and Perspectives

Anastasia V. Mitrofanova

Historically, solidarity has been a precondition for the survival of human communities. For ages, religion consolidated people through shared values and rituals; however, our contemporaries appear much less interested in professing their faith collectively. Large corporations try to "buy" their employees' solidarity—that is, their solidarity with the company, not with one another. The state makes solidarity among its citizens compulsory, but, as state institutions become weaker, society reveals its inability to maintain its own integrity. Civil solidarity is displaced by socially destructive forms of networking, such as clans, sectarian ideological groupings, and diffuse criminal communities. Against this background, the place of integrity-facilitating social structures is uncertain—that place being located between primary collectives (e.g., families and circles of friends) and the state with its coercive apparatus.

In twentieth-century Russia, civic solidarity experienced a particularly serious crisis caused by a series of devastating blows, some intentional and some unexpected. The author's task in this chapter is to evaluate the scale of damage and the restoration prospects of these social solidarity structures. Conceptually, the chapter is based on the theory of civil society developed by the Canadian philosopher Charles Taylor. My research methodology combines a critical analysis of texts and historical data; in addition, I use the results of the qualitative sociological research that I carried out either independently or as part of various research groups.

1   The Constitutive Structures of Society as Agent

In "Modes of Civil Society," Charles Taylor has suggested that social solidarity is sustained by two kinds of structures (or "streams," in his own terminology), named after John Locke and Charles Montesquieu:[1]

---

[1] Charles Taylor, "Modes of Civil Society," *Public Culture*, 1990 (3), No. 1, 115.

(1) Lockean structures (L-structures) are pre-state or non-state communities bound by common ethical values (e.g., parish churches, rural and urban neighborhoods). L-structures are linked to territories or to common ancestry, which makes them reminiscent of the family and other primary social institutions.

(2) Montesquieu structures (M-structures) are voluntary associations of citizens bound by shared values, which shape society as an agent under the conditions of a strong centralized state (e.g., non-parochial religious fraternities, volunteer groups, and co-operatives). M-structures are not territorial; they are subordinate to L-structures and comprise a superstructure over the latter.

When linked together, L- and M-structures comprise the society as an agent that is independent of the state and has its own values and vision. Taylor juxtaposes this agent with the state. He does not mention corporations, although they serve as another exceptionally powerful actor, in confrontation with whom the state exercises its agency (e.g., when confronting corporate pollution of the natural environment or protecting historic buildings). Here we must differentiate the structures of social solidarity from those anti-social communities and networks that do not strengthen social integrity but have, instead, a devastative effect on it. In my opinion, the socially formative L- and M-structures are constitutive for society as an independent agent in its opposition to the state, corporations, and socially destructive networks.

Lockean structures exist in all societies and are, in most cases, the holdovers from the preindustrial period. In Russian social thought, beginning with the older generation of Slavophiles, we find a tendency to see the peasant village community (*obshchina*) as a Lockean structure. First the Slavophiles, and later the Narodniks ("Populists") thought of the *obshchina* as of an ethical community. Konstantin Aksakov called it a "moral choir," where each personality "renouncing its exclusiveness for the harmony of the whole … finds itself in accord with personalities who have made an equal self-sacrifice."[2] This vision was popular, and even authors speaking out against the preservation of the village community admitted that the latter was based on "very high moral principles of mutual assistance."[3]

Beginning in the second half of the nineteenth century, some authors considered the traditional Russian cooperative (*artel*) to be a Lockean structure.

---

2 Quoted in: Sergey Pushkarev, *Self-Government and Freedom in Russia* (Boulder, CO: Westview, 1988), 46.

3 Aleksandr A. Rittich, *Зависимость крестьян от общины и мира* [*Peasants' Dependence on Community and Society*] (St. Petersburg: Kirschbaum, 1903), 50.

They understood *artel* not just as a unit of production but also as an ethical community that aimed at shaping and perfecting the human being as a member of society.[4] As in the case of the *obshchina*, the admirers of the *artel* exaggerated that institution's moral potential; at the same time, the *artel* was analogous to the cooperative, generally recognized as one of its constitutive social structures (since its inception, the cooperative represented an ethical collective).

In addition, the older generation of Slavophiles envisioned the traditional multigenerational family as an ethical community. In this, they relied on the Biblical concept of family as a church "in their house" (as in Romans 16:5), which can be established only with like-minded partners, otherwise "they of his own household" become one's "foes" (Matthew 10:36). Aksakov wrote that the Russian family is united neither by blood, nor by economic ties, but by ethical bonds—that is, by a sincere intent to perform the will of the father, freely and lovingly.[5] Such formulas should definitely be taken critically; at the same time, we need to keep in mind that, even in the last quarter of the nineteenth century (and all the more so later), those institutions of village community—the *artel* and the traditional family—were already in various stages of decay. Against this background, it was hard to decipher their meaning as socially constitutive structures bound by ethical principles. When speaking about the family, we should also keep in mind that this is a complex phenomenon that cannot be comprehensively defined within one explanatory paradigm; among other things, the family definitely constitutes a Lockean structure.

According to Taylor, M-structures were best represented by the Christian fraternities that emerged in Europe in the course of the confrontation between the Roman Catholic Church and the secularized state apparatus. Initially, they were something like a superstructure over the Lockean structures of church parishes, but, as their activities gradually embraced society as a whole, they became constitutive for the society as a sovereign agent.[6] These Catholic M-structures became a model for their ethical competitors—above all, the socialists. Orthodox fraternities first emerged in the late sixteenth century on the territory of Rzeczpospolita. The formation of Catholic and Orthodox fraterni-

---

4 Vitaly Averiyanov, V. Venediktov, and A. Kozlov, Артель и артельный человек [*The Artel and the Artel Individual*] (Moscow: Institute of Russian Civilization, 2014), 580.
5 Vasily Schukin, "Концепция Дома у ранних славянофилов" ["The Concept of the Home Among the Early Slavophiles"], in Славянофильство и современность [*Slavophilia and the Present*], edited by B. F. Yegorov (St. Petersburg: Nauka, 1994), 40–41.
6 Oleg Kharkhordin, "Civil Society and Orthodox Christianity," Europe–Asia Studies, 1998 (50), No 6, 953–54.

ties directly depended on the state's encroachment on the Lockean structures represented by parish communities.

In the nineteenth century, L-structures were disintegrating as a result of the Industrial Revolution. They were no longer able to perform their conventional socially beneficial functions (such as caring for the destitute, orphans, and the elderly). M-structures started to fill the emerging lacunas, provoking the concern of the state. Although M-structures are not always hostile to the state, in the case of the state's abrupt weakening, they are transformed into an alternative source of power, which can be helpful in transferring the state apparatuses into new hands. To protect itself, the state becomes socialized, taking on some functions that had been previously performed by non-state actors. Germany became the pioneer of this development. In the second half of the twentieth century, the progressive socialization of states led to the emergence of the welfare state, one that aims at performing all the functions of both L- and M-structures (caring for children, assistance to the elderly and the disabled, etc.). This was, in fact, a great civilizational achievement, because the enormous resources of the state were now redirected towards protecting the weakest members of society. Yet, this socialization of the state (or, in a sense, the conflation of state and society) also had a negative side. The welfare state risked undermining the integrity of some preceding structures—including the family—that used to be constitutive for the agency of society. (In this way, Chad Freidrich's 2011 documentary *The Pruitt Igoe Myth: An Urban History* has footage of Pruitt Igoe's former inhabitants recalling their fathers having to hide from social workers, since only single-parent households were eligible for the apartments.) Human beings came to depend on the state, and this made them extremely vulnerable in the face of possible abuses by state authorities, as well as in the event of state power's collapse.

2 The Crisis of Non-State Solidarity Structures in Twentieth-Century Russia

Initially, Russia lagged significantly behind Western countries in the sphere of state socialization. As a result, Lockean structures performed a significant share of the socially beneficial functions in the first quarter of the twentieth century. We find a complete destruction of these old structures after the rapid industrialization took place at the end of the 1920s, followed by the state-sponsored repressions against various social groups. At the same time, achieving a stateless Communist society was proclaimed to be the end goal;

this meant that some new L- and M-structures had to be constructed. This will be discussed in greater detail later on.

When considering the structures that used to be formative for society as an agent, I should mention, first of all, the various Orthodox-Christian civic associations. In the early years following the Socialist revolution, multiple lay fraternities and M-structures emerged on the basis of the parochial L-structures. The latter formed a protective layer between the believers and the atheist state. Their activities immediately surpassed their initial aims (such as protecting the holy relics) and became socially beneficial—lately, due to the ways in which they addressed the external social environment. Fraternities, for instance, were widely involved in providing relief for the victims of the 1922 famine.[7] In 1929, "the year of the Great Turn," the state initiated an anti-religious campaign to eliminate both parishes and lay associations—a move connected to collectivization and to the struggle against the "kulaks."[8] State-induced repression of believers sent Orthodox associations underground, turning them into anti-social, rather than social, organizations.[9] Non-confessional M-structures built on diverse ethical foundations (e.g., Tolstoyans, Esperantists, vegetarians, etc.) were concurrently wiped out.

Confrontations between the state and L-structures led to the gradual destruction of the family institution, thereby affecting both the traditional, multigenerational family and the more modern, nuclear family limited to spouses and their children. Immediately after the revolution, an attempt was made to eliminate the family as such "with one blow," but state resources were so scarce that some of the socially beneficial functions had to be returned by the state to the family, as the latter was the only social institution willing to perform those functions free of charge. (In 1918, adoption of children by families was made illegal, but in 1926 it was once again allowed, since the state could not cope with caring for the orphans.) The Soviet social security system remained weak and covered only an insignificant part of the population: for instance, no social security guarantees existed for peasants and for people deprived of civil rights due to improper class origins or for other reasons.[10]

---

7   Alexey Beglov, "Объединения православных верующих в СССР в 1920-1930-е годы: причины возникновения, типология и направления развития" ["Associations of Orthodox Believers in the 1920s–1930s USSR: Causes of Emergence, Typology, and Directions of Development"], *Rossiyskaya istoriya*, 2012, No. 3, 95.

8   Alexey Beglov, "Русская Православная Церковь в годы 'Великого перелома': приходской аспект," ["Russian Orthodox Church in the Years of the 'Great Watershed' under the Aspect of Parish Life"] in *1929: "Великий перелом" и его последствия* [*1929: The "Great Watershed" and Its Consequences*] (Moscow: RossPEn, 2020), 369–81.

9   Alexey Beglov, "Associations of Orthodox Believers," 100.

The rise of crime rates and deviant behavior turned out to be the side-effect of the destruction of the family, and these negative consequences could not be successfully deterred by state law enforcement.

The most serious threat to the family appeared not in the period of the socialization of the state, but during the time of state-induced repression. This was destructive, and not solely for individual household: the damage was much more severe, as repressive measures and their consequences quickly and all but inevitably broke up the intergenerational ties within families. Repression was equally destructive for the future generations, since family members did not simply disappear without a trace: they were also erased from family memory.

In that time, the basic act of keeping in touch with one's family could be dangerous—for example, to people of "questionable" class origins. Some people in that situation chose to renounce their families; more often, they concealed or intentionally distorted their backgrounds, sometimes altering their names and places of origin.[11] Many people were afraid of making inquiries about their arrested or exiled relatives. The mechanism of transmitting family memory between generations thus disintegrated. The result was that "blank spots" took the place of specific events, people, and time periods erased from the earlier versions of family history passed down to the previous generations.[12] The political campaigns of the 1920s and 1930s were especially destructive for peasant families. This claim is supported by the empirical evidence collected by our research team, through in-depth interviews with the descendants of the victims of state-sponsored repression.[13] Even people who showed

---

10   Natalia Lebina, Pavel Romanov, and Yelena Yarskaya-Smirnova, "Забота и контроль: социальная политика в советской действительности" ["Care and Control: The Social Policies of Soviet Reality"], in *Советская социальная политика 1920-х-1930-х годов: идеология и повседневность* [*Soviet Social Policies in the 1920s and 1930s: The Ideology of Everyday*] (Moscow: Variant, 2007), 21–67; Galina Ivanova, "На пороге 'Государства всеобщего благосостояния'" ["On the Threshold of a 'State of Total Prosperity'"] in *Социальная политика в СССР (середина 1950-х—начало 1970-х годов* [*Social Policies in USSR, Mid-1950s to Early 1970s*] (Moscow: IRI RAN, 2011), 11–12.

11   Anna Kimerling and Oleg Leibovich, *"Я вырос в сталинскую эпоху": Политический автопортрет советского журналиста* [*"I Grew Up in Stalin's Era": A Political Portrait of a Soviet Journalist*] (Moscow: Higher School of Economics, 2019), 22–27.

12   Veronika Duprat-Kushtanina, "Remembering the Repression of the Stalin Era in Russia: On the Non-Transmission of Family Memory," *Nationalities Papers: The Journal of Nationalism and Ethnicity*, 2013 (41), No. 2, 226.

13   "Legacies of Dehumanization: The Transnational Perspective" (2019–2021) is a research project aimed at understanding the dynamics of family memory of state-sponsored repression. Hereafter, the codes that protect the privacy of interviewees include infor-

interest in their familial past often had no information about their relatives who had "disappeared":

> "Afterwards, we never told anyone that our parents had been repressed. That was something no one ever did afterwards; it was as if it never happened." (f91)

> "Although [their parents] had been repressed, it's as if [the grandparents] don't remember." (m19)

> "The parents, too, don't remember especially what has happened. Even family members did not go on about that." (m51)

> "How Mom must have been frightened that she never said anything... And my grandma... We don't know when she died or anything." (f70–OB)

> "I received a letter about granddad's rehabilitation and grandma's rehabilitation, with a photo of grandma in profile and full face... But they did not say where and when [they died]." (f62–OB).

> "Their photos are nowhere to be found; everything has been destroyed—confiscated and destroyed. Here I am: no photos, none of the grandfather, none of the great-grandfather. Nothing anywhere, no traces whatsoever. No matter how I searched, I found nothing." (m79–OB).

Our respondents, up to five generations removed from the events, noted the rupture of family ties as a result of the repressions:

> "What is most painful is that families were destroyed, that family ties were undermined." (f51)

> "Here's something else I want to say: when I received those letters of rehabilitation—oh Lord—how I cried, how I cried. I think: my Lord, I lived my whole life without grandma, without grandpa; they were liquidated for no reason—and these two pieces of paper came, without apology, without anything." (f62–OB)

---

mation about their gender and age. Approximate age is designated by a "~" sign. When quoting the interviews taken by my collaborator, Olga Bogatova, I include her initials in the code.

In the postwar period, the Soviet state gradually became socialized. The Lockean structures, which were seriously damaged by the repressions in the 1920s and 1930s, and by the Second World War, could no longer fulfill their socially beneficial tasks. (The war had been less destructive for the family institution, since soldiers killed and wounded in battle were not erased from family memory, and those family ties did not have to be concealed.) This proto-welfare state was, on the one hand, progressive and able to improve the everyday lives of its citizens. On the other hand, it consumed very scarce resources, thereby overextending the state.[14] In fact, state institutions of care proved to be so successful in demolishing the remains of Lockean structures that by the beginning of the 1970s the Russian Soviet Federative Socialist Republic and some other parts of the USSR experienced a severe demographic crisis. The state had to deal not only with the plummeting fertility rate, but also with problems of social morality, including an overly casual approach to marriage and the spread of harmful habits and anti-social behavior. The paradox was that the more the Soviet state promoted family values, the greater were the resources it channeled into social security, thereby enabling each private citizen to survive outside of a family network.

Did any novel structures of social solidarity emerge to replace the old ones? And did these novel structures offer even a distant possibility of the state's withering away, in order for society to become self-regulated? This question has been taken up in contemporary historical sociology. According to Oleg Kharkhordin, as a result of the revolution, all small contact groups were transformed into collectives—quasi-religious congregations held together by shared ethical norms.[15] According to this conception, the collective is an L-structure functionally replacing the church parish and performing, at the same time, the M-function of protecting individuals from the state.[16] Vadim Volkov argues that Soviet civil society (*obshchestvennost*), which united diverse forms of organization (and self-organization) from below (voluntary people's guards, civil courts, volunteer organizations), is a functional equivalent of M-structures.[17] The question remains open whether these structures—which would have been unlikely to emerge without state encouragement—can be treated as socially constitutive.

---

14 Ivanova, "On the Threshold," 14.
15 Kharkhordin, "Civil Society and Orthodox Christianity," 958.
16 Kharkhordin, "Civil Society and Orthodox Christianity," 960.
17 Vadim Volkov, "Общественность: забытая практика гражданского общества" ["*Obshchestvennost*: The Forgotten Civic Practice"], *Pro et Contra, a Journal of the Carnegie Foundation*, 1997 (2), No. 4, 77–90.

Beginning in the late 1950s, informal groups began to appear in the Soviet Union, and—unlike *obshchestvennost*—these groups were tolerated, rather than supported, by the state. These were groups of idealists, formed on the basis of shared ethical principles, and oriented towards performing socially-beneficial functions (for instance, the trackers' movement, dedicated to the discovery and burial of fallen soldiers, and movements dedicated to preserving cultural heritage). There were also youth initiatives, such as the Communards' movement, whose participants were united by the same communist values that were being propagated in the rest of society. In her publication on the commune of Young Frunzenists, Daria Dimke observed that the Communards inhabited a world that was psychologically alternative to the rest of the Soviet society; and yet, at the personal level, they did not feel apart from society and considered themselves to be its "vanguard."[18] At first glance, there should not have been conflicts between the Communards and the rest of society. In reality, though, conflict was inevitable, and conflicts between informal youth movements and their Soviet environment normally resolved in favor of the latter. Such conflicts were devastating for these groups' pro-social position and their social utility. (A good example of this is furnished the novels by Vyacheslav Krapivin (1938–2020), a famous Soviet children's author and the organizer of "Caravel," a children's flotilla, in some ways reminiscent of the Communards' movement. Although Krapivin's characters always have a strong sense of social responsibility, they remain in a permanent and inevitable state of conflict, not so much with the state, as with the notorious Soviet *obshchestvennost*.)

During the postwar period, Soviet M-structures were weak, and their ability to perform socially constitutive functions were dubious. Some of them were openly state-initiated and engendered no particularly strong social solidarity. Others possessed some superficial social utility and were loaded with the possibility of transformation into hermetically-sealed "islands of utopia" (to recall an eponymous edited volume). And yet, such "islands" did not contribute much to social solidarity.

The destruction of L-structures and the weakness of nascent M-structures in Soviet society caused an irreversible and very dangerous developmental

---

18   Daria Dimke, "Юные коммунары, или Крестовый поход детей: между утопией декларируемой и утопией реальной" ["Young Communards, or The Children's Crusade: Between Utopias Declared and Real"], in *Острова утопии: педагогическое и социальное проектирование послевоенной школы (1940–1980-е)* [*The Islands of Utopia: The Postwar Approach to Pedagogical and Social Planning (1940s–1980s)*] (Moscow: NLO, 2015), 377–78.

trend. Ilya Kukulin writes that, although multiple and sometimes very complex practices of social self-regulation were emerging, most of them had a generally anti-disciplinary character.[19] He talks about what I designated earlier as the structures of "bad," or socially destructive, solidarity. This form of solidarity took the forms of organized crime and the anti-Soviet underground, whose antagonism to Soviet society was self-evident. The problem was that in late Soviet society, virtually all forms of non-state solidarity acquired socially destructive characteristics.

Lev Gudkov emphasized that in Soviet society, the word loosely equivalent to "us" (*svoi*, "our own") meant those placed in the domain of ethical principles, while "them" (*chuzhiye*, "the outsiders") inhabited a sphere where no norms of solidary and responsibility applied.[20] Informal networks of "us," even if not openly antisocial (e.g., classmates and college friends), could not function as socially beneficial: instead of reinforcing solidarity between citizens, they eroded it. People preferred to discuss this issue in terms of friendship and mutual help, but their friendly interactions were gradually transformed into a system of *blat*—a form of nepotism that caused massive social corruption.[21] (Soviet networks of *blat*, disguised as friendships, were shown in *A Blonde Behind the Corner*, Vladimir Bortko's 1984 comedy, whose genre is owed to the obvious reason that no serious sociological film on the topic would have been financed at the time. Alyona Ledenyova defines *blat* as using private contacts, channels, and networks to access public resources.)[22] Volkov, too admits that the influence of the informal networks of *blat* led to the "privatization" and erosion of the state.[23] The main idea here is that the state, at that moment, remained the only capable guardian of social solidarity. Its alternatives were limited to weak M- and L-structures, unable to counter the "bad" networks of

---

19 Ilya Kukulin, "Продисциплинарные и антидисциплинарные сети в позднесоветском обществе" ["Pro-Disciplinary and Anti-Disciplinary Networks in the Late-Soviet Society"], *Sotsiologicheskoye obozreniye*, 2017 (16), No. 3, 145.

20 Lev Gudkov, "Доверие в России: смысл, функции, структура" ["Trust in Russia: Its Meaning, Functions, and Structure"], *Novoye literaturnoye obozreniye*, 2012, No. 5, https://www.nlobooks.ru/magazines/novoe_literaturnoe_obozrenie/117_nlo_5_2012/article/18937/.

21 Geoffrey Hosking, "Структуры доверия в последние десятилетия Советского Союза" ["Structures of Trust in the Final Decades of the Soviet Union"], *Neprikosnovenny zapas*, 2007, No. 4, https://magazines.gorky.media/nz/2007/4/struktury-doveriya-v-poslednie-desyatiletiya-sovetskogo-soyuza.html.

22 Alyona Ledenyova, "Личные связи и неформальные сообщества: трансформация блата в постсоветском обществе" ["Personal Connections and Informal Associations: The Transformation of *Blat* in Post-Soviet Society"], *Mir Rossii*, 1997, No. 2, 90.

23 Volkov, "*Obshchestvennost*."

non-state and anti-social solidarity. The only possible result of this disposition was a massive crisis of solidarity like the subsequent social collapse.

These "bad" networks did not outlive the state in whose shadow they had first emerged. According to Gudkov, Soviet forms of trust that used to bind members of small groups and communities—while simultaneously representing the mechanism of social fragmentation—deteriorated and were no longer meaningful and active.[24] Alyona Ledenyova has shown that the market reforms of the 1990s undermined the foundations of *blat* and deprived it of its humane elements, which were then replaced with monetary exchange.[25] This transformation robbed the system of *blat* of its air of solidarity, friendship, and mutual help, thereby revealing its antisocial nature. The "bad" networks persisted, partly, in the form of criminal associations and webs of corruption. Later, they were joined by the remainders of the Soviet Lockean structures (family clans and ethnic criminal groups) and those M-structures that accidentally survived the state collapse and grew into criminal organizations (for example, some former sports clubs).

The collapse of Soviet statehood provoked a total crisis of sociality and disrupted all social interactions. According to some surveys, at the end of the twentieth century, solidarity and ethical obligations could be detected only at the level of the person's closest environment.[26] Socially responsible behavior became an exception, and Russian society thus ceased to exist as a sovereign agent.

3   The Twenty-First Century: On the Path to "The New Social"

It remains unclear whether the ruined structures of non-state solidarity have the capacity to regenerate. At the beginning of the twenty-first century, two trends became visible in Russia. One of them was the attempt to recreate Lockean structures, such as the family and the faith community (the parish). In theory, the state could have transferred its social obligations to them, since it was unable to fulfill them itself. At the turn of the millennium, family becomes part of the state's rhetoric as one of the fundamental moral and spiritual values of Russian society. In reality, however, few families (either multigenerational or nuclear) managed to avoid the catastrophe of the twentieth century.

---

24   Gudkov, "Trust in Russia."
25   Ledenyova, "Personal Connections," 94.
26   Gudkov, "Trust in Russia."

Many Orthodox Christian authors now promote the family by encouraging people to have multiple children, yet they rarely speak about the necessity of restoring the intergenerational ties, or of knowing one's ancestry and family history. This, in my opinion, is indirect evidence of the devastating results of the total break-up of intergenerational ties in the previous century. Very few people are receptive to the propaganda of having more children; no large-scale restoration of large, multigenerational families looks possible in Russia's foreseeable future. Accordingly, the prospects of traditional faith communities as Lockean structures consisting of multigenerational families are equally vague. The more the family is discussed in the contemporary Russian society, the less is its role in real life. Restoring the family institution would require massive financial inflows from the state (e.g., the so-called "maternity capital," etc.) and consistent social assistance. This would make the family a burden for the state, instead of a utilizable resource.

The so-called "religious revival" of the 1990s has offered hope in restoring L-structures in the form of church parishes. But the process of transforming the parish from a formal administrative unit of the church into a consolidated community is marked by some serious obstacles. Ivan Zabaev has proposed the concept of "sacral individualism" among Russian Orthodox believers, for whom the church is a place of private communion with God, not a consolidated community of people.[27] This problem is evident to the believers themselves. For example, Andrei Kormukhin, the leader of the para-ecclesiastical social movement *Sorok Sorokov*, stresses that

> we do not live in our churches as one big family. We are, rather, living as Orthodox Christians who love Christ and enter churches to meet Christ, to address Him, to participate in His sacraments, to confess, to take communion; and then we leave the church; we leave the church walls behind, and plunge, once again, into this world that atomizes and individualizes us.[28]

---

[27] Ivan Zabaev, "'Сакральный индивидуализм' и община в современном русском православии" ["'Sacral individualism' and Community in Contemporary Russian Orthodox Christianity], in *Приход и община в современном православии: корневая система российской религиозности* [*Parish and Community in Contemporary Orthodox Christianity: The Root System of Russian Religiosity*], edited by Alexander Agajanian and Kathy Rousselet (Moscow: Ves mir, 2011), 347.

[28] "Прямой эфир с Андреем Кормухиным. Движение Сорок Сороков" ["Live with Andrei Kormukhin. The *Sorok Sorokov* Movement"], DSS, April 6, 2020, https://vk.com/videos-53664310?z=video-53664310_456240982%2Fpl_-53664310_-2.

Most likely, many believers attend sacred services individually, following their own spiritual impulses and without any intent to join a parish community. Alexander Agajanian argues that the average parish consists of a small "core" of activists, known to each other and to the priest, and of a diffuse "periphery" made of believers who do not intend to befriend others at a parish.[29] Religious conversion in Russia remains individual; it tears people from their usual social environment, and often from their families. This type of interaction between believers and organized religion is known as the "temple model": the congregation of a temple consists of individuals carrying out no common liturgical or extra-liturgical activities.[30] Solidarity between them emerges only accidentally, and does not lead to the formation of community as a sovereign agent.

Both the priests and the researchers emphasize the connection between the insufficient solidarity of Orthodox congregations and the anti-church policies of the past: "the whole life of a parish in the Soviet time was focused on welcoming a single, individual ... parishioner. She came, she confessed, took communion, and left: no further contact."[31] Eventually, the very idea of a parish community became suspicious. When speaking about consolidated parishes, some researchers use terms like "the Orthodox guruism" and "the ashramization of Orthodoxy."[32] Still, some contemporary parishes have managed to become consolidated. This makes them unlike traditional church congregations; they are tied to specific territories and their inhabitants and serve to unite individuals around the locus of the given church. Such parishes do a lot of socially beneficial work.[33]

---

29 Alexander Agajanian, "Приход и община в современном православии: современные процессы в ретроспективе последнего столетия" ["Parish and Community in Contemporary Orthodox Christianity: Contemporary Processes in the Retrospect of the Last Century"], in *Parish and Community in Contemporary Orthodox Christianity*, 347.

30 Ram A. Cnaan and Daniel W. Curtis, "Religious Congregations as Voluntary Associations: An Overview," *Nonprofit and Voluntary Sector Quarterly*, 2012 (42), No. 1, 16–17.

31 Oxana Golovko and Fyodor Borodin, "Если священник не умеет дружить, общины не получится" ["If the Priest Cannot Be a Good Friend, There Will Be No Community"], *Pravmir*, September 26, 2019, https://www.pravmir.ru/esli-svyashhennik-ne-umeet-druzhit-obshhiny-ne-poluchitsya-i-pochemu-inogda-v-hrame-ne-gotovy-prinyat-postoronnih/.

32 Yevgeny Klyachenkov, "К вопросу о новых формах самоорганизации в Русской Православной Церкви" ["Towards the Question of New Forms of Self-Organization in the Russian 'Orthodox Church'"], *Mezhdunarodny zhurnal gumanitarnykh i estestvennykh nauk* [*International Journal of Humanities and Natural Sciences*], 2019, No. 6–1, 77–83.

33 See: Polina Batanova, Ivan Zabaev et al., *"Партнерский приход": сотрудничество священников и мирян в развитии социальной деятельности в приходах РПЦ в начале*

The second trend is the emergence of new M-structures, such as volunteer organizations built on religious or secular ethical foundations and performing socially-beneficial functions. My empirical research confirms that people involved with social volunteering envision the destruction of sociality as an ethical problem.[34] Many speak of their feelings and psychological crises:

"Everyone is on their own; this is very obvious." (m30)

"Family ties are now weakening more and more, and this allows people to be more independent, if they have the resources for it. But if something catastrophic happens in a person's life, he has no help or buttress from the family, as in the former days, when the extended family still existed." (m~35)

"These ideas do not resound in the society in principle—that one should live for more than just oneself, not just to build a carrier, not just to wander around supermarkets looking for a discount." (w~25)

[The respondent speaks on behalf of a friend.] "By his doors, over there, by the apartment-building entrance, in the space between the two sets of doors, there lived some homeless, awful, simply hideous, foul-smelling woman who drove everyone wild and mad, all the neighbors who entered the building through those doors. He would walk past her and you can imagine that smell and how unpleasant that was. Where had she come from? She was like some vermin, like some mouse that moves in. And once, he was leaving... And he looked, and she was acting a bit strange, twitching or something. So he just walked by without paying attention, not quite without paying attention, but it was unpleasant. And it turned out that she died. (m~30)

Volunteers appear to be motivated not only by their wish to help others, but also by their aspiration to find a social milieu congruent with their own values:

XXI века ['A Parish Partnership': Cooperation of Priests and Lay-People in the Development of ROC's Social Activities in the Early Twenty-First Century] (Moscow: St. Tikhon Orthodox University, 2018).

34 Volunteer initiatives were studied in 2018–2019. See: Olga Bogatova, E. Dolgaeva, and Anastasia Mitrofanova, "Деятельность социально ориентированных организаций Русской православной церкви: региональные аспекты" ["The Activities of the Socially-Oriented Organizations of the Russian Orthodox Church: Regional Aspects"], *Regionologiya*, 2019 (27), No. 3, 489–512.

"You expect that there are people there who share, so to speak, your own worldview—the volunteers—and that it'll just be easier to find a common language with them... I felt very comfortable and natural there." (w~25)

"It was more comfortable for me to deal with those people, because we were on the same wave-length, and we had a common goal." (w~22)

"All people are kind; everything is done in kindness; everyone is with God." (m40)

"We do not just have some similar interests, but ... It is that we are spiritually a bit higher, so that, apart from our personal interests, we are ready to take part in disinterested activities." (w~28)

Volunteer initiatives in contemporary Russia represent the most promising venue for recreating the non-state sociality. At the end of the 1990s, Oleg Kharkhordin mentioned that in the conditions of a collapsed state, the main task of M-structures is to protect individuals, not so much from state despotism, but generally from "uncivil means of interaction."[35] No longer does the state pose the main threat to the individual; quite the opposite, it would not object to getting rid of its obligations in the sphere of social security. Corporations and destructive non-state associations now pose a much bigger threat. Currently, volunteers perform many social functions that were previously handled either by L-structures or by the state (e.g., assisting the homeless, rehabilitating addicts, supporting single mothers, etc.). What is even more important is that they represent M-structures and reproduce sociality as such, thereby constituting society as a sovereign agent independent of the state.[36]

The collapse of the Soviet state—the state that formerly served as the sole protector of social solidarity—transformed the prospect of the restoration of non-state structures of social sovereignty from a mere possibility into a necessity. At present, M-structures give rise to society as an independent agent (*obshchestvennost*), but must emerge "from below," and are not inspired by the state. This kind of independent society produces and articulates a nascent

---

35 Kharkhordin, "Civil Society and Orthodox Christianity," 963.
36 Anastasia Mitrofanova, "Православные инициативы как пункты социальной сборки: преодоление исторического разлома" ["Orthodox Initiatives as Social Assembly-Points: Overcoming the Historic Divide"], *Tekhnologos*, 2019, No. 1, 118.

public opinion (which can already be heard in contemporary Russia), able to confront not just the forces of social destruction represented by the "bad" networks and criminal organizations, but also the tremendous might of the state and corporations. Charles Taylor mentions that M-structures coordinate the actions of society as a whole, and by doing this they are able to significantly determine the course of state policy.[37] The moment is approaching when Russian society as a full-fledged agent will enter the political scene and speak loudly about its interests, demanding equal participation in the process of making important decisions.

37   Taylor, "Modes of Civil Society," 98.

The Philosophical Potential of Russian Cosmism in the Context of Contemporary Interdisciplinary Global Studies

Alexander M. Starostin

The concept of the *globalization of society* is well established and has assumed its place in modern scholarship, among experts in relevant fields, and in public opinion. This concept is commonly defined as "the process of universalization and formation of structures uniformly applicable to the entire planet Earth, and of connections and relations among various spheres of society."[1] It is also defined as the "processes of planetary-scale integration and disintegration in the economy, politics, and culture, as well as anthropogenic environmental changes that are comprehensive in their form and affect the interests of the entire world community."[2] Research and interpretation of globalization have been concentrated in the interdisciplinary field called "global studies." The efforts of this field are aimed at "identifying the essence of globalization, the causes of its emergence and its development tendencies," and also at "analyzing the positive and negative effects it generates."[3]

In recent years, the field of global studies has been concerned with several acute problems, as reflected by the work of contemporary scholars in the field. Scholars working in the areas of global modeling (some of the well-known figures being the organizers and coordinators of the Club of Rome) have highlighted the paramount importance of reorienting our approaches to the social sphere and globalization, as evidenced by the Club's 2018 anniversary report, *Come On! Capitalism, Short-Termism, Population and the Destruction of the Planet*.[4] This report called for the development of a new strategy for the "guaranteed planetary security and survival," in the context of the idea of the "Whole World," which requires the formation of a new worldview based on

---

1 Alexander Chumakov and Ivan Mazour, eds., *Global Studies: International Interdisciplinary Encyclopedic Dictionary* (New York: Piter, 2006), 163.
2 Alexander Chumakov, "Global Studies in the System of Modern Scientific Knowledge," *Problems of Philosophy*, 2012, No. 7, 5.
3 Chumakov, "Global Studies in the System of Modern Scientific Knowledge," 4.
4 Ernst U. von Weizsäcker and Anders Wijkman, *Come On! Capitalism, Short-Termism, Population and the Destruction of the Planet: A Report to the Club of Rome* (New York: Springer, 2018).

a "new Enlightenment." It unconditionally emphasized the need for a new generation of humanistic values and demanded that we critically reconsider the mounting global risks engendered by modern speculative capitalism.

The authors, nevertheless, did not propose a new model of globalization that might lead to changes in social attitudes; nor did they propose a model that might respond to the rising wave of mass consumption and replace the economic and political institutions of the global capitalist market. Therefore, just as the authors of the anniversary report to the Club of Rome, the author puts forward the claim that the new advances in our global worldview should be based both on representations of the contemporary global agenda and on developing the worldview already well-defined in world culture, with its significant spiritual potential.

This invites us to consider the concept of "alternative global studies."[5] This concept is based on research in the field of contemporary global studies, including questions of the correlation of paradigms and the collision of concepts. By considering the synthesis-driven movement of these collisions, we will achieve a deeper understanding of the essence of globalization and the development of an *interdisciplinary* view of its processes.

The very idea of "alternative globalization models," as well as the work of Russian Cosmism, is based on a particular approach, wherein "research philosophy" is understood as a set of philosophical segments and tools, and as a set of philosophical activities, that allow one to obtain new knowledge and to form research strategies. In the author's view, this includes the strategies of philosophical diatropy, philosophical alternativism, and philosophical innovation studies (i.e., applied philosophy). Thus, research philosophy is a dynamic, productive, and innovative part of the present-day system of philosophical knowledge and methods.[6]

An analysis of the conceptual foundations of alternative globalization models makes it possible to identify several major trends of their development,

---

5 Alexander Starostin, *Глобализация современного мира: концептуальная репрезентация* [*Globalization of the Modern World: A Conceptual Representation*] (Rostov-on-Don: Rostov State University of Economics, 2018), 31–48.

6 Alexander Starostin, *Исследовательская философия в системном и инструментальном измерении* [*Philosophical Scholarship in Systemic and Instrumental Dimensions*] (Rostov-on-Don: Rostov State University of Economics, 2018), 7–24; Alexander Starostin, *Философские инновации: концепция и основные сферы проявлений* [*Philosophical Innovations: The Concept and Its Main Spheres of Manifestation*] (Rostov-on-Don: SKAGS, 2009); E. V. Zolotukhina-Abolina, "Поиск системы философских знаний (Размышления над книгой А. М. Старостина *Исследовательская философия*)" ["The Search for a System of Philosophical Knowledge (Reflections on A. M. Starostin's *Research Philosophy*)"], *Economic Science of Modern Russia*, 2019. No. 3, 152–57.

which are either established, manifest, or may become the norm in the next few decades. The foundations of alternative globalization models can be represented as follows:

(a) a continued sector-based approach (primarily, in macroeconomics and geopolitics), with attributes of the new world economic and technological paradigm, and with the inclusion of political multipolarity in the analysis;
(b) globalization as a new anthropological revolution (similar to the Neolithic and Industrial Revolutions), with similar mass-level qualitative changes in the production, value-motivational, and cognitive spheres;
(c) globalization in the context of cosmism and global evolutionism (Nikolay Fyodorov, Konstantin Tsiolkovsky, Teilhard de Chardin, Vladimir Vernadsky, Nikolay Kardashev), with the formation of a first-level space civilization.

The projection of global development in the context of cosmism and global evolutionism has significant implications. In the philosophical and ideological quest of Russian philosophical and humanistic thought, the school of cosmism has been developing for several centuries. It is of particular interest to consider the ideas of cosmism in light of the Club of Rome's quest for a new worldview.

A nation's search for the meaning of life and for national identity represents a key motif in cosmism. As a particular instance of this, the Russian Idea plays a special role in the formation of the Russian national identity. Here we would like to draw attention not only to the content of this quest, which has been the object of Russian philosophers' attention for almost two centuries, but also to the sophisticated context behind this idea, which includes national and civilizational dimensions, as well as those connected with the ideas of universal humanity and the natural-cosmic sphere.

The Russian Idea is the development of one version of national identity, and is a response to the need for a unique philosophy of history. It is characterized by a global evolutionary approach and by the idea of intercultural, interethnic, and moral *sobornost*; by anthropo-cosmism as the search for ways to overcome physical, spatial, and temporal limitations; and by the search for the "kingdom of God" and for the means of overcoming spiritual limitations and resistances. These components serve as the philosophical, ethical, and theological justification of the Russian Idea. Russia's historical path, including its future, is viewed here as distinctive, and messianic motifs are quite apparent in this view. Unlike many other manifestations of messianism, the Russian Idea is characterized by the preservation of Orthodox Christian spirituality, humanistic openness, and tolerance.

In order to define the Russian Idea, it is necessary to look at its ethnogenetic roots. The Russian "super-ethnos" (according to Lev Gumilyov and his terminology) is relatively new and quite "passionate," and is in the acme phase of its development. On the one hand, we can observe the gigantic spatial and geographical scale of the super-ethnos's settlement, with spatial redundancy (such that eliminates the need for further territorial expansion). On the other hand, when comparing this situation with the planetary context, we find that this excess of passionate energy gave no impulse for geopolitical and socioeconomic quests (as was the case with Western ethnic groups in the industrial period), but led immediately to the search for the ultimate socio-ecological, moral, worldview foundations of social existence—the search for its cosmic meaning. In this regard, Russian Cosmism can be seen as the logical continuation of the Russian Idea. In any case, Western cosmism is natural, objectified, and not anthropo-cosmic, unlike Russian cosmism.

Russian Cosmism thereby continues the Russian Idea by ontologizing the historiosophic, moral, and socio-ecological intuitions of Russia's historical mission, so beloved by some circles of the Russian liberal intelligentsia. One might say that cosmism is the cosmic substantiation of the Russian Idea—its cosmic level. The ethno-genetic, social, and spiritual messages of the Russian Idea and Russian Cosmism have become so universal that they are reproduced in philosophical, religious, artistic, scientific, and mystical forms by different, sometimes completely independent groups of intellectuals. Today, this aspect of the Russian natural sciences and of the Russian humanities continues to be one of the most original manifestations of world culture.

It should be emphasized that modern philosophical, scientific, theological, and journalistic literature demonstrate an intense and unwavering interest in the phenomenon of Russian Cosmism. This worldview is considered one of the fundamental and original manifestations of nineteenth- and and twentieth-century Russian culture. Indeed, when attempting to highlight the most striking and unique manifestations of the Russian humanities, including philosophical thought, both Russian and non-Russian researchers most often pay attention to the following well-known triad: the civilizational approach (represented by Nikolai Danilevsky), the existential view of humanity (e.g., Lev Tolstoy and Fyodor Dostoyevsky), and cosmism (e.g., Nikolai Fyodorov, Konstantin Tsiolkovsky, Vladimir Vernadsky, Aleksandr Chizhevsky).

The extensive publications that have been devoted to the study of Russian Cosmism provide various definitions and interpretations, identify its different forms, and examine the evolution of its ideas.[7] Generally, the phenomenon of Russian Cosmism cannot be said to suffer from neglect, be it from philosophers, natural scientists, theologians, or journalists. And yet, we should note a detail that researchers and advocates of Russian Cosmism either pass over unintentionally or evade deliberately: the fact that the main manifestations of Russian Cosmism ended abruptly with the work of Tsiolkovsky, Vernadsky, and Alexander Chizhevsky. There is, allegedly, no continuation of cosmist thought beyond these figures. In the present author's opinion, though, it is necessary to talk about the evolutionary development of Russian Cosmism in its transformation from its classical form into the modern Russian or "Soviet" cosmism. Soviet cosmism enriched the Russian cosmist paradigm with new layer of philosophical, socio-political, scientific, artistic, and journalistic publications related to the new era of space exploration and its concerns with the outer space, its study and exploration, and even travel there.

Notably, modern forms of Russian Cosmism came about in connection with the advent of the Space Age and with the need to comprehend a fundamentally new kind of human experience, and to anticipate new developments in that sphere. It is in connection with the formation of this new agenda that we see, in the 1960s–1980s, the emergence of several leading research centers dedicated to new developments in this worldview. These included the Department of Philosophical Problems of Natural Science of the USSR Academy of Sciences Institute of Philosophy, and the Institute of History of Natural Science and Technology of the USSR Academy of Sciences. In addition, special conference sessions (or "readings") were held annually in Kaluga, at the Konstantin Tsiolkovsky Museum of History of Cosmonautics. The Kaluga readings served as the main forum for the discussion of scientific, technological, philosophical, social, political, and legal problems of space exploration. Over fifty such sessions were held.

---

7   See: Svetlana G. Semyonova and Anastasia G. Gacheva, eds., *Русский космизм: Антология философской мысли* [*Russian Cosmism: An Anthology of Philosophical Thought*] (Moscow: Pedagogika, 1993); Alexander P. Ogurtsov and V. V. Fesenkova, eds., *Философия русского космизма* [*Philosophy of Russian Cosmism*] (Moscow: New Milennium, 1996); Olga D. Kurakina, *Русский космизм как социокультурный феномен* [*Russian Cosmism as a Socio-Cultural Phenomenon*] (Moscow: MFTI, 1993); Natalia M. Nikolayenko, *Космизм в контексте отечественной философской культуры* [*Cosmism in the Context of Russian Philosophical Culture*] (Omsk: Omsk State Institute of Business, 2006); Kamil H. Khairullin, Философия космизма [*The Philosophy of Cosmism*] (Kazan: House of Print, 2003); *Философская инноватика и русский космизм* [*Philosophical Innovation and Russian Cosmism*] (Rostov-on-Don: SKAGS, 2011).

In the middle of the 1980s, the Institute of Philosophy of the USSR Academy of Sciences prepared and published a five-volume *History of Philosophy in USSR*—a *summa* of what had been accomplished in this field. One chapter of this publication was devoted to philosophical and ideological interpretation of outer-space research.[8] The authors noted:

> The topic of philosophical problems of space exploration has included the most general patterns and tendencies in the interactions between society and space, and the study of the general characteristics of "man–universe," "society–space," "humanity–space–civilization" relations. Consistent development of the philosophical and sociological problems of cosmonautics began in the early 1960s, after the first manned space flights. Currently, a large team of scientists is working on this problem in the Soviet Union, with over 300 works published.... Expansion of the overall scope of space activities has further attracted the attention of philosophers and social scientists (V. E. Davidovich, B. M. Kedrov, V. V. Rubtsov, A. M. Starostin, Y. N. Stempursky, A. I. Tukmacheva, P. F. Tukmachev, E. T. Faddeyev, Y. A. Shkolenko, K. H. Khairullin, and others), scientists, rocket- and space-technology professionals, specialists engaged in space research, space biology and medicine, astronomy, astrophysics (O. M. Belotserkovsky, O. T. Gazenko, V. P. Glushko, N. S. Kardashev, K. Ya. Kondratyev, B. N. Petrov, R. Z. Sagdeev, B. V. Rauschenbach, I. S. Shklovsky, etc.), Soviet astronaut-pilots (G. T. Beregovoy, A. A. Leonov, V. I. Sevastianov, K. P. Feoktistov, etc.), and those working on the general theoretical problems of cosmonautics.[9]

Many works published in the 1960 and through 1980s touched upon the general philosophical and ontological problems of the interaction of humanity and its spirit with the outer space.[10] This work, in fact, continued the worldview pursuits of Tsiolkovsky, Teilhard de Chardin, and Vernadsky, and addresses specific questions regarding the best practices of outer space activities. At the same time, it brought up and discussed scenarios that might occur

---

8 V. E. Evgrafov et al., eds., История философии в СССР [*History of Philosophy in USSR*], v. 5, Book 1 (Moscow: Nauka, 1985), 782–97.
9 Evgrafov, История философии в СССР, 784–85.
10 Evald V. Ilyenkov, "Космология духа" ["Cosmology of Spirit"], *Nauka i religiya*, 1988, No. 8, 9; Vlail P. Kaznacheev and Evgeny A. Spirin, Космопланетарный феномен человека [*The Cosmo-Planetary Phenomenon of Humanity*] (Novosibirsk: Nauka, 1991).

in the course of research and exploration of near and far space. Such questions included the analysis of promising avenues of space exploration and habitation, possible positive and negative impacts on the Earth's ecology, and the search for intelligent life in the Universe and establishing contact with extraterrestrial civilizations (e.g., the CETI and SETI initiatives).[11]

It should be noted that, to a large extent, this agenda was ideologically loaded, and a considerable part of its scope was involved in the Cold-War ideological campaigns. The fundamental propaganda thesis was that socialism would be "the launching pad for Soviet space-crafts." By the end of the 1980s, the USSR significantly reduced its multifaceted and large-scale activities in this area. Mass media began publishing attacks on the Soviet rocket and space industry, claiming that it diverted massive resources from meeting the needs of the Soviet people.

After the collapse of the USSR in the 1990s, space activities declined drastically. By the mid-1990s, financing of space activities was estimated to have decreased more than twenty-fold. Even now, funding for space research remains more than ten times less than the Soviet financing of space programs in the mid-1980s. In that period, the Soviet government began to dismantle everything connected with the earlier idea of "socialism as a launching pad for space exploration." Nevertheless, it is worth noting that the organizational, managerial, and logistical efficiencies of large Soviet space projects were three to four times higher than the American indicators of efficiency, mostly attributable to the higher level of centralization, resulting in the reduction of competitive and transactional costs under the state management of such large projects.[12]

The scope of humanities research and the number of publications on the subject of space has also decreased significantly. New research in this area is mostly related to the development of extra-rational ways of reflecting on space and space activities. This has greatly influenced public opinion in these matters, which is mostly formed on an extra-rational and irrationally mystical basis.

---

11   See: *Проблема CETI (связь с внеземными цивилизациями)* [*The Problem of CETI (Communication with Extraterrestrial Intelligence)*] (Moscow: Mir, 1975); Iosif S. Shklovsky, *Вселенная, жизнь, разум* [*Universe, Life, Reason*], third ed. (Moscow: Nauka, 1973); Nikolay S. Kardashev "Астрофизический аспект проблемы поиска внеземных цивилизаций" ["The Astrophysical Aspect of Searching for Extraterrestrial Civilizations"], in *Внеземные цивилизации: Проблемы межзвездной связи* [*Extraterrestrial Civilizations: Problems of Inter-Star Communication*], edited by S. A. Kaplan (Moscow: Nauka, 1969).

12   Mikhail Delyagin and Vyacheslav Sheyanov, *Русский космос: победы и поражения* [*The Russian Deep Space: Victories and Defeats*] (Moscow: Eksmo, 2011), 156–88.

Nevertheless, beginning in the mid-1990s, Russian historical writing, philosophy, and memoirs all began to show a significant interest in the classical tradition of Russian Cosmism, and in the idea of developing and popularizing irrational forms of spiritual space exploration. This flourishing was a reaction to prior censorship and to Soviet-era ideological obstacles. For example, the legacy of the little-known, though distinctive, Russian discipline of *biocosmism* did not see further development, since in the 1920s and the 1930s its proponents had been subjected to political persecution. The legacy of thinkers like Nikolay Fyodorov, Pavel Florensky, and Alexander Chizhevsky has yet to be properly appreciated. Most of Tsiolkovsky's work in philosophy and in the humanities were published during that period.

Nevertheless, by the beginning of the twenty-first century, scholars began to develop contemporary forms of the Russian cosmist agenda. These years saw the emergence of important works that summarized and consolidated the research findings of the 1970s, 1980s, and 1990s. At the turn of the twenty-first century, multiple doctoral theses were defended on various aspects of the topic of space activity.

Both classical and modern varieties of Russian Cosmism encompass an anthropo-cosmic aspect corresponding to the second position on the list of alternative globalization vectors—namely, to the global anthropological revolution. This aspect of modern cosmism found its development in Soviet science fiction. After the collapse of the Soviet Union, that work came to be suspended, for a long time. As for contemporary reality (as opposed to fiction), one must emphasize the significant impact of cultural and anthropological factors *on the formation of a new global context*. What one has in mind is the increasing population of the planet. After the Second World War, the world population reached the stage of mass product consumption; in some parts of the world, up to 15%–20% of the population rose to a stage of personal and spiritual development in which their focus shifted to spiritual and cultural priorities in consumption.

One can assume that over the next 25–30 years (the span of one generation), the priorities of spiritual personal fulfillment will become the standard, not only for the elites and the middle stratum, but also for the masses. The implementation of the principle of social justice plays an important role in labor relations and economic interests, in the power structure, in post-material interests and values, and at the deepest foundations of human existence.

One should like to touch upon the renewed social axiological and person-centered egalitarian matrix.[13] In addition to the traditional values of individual rights and freedoms, and of social justice, this matrix includes the values of *altruism, humanism, solidarity, social and personal responsibility, common cause, and common good* that are necessary for a well-developed social egalitarian culture. These values and orientations are supported mostly by contemporary socialist and post-socialist movements (neo-communism, social democracy, Christian democratic movements, and other similar religious movements); we also find them represented in the new secular neo-egalitarian currents of science, culture, and education.[14]

In conclusion, to return to the ideas of the Club of Rome's anniversary report on the "full world" and the "limits to growth," we should emphasize the relative nature of such value judgments and their dependence on the system of worldview coordinates. In terms of prehistoric and historical global ecology, humanity has already experienced three or four milestone stages of the "full world," over the course of its post-flood history, in moving from hunting and gathering to agriculture and cattle breeding; then to proto-state and state systems, the era of early and mature industrialism; and finally to the post-industrial and information era. These steps align with qualitative environmental, demographic, economic, and cognitive milestones.

Upon entering the milestone associated with the full development of the Earth and the near-Earth space, we must once again qualitatively revise our norms, values, and standards of conduct, so as to align them with our more dimensionally and structurally complex environment. New risks and dangers are in store for us there, and a new worldview system of coordinates—the cosmic worldview—is necessary, since global geo-centrism is already "losing traction." Yet such a "new" system of worldview coordinates has long been in existence.

---

13   Alexander Starostin, "Элитарный и эгалитарный контекст социальной справедливости: возможна ли конвергенция?" ["Elitist and Egalitarian Contexts of Social Justice: Is Convergence Possible?"] in *Социальная справедливость в современном мире*, edited by L. I. Nikovskaya et al. [*Social Justice in the Modern World*] (Moscow: Klyuch-S, 2017); L. G. Shvets, "Справедливость в гендерном измерении" ["Justice in the Gender Dimension"], ibid.

14   Alexander Starostin, *Прикладная философия как философская инноватика* [*Applied Philosophy as Philosophical Innovation*] (Rostov-on-Don: Southern Russian Institute of Management, 2015), 42–43.

PART 5

Humanistic Aspects of Global Civilization

∴

Civilizational Values in the Age of Global Social Transformations

Ivan A. Aleshkovski and Alexander T. Gasparishvili

1 Civilizations and Civilizational Values

Human beings have always defined themselves using such concepts as origin, religion, language, history, values, customs, and social institutions. They have identified themselves with different social groups—ethnic groups, religious communities, nations, and, at the broadest level, civilizations. Civilization itself should be regarded as a kind of cultural community, the highest level of grouping of people according to culture and the broadest category of cultural identity, subordinate to what separates the human from other biological species. It is civilization that takes care of the whole variety of material and non-material problems pertinent to human life. All human history is essentially the history of civilizations.[1]

The world of civilizations forms a single, closely interconnected system, where the interrelations of civilizations form the content of world history. The diversity of civilizations itself is the basis of the vitality of humankind as a single, diverse, and dynamic whole, and of its ability to adapt to different conditions of life and activity in different parts of the Earth.

The subject matter of civilization is always the human being, and it is he or she who occupies a central place in the civilization's value system. In this sense, civilization is anthropocentric, that is, all its peculiarities proceed from the fact that the center of its interests is precisely the person and his or her value-based attitudes, and not abstract ideas or material and technical problems of its own development.

By "world civilizations" we will understand the historical stages in the development of mankind, characterized by significant differences in the level and nature of the demographic, environmental, technological, and economic dynamics, geopolitical relations, and the sociocultural system conditioned by cultural heritage based on its supreme values and main goals.[2]

---

1 Samuel Huntington, "The Clash of the Civilizations?" *Foreign Affairs*, 1993 (72), No. 3, 29–49.
2 Yury Yakovets and Suheil Farah, *Диалог и партнерство цивилизаций* [*Dialogue and Partnership of Civilizations*] (Moscow: Pitirim Sorokin, 2014), 24–25.

Arnold Toynbee, in his *Study of History*, had argued that humankind, as a natural phenomenon, appears as an assembly of individual local civilizations, while the historical process represents a cycle of such formations. In total, he counted twenty-one major civilizations in the history of humankind.[3]

At present, the question of how many civilizations are there in the world is answered differently by different authors, whereas the principles of selection of modern civilizations are still debatable. A civilization can embrace a large mass of people like China, about which the famous American political scientist Lucian Pye once said: "This is a civilization that impersonates a country."[4] But a civilization can also be very small, like the civilization of the English-speaking Caribbean. A civilization can be determined by objective criteria (e.g., history, religion, language, traditions, and institutions) as well as subjectively, via self-identification. It can span over multiple states (like the West-European and Arabic civilizations) or just one (such as China or Japan). Each civilization is distinguished by its own unique specificity and particular internal structure. In this way, the Japanese civilization has but one variant, while the Western civilization has two main variants, European and North American. The Islamic civilization has at least three: the Arabic, Turkish, and Malay variants.

Given this diversity of civilizations, a number of elements are common to all types of civilization. These are

- a certain path of historical formation and development in spiritual and material culture;
- a common worldview and common values within the existing framework of cultural and historical shared identity;
- patterns of relationships between society and individuals, etc.

What is common to all civilizations is their pragmatic nature. This does not cause much doubt, since everything that a civilization does has a clear utilitarian-pragmatic meaning, in relation to material and spiritual problems alike. This pragmatic character of civilization manifests in the formation of a certain system of civilizational values.

From this point of view, values represent a relatively stable, socially determined selective attitude to the totality of material and spiritual public goods. In essence, values are what people need in order to satisfy their appetites and interests, together with ideas and motivating norms, goals and ideals. At the same time, *value* is among the key concepts that designate objects, phenomena, their properties, and abstract ideas that embody moral ideals and supply

---

3   See: Arnold J. Toynbee, *A Study of History* (Oxford: Oxford University Press, 1987).
4   Lucian W. Pye, "The Non-Western Political Process," *Journal of Politics*, 1958, No. 3, 468–96.

the standards of "what ought to be." In fact, the whole variety of objects of human activity, social relations, and natural phenomena can serve as values, as traditionally considered within the dichotomies of good and evil, truth and error, beauty and ugliness, the permissible and the forbidden, the just and the unjust.[5]

The value-based world of civilizations is vast and diverse. At the same time, there are some "cross-cutting" values that are practically pivotal in any field of activity. These are the values that, either directly or indirectly, affect the behavior of people in all areas of their lives. Their specific objective content becomes the basis of their typology, via the arising distinctions.

Values can be social, economic, political, spiritual, etc. Experts count dozens and even hundreds of different values in existence. For example, scientific analysis of the problem of social values might be based on the study of people's attitudes to various facets of their life. According to such a classification, the "value of the family," the "value of labor," the "value of education," and many others can be classified as varieties of value.[6]

Civilizational values are fixed in the system of categories constitutive of a civilizational worldview. They are deeply rooted in each individual's material and spiritual activities, and in the activities of all the people who belong to this civilization. Culture is invariably included in the value system, often understood as the totality of spiritual values, while civilization is often perceived chiefly as a totality of material values. In reality, the objects of culture and civilization do not exist independently of each other. This interconnection does not rule out, but, in a certain sense, presupposes and engenders both the opposition of material and spiritual values and the contradictions within the systems of material and spiritual values themselves.

A typical example of the sometimes diametric opposition of civilizational values is the advice issued by the East and the West in connection with the periodically arising contradictions between a person and the world around him or her. "Change the world," the West insists. "Change yourself," the East teaches.[7]

---

5   Ivan Aleshkovski, Alexander Gasparishvili, and Natalia Smakotina, "Global Values in the Context of Civilizational Dialogue," *Journal of Globalization Studies*, 2020 (11), No. 1, 74, https://doi.org/10.30884/jogs/2020.01.05.
6   See: Hilary Putnam, *The Collapse of the Fact/Value Dichotomy and Other Essays* (Cambridge: Harvard University Press, 2002).
7   Vadim Kortunov, "The Values of Culture and Civilization Do Not Coincide," *Modern Studies of Social Problems*, 2013 (30), No. 10, https://cyberleninka.ru/article/v/tsennosti-kultury-i-tsivilizatsii-ne-sovpadayut.

Despite the differences in the different civilizations' value systems, there has always been a certain inevitable unity; we might say that the similarity of common values is formed by the commonality of essential features of civilizations themselves, since these shared identities inevitably inhabit a context of interrelations formed by the peoples' need for co-existence and by their interactions in an increasingly complicated society. The same need for co-existence can be traced with regard to the interaction of civilizations.

Still, the unity and commonality of interests among modern civilizations are not yet sufficiently realized. The world of civilizations is torn by contradictions and armed conflicts, and by global and local wars. It is fraught with threats that can result in the death of civilizations. These threats can become a reality, if the leaders of humankind do not promptly realize their danger and join forces on the basis of dialogue and partnership instead of confrontation and conflict.

Throughout the history of humankind, the clash of civilizations and their rivalry over the resources necessary at home, to ensure one's own survival and development, has been only one aspect of their interaction. But there has been another very important aspect of constant dialogue and exchange of values between them. Millennia of human history present numerous examples of peaceful and positive interaction that benefited its sides and all of humanity as a whole.

The power of modern civilizations has reached such a level that it can lead to their own destruction and to the end of human history as such. It is now globally recognized as necessary to establish a dialogue between civilizations, for the sake of preserving humanity and continuing its advancement on the path of social progress. Today, the fate of humankind depends on the fate of the great modern civilizations. It is possible that they might unite into a single world civilization, or manage, despite the differences in their main values and ultimate goals, to peacefully settle their contradictions while maintaining their basic values.[8]

2   Dialogue among Civilizations

The UN General Assembly proclaimed 2001 the Year of Dialogue among Civilizations. Resolution 53/22 of the UN General Assembly pointed to the "impor-

---

8   Jan Such and Janusz Vishnevsky, "Судьба современных цивилизаций в перспективе унификации мировой экономики" ["The Fate of Modern Civilizations at the Prospect of Unification of the World Economy"], *History and Modernity*, 2006, No. 1, 89.

tance of displaying tolerance in international relations and the significant role of dialogue as a means of achieving mutual understanding, eliminating threats to peace and enhancing interaction and exchanges between civilizations." In addition, it was noted that the "achievements of civilizations are the collective heritage of humanity providing a source of inspiration and progress for all of humanity."[9] Subsequently, in connection with the processes of globalization unfolding around the world, a need for a deeper study of these problems emerged, since globalization created new conditions for cooperation and required building bridges between civilizations, cultures, and peoples as a necessary condition for the survival of humankind.

A number of UN and UNESCO documents of the early twenty-first century pay special attention to the problems of dialogue between civilizations. Regional and international conferences and roundtables on this question have also been held throughout the world.[10] It was seen as a process unfolding both within civilizations and at their boundaries, and based on general participation and a collective desire to learn, to discover and investigate concepts, to identify areas of common understanding and core values, and to bring different approaches into a single whole. The dialogue was supposed to be constant and continuous.

Within the framework of the UN, from the very inception of this international organization, measures were taken to unite the international community's efforts to protect the spiritual and cultural values of humankind and to organize a constructive dialogue between the main civilizations of the modern world, promoting multilateral relations in all spheres of public life.

The development of these efforts led to the adoption by UNESCO member states, in November 2001, of the "UNESCO Universal Declaration on Cultural Diversity" and the United Nations-developed "Global Agenda for Dialogue Among Civilizations." This document outlined the basic principles of intercultural dialogue, which should be protected and cultivated.[11]

This process was assumed to be aimed at the following goals:
- promotion of general participation, equality and equity, justice and tolerance in human relations;

---

9 "United Nations Year of Dialogue Among Civilizations," a resolution adopted by the General Assembly, United Nations, November 16, 1998, https://undocs.org/en/A/RES/53/22.

10 Mohammad R. Hafeznia, "Dialogue Among Civilizations as a New Approach for International Relations," *The Future of Life and the Future of Our Civilization*, edited by Vladimir Burdyuzha (Berlin: Springer, 2006), 355.

11 "Universal Declaration on Cultural Diversity," General Conference of the United Nations Educational, Scientific, and Cultural Organization, November 2, 2001, https://www.ohchr.org/Documents/professionalinterest/diversity.pdf.

- strengthening of mutual understanding and mutual respect through the interaction between civilizations;
- mutual enrichment and development of an understanding of the richness and wisdom of all civilizations;
- identification and promotion of what unites civilizations, in order to eliminate common threats to shared values, universal human rights, and achievements of human society in various fields;
- promotion and protection of all human rights and fundamental freedoms and the achievement of a deeper common understanding of human rights;
- promotion of a deeper understanding of common ethical standards and universal human values;
- ensuring greater respect for cultural diversity and cultural heritage;[12]

Dialogue among civilizations makes an important contribution to progress in the following areas:[13]
- building confidence at local, national, regional, and international levels;
- deepening mutual understanding and knowledge among various social groups, cultures, and civilizations in various fields, including culture, religion, education, information, science, and technology;
- eliminating threats to peace and security;
- promotion and protection of human rights;
- development of common ethical standards.

By now, the "Global Agenda for Dialogue Among Civilizations" has become an important foundation for enhancing understanding between nations. As part of it, various innovative approaches are being developed towards strengthening mutual understanding and promoting constructive interaction between peoples with different cultural traditions. From the beginning of the millennium and until the present, one of the main goals and objectives of the United Nations and UNESCO has been to facilitate the dialogue of civilizations, and to take account of intercultural differences in order to find compromises and areas of common interest.

The true goal of dialogue among civilizations is to take possession of the hearts and minds of the next generation. In order for new attitudes to take

---

12   "Global Agenda for Dialogue Among Civilizations," a resolution adopted by the General Assembly, United Nations, November 21, 2001, https://www.un.org/en/documents/decl_conv/conventions/dac_agenda.shtml.
13   Hans Koechler, "The Dialogue of Civilizations: Philosophical Basis, Current State and Prospects," *Asia Europe Journal*, 2003 (1), 315–20, https://doi.org/10.1007/s10308-003-0037-9.

root, they must be accepted by those who can inspire young people and stimulate their imagination. The efforts of these people, the role models of our societies, must be mobilized by the international community.

3 Globalization and the Transformation of Civilizational Values

One of the characteristic features of the modern approaches to the study of the processes of development of civilizations is that all the transformations of the world-civilizational space are almost everywhere considered in connection with the processes of globalization. Without a doubt, they are inextricably linked, since globalization has the greatest influence on the development of modern civilizations. At the same time, while studying the characteristic features of the modern development of civilizations and the transformations of civilizational values, one should not forget that "globalization" is still but an emblematic word, commonly used to denote a great many processes taking place in the modern world.

In the context of the problems of the modern development of civilizations, the processes of globalization are often regarded as processes of global economic and political integration and unification, as a general trend of planetary unification of people, countries, peoples, and cultures, and as processes of cultural integration and unification taking place on the basis of their economic integration in the conditions of the formation of a global informational space. Here, one cannot turn a blind eye to the fact that modern views of the essential features of globalization have replaced the old and, one would think, forgotten futuristic forecasts of the imminent onset of the technetronic era, prophesied to bring about the unification of most values inherent in the existing civilizations. This new era was supposed to lead to the creation of a new transnational elite especially concerned with world problems, with its own language of interethnic communication, a single information environment, a single culture, etc. At the same time, nation-states were doomed to lose political weight.[14] Yet the reality of world development has proved to be not only different, but to pursue the opposite direction.

In the course of the ongoing development of globalization processes, the situation with the interpenetration and mutual influence of cultures and civilizations heavily impacted by the declared values of Western civilization

---

14   See: Zbigniew Brzezinski, *Between Two Ages: America's Role in the Technetronic Era* (New York: Viking, 1970).

associated with americanized mass culture has not yet resulted in the unification of the world civilization space. Certainly, modern civilizations experience powerful pressure from the outside and must respond to very diverse challenges, each of which, to a varying degree, changes and even deforms their identity (or, at least, poses a certain threat to it). However, civilizational traditions and values persist. The Occident has not turned into the Orient, neither is the reverse the case; civilizational differences between, say, Confucian, Islamic, and Indo-Buddhist worlds are still strong.

In this connection, the ongoing transformations of civilizational space should be considered in the context of not only globalization, but also the evolutionary processes of human civilization as a whole and its constituent local civilizations. These processes manifest themselves in a very peculiar way, since any civilization represents an extremely complex object. They can evolve towards differentiation, manifesting in an increase in the number of local civilizations; but, to a certain extent, they can also drift towards a certain kind of unification, with common features emerging across various civilizations. The latter tendency is the result of diverse and overlapping integration processes stimulated by the strengthening of cultural contacts and by the enlargement of civilizations themselves.[15] This is especially noticeable when studying the transformation of civilizational values that occurs in the conditions of unfolding globalization.

There is no doubt that the impact of globalization on human values is very significant in its sociocultural consequences.[16] If we proceed from the understanding of globalization as the desire of humankind to preserve the diversity of its cultures while achieving a civilizational synthesis (i.e., unity in diversity), then this process will be impossible without changes in the developmental trends and the formation of a new paradigm of culture. Given that any culture is based on a certain system of values, changes in the cultural paradigm entail changes in the value system. If we positively accept the idea of globalization of humankind, then we should be ready for the establishment of a new cultural paradigm with a qualitatively different system of values.[17]

Globalization processes create a new sociocultural context that has a significant impact on the vector of change in the value system. We can already say

---

15 William McNeill, "The Changing Shape of World History," *History and Theory*, 1995 (34), 26.

16 Kofi Annan, "Do We Still Have Universal Values?" An Ethics, Human Rights and Globalization speech, given at the University of Tübingen, Germany, December 12, 2003, https://www.un.org/press/en/2003/sgsm9076.doc.htm.

17 Anthony F. Lang, "Constructing Universal Values? A Practical Approach," *Ethics & International Affairs*, 2020 (34), No. 3, 267–77.

that the changes are directed towards creating conditions for the formation of universally accepted values that can determine the life strategy of the entire world community.

Certainly, the unfolding of global processes implies a change in the sociocultural space for the formation of various new forms of interaction between civilizations. Under these conditions, a clash between different value systems is inevitable; among other things, there is a contradiction between the traditional values inherent in existing civilizations and the new values emerging on the basis of recognition of the objectivity of global processes and the adaptation of civilizations' life-sustaining activity to those processes.

The interaction of civilizations in these conditions can be facilitated by the process of "positive globalization," in which each civilization, while striving to preserve its individuality and uniqueness, nevertheless capitalizes on modern communication and information exchange technologies to assimilate the values of other civilizations, thereby enriching both itself and others. This mutual exchange of values should not occur involuntarily, under the pressure of Western values claiming generality and universality, but as dictated by the needs and interest of non-Western societies and civilizations. These new universal values may include, for example, awareness of the need to participate in solving global problems, respect for the basic values of other peoples and civilizations, preservation of the environment, and many others.[18]

Mutual exchange of values may result in the formation of such common values as part of the dialogue of civilizations. At present, most experts professionally engaged in comparative political science and philosophy consider only the synthetic option desirable. Such an option implies borrowing, by one culture from another, of ideas useful for its own development. Designated as a "new synthesis," it should replace the "Western cultural synthesis based on the ideas of individualism, rationalism, scientism and faith in progress. A synthesis that previously seemed self-evident and attractive, but which now has ceased to be a reliable guide to the prosperity of humankind."[19]

As once suggested by Samuel Huntington, the West will have to reckon more and more with civilizations similar to it in their power but quite different in

---

18 Bertrand Ramcharan and Robin Ramcharan, "Crafting Universal Values: The UDHR Model, Context, and Process," in *Asia and the Drafting of the Universal Declaration of Human Rights* (Singapore: Palgrave Macmillan, 2019), https://doi.org/10.1007/978-981-13-2104-7_2.

19 Yersu Kim, "World Change and the Cultural Synthesis of the West," in *Justice and Democracy: Cross-Cultural Perspectives*, edited by Engelbert Kaempfer and Marietta Stepaniants (Honolulu: University of Hawai'i Press, 1997), 431–42.

their values and interests. This will require the West to develop a deeper understanding of the fundamental religious and philosophical foundations of other civilizations, and it will have to understand how the people of these civilizations see their own interests. It will be necessary to find elements of similarity between Western and other civilizations, because a single universal civilization is not going to emerge in the foreseeable future. On the contrary, the world will consist of dissimilar civilizations, and each of them will have to learn to coexist with the rest.[20]

In other words, at present, as the processes of globalization and the formation of a new value system are gradually unfolding, and as the sociocultural context of the development of local societies is renewed, this has a significant impact on the vector of value-system change, which points to the formation of universal civilizational values. Klaus Leisinger has noted that "there are shared fundamental values, universal normative imperatives" and that "a new political, economic and societal framework, designed in the light of global values, must be developed with the objective of making the necessary adaptations in individual and institutional practices also beneficial from a self-serving perspective."[21] This represents a strategy for the peaceful existence of the human community as part of the unity of its constituent civilizations.

Among the universal values common for all modern civilizations are, first of all, those necessary for the civilizations' subjects, in order to live in a single, global civilized community. Foremost of these are the vital values (i.e., the right to life and procreation, health, and personal security). These are followed by environmental values (i.e., clean soil, water, and air, and the basic resource sufficiency). There are primary civil rights (i.e., protection from unlawful violence and coercion, freedom of movement, inviolability of the home, and freedom of thought, speech, assembly, and association). There are universal political and legal values (i.e., judicial independence, freedom and independence of the media, and various forms of civic participation in political life). Finally, there are universal socio-economic values (i.e., the right of every person to self-sufficiency).[22]

---

20   Huntington, "The Clash of the Civilizations?", 49.
21   Klaus M. Leisinger, "Global Values for Global Development," Sustainable Development Solutions Network, 2014, http://www.jstor.org/stable/resrep16087.
22   Valentina V. Gorshkova, "Ценностный релятивизм в контексте диалога культур" ["Value Relativism in the Context of the Dialogue of Cultures"] in *XIII Международные Лихачевские научные чтения. Диалог культур: ценности, смыслы, коммуникации* [*The Dialogue of Cultures: Values, Meanings, Communications. Thirteenth International Likhachev Scientific Readings*] (St. Petersburg: SPBGUP, 2013), 285.

All the above-mentioned values serve as the basis for the implementation of civilizational values proper, which pertain to the particular lifestyle and thinking of each civilization. This leaves open the question of the formation of the value system of each existing civilization with the preservation of the basic cultural values constitutive of its persistent core. It is unlikely that each civilization would be able to fully preserve its basic values in their traditional form, since globalization itself is evolving in the context of another, no less significant global planetary process of further development and differentiation of local civilizations, as pointed out by Samuel Huntington.

In this connection, the grounds for the formation of a new system of values can differ widely and must be examined with vigilance. Presently, it can only be asserted that this new system of values will express a new image or model of the world, formed by the modern person as a result of globalization.[23]

Now that individual civilizations have reached a level at which they are able to annihilate each other, it is precisely "partnership"—the highest, constructive form of interaction between equal and sovereign individuals, collective bodies, generations, states, and civilizations—that should determine the main tendency of humankind's future development. It is the way of civilizational interaction within the dilemma of choice between confrontation and partnership that will determine the fate of humanity in the twenty-first and subsequent centuries.[24]

In such conditions, the transformation of values should not occur in a clash, but in the context of civilizational exchange, built on the basis of equality and partnership. On the whole, however, the transformation of the value systems of modern civilizations will most likely proceed in the direction of mutual exchange and mutual enrichment achieved through acknowledging the inevitability of further development of global interconnections in the course of changes in the worldviews of people belonging to different civilizations. In the final analysis, it is hoped that the formation of a global panhuman consciousness will persuade people that they are all equal inhabitants of planet Earth, equally responsible for its preservation.

23   Gulnar K. Kasumova, "Социокультурная реальность глобализирующегося мира" ["The Sociocultural Reality of a Globalizing World"], *Bulletin of Moscow University*, Series 7, 2011, No. 3, 87–98; Deshun Li, "The Conflict of Value and Contemporary Civilization," in *Value Theory: A Research into Subjectivity* (Berlin: Springer, 2014), 322–30.
24   Huntington, "The Clash of Civilizations?", 47.

Towards a Theory of Global Security

Igor F. Kefeli

1   Towards a General Understanding of Global Security

In the course of my research, I have come to the conclusion that global studies should contain a relatively independent area—the theory of global security, which we might call *asphatronics*, after the Greek ασφάλεια for "security" and ηλεκτρόνιο for "electron."[1] Russian scholarly literature frequently interprets "security" as the state of protecting a person, society, nation, or living environment from internal or external threats or hazards, as well as the capability of a system to exist in the presence of hazardous effects, and to counteract danger. This definition is more likely to be *functional*, which characterizes the need to solve certain problems, than it is to be *substrate*, which refers to the search for the ontological grounds of the security phenomenon in its partial manifestations (e.g., national, military, social or environmental security).

When it comes to global security, it has been suggested that we should interpret this concept in global studies as the "political regulation of global processes, the aiming of policy at growing global dangers"; "in a broad sense, a security policy is the policy of reducing global risk."[2] Yet this interpretation of global security seems out-of-date and inconsistent with current research into global risks. Since 2006, the organizers of the Davos Economic Forum have published their annual "Global Risks" reports, presenting a substantial analysis of a stable set of global risks, including geopolitical, social, economic, environmental, and technological. In the preface to the "The Global Risks Report 2021," recently published by the World Economic Forum, Klaus Schwab and Saadia Zahidi anxiously point out that "inaction on economic inequalities and societal divisiveness may further stall action on climate change—still an existential threat to humanity."[3] The authors of the report highlight the drawbacks in fighting economic inequalities and growing societal fragmentation, which represent an existential threat for humanity. The report also highlights the risk of

---

1   See: Igor F. Kefeli, *Асфатроника: на пути к теории глобальной безопасности* [*Asphatronics: Towards a Theory of Global Security*] (St. Petersburg: RANEPA, 2020).
2   Alexander I. Kostin, "Global Security," in *Global Studies: International Interdisciplinary Encyclopedic Dictionary*, edited by Alexander Chumakov and Ivan Mazour (New York: Piter, 2006), 200.
3   "The Global Risks Report," sixteenth ed., World Economic Forum, 2021, https://www.marsh.com/es/en/risks/global-risk/insights/global-risks-report-2021.html.

"youth disillusionment," which the world community has been ignoring, and some other factors that increase global risks. In response to COVID-19 there are four governance opportunities that can be employed to strengthen the overall resilience of countries, businesses, and the international community, including one directly related to the topic under discussion here: "formulating analytical frameworks that take a holistic and systems-based view of risk impacts."[4] As first approximation, asphatronics can be seen as a way to meet this challenge.

Some efforts are already underway towards developing an understanding of security as an individual's sense of safety within society, state, or living environment. In this regard, Vladimir Yarochkin's key contribution has been his assertion that "securitology" is the science of safety for the lives of human beings.[5] However, we run into problems when considering the ontological fullness of Yarochkin's security philosophy, since his position does not cover the technosphere as a sort of "alpha and omega" of human activities, including all kinds of possible and impossible dangers—from physical to social and cognitive.

We find a more constructive position in interpreting global security in the work of Konstantin Kolin, who rightly claims that in the twenty-first century the most important issues faced by civilization include a set of problems related to providing global security. These problems are caused by accelerating global processes, such as: the rising geopolitical tension in international relations; increasing environmental and biospheric threats due to anthropogenic causes; the growth of world population; degradation of basic spiritual values; and changes in humans as a biological species. In Kolin's opinion, contemporary civilization requires a global developmental strategy and a system for governing its development—one based on an international system of monitoring and analyzing global threats to the development of the civilization, which would take into account the achievements in nano-, bio-, info-, and cognitive technologies. One should highlight that by asserting "the military security, disarmament and demilitarization of the economy" as a top priority of global security strategy, Kolin argues that the following areas must be considered as the key aims of global security: "military geopolitical balance," "the US military withdrawal from Europe and other countries," "the formation of a multipolar word order," "NATO's military withdrawal from Russia's borders," "reducing NATO's military potential," and others.

---

4 "The Global Risks Report."
5 Vladimir I. Yarochkin, "Секьюритология: Наука о безопасности жизнедеятельности" ["Securitology: The Science of Life and Safety"] (Moscow: Os–89, 2000), 4–8.

Indeed, the contemporary situation demands constructive suggestions that might be implemented in the context of international legal relations. Such suggestions are necessary for providing international security. One should note that *international security* is often seen as equivalent to *global security* and viewed in the context of methods for exerting force using global weapons.[6] And yet, these are merely political suggestions that result from equating global and international security. In addition, it should be noted that "national and international security" (in the position of the UN General Assembly)

> have become increasingly interrelated, which accordingly makes it necessary for states to approach international security in a comprehensive and cooperative manner ... Traditionally, the concept of international security has been perceived as primarily a problem of state security. Within recent years, however, an additional concept has emerged—that of human security, which acknowledges that threat come not only come from states and non-state actors but can also challenge the security of both states and people. There are more and more appeals according to which international law must become an international law of security and protection.[7]

A comprehensive solution to the problem of global security calls for an interdisciplinary approach—for the initiation of "Industrial Revolution 4.0" and the establishment of a new, sixth technological paradigm (whose achievements are primarily noticeable in the sphere of military technology)—but one focused on perceiving the ever-expanding range of existential risks.

Data on the contemporary crisis of the world order is now supplemented with research into the long-term trajectory of human civilization during *the entire future time period in which human civilization could continue to exist*. Below we have summarized how the authors of one such analytical report compared four types of such a trajectory for human civilization:

1) *Status quo trajectories*, in which human civilization persists in a state broadly similar to its current state into the distant future.

---

6 Konstantin K. Kolin, "Структура и приоритеты глобальной безопасности" ["The Structure and Priorities of Global Security"], *Kultura i bezopasnost*, April 26, 2018, http://sec.chgik.ru/struktura-i-prioritetyi-globalnoy-bezopasnosti-2/.

7 Bertrand Ramcharan, "Новое международное право в области защиты безопасности" [New Security Defense International Law], United Nations, 2015, https://www.un.org/ru/chronicle/article/21998.

2) *Catastrophic trajectories*, in which one or more events cause significant harm to human civilization.
3) *Technological transformation trajectories*, in which radical technological breakthroughs put human civilization on a fundamentally different course.
4) *Astronomical trajectories*, in which human civilization expands beyond its home planet and into the accessible regions of the cosmos.

The authors of this report argue that it is important to focus on the selection of attributes for a quantitative assessment of long-term, rather than short-term, trajectories. Moreover, they believe that more attention must be paid to qualitative descriptions as a way to define different trajectories, since

> over the long-term, human civilization may not be using the same natural resources as it currently is, and the environment may change sufficiently such that near-term environmental parameters are unimportant. The form of civilization may likewise change enough that current conceptions of economic production, security, and quality of life do not meaningfully apply.[8]

2 Will There Be a Place for Spiritual Values in the Chaos of Big Data?

The Norwegian anthropologist Thomas Eriksen, author of the fascinating book *Tyranny of the Moment*, posed the following question: How can we sleep soundly if every day we reject 99.99% of information that we have the potential to absorb?[9] The transition from the analog to the digital age in the early twenty-first century has meant a revolution brought about by the advent of Big Data. One of the characteristics of this transition has been the appearance of a new quality information data. While data used to be expressed as the digitization of analog data and as statistical analysis of various information, now we find that data have a *prognostic* quality.

At the present moment, we see the creation of an enormous digital platform for media constructions, simultaneous with a destruction of societal values. This is occurring as *small* (i.e., analog) data are exchanged for *Big Data*, whose stewards seek to digitalize all spheres of human activity, and, consequently,

---

8 Seth D. Baum et al., "Long-Term Trajectories of Human Civilization," *Foresight*, 2019 (21), No. 1, 53–83, http://gcrinstitute.org/papers/trajectories.pdf.
9 See: Thomas H. Eriksen, *Tyranny of the Moment: Fast and Slow Time in the Information Age* (London: Pluto, 2001).

be able to govern these spheres. Here we cannot but remember *RUR*, a play written by the Czech writer and dramatist Karel Čapek, which depicts a conversation between Alquist, the last human being on Earth, and the robots he had created:

> *Fourth Robot*: Teach us how to make robots.
>
> *Damon*: We will give birth with the aid of machines. We shall build thousands of steam-powered uteruses. They will bring forth torrents of life. Life! Robots! Nothing but robots!
>
> *Alquist*: Robots are not life. Robots are machines.
>
> *Second Robot*: We were machines, Sir; but through terror and suffering we have become...
>
> *Alquist*: What?
>
> *Second Robot*: We have obtained a soul.
>
> *Fourth Robot*: There is something struggling within us. There are moments when we are possessed by something. Thoughts arrive, such as have not been before.
>
> *Third Robot*: Listen, oh, listen! People are our fathers! This voice that heralds your desire for life—the voice that laments, thinks, the voice that speaks to us of eternity—it is their voice! We are their sons!

Čapek's wife, Olga Scheinpflugová, recalled the author's experiences after the completion of the play:

> Writing about people is more pleasant, they are always around us... The robots, devoid of everything human, were completely dependent on me. It's a terrible feeling... I realized with horror that I could do whatever I wanted with them, because they did not have a soul of their own. I ordered them to push humanity out of the sphere of labor—and they did it without question, instantly and easily, in two or three pages of concise dialogue; I sent them to the scrap pile—they only nodded; I made them rebel against humanity—they went, without hesitation, without a single doubt, without a thought of what might happen with the world

and with them. While working on the play, I was seized with an incredible fear; I wanted it to warn somehow against the production of an unthinking mass, against inhumane slogans; and suddenly I was seized by a painful premonition that some day this will all happen, and maybe even soon, that I will save nothing with my warning: just as I, the author, directed the power of these mindless mechanisms wherever I wanted, so someone else, one day, will lead the stupid herd man against the world and against god.[10]

This "someone" is already emerging, in the form of programming platforms and social control systems based on Big Data. These conditions demand a proper analysis of the dialectic of analog-digital dualism in the processes and structures of the biosphere, society, and human-machine intelligent systems.

The most important thing to consider is not the quantitative growth of Big Data, although this rapid growth indeed exceeds our wildest imaginings. Rather, we need to consider that the growth of Big Data contains a vast potential for creating new knowledge and for bringing about radical qualitative changes. Big Data will change everything: science and education, health care and people's living environment, state governance and business. Quantity develops into new qualities, which implies possibilities for forecasting the future progress of these areas and its effects on the lives of human beings. Viktor Mayer-Schönberger and Kenneth Cukier have suggested three areas for analyzing the information that transforms our concept of society and its organization—our perceptions of the spiritual world and of concepts like justice, heroism, truth, faith, and many other values. These areas of possibility are:

– The possibility of analyzing a vast quantity of information and processing *all* the data about a phenomenon, instead of a random sample. Big Data allows us to better understand details that we would typically never see or consider when relying on the analog-age methods of random sampling.
– The opportunity to "leap" from the sphere of small data to Big Data, which thereby reduces the requirements for accuracy. According to the authors, the bigger the scale, the bigger the acceptable margin of error. For higher accuracy, small data must be checked carefully; but, in the world of Big Data, strict precision is not possible and sometimes may even be undesirable, so absolute accuracy—together with many nuances of the subtler

---

10   Oleg M. Malevich, ed., *Карел Чапек в воспоминаниях современников* [*Karel Čapek in the Memoirs of His Contemporaries*] (Moscow: Khudozhestvennaya Literatura, 1983), 126–27.

kind—recedes to the background. When we work with Big Data, we must do so in general terms. We do not reject accuracy per se, but we reduce our commitment to it, which allows us to make discoveries at the macro level.

– In the world of Big Data, information is analyzed with a focus on the correlations between the data, thereby revealing new and valuable knowledge. Correlations cannot tell us for sure *why* things happen, but they tell us *what* they are. When working with Big Data, we do not always have to know the causality between processes and phenomena, because data in all their diversity can "speak for themselves."

Thus, the new source of value is not the capacity of the computer, but the data it obtains and the predictive method of their analysis. According to Mayer-Schönberger and Cukier, we are entering a world of continuous data-based prediction, where we might not always be able to explain the reasons for our decisions.[11] The emphasis on the priority of predictive analytics invites a reconsideration of the very phenomenon of global security, including information-psychological and cognitive security.

3   The Ideal at the Boundary of Natural and Artificial Intelligence

The 2019 annual "Global Risks Report" mentioned the "Digital Panopticon" as a serious problem of the future, thanks to which "we move into a world in which everything about us is captured, stored and subjected to artificial intelligence (AI) algorithms," and "geopolitically, the future may hinge in part on how societies with different values treat new reservoirs of data."[12] The 2020 report of the Davos Club expressed these fears in even stronger terms: with the expansion of AI in the human world, we will approach a "human dystopia." Given the growing societal awareness of problems such as biased algorithms and cyber-bullying, many scholars have called for deeper engagement with ethical questions in the development and use of AI technologies. AI is seen not only as "the most impactful invention" (resulting in manipulation through fake news and "deep fakes") but also as "our biggest existential threat."[13]

For all the reasons just mentioned, we believe that the technology of autonomous and intelligent systems (A/IS) is not limited to solving ethical

---

11   Viktor Mayer-Schönberger, Kenneth Cukier, *Big Data: A Revolution That Will Transform How We Live, Work, and Think* (Boston: Houghton Mifflin Harcourt, 2012).
12   "The Global Risks Report," fourteenth ed. (Geneva: World Economic Forum, 2019), 70.
13   "The Global Risks Report," fifteenth ed. (Geneva: World Economic Forum, 2020), 63.

problems. We must place the category of the "ideal" at the epicenter of discussions on artificial intelligence. This category is not only the basis for comparing natural and artificial intelligence, which researchers have been doing for many decades. It also gives grounds for comprehending and finding organizational and technological solutions and for providing information-psychological and cognitive security based on NBIC-technologies. When we include the category of the ideal into information-cybernetic discourse, we are able to step outside the narrow constrains of the artificial and the natural in the information space. AI can be used to simulate those manifestations of human intellectual activity that are limited by its rational, abstract-logical functions, whereas the ideal is an umbrella term in relation to all forms and types of human spiritual activity, whether it be consciousness and worldview, beliefs and will, view of life and world perception, faith and doubt, etc.

According to the strong conviction of the philosopher Evald Ilyenkov, the main difficulty (and, correspondingly, the main problem of philosophy) is to distinguish the world of collectively preached ideas (i.e., the entire socially-organized world of spiritual culture, with all the stable and materially-committed universal schemes of its structure and organization) from the real, tangible world that exists outside of the socially-authorized forms of "experience," and in objective forms of "spirit." Here and only here, the distinction of the "ideal" from the "real" ("material") makes serious scientific sense, since, in practice, these two terms are regularly confused.[14] The ideal, or ideality, appears in social space and in social and interpersonal relations, and turns out to be the product of this space in all its endless diversity. Ideality has an exceptionally social nature and origin, and it objectifies the uniqueness and individuality of a person in human spiritual activity. However strange it might seem, for reasons that we do not understand, the problem of the ideal (and hence that of an idea and ideology) seems to have slipped out of philosophical, general scientific, and political discourse. The category of the "ideal" is not addressed either in the *Big Russian Encyclopedia*, nor in the specialized in the 2007 Russian *Dictionary of Philosophical Terms*, while the 2010 *Philosophical Encyclopedic Dictionary* contains the following "gem": "ideality is being as a are idea or representation, as contrasted to reality, being in objective actuality." The category of the "ideal" plays the same fundamental role in the socio-philosophical perception of the surrounding world and human life activities as "material," "space," "time," "movement," and "development." Each of them is instantiated in the studies of artificial intelligence, and its place and role in

---

14 Evald Ilyenkov, "Диалектика идеального" ["Dialectic of the Ideal"], *Logos*, 2009, No. 1, 41.

society. Thus, it is critical to recognize *the ideal* as an umbrella term both in interpretation and in modern cognitive research studies, in the manner flawlessly presented by Ilyenkov.

The ideal is an umbrella term in relation to consciousness, thinking, intelligence, and meaning, which, in turn, records various aspects and planes of the human spiritual world—human thoughts and feelings, will and beliefs, doubts, and mindset. AI is just beginning to "compete" with one of the fragments of the ideal in general, the one embodied in human intelligence. Natural intelligence is the edge of the intellectual abilities of a human being; it is that capacity develops and forms in the process of all stages of learning and can be implemented in their professional fields. Multiple research studies in the field of psychology of human intelligence have provided rich food for thought for the developers of AI. However, many other areas of the spiritual world of man remain outside the boundaries of the psychology of intelligence. Primarily, here we have in mind the view of life as a synthesis of various features of the spiritual activities of human beings, whose emotional-psychological apex (at the level of moods, experiences, and feelings) is worldview and world perception.[15] Mindset is one cognitive-intellectual side of worldview and it determines the method and nature of a human being's thinking activity while representing an essential component of worldview. In turn, worldview encompasses one's view of life (an absolutely individual phenomenon, as humans experience through sense organs that which affects them directly) and world perception (which has quite a range of characteristics). The level of intelligence, as well as the degree of emotional intensity, of worldview vary. But, to a point, both of these "poles" are inherent in worldview. Even the most mature forms of worldview do not only comprise intellectual components. Worldview is not just a set of neutral knowledge, indifferent evaluations, and cautious actions. It is formed not only by the passionless work of mind, which is of primary interest for AI creators. It is also formed by human feelings, emotions, and doubts, which "intersect" in the view of life and mindset of a human being.

The fabric of worldview is where mind and feelings come together organically, together with the idea of will. Worldview, at least in its key moments,

---

15   Igor Kefeli, "Информационно-психологическая и когнитивная безопасность: в поисках мировоззренческих и теоретико-методологических оснований" ["Information-Psychological and Cognitive Security: In Search of Worldview, Theoretical, and Methodological Foundations"], in *Информационно-психологическая и когнитивная безопасность* [*Information-Psychological and Cognitive Security*], edited by Igor Kefeli and R. M. Yusupov (St. Petersburg: Petropolis, 2017), 196–220.

is considered a more or less integral set of beliefs. Thus, various components of worldview acquire a new status: they absorb the content side of human relationships, are colored with emotions, and are implemented in volitional actions. Even knowledge in the context of worldview acquires a special tonality. It fuses with an entire set of views, positions, and feelings, thereby becoming more than knowledge and transforming into beliefs as an integral way of seeing and understanding the world and orienting oneself in it. Moral, legal, political, and other views—values, standards, and ideals—acquire the strength of conviction. In comparison with volitional factors, they are the basis of life and of the behavior and actions of individuals, social groups, nations, peoples, and, ultimately, the entire world community. The essential elements of mindset are faith and doubt. The range of human faith is broad. It includes everything from practical, living cognitive factors to religious beliefs or even the gullible acceptance of absurd fictions, which human minds of a certain type are inclined to believe. A person who was once an atheist suddenly turns (or pretends in the public eye) to truly believe in God. Is this an independent action? Did this person change their point of view or socio-political situation? Or is this the result of some manipulative external effect?

Doubt is always part of the system of worldview. And it is for this reason that we should pay attention to the condition that I would define as the "bifurcation of mindset." We are all inclined to doubt some information—be it the sincerity of the feelings and friendship of those around us, the fairness of actions or decisions, or the truthfulness of interpreted historical events. It may be quite easy to accept doubt as to the correctness of certain historical interpretation, which can fundamentally transform the essence of the outlook of the past, present and future. In this case, doubt is a "bifurcated imprint of mindset," which leads to a fundamental transformation of the worldview and axiological attitudes of an individual and his actions. A person can become lost trying to make sense of what is going on, while society appeals to those who are capable of speculating on the meaning of life and history. It is important to consider that doubt is the mental condition of the mental process that leads to the inability of making a concrete judgement or the lack of an unambiguous conclusion. Doubt is negative if the individual does not find reasons for deciding unambiguously whether the decision is right or wrong. In this case, any further analysis of the situation is blocked. However, if a person reveals reasons that give grounds for considering one decision option impossible, then doubt is positive: it allows for invariance in decision-making. In both cases the outcome is the inability to make a final judgement, and abstinence from such.

The same "bifurcated imprint of mindset" can easily activate the mechanisms for manipulating consciousness. In order to stop this from happening, we must set about developing preventive mechanisms and methods of information-psychological security. Of course, the doubt inherent in the human mind is unattainable to AI. Any problem an individual faces requires that he choose among some variants by "weighing" them with a certain degree of error. This state raises doubts as to whether the solution to the problem is reliable. Doubt is not inherent in an AI system, because a state of uncertainty paralyzes the action of the system. Hence there are two ways to "resolve doubt":

a) The individual is in the AI state, implying the unambiguity of problem-solving. In this case, the target function of information-psychological security is reduced to blocking one of the two variants of the solution to the problem (leaving state $2^0 = 1:2$ to the power of o).
b) The individual uses his own reason and comes to the AI state ($2^n \rightarrow 2^{n-1} \rightarrow \cdots 2^0$). Then variant (a) is implemented.

The solution to the problem (doubt-resolving) can be considered final or absolutely certain only when it is attached to a certain point of view or a single coordinate system. This is what we call "ideology" in the broad sense. World perception is regulated by the ethical norms and values intrinsic to a society, and thus it can be considered the most differentiated form of worldview, one that is most vulnerable to external influences like education, teaching or programmed psychological influence.

Meaning is one of such phenomena. On the one hand, it is enigmatic to many; on the other, it is treated as something about which there is "common knowledge," since it is regularly employed both in scientific and everyday communication. Alongside semantic definitions of meaning, there are also pragmatic definitions that evaluate this phenomenon from the position of the individual as an actor. In this case, meaning acquires the status of value, or significance—it acquires the status of a characteristic of the utility of a thing. Meaning is assigned in the context of a certain living situation, be it needs, self-preservation or projective activity. Meaning embraces not only knowledge about an item, but also the attitude toward it. To understand the meaning of what is happening, whether that be natural or sociopolitical processes or a narrative, is the outcome of cognition of a certain value characteristic, whose reliability and truthfulness have been evaluated based on a certain norms, standards, or principles. It is possible to understand something when it can be compared to something else that already exists. The function of understanding is to attribute a certain meaning to objects of socio-cultural reality and to include them in the spiritual world of the individual and his everyday life. In some cases, this is a question of the substantial essence of meaning; in other cases, it is a question of programming meaning into a text; and in still others, it concerns methods of decoding. Meaning has to be "looked for" and "understood," which is evidence of its creative (rather than routine) nature.

Meaning is the result of understanding and is its ultimate purpose. Understanding, in turn, occurs in the search for meaning. Thus, a question arises as to how the concepts of "meaning-tool" and "meaning-result" relate to each other in issues of psychological security and information-psychological and cognitive security—the context we have addressed in this article. In some cases, the answers to these questions can be quite simple; still in other cases, they require special research, as human beings are always looking for a meaning that serves their individual purposes, and that serves as a motive and means. In this case, we should look at contemporary research on this topic in psychology, on the one hand, and in the context of sociology as a theoretical-methodological basis for investigating the living world of the human being, on the other.

Meaning is an integrating factor of human life and, for this reason, the problem of meaning has a complex nature that can be addressed only at the meeting point of psychology, sociology, and philosophy. At this rich meeting point of humanities research, philosophical reflection relies on the generic concept of the "ideal" and works to distinguish a sphere of the intellectual activities of man—those that are "aimed" at solving a range of tasks in the field of learning and professional activities, as well as in the sphere of everyday human life like participation in family education, going to church, taking part in social and political life, etc. If the first of these spheres of spiritual activities (the strictly intellectual, the one we have defined as natural intelligence) has become the subject of AI technologies, then in order to apply these technologies to the second of them (either social control or the rights of robots and AI) we must consider all the expected and unexpected risks. In my opinion, everything just stated serves as a confirmation of the ideas of Evald Ilyenkov. We should consider his work to be the philosophical-methodological basis for the further development of AI.

In closing, I should note that Big Data technologies will bring about many new and unpredicted phenomena in the future, but it would be unforgivable to fail to consider the concept of the "ideal" in cognitive science. The dispute between the "physicists" and the "lyricists" has now become an omen of the twentieth century, since today the "physicists" have been replaced by IT specialists. As they debate existential risks and global security, asphatronics can help them in their work.

Modern Challenges of Global Sports Development
A Philosophical and Methodological Analysis

Vladislav I. Stolyarov and Sergey G. Seyranov

1   Introduction

Both theoretical analysis and the real practice of sports development indicate that sporting activities present opportunities for personal development, self-realization, and self-affirmation, as well as for developing health, fitness, physical strength and the formation of physical culture and a healthy lifestyle. Sports assist the development of mental abilities, familiarize us with the values of aesthetic and moral culture, supply opportunities for creative leisure, recreation, entertainment, and community. They encourage humane social relations by performing integrative and peacemaking functions and by familiarizing children and young people with the values of peace, sustainable development, etc. This potential of sport and the positive results of its wide implementation in people's lives gave rise to a certain euphoria, both in public consciousness and among specialists, about the merits of sport.

But theoretical analysis also reveals some negative aspects of this potential, determined by the very nature of sport as a social system oriented toward competition and rivalry. Within such a system, each competing party tends to focus on its own interest, instead of the common good. The competitive nature of sports encourages athletes and coaches to direct their efforts towards a pragmatic goal: winning. This focus is generally encouraged, and not just morally, but also financially. The desire to win is fueled by the media, coaches, sports functionaries, and political figures who seek to use sports in their own interests. This strong focus on success, the pursuit of high results, records, the desire to win at all costs can all have a negative impact on personality development, leading to violations of moral standards and to the use of such means of sports training (including medical and pharmaceutical means) as have a detrimental effect on the health of athletes.

As sports develop, we witness not only the possible, but also the real negative impacts of sports on the personalities and social relations of those involved. This especially concerns the role of sports in the formation and development of spiritual, moral, aesthetic, and creative abilities of children and youth, and in the evolution of their moral, communicative, and ecological culture. A passion for sports often leads to one-sided personal development.

Numerous facts show also that sports activities often have a negative impact on the athletes' health.[1]

Based on philosophical and sociological analysis of this situation, scholars and practitioners have come to the following conclusions. First, the negative influence of sports on the players' personalities and social relations is connected primarily with high-achievement types of sport (elite sports), because of the priority, in this kind of sport, of elite athletes, their high achievements, victories in competitions, setting new records, and other related utilitarian-pragmatic values (successful careers, fame, financial well-being, etc.). Second, the realization of sport's positive potential (i.e., health improvement, personal integral development, exciting and creative leisure, entertainment, humane communications with other people and with nature, positive emotions, aesthetic pleasure, etc.) relies on a special kind of sport, which promotes recreation and mass participation, instead of elite achievement.

This type of sport is called "sport for all," or "mass sport." This concept has been developing worldwide on the basis of the international movement Sport for All, which first appeared on the policy agenda of industrialized countries in the 1960s. By the end of the 1990s, Sport for All embraced more than one hundred countries on all continents. It is developing intensively in Russia.[2]

---

1 Volkamer H. Zur, "Aggressivität in konkurrenzorientierten sozialen Systemen," *Sportwissenschaft*, 1971, No. 1, 33–64; C. Sherif, "The Social Context of Competition," in *Social Problems in Athletics*, edited by D. M. Landers (Urbana: University of Illinois Press, 1976), 18–36. See also: Vladislav I. Stolyarov, *Основы социологии физкультурно-спортивной деятельности и телесности человека* [*Fundamentals of Sociology of Physical Education, Sports, and Human Embodiment*] (Moscow: Ru-Science, 2017); *Современное олимпийское движение: гуманистическая миссия ("храм") или "рынок"?* [*The Contemporary Olympic Movement: A Humanistic "Temple" or a "Market"?*] (Moscow: Ru-Science, 2017); *Социальные проблемы современного спорта и олимпийского движения (гуманистический и диалектический анализ)* [*Social Problems of Contemporary Sports and the Olympic Movement*] (Bishkek: Maksat, 2015).

2 Tamasz Dotsi, "Спорт для всех" ["Sport for All"] in *Наука о спорте. Энциклопедия систем жизнеобеспечения* [*Sports Science: An Encyclopedia of Life Systems*], edited by Vladislav Stolyarov (Moscow: Magist, 2011), 422–41. See also: Lamartine DaCosta and A. Miragaya, eds., *Worldwide Experiences and Trends in Sport for All* (Oxford: Meyer & Meyer Sport, 2002); "Promoting Sport for All: Benefits and Strategies for the 21st Century," a declaration at the Thirteenth World Sport for All Congress, International Olympic Committee, https://stillmed.olympic.org/media/Document%20Library/OlympicOrg/IOC/What-We-Do/Promote-Olympism/Sport-And-Active-Society/Conferences/2010/EN-13th-World-Sport-for-All-Conference-Declaration.pdf; Kazunobu P. Fujimoto, ed., *TAFISA World 2001: The Global Almanac on Sport for All* (Tokyo: Sasakawa Sports Foundation, 2001).

2 Sports for All as a Concept and a Program

The first official document of the Sport for All movement (adopted by the Council of Europe in 1966), when explaining the concept of "sport for all" and the movement's philosophy, stated that it aims at mass sporting activity—that is, at involving all people in active sporting activities, regardless of gender, motor ability, nationality, income level, profession, place of residence, etc.—and at helping those involved in sports to realize the lifelong importance of exercise. According to the European Sport for All Charter, the movement's mission is to enable everyone to participate in sport, to protect and develop the moral and ethical foundations of sport and human dignity, and to ensure the safety of people involved in sport.[3] Official documents also emphasize that an important objective of Sport for All is to increase the athletes' orientation towards the values of health, recreation, personal development, humane social relations, etc. Scientific literature contains similar characterizations of the movement's objectives.[4]

The practical realization of these complex social and pedagogical aims relies on certain methods and approaches, the most significant among them taking the form of annual international events within the Sport for All framework. These include the World Challenge Day (WCD, formerly called the International Challenge Day) and the World Walking Day.

The WCD is an international friendly competition held as part of the Sport for All movement and involving communities of people from all over the world, which compete against each other by comparing the percentage of people living in a given country and doing any kind of physical activity for fifteen consecutive minutes on the last Wednesday of May, in order to get as many people as possible to be physically active. The purpose of this sporting event is to promote awareness of the need for physical activity and a healthy lifestyle.

The World Walking Day is held on the first weekend of October every year since 1991. Millions of people all over the world go out into the streets to celebrate the World Walking Day together. This event is held under the auspices of TAFISA (the Association for International Sport for All).

Also under the aegis of TAFISA, World Sport for All Games are held every four years. These include the traditional national games, dances, and sport events characteristic of different countries and nations. The first such event

---

3 Pekka Oja and Risto Telama, eds., *Sport for All: Proceedings of the World Congress on Sport for All* (New York: Elsevier Science Publishers, 1991), 427.
4 Oja and Telama, 111–21, 425–38.

was held in Bonn in 1992; later, its guests were received in Bangkok (1996), Hanover (2000), Busan, South Korea (2008), and Siauliai, Lithuania (2012).[5]

In addition, Sport for All programs in different countries include a variety of sports games and competitions, training exercises for the purpose of long-term improvement of physical performance and general well-being, open-air recreation with outdoor games, and exercises involving aesthetic pleasure (e.g., figure skating, rhythmic gymnastics, and synchronized swimming).

The program's focus is on nationally-oriented forms and methods of sports activity, reliant on the socio-cultural characteristics of each particular country. For this reason, special attention is paid to folk games and national sports, and to sports clubs that permit a differentiated consideration of the athletes' interests and needs, promote community, social life, respect for the principles of democracy, and collective and personal responsibility, increase—and, most important, *maintain*—people's interest in sports.

3   Positive Aspects of Sports for All as a Concept and an Approach

Analysis reveals the following positive aspects (from a humanistic point of view) of the concept of Sport for All and the means of its realization:

- The aim to involve in sports as a way of active pastime not just some narrow group like children or young people, but *all* social groups and generations. Particular attention is paid to groups such as the poor, women, the elderly, immigrants and minorities, as well as people with disabilities, whose involvement in sport requires more intensive effort.[6]
- It is recognized that different individuals and socio-demographic groups have different motives and opportunities to engage in sports. Consequently, the task of developing various types of organizations and models of sports activity is set.
- Sports for All is primarily oriented towards the use of sports as the solution of humanistic tasks like health improvement, physical and mental improvement, integral personality development, active and creative recreation, humane communication with other people and with nature, etc.
- Forms and methods of solving these problems are developed and put into practice. Special attention is paid to the revival of folk games and national sports, in order to preserve the cultural heritage of countries, regions, and nations.

---

5   Dotsi, "Sport for All," 438.
6   Dotsi., 430–34.

4   Substantive and Terminological Issues in the Concept of "Sport for All"

Analysis of the theory and practice of Sport for All reveals not only the achievements just listed, but also a number of problems in the conceptual basis of the movement's objectives and its means for their achievement. These conceptual problems affect the effectiveness of the implementation of the program's declared objectives, and can be divided into two groups: *substantive* and *terminological*. Generally, these problems stem from the fact that the basic idea of "sport for all," which informs the program's goals and objectives, is defined as "sport for all." But how, exactly, should we understand the content of this concept? Official documents and scientific publications offer different readings.

4.1   *The First Possibility*

By "sport for all" we do not mean a special kind of sport, but sport as such (sport in general). In this case, first, the concept of "sport" is interpreted in the sense that sport includes not only certain competitions, but also non-competitive forms of motor activity. Second, it is assumed that "sport for all" includes all kinds and varieties of sport, including high-performance sport.

In accordance with this concept, the task of Sport for All is seen as involving as many people as possible—ideally all people, regardless of gender, age, social background, etc.—in active and regular sports activities based on the creation of conditions in which sports activity is accessible to all comers: conditions in which all individuals and groups can draw on sport to satisfy their interests, needs, etc. For this purpose, the formation and development of various types, varieties, organizational forms, and models of sports activities, including those related to high-achievement sports, is envisaged. Tamasz Dotsi characterizes this idea of "sport for all" as follows:

> Today, "sport for all" is a general concept that implies active recreation, development of sports, programs with the participation of large masses of the population, and cultural and health-improving activities in order to organize leisure time and improve health of all social groups that support this movement.[7]

This conception has some positive aspects.

---

7   Dotsi., 423.

- It encompasses not only all kinds of sports activities related to sports competitions, but also a variety of other types of motor activity. The latter can be very attractive to different groups within the population. On that basis, great achievements are possible in involving the population. The Sport for All framework is reported to have a billion participants in active sports activities worldwide and more than 400 million in Europe.[8]
- A broad understanding of "sport for all" elevates its image as a vehicle for health, education, personal development, and improvement of social relationships, while diffusing attention from the inherently negative aspects of certain kinds of sporting rivalry.
- This understanding of "sport for all" makes it possible to use attractive slogans for its promotion and prestige. In this way, the Association for International Sport for All (TAFISA) was founded in 1991 at a conference in Bordeaux, France, under the slogan "Preparedness and Endurance."

Yet, the general and unspecific characteristics of "sport for all" and the priority of massiveness, based on the involvement of all varieties of sport, including high-performance sport, create uncertainties in this program's value orientation. For the Sport for All movement, writes the Canadian researcher Peter Donnelly, "the main task is to achieve the greatest massiveness" in the practice of sport. But sport, he continues, can have very different meanings for participants and groups involved, and it is therefore important to clarify the value of sports activities and mass participation towards which this movement orients itself.[9]

We see that this approach does not differentiate among the value orientations inherent in different varieties of sports: those focused on the solution of health and recreational tasks, and those that do not have this orientation or even are opposed to it. At the same time, politicians and sports officials, when determining the priorities of social policy in the field of sport, get an opportunity to focus (in financial terms, too) on high-performance sport, instead of varieties of sports activity oriented towards health and recreational objectives. Donnelly rightly notes that the democratic value orientations of the Sport for All movement go far beyond leisure and pleasure, physical readiness and health, which can be used and reinterpreted in a less democratic way by the interested forces (the state, the sports bureaucracy, corporations, etc.).

---

8 Klaus Bös, "Health-Related Sport-for-All and Fitness Assessment: European Experiences," in *Sport for All*, ed. Oja and Telama, 111–21.
9 Peter Donnelly, "Sport for All: Concerns for the Future," op. cit., 428.

4.2   The Second Possibility

Along with the just-described understanding of "sport for all," there is another common interpretation of this phrase. It is then understood as a special kind of sport and sometimes used interchangeably with the term "mass sport." On this basis, corresponding concepts are introduced. These concepts are intended to distinguish "sport for all" (or "mass sport") as a particular kind of sport among sport's other varieties, denoted by the terms "high-achievement sports," "record sports," etc. But the notion of "sport for all" ("mass sport"), as used to characterize a special kind of sport, is vague and ambiguous, which makes it impossible to distinguish "sport for all" from other sports varieties.

Often the main distinction between "mass sports" and "elite sport" is seen to be the greater number of athletes or the lower performance of athletes. This amounts to a purely quantitative distinction, and in qualitative terms one ("high-performance sport") is understood to hold the other ("mass sport") in reserve, so to speak. This approach allows sports bureaucrats and politicians to proclaim a commitment to "sport for all" as a special kind of sport, supposedly designed to improve public health and solve other social problems, while actually focusing on elite sports and winning competitions.

Recently, it was realized that the difference between "sport for all" and high-achievement sports lies primarily in the aims of these sports varieties. Elite sport provides systematic training and participation in competitions in a certain sport in order to produce the highest results and win the competitions. Varieties of this sport—professional, spectator-commercial sport, and the sort represented by the modern Olympics—represent commercial sport activity used for economic profit. The aims of "sport for all" are not the same. It is focused primarily on the use of sports activities to address health and recreational goals (e.g., health promotion, holistic development of the individual, active recreation, and community).

Still, there is a widespread belief that it is possible to address these different aims on the basis of a single organization of sports activities, including competitions. This opinion does not take into account (a) the possibility of organizing sports rivalry on the basis of different principles governing the formation of the competition program and the composition of its participants, determining the winners, and encouraging their cooperation, or (b) the need to apply appropriate principles of sports rivalry organization in order to address specific tasks of sports activity. As a rule, modern sports competitions are organized on the basis of the following principles:

– Competitors are divided into groups (according to sex, age, level of fitness, etc.), and competitions are held separately, within these groups (the disabled in particular compete separately from others).

- In competitions, each team, as a rule, is made up of representatives of one country, one region, one city, one educational or labor or sports organization.
- The competition program assumes its participants' narrow specialization in one kind of sports activity (e.g., running, swimming, etc.), or in several kinds but reliant on one-sided training (such as physical ability in decathlon or intellectual in chess). As a result, sports competition is isolated from artistic, scholarly, and other forms of creative competition, even though it can be supplemented by a cultural program (concerts, etc.).
- Rules are established to strictly define what objects can be used (e.g., balls, pucks, rackets, etc.) and how they can be used during the competition.
- At the end of the competition, all the participants are assigned a certain place, and the number of places is equal to the number of participants. Several contestants cannot share a single place: the task is to compare their results on the basis of one or more criteria and to establish—taking into account sometimes minimal differences in performance indices—who did better and who did worse. When determining the participants' places, only their results and compliance with the rules of the sport are taken into account; the moral aspects of their behavior are not taken into account.
- Those who win first place, or several first places (usually three first places), are fulsomely praised and encouraged (sometimes with prizes and awards of great material value), while others usually receive but reproaches and taunts.
- There is a limited range of cooperation between competitors—usually, it is confined to cooperation and mutual assistance between teammates and communication with athletes from other teams.

These principles of organizing an athletic competition may be called "traditional," since they have long been used in organizing sports competitions in all kinds of sports. These principles are adequate to the objectives of high-achievement sports—of Olympic, professional, and commercial sports. They make it possible to (a) compare objectively the qualities and abilities exhibited by athletes in a competition; (b) to foster in the athletes an orientation towards high achievement, records, and victory, and an aspiration towards constant improvement of sportsmanship on the basis of developing and refining physical ability and other necessary qualities; and (c) to use intense sports rivalry to heighten the attractiveness of sports competitions to spectators, resulting in a commercially profitable mass spectacle.

To some extent, sports competitions organized on the basis of traditional principles can also be used for the purposes of public health, recreation, entertainment, and athletic community. But since the main aim of these principles is to determine the best athletes and to encourage them towards high achievements and victories, competitions organized on this basis do not effectively address the needs of public health and recreation, and can even preclude their being addressed, while contributing to a number of negative phenomena.

Many people (especially children and adolescents) do not want to participate in sports competitions organized on the basis of these principles, fearing defeat and its negative consequences. On the other hand, those who actively and regularly participate in these competitions often have such a strong motivation for high achievement and victory that they strive to achieve them at any cost—even at the expense of one-sided (and primarily physical) personal development, or in violation of fair play principles, anti-doping regulations, etc. Their main orientation in this case is to achieve victory over their opponents, to demonstrate their superiority, to win valuable prizes, to obtain other material benefits connected with victory, and to acquire fame. In this manner, the traditional principles of sports competition promote one-sided personal development among athletes, limit their creativity, and lead to stress and to the emergence of negative personal qualities like self-centeredness, aggressiveness, and envy. Frequently, they contribute to manifestations of nationalism.

When sports competitions are organized on the basis of these traditional principles, athletes are divided into groups based on their age, gender, physical and mental condition, their performance level, etc., in order to ensure the comparability of results. Under this approach, persons with motor or intellectual impairments, even if they are involved in sport, are singled out into a special group of athletes with disabilities. They compete apart from others, which emphasizes their socially-perceived "inferiority" and contributes to their social exclusion.

Evidently, the difficulties of "sport for all" in meeting its declared humanistic sociocultural objectives are primarily related to the means used for that purpose (sport events, forms of sports activity, and organizational methods). An important condition for overcoming these difficulties is the organization of competition in "sport for all" based on innovative principles that would promote positive emotions, pleasure, the joy of sports competition, and cooperation among participants, fostering health, fitness, morality in competition, holistic personal development, social integration, and rehabilitation of persons with disabilities. In sum, these new principles would contribute to the development of humane social relations.

These new principles of sports organization were formulated by the author of this article as part of an innovative project called "SPART," developed in 1990 and implemented since 1991.[10] The main idea of that project was to enlarge the cultural aspect of sports by integrating them with the arts. The project title "SPART"—a portmanteau of "spirit," "sport," and "art"—was invented by the author to reflect the rich unity envisioned by this initiative.

The implementation of the project involves, first of all, the organization of special games, called SPART Games. These games have been held in our country since 1991—that is, for almost three decades. Their main feature is the use of innovative principles in planning the program and the games' participants, evaluating their performance, determining their achievements, and encouraging cooperation. These principles include the following:

(1) SPART Games are to include *competitions and contests* that
– require the participants to show multifaceted abilities (physical, sports, and artistic skills, knowledge, a sense of humor, etc.) in different kinds of games connected with sports, the arts, science and technology, etc.;
– are designed primarily to promote the manifestation and development of creative abilities of the participants;
– are unique in comparison with usual, traditional competitions in certain kinds of sports, art competitions in different kinds of art (singing, dancing, drawing, etc.) and other similar competitions and contests
– allow comparing and evaluating the level of holistic (harmonious and versatile) development of participants.

(2) Innovative approach to *determining and rewarding the winners*:
– when evaluating the participants' performance, their behavior is evaluated first (based on clear criteria);
– every participant's individual peculiarities (e.g., sex, age, disability and its nature, etc.) are taken into consideration;
– in determining the participants' place in individual competitions, only significant differences in their results are considered; the number of places they can take is insignificant (usually, no more than five), and each place can take not one, but several participants;

---

10   Vladislav Stolyarov, "Проект 'СпАрт'" ["The SPART Project"] in *Спортивно-гуманистическое движение СССР. Основные документы* [*The USSR Humanistic Sports Movement: Foundational Documents*] (Moscow: SPART, 1990), 13–16; Vladislav Stolyarov, *Теория и практика гуманистического спортивного движения в современном обществе (критический анализ состояния и новые концепции)* [*Theory and Practice of the Humanistic Sports Movement in Modern Society (Critical Analysis of Its State and New Concepts)*] (Moscow: Ru-Science, 2019).

- in determining the overall winners, a participant's performance in all competitions and contests in the program is considered;
- achievements across various categories are additionally encouraged: a participant's overcoming of her own earlier results, integrity in competition, creativity, humor, physical brilliance and sportsmanship, aestheticism, and erudition are all valued.

(3) Innovative forms of *encouraging cooperation among participants*. Besides the traditional forms of cooperation between the participants of a competition (cooperation among teammates, community with members of other teams, etc.), the following innovative forms are used:
- organizing non-competitive games that focus on cooperation instead of competition, on "competing with oneself" instead of an opponent, on creativity, wit and jokes, fun and joy;
- competitions (e.g., relay races) between teams with a "mixed" composition—that is, between newly-assembled teams, each of which includes representatives of teams participating in the Games.

(4) Innovative approach to the *composition of the participants* of the Games. Persons of different sex, age, physical ability, etc., including people with and without disabilities, take part in SPART Games and compete on equal terms.

(5) *Integrating sports and the arts*, not only in traditional but also in entirely new forms.

The SPART Games are connected with health-and-recreational SPART clubs, schools, and game camps. The complex use of these activities is an effective solution to the humanistic tasks of "sports for all"—not only recreation, entertainment, and community, but also the harmonious and versatile development of the individual, and the formation of humane social relations.[11]

Specialists in other countries have accumulated considerable experience in developing innovative principles for organizing athletic competitions. Still, typically this involves altering the traditional way in some part (e.g., the competition program, the composition of participants, or the system of determining the winners).[12] A holistic system of specific means to ensure the effective

---

11   Vladislav Stolyarov, "Спартианские игры—новая гуманистически ориентированная модель спорта в его интеграции с искусством" ["Spartan Games: A New Humanistically-Oriented Model of Sport in Its Integration with the Arts"], in *Спорт, духовные ценности, культура*, v. 4 (Moscow: SPART, 1998), 54–279.

12   See: Vladislav Stolyarov, *Инновационные направления, формы и методы физкультурно-спортивной работы с населением (отечественный и зарубежный опыт)* [*Innovative Directions, Forms, and Methods of Physical Education and Sports*

solution of the problems of "sport for all" includes not only sports competitions based on innovative principles of organizing competition, but also a set of other forms and methods, including:
- non-competitive forms of sports game activities that orient participants not towards competition, but towards cooperation, creativity, humor, etc.;
- non-game and non-competitive forms of motor and body-oriented activity (health gymnastics, health fitness, etc.);
- activities, forms, and methods of health and recreational tourism;
- aesthetic body-oriented technologies, forms, and methods;
- sports health-recreational games and festivals, an integrative program that includes both competitive and noncompetitive sports;
- forms and methods of outreach aimed at advancing the sports, humanistic, health, and recreational education of athletes;
- sports clubs, schools, camps, etc., whose activities employ all of these approaches and focus not on training high-class athletes, but on addressing the needs of health and recreation.[13]

5 Terminological Problems of "Sport for All"

In order to solve the substantive problems of "sport for all" and its practical implementation, some terminological changes are advisable. "Sport for all" has many meanings; in addition, the phrase itself contributes to the view that the main distinction of "sport for all" (as compared with high-performance sport) does not lie in its aims and means of addressing them, but only in mass participation. This leads to muddling of the two categories, and calls for a refinement of terms.

There are different replacements for the term "sport for all." The term "mass sport" is widespread, especially in Russia, but it has the same drawbacks as the term "sport for all." The author would like to propose another option: to replace the terms "sport for all" and "mass sport" with the term "health and recreational sport," or "sport for health and recreation." This would take into account the specific goals and objectives of the discussed kind of sport—the

---

Work with the Population (Domestic and International Experience)] (Moscow: Ru-Science, 2017).

[13] See: Vladislav Stolyarov, *Новая российская модель массового спорта—спорт для здоровья и рекреации (концепция, опыт реализации, значение)*) [*The New Russian Model of Mass Sport: Sport for Health and Recreation (Concept, Implementation, and Significance)*] (Smolensk: Print-Express, 2019).

goals of health promotion and athletic recreation, which fundamentally distinguish it from high-achievement sports. What is being proposed, then, is to change not solely the meaning of the term, but also the content of the concept of discussion.

Recreational sport prioritizes health improvement, harmonious and versatile personal development, the organization of active and creative recreation and community live and the formation of humane social relations. To address these aims, we use specific approaches and methods: innovative principles of sports organization, forms of physical-motor and body-oriented activity, etc. These features of *health-recreational sport* determine its other features: its mass orientation, its inclusiveness of all people (regardless of sex, age, level of physical and sports training, etc.) in sport activity, and the lower levels of achievement among participants when compared to high-achieving professional athletes.

In this way, *recreational sport* has a pronounced humanistic orientation. It is addresses all population groups and people of different sex, age, physical condition, etc. Above all, this kind of sport is intended for the "sports-romantics": people for whom the most attractive aspects of sports involvement are not achievement, victory, or the related material benefits of fame and career—but, instead, an opportunity to engage in sport for humane purposes, in the relaxed atmosphere of physical activity and friendly rivalry. What these people want is to relax and have fun, to enjoy positive emotions, and to take pleasure in communing with friends and nature. This brings up another possibility for solving the terminological problem under discussion. It is to replace the terms "sport for all" and "mass sport" with the term "romantic sport."

Other solutions to this terminological problem are possible. What matters is that we solve the substantive problems of sports under discussion.

6 Conclusion

The rise of Sport for All and its worldwide development is connected with the social need to realize the enormous positive potential of sports activities—opportunities for health improvement, integral personal development, exciting and creative recreation, entertainment, humane communion with other people and with nature, and for reaping the benefits of positive emotions and aesthetic pleasure. Analysis in the field of sports reveals the modern people's tendency to increasingly orient towards these values instead of competitive victories and records. This determines the increasing global socio-cultural importance of Sport for All and what this movement represents in terms of values and ideas. That is why it is so important, at present, to identify ways to improve the activities in this particular sphere of sport. It is practically advisable, apart from pragmatic discussion, but also to facilitate it, to engage with the terminological problem of "sport for all" as presently understood, in order to arrive at a new vision, as encapsulated by the idea of "romantic sport."

The Dialectic of Civilization
From Ethnic-Religious to Global Civilization

Ilham R. Mamedzade and Tair M. Makhamatov

1 Introduction: Modern Discourse on the Concept of Civilization

By intensifying the reciprocities and interrelations of countries and peoples on the planet in every sphere of life, the ongoing process of globalization facilitates an intensive exchange of technological, socio-political, cultural, and other civilizational advances. One of the crucial outcomes of globalization in the near future will be the formation of a global human civilization, which presently has real preconditions and should not be conceived in Eurocentric terms, even though a number of key social institutions and ideas—such as democracy, liberalism, tolerance, equality, freedom of speech, human rights, civil society and others—emerged and obtained conceptual definition and full expression in the West. By virtue of globalization, these ideas have spread throughout the world—to be refracted through the optics of any given country's particular national characteristics. Francis Fukuyama was therefore partly correct in proposing his concept of "the end of history," which regards liberal democracy as the pinnacle and the final form in the succession of progressive developments in social organization. Drawing upon the ideas of Hegel, Marx, and Fukuyama concerning the highest stage of humanity's historical development (but without treating them with absolute deference), we presently propose the concept of global civilization. In developing our conception, we have creatively deployed, systematized and developed the ideas of Zaid Orudzhev, Alexander Chumakov, and Johann Pall Arnason.

We view global civilization as the result of the dialectical synthesis of ethnic and regional civilizations and their achievements. The universal principles of humanism, anthropocentrism, equality, and freedom for people of all races and religions, justice, etc., are refracted through the optics of each such civilization's specific cultural and historical characteristics. The fundamental values and principles of civilization, having a universal essence, emerge originally within the framework of nation-states and of regional and ethnic cultural microcosms; drawing upon local material and spiritual attainments, they manifest in forms inflected by their specific native culture. The contradictory, but ever-ascending trajectory of human evolution and its historical prospects suggest that, in the words of Alexander Chumakov, "there is every reason to speak of common civilizational features for different societies, which, sooner or later, must appear in every nation that has reached a certain degree of maturity in its cultural development."[1] The ontological factors for the emergence of universal civilizational values are initially formed within the framework of national cultures, and can be expressed in different degrees, varying also in conceptual form and prevalence.

In order to delineate the historical and logical stages of the formation of civilization, to remove the question of the multiplicity of civilizations, and to identify the contribution of each subject of world history to the formation of a *global civilization*, it is necessary to define the contents of this concept. Since its first appearance in scholarship, it was all but universally invoked as synonymous with culture—a conflation that complicates objective analysis of phenomena like civilizational convergences and clashes. Although the concepts of culture and of civilization are closely related, they have some significant differences. The philosophical concept of culture reflects the historic forms, means and the material and spiritual fruits of creative human activity in all spheres of existence, aimed at attaining knowledge of reality, as well as transforming it. "Culture," writes Chumakov, "is what fundamentally distinguishes man and various human communities from the animal world."[2] To this, we would like to adduce that culture also means a specific national or ethnic group's historically developed way of life, which finds expression through customs, traditions, beliefs, philosophies, art and science, everyday life, technology, manufacture, etc. Every nation and every ethnic group has its own historically consolidated culture, which is the basis of its ethnic identity. Thus, culture is by definition diverse and multiple.

Is it tenable to insist on the plurality of civilization—as did, for example, Nikolai Danilevsky, Oswald Spengler, Arnold J. Toynbee, or Samuel P. Huntington? What is the essential difference between the concepts of culture and civilization? Could they be synonymous? In his study of the history of the debates over the theory of civilization, Johann Pall Arnason concluded that "to stress the wide scope of civilizational analysis is also to admit the underdeveloped and provisional character of its current theoretical models."[3] It

---

1 Alexander Chumakov, *Путь в философию. Работы разных лет* [*The Way to Philosophy: Collected Works*] (Moscow: Prospect, 2020), 301.
2 Alexander Chumakov, "Культурно-цивилизационные разломы глобального мира"["Cultural and Civilizational Faultlines of the Global World"], *Vek globalizatsii*, 2015 (16), No. 2, 40–41.
3 Johann P. Arnason, "Civilizations in Dispute: Historical Questions and Theoretical Traditions," *International Comparative Social Studies*, 2003 (8), 357.

remains true that among the numerous publications devoted to the problems of civilization, it is difficult to spot a work that would clearly define civilization as such, and what, if anything, distinguishes it from culture. In his fundamental study of the concept of civilization, the French linguist Jean Starobinski noted that civilization has been identified with culture ever since the time of Mirabeau.[4] This logic of identification was perpetuated and deepened by Danilevsky, Spengler, Toynbee, and others, even though they would all point to various inconsequential differences between civilization and culture. Their understanding of civilization differed as well. For Danilevsky, "cultural-historical types" of societies were in themselves constitutive of the so-called civilization."[5] For Spengler, meanwhile, the main features of civilization were the global city and province, for civilization means total and sovereign domination of the rural by the urban.[6] According to Toynbee, civilization is a society that includes, as constituents, independent states with a greater extension, both in space and in time, than that of the nation-state, as well as city-states or other political unions. In his view, it is the society, not the state, that represents the social "atom" to which historians must attend in the first place.[7]

In his work *Civilization and Capitalism, 15th–18th Century*, the French historian Fernand Braudel considered civilization as a complex unity of a society's material and spiritual values, "created out of a multitude of riches, material and spiritual."[8] Jacques Le Goff thought of civilization as "total history," inclusive, along with intellectual and spiritual culture, of "material culture—technology, economy, everyday life (since, within the historic process, people build houses, eat, dress, and function in general)."[9] Finally, the Russian researcher Lev Skvortsov believes that "civilizational truth can be understood as a form of adequate adaptation of man and society to Nature.... Civilizational truth can refer to the realization of self-preservation in the here and now, the realization of the real interests of the individual, the social group,

---

4 See: Jean Starobinski, *Poetry and Knowledge. History of Literature and Culture*, translated into Russian (Moscow: The Languages of Slavic Culture, 2002).
5 Nikolay Danilevsky, *Россия и Европа* [*Russia and Europe*] (Moscow: Mysl, 1991), 85.
6 Oswald Spengler, *The Decline of the West*, translated into Russian, v. 1 (Moscow: Mysl, 1993), 131.
7 Arnold J. Toynbee, *A Study of History*, translated into Russian (Moscow: Progress, 1991), 40.
8 Fernand Braudel, *Civilization and Capitalism, 15th–18th Century*, translated into Russian, v. 3 (Moscow: Progress, 1992), 62.
9 Jacques Le Goff, *Medieval Civilization, 400–1500*, translated into Russian (Moscow: Progress, 1992), 6.

the nation, and the state."[10] When asked about the essence of civilization, Skvortsov answers that it "receives expression in various forms of activity, generating that visible "product" which is perceived as a civilizational reality."[11] These disquisitions do not answer the question of what civilization is, what type of activity and what results are meant.

Arnason is quite right that

> The problems of civilizational theory begin with the ambiguities of its most basic concept. It is a commonplace that there are two obviously different ideas of civilization: the one we use when we speak of the origins, achievements, or prospects of civilization in the singular, and the other that is invoked when we discuss the criteria for distinguishing and comparing civilizations, the ways of drawing boundaries between them, or the various inventories and typologies which have been proposed by analysts of the field.[12]

Huntington's muddled discussion of the clash of civilizations confirms the correctness of Arnason's words about the uncertainty of the concept of civilization. When examining the problems of interaction among modern societies, Huntington wrote that the Western world, the Arab region, and China do not constitute a more inclusive cultural unity—but are instead separate civilizations. Civilization is, to him, "a cultural unity of the highest order," which leads him to conclude that the clash of Eastern and Western civilizations is inevitable and is bound to become become the dominant factor in world politics. Huntington saw the fault-line between civilizations as the front-line of the future. The coming conflict between civilizations was seen by him as the final phase of the evolution of global conflicts in the modern world.[13]

But would not a "cultural unity of the highest order" issue in humanism and tolerance? What kind of a "high-order" culture could possibly lead to such a clash? And are not "the presence of common features of an objective order, such as language, history, religion, customs, institutions, as well as the subjective self-identification of the people," which Huntington enumerates as the attributes of civilization, in fact the attributes of culture?

---

10   Lev Skvortsov, *Цивилизационные размышления: концепции и категории постцивилизационной эволюции* [*Civilizational Reflections: Concepts and Categories of Post-Civilizational Evolution*] (Moscow: Center for Initiatives in the Humanities, 2016), 13.
11   Skvortsov, *Цивилизационные размышления*, 95.
12   Arnason, "Civilizations in Dispute."
13   Samuel P. Huntington, "The Clash of Civilizations?," translated into Russian, *Polis*, 1, 33–34.

The increasing migration of hundreds of thousands of people from underdeveloped to more developed countries and the vandalism of street protests in large cities both East and West represent a clash not only of political interests, but also of cultures that differ in their contents. The intensification of multidimensional globalization and its gradual transition to the phase of neo-globalization, according to the Chinese author Jin Li, "increases rather than decreases the need to understand cultural differences."[14]

We must not, nevertheless, lose sight of historic cases in which states with high levels of technical, scientific, and military culture waged merciless wars against other states and their populations. This is exemplified by the colonial wars of developed European states against Asian and African peoples, the war waged by Nazi Germany against its European neighbors, including the USSR, etc. It follows that a war can be initiated by a party endowed with high culture but a low level of civilization. Zaid Orudzhev is quite right in this respect when he writes that "civilization is a characteristic of the force that unites people, as against placing them in opposition, although the forms in which this occurs often take a conflictual character, whose cause is not, nevertheless, civilization in itself."[15]

Alexander Chumakov and Maxim Stychinsky have identified a more specific distinction between culture and civilization:

> The difference between civilization and culture lies in the society's elevation of civic and individual values and virtues of compassion and solidarity—that is, the principles of practical humanism and anthropocentrism. The civilizational component of such systems is nothing but a fragment, an integral part of the cultural context of this or that society, which expresses a certain type of relations within society, founded upon human rights, separation of powers, the rule of law and equality of all before it.[16]

During the Age of Enlightenment, when the features of civilization emerged from the material, spiritual and artistic accomplishments of culture, Kant for-

---

14   Jin Li, *Cultural Foundations of Learning: East and West*, translated into Russian (Moscow: Higher School of Economics, 2017), 431.
15   Zaid M. Orudzhev, *Природа человека и смысл истории* [*Human Nature and the Meaning of History*] (Moscow: Librokom, 2009), 393.
16   Alexander Chumakov and Maxim S. Stychinsky, "Культурно-цивилизационный диалог и его возможности в условиях глобального мира"["Cultural-Civilizational Dialogue and Its Possibilities in the Conditions of the Global World"], *Vek globalizatsii*, 2018 (25), No. 1, 5.

mulated his categorical imperative in the *Critique of Practical Reason*: "Act so that you always treat humanity, both in your person and in any other, as an end, and never as a means only." It is this that enables Anne Norton to justly state that there is no "clash of civilizations," and that civilized world is 'stronger, more beautiful, more demanding, and more just than the world Huntington saw."[17]

Our own understanding of the relationship between culture and civilization stems from Fareed Zakaria's concept of illiberal democracy and from Marc Plattner's observations regarding the ineliminable connection of liberalism and democracy. Plattner writes that "liberalism is unlikely to survive in the contemporary world unless accompanied by democracy," and it is true that a given national or ethnic culture may have but the rudiments of civilization, but civilization itself cannot exist without a certain level of cultural development—material, spiritual and political.[18]

2 Historical Stages in the Evolution of Civilization

We shall proceed from the principle stated by Alexander Chumakov, that "there is every reason to speak of common civilizational attributes for different societies, which sooner or later appear in every nation that has reached a certain level of maturity in its cultural development."[19] The formation of fundamental principles and values of civilization in global history unfolded initially in the context of national and ethnic regional frameworks.[20]

In the first historical stage, which unfolded in ancient Greece, the individual was first elevated, and the concept of citizenship also emerged, together with the relationship of equality among citizens and the respect accorded to individual freedoms by the society. Crucially, these values were enshrined by the law. According to Zaid Orudzhev, this constitutes "the first level of civilization,

---

17 Anne Norton, *On the Muslim Question*, translated into Russian (Moscow: Higher School of Economics, 2016), 225–27.
18 Fareed Zakaria, "The Rise of Illiberal Democracy," *Foreign Affairs*, 76 (November–December 1997), 22–43; Marc F. Plattner, "Liberalism and Democracy: Can't Have One Without the Other," *Foreign Affairs*, 77 (March–April 1998), 171–80.
19 Alexander Chumakov, *The Way to Philosophy*, 301.
20 Ilham R. Mammadzadeh and Tair M. Makhamatov, "Вклад тюрко-мусульманского мира в становление общечеловеческой цивилизации" ["The Contribution of the Turko-Islamic World to the Formation of Universal Civilization"], *Vek globalizatsii*, 2020 (36), No. 4, 36–46.

and its significance is in its being the first limitation of force and the affirmation of human rights, instead of force. Written legal code became a stabilizing factor in relation to achieved ethical norms, that is, rules governing the multitude."[21] In solving whatever practical problems that arose between them, people were now relying on a legal code, rather than brute force. During the same period, the first elements of democracy were formed in the ancient Greek polis. As the earliest beginnings of civilized society, these factors assisted the development of a new rational and logical way of thinking—philosophy. The birth of philosophy concretized and consolidated in the public consciousness such categories of civilization as friendship, virtue, morality, etc.

Here, we must note the historically inevitable limitations of this stage of civilization. Civil rights, equality and other values of civilization applied only to the native citizens of a given polis and to Hellenes. This circumstance was predetermined by the very genesis of civilization and by the necessary of preserving the integrity and stability of the polis.

The inception of the second historical stage of civilization's development is associated with the formulation of the principle of universal equality of all people before God, which is one of the main postulates of the world's great religions—Buddhism, Christianity, and Islam. At this stage, the limitations of the principle of equality observed in ancient Greece and Rome are dialectically removed. The Sutras, the Gospels, and the Koran treat all people, regardless of their race and nationality, as equal before God and as God's creatures whose lives can only be taken by God himself.

The French philosopher of Islam Henry Corbin pointed to the universality of Islam as a religious concept.[22] Nevertheless, due to primitive material production as well as the general illiteracy of the population of Western Europe and the struggle between the heirs of the Prophet Muhammad in the Arab-Muslim world, the new civilizational principles formulated in the New Testament and the Koran remained but ideological provisions that could not be realized in practice.[23] Civilizational values, expressed in ethical principles like "thou shalt not kill," "thou shalt not steal," "love thy neighbor," etc., as well as the insistence upon equality before god, were asserted for quite a long time—throughout the Middle Ages. As they gradually penetrated the philosophical consciousness and the minds of the creators of culture, the work of the latter began to emancipate those principles from their original religious context and

---

21 Orudzhev, *Human Nature*, 384.
22 Henry Corbin, *History of Islamic Philosophy*, translated into Russian (Moscow: Academic Project, 2018), 13.
23 Le Goff, 35–40.

to lend them a rational and intellectual character. The moral and ethical principles of the Gospels were thus transformed into the basic principles of Renaissance humanism and anthropocentrism, to be further concretized, developed, and transmitted to the masses in order to supply the spiritual foundations for the Enlightenment. In the European Enlightenment, the civilizational norms and principles elaborated by Montaigne, Rabelais, Molière, Erasmus of Rotterdam, Shakespeare, Cervantes and other Renaissance geniuses were conjoined with the idea of progress, forming a substantive basis for their subsequent development.

Zaid Orudzhev believes that the third stage of historical evolution and the corresponding third principle of civilization is the establishment of the domination of money. "The equalizing function of money," he writes, "played here its decisive civilizing role." "Money in the form of financial capital," according to Orudzhev, equalized "all people and their activities across caste and class differences, and the creativity of the entire world of objects," representing "the highest stage of civilization achieved in the course of human development."[24] We find it difficult to agree with this statement. First of all, money is an economic category, a universal equivalent in the commodity market. Orudzhev is nevertheless correct in observing that money is a material manifestation of value, whose prevalence signals the triumph of abstract equality and of the principle that no one is irreplaceable. Meanwhile, the values of civilization are tied to a recognition of individual uniqueness and to the principle that each person is irreplaceable.[25] For this reason, it can hardly be legitimate to elevate money into a principle of civilization operant in defining morality, justice, freedom, and tolerance. Further, the domination of financial capital reinforces inequality, thereby violating the principles of justice. This has been amply demonstrated by the findings of Joseph Stiglitz (*The Price of Inequality*), Tony Atkinson (*Inequality: What Can Be Done?*), Michael Sandel (*Justice: What's the Right Thing to Do?*) and numerous other researchers. The transformation of money into a financial commodity aggravates the consequences of global financial and economic crises, and the activities of international finance giants increase global economic inequality.

In our view, the third historical stage, or principle, of civilization consists in democracy, liberalism, and their core values. The motto of the French Revolution, "liberty, equality, fraternity," was rooted in the necessity of casting off the

---

24 Orudzhev, 392.
25 Saida T. Makhamatova et al., "Dialectics of Equality and Justice in the Economic Theory of Karl Marx," in *Marx and Modernity: A Political and Economic Analysis of Social Systems Management*, edited by M. Alpidovskaya and E. Popkova (Charlotte: Information Age Publishing, 2019), 215–24.

fetters of feudalism, of liberalizing the ways of life, of recognizing the right of citizens to expect state protections for private life and property, as well as for public order. When authorities prove inconsistent and unreliable in meeting these demands, the politically active part of the citizenry shall seek to participate in public affairs by electing representatives of the authority via universal suffrage.

Marc Plattner, an American scholar of political philosophy, observes that, today, "wherever we encounter liberalism (understood as constitutional and limited government, the rule of law and the protection of individual rights), it is almost always combined with democracy (understood as the election of public officials by universal suffrage)."[26] Liberalism, and not money in the form of financial capital, is what promotes the expansion of the boundaries of legal equality and freedom, which is the prerequisite for the modern function of capital.

3   The Origins of Civilizational Principles in the Turko-Islamic World

By the objective logic of history, each national-ethnic region in its cultural and religious scope contributes to the evolution of global civilization. In *The Philosophy of History*, Hegel wrote that history constitutes progress in the consciousness of freedom—a progress that must be understood in its necessity. This cognizance of the necessity of freedom is among the fundamentals of civilization, and here the Islamic world has made its own significant contribution, particularly in the period of its revival in the Arab and Turkic worlds.

Just as the European Renaissance saw the development of the nation state and the corresponding growth of national languages—Italian, French, English, etc.—so did the Turkic-Muslim region witness the development of national literary languages—Uzbek, Azerbaijani, Turkish—while the national identities of their bearers developed along the lineaments supplied by language. Late in the thirteenth century, the Ottoman state developed in northwest Asia Minor, and by the middle of the next century, the Timurid Empire in Central Asia also emerged. This period opened a new stage in the history of the Islamic Renaissance. This was the stage of the emergence of the Turkic Muslim world, with its socio-political, material, and spiritual culture and the original rudiments of civilizational thought and of ideas concerning the value of human life in this,

---

26   Marc F. Plattner, "From Liberalism to Liberal Democracy," *Journal of Democracy*, July 1999 (10), No. 3, 121.

earthly existence. This process manifested as a continuation and expansion of the religious-philosophical currents of Sufism, Arab Islamic philosophy, history, mathematics, and other scholarly achievements of Medieval Islam.

The emergence of the Turkic-Muslim civilization initially took shape as the establishment of the basic concepts and principles of its philosophy, as set forth in its poetry, in terms of ethnic and national self-consciousness. The ideas of humanism, tolerance, and the unity of the human race, which it proclaimed, were the "bricks" from which the edifice of Turko-Islamic civilization was constructed.

4 Civilizational Ideas in Nasimi's Work

One of the most vivid examples of the emergence of civilizing ideas is the work of the great Azerbaijani thinker Seyyid Imadaddin Nasimi. The German researcher of Nasimi's work, Michael Reinhard Hess, noted that Nasimi's ideas of humanism and of the unity of humankind, tolerance and enlightenment distinguish Nasimi's reflections as deeply germane for readers in the West as in the East, in Asia as in Europe.[27] The President of the International Turkic Academy Darkhan Kydyrali observed that Nasimi made an invaluable contribution to the substantial enrichment of Medieval Turkic poetry with humanistic ideas. His poetry's investigations concerned "the perfect man" and human perfection, which Ni extolled.[28] Nasimi's writings abound in thoughts on the spiritual and religious foundations of the humanity, which he conceived as a unity. It is his characteristic thought "that God is any one of us, the sons of Adam." What follows is that the basis for the equality of all religions is in each person's successorship to Adam's lineage, in the unity of the god that lives in every person's soul—"for God is one, and he is everywhere." Nasimi's pantheistic doctrine is, then, that the Gospels and the Qur'an do not contradict each other. Both scriptures indeed contain humanistic and peace-loving principles, which can promote cooperation across religious difference and the formation of a global civilization. Only incompatible interpretations of these scriptures,

---

27 Michael Reinhard Hess, "Zum Stammbaum einiger türkischer Nesimi-Handschriften," *Archivum Ottomanicum*, 2003 (21), 245–58; "Subversive Eulogies: A *Medḥiye* about the Prophet and the Twelve Imams by ʿImād ed-Dīn Nesīmī," *Turcica*, 2006 (38), 3–45.

28 Darkhan Kydyrali, "К 650-летию поэта: Творчество тюркского мыслителя Имадеддина Насими поражает своей глубиной" ["On the 650th Anniversary of the Poet: The Art of Turkic Thinker Imadaddin Nasimi Astonishes with Its Depth"], *Liter*, 2019, https://bit.ly/2PI11Aj.

together with conflicting political interests, present an obstacle to this mutuality.

Nasimi is one of the very rare and brilliant Medieval Turkic-Muslim thinkers who extolled the values constitutive of our criteria of civilization and reflective of a new attitude towards the human being, human individuality, and human life as the highest value of society. Human magnificence was central to his work: "God is the son of man, and man is great; behold: the pillar of the world is man."[29] The poet-thinker never tired of asserting the value of man and its inextricable connection to knowledge. "I have found the truth, and have become God's likeness," he wrote. Ignorance, meanwhile, makes man hard-hearted and likens him to Satan. Indeed, it is ignorance, or even semi-literacy, that precludes the emergence of civility. The knowledge of truth exalts the human being and allows the realization of the human being's divine essence. Nasimi's vision is such that humanity, in its thought and comprehension of the ways of the world, is higher, richer, and greater than the rest of existence—for man was created by God to be a creator. Nasimi's thoughts, grounded in the profoundly progressive humanist and democratic provisions of the Qur'an, emphasizing that man is the highest value of the world and the engine of progress, eventually become the central tenets of Turkic-Muslim civilization.

5   Babur's Contribution to Turkic-Muslim Civilization

Such representatives of Central-Asian Turks as the thinker and politician Alisher Navoi and the Mughal Empire's founder, the historian, humanist, educator, and statesman Zahiriddin Muhammad Babur made immense contributions to the history of the Turkic-Muslim civilization and its emergence. Babur in particular represents a unique phenomenon at the dawn of Turkic-Muslim civilization—singular by virtue of his participation not only in the Islamic Renaissance, but also in its European counterpart. Both Babur's politics and his creative works were marked by the civilizational principles of humanism and tolerance. Before Babur, those principles inhabited the imaginations of artists, poets, writers, and philosophers, and were perhaps dreamt of, but were never before realized in the proposals of a statesman.

---

29   Imadeddin Nasimi, *Selected Poems*, translated from Azeri into Russian by Naum Grebnev (Baku: Azernashr, 1973).

Unlike Timur's empire, the Baburid Empire lasted more than 300 years. Its longevity was assisted by its improvements of infrastructure with the construction of irrigation systems, roads, caravanserais, etc., and also by the policies of tolerance with respect to the ethnic and religious self-determination of local populations. In his historical work *Baburnama*, Babur described in detail the preparations for the festivities, before which he "gathered representatives of the Turks and the Hindus in order to hold a council"; then, "representatives of the Indian Gypsies arrived to join the festivities, and demonstrated their arts."[30] With his humanistic and tolerant policies, Babur achieved his goal of creating a centralized, unified, prosperous state. That is why the people of India honor Babur's role in the creation of their state. This veneration is potently evident in Jawaharlal Nehru's letter to his daughter, Indira Gandhi, written from prison in 1932. Nehru wrote that Babur was among the most cultivated and enchanting people who ever lived. He was free from all small-minded sectarianism and religious fanaticism and did not engage in destruction, as his ancestors had done before him. Nehru also thought that after Babur's stay in India great changes took place, with reforms that improved the lives of the population and enriched both art and architecture.[31]

Babur's political tolerance towards manifestations of national and ethnic identity should be considered in parallel with the art and politics of his kindred spirit—the earlier thinker and statesman Alisher Navoi, known as the founder of Uzbek literature. Navoi's poems "The Confounding of the Virtuous," "Farhad and Shirin," "The Wall of Iskandar" praised mercy, humanism, tolerance, and friendship among people committed to different religions: his philosophical poems featured Shirin, an Armenian princess, Farhad, a Chinese prince, his friend Shapur, who was a Hindu. Babur was in sympathy with Navoi in his thought and in his veneration of justice, virtue, friendship, and related values. Babur's art and his statesmanship assisted the formation a special spiritual and intellectual world within his empire and its society—a world that combined the achievements of the Turkic-Muslim world with the cultural riches of the peoples of India. In this way, Babur made his substantial contribution to the civilizational beginnings of both Turkic-Muslim and Hindu worlds.

---

30   Bobur, *Boburnama*, in Uzbek (Toshkent: Yulduzcha, 1989), 322–24.
31   Jawaharlal Nehru, *The Discovery of India*, translated into Russian (Moscow: Foreign Literature, 1955), 272.

6 Civilizational Factors in Ottoman Policy

The Ottoman Empire's national-religious policy also contributed greatly to the emergence of civilization in the Turkic-Muslim world, despite all the contradictions of the politics of conquest. As stated by the Russia-based historian Mahir Aslan, "the heritage of the Ottoman Turks, Persians, Byzantines and Arabs only increased the tolerance, harmony and mutual understanding within the empire. Eventually, the Ottomans abandoned all discrimination based in the sense of 'us versus them.'"[32] The Ottoman Empire's generous reception of large numbers of Sephardic Jews, expelled from Spain in 1492 and from Portugal in 1497, the freedom of religion and business in its domain, and its permission to build synagogues are also striking examples of civilization's progress in the Turkic-Muslim region.[33]

The Edict of Gulhane of 1839 (Hatt-ı Şerif) affirmed the equality of all subjects, who were now considered citizens, regardless of religion. These ideas and the fundamental civil rights were then formulated more broadly in the Imperial Edict of 1856 (Hatt-ı Hümayün). In the context of the discourse on religious freedom as proclaimed during the Tanzimat period, the Ottoman idea relied on the concept of equality for all of the Empire's citizens and their rights and duties, regardless of religious and ethnic ties. By virtue of these policies, the Turko-Islamic civilization attained a systemic and stable character.

Nevertheless, by late seventeenth century, in the absence of liberalization and democratization in the social and political spheres, further evolution of civilizational principles and values in Central Asia and the Ottoman region had all but ceased. As evidenced by contemporary socio-political reforms aimed at liberalizing and democratizing societies in Turkic-speaking countries, the development of civilization in the Turkic-Muslim world is now being revived and, thanks to the processes of globalization, its achievements are now merging with the currents of universal civilization.

---

32   Mahir Aslan, "Османская империя: национальная система" ["Ottoman Empire as a National System"], *Turkologiya*, 2019, No. 2, 73.

33   Ümit Eser, "Millet sistemi'nin Tarihi Arka Planı: Gayrimüslim Cemaatlar icin Özerk bir Alan" ["Background of the Millet System: An Autonomous Realm for non-Muslim Communities"], *Balıkesir Üniversitesi Sosyal Bilimler Enistitüsü Dergisi*, Vol. 13, 24, 204–12; Balıkesir; Gülcan Avşin Güneş, "Osmanlı Devleti'nin Gayrimüslimlere Bakışı ve Klasik Dönem Millet Sistemi", *Sosyal ve Kültürel Araştırmalar Dergisi*, 2015 (1), No. 2, 16–18; M. Şükrü Hanioğlu, *A Brief History of Late Ottoman Empire* (Princeton: Princeton University Press, 2008); Stanford Shaw, "Osmanlı İmparatorluğunda Yahudi Milleti," *Osmanlı Ansiklopedisi*, edited by Güler Eren (Ankara: Yeni Türkiye Yayınları, 1999).

7 Conclusion

Humanity differs from the animal in being aware of its past and in drawing upon it, learning the necessary lessons, and discovering the roots of the present and the future in the past. Humanity's interest in the past therefore conceals its lively interest in the present and the contemporary.[34] By examining the emergence of civilization values over the seven centuries in the history of the Turkic-Muslim world and its Renaissance, and dwelling especially on the thought of Nasimi, Navoi, and Babur, we arrive at a new sense of their significance, not as peculiar Turkic museum rarities, but as theoretical substantiators of universal civilization. While modernity continues to confront the same problems that occupied Seyyid Imadaddin Nasimi, Alisher Navoi, and Zahiruddin Babur, it continues also to benefit from their striving to realize the value of human life, to find the grounds for the unity of the human race, to enlighten humanity and to improve the world for the good of every living person.

The philosophical analysis of the history of civilizational principles and their emergence, via the Baburid imperial policies and those of the Ottoman Empire, permits us to conclude that, during a specific period, those policies successfully systematized civilizational factors first elaborated in the sphere of creative speculative thought and the arts, lending them practical import and stabilizing them through public dissemination and legal formalization. Consequently, the continued development of the civilizational achievements of the modern Turkic world and their unification with the global civilization depend on policies of liberalization, democracy, public education, on social and cultural initiatives, and on the activity of the various institutions of civil society.[35]

In our view, the emergence of a global civilization is among the highest achievements of globalization, constituting an essential element of human progress, which, in the thought of Robert Nisbet, can be transferred from the category of merely desirable to that of historic necessity.[36] In our study we have attempted to demonstrate that global civilization is not reducible

---

34 Ilham R. Mamedzade, *О философии (Современные подходы, тенденции и перспективы)* [*On Philosophy: Modern Approaches, Trends and Perspectives*] (Baku: Teknur, 2011), 41.

35 Tair M. Makhamatov et al., "Principles of Democracy as the Foundation of the Market Economy," in *Human and Technological Progress Towards the Socio-Economic Paradigm of the Future*, edited by M. Alpidovskaya and E. Popkova (Boston: Walter de Gruyter, 2020).

36 Robert Nisbet, *History of the Idea of Progress*, translated into Russian (Moscow: Irisen, 2007), 34.

to a Eurocentric understanding of civilization, nor does it deny the national and cultural differences among the various nations" civilizational achievements; civilization, we believe, emerges, develops and manifests as mediated by national cultures and by each nation's characteristic way of life. It is only in this sense, in our opinion, that we can speak of a plurality of civilizations.

Global civilization, whose emergence is objectively preconditioned by the achievements of national and ethnic cultures, coupled with globalization, cannot appear spontaneously, at once, as an integral system. The prerequisites for such an emergence are supplied by democratic cultural and educational policies of the states, by a democratic international legal space, by the effectiveness of international institutions (from the UN and the Security Council to UNESCO, etc.). Only the active and impartial work of key institutions can transform the humanistic principles of national cultures and the universal values of civilization into universal norms of international community and of unified humanity.

Civil society in a given country requires civility not only within, but also without, in the international arena. The processes of globalization will gradually transform the civilizational achievements in the culture and politics of individual peoples and regions into a single, global civilization. This appears to be objectively necessary for the survival of humanity.

The Essence of Globalization in the Spiritual Dimension

Anatoliy G. Kossichenko

Globalization is the dominant civilizational process of our time. We can have endless debates about the definitions of globalization, its relationship to global integration and modernization, the moment of its inception, and the beginnings of its active influence on global processes. Clarifying such definitions is beneficial, especially in the early stages of research on such a large-scale and multidimensional phenomenon. At the same time, globalization is a modern phenomenon that incorporates many properties of different universal processes. As such, it is a fundamentally new phenomenon in the history of humankind, and not a simple continuation of the prior global integration trends.

The fundamental novelty of globalization lies not in its scale or sphere of influence (although they are indeed unprecedented), but in its very orientation. It only *appears* to be a diffuse process—spontaneous, natural, and independent of human will and intentions. But processes of this kind cannot randomly occur by themselves and, in this sense, cannot be considered "natural." Such processes have initiators and subjects. Though at first globalization took shape as a natural, historical, pragmatic, and economic process, it was soon "reformatted" into a managed project governed by the designers of the new world order. Globalization is a multidimensional project, and it contains a variety of constituent parts, including some that are quite random. The sporadic presence of such random elements (that can be autonomous from the main goal of globalization) obscures the planned elements of its nature and its objectives from outside scrutiny, contributing to the concealment of the ultimate goal of globalization. Globalization is designed as a series of non-systemic processes with dynamic and changing priorities within the framework of a common goal, which allows it to shift the emphasis of its content at various stages of its implementation.

Globalization earned its name because it, quite literally, globalizes everything and everyone. All processes and events, all actions and relationships—everything becomes global: only in this way can globalization sustain its own global trend. Everything that remains outside the global processes, everything that is unique, private, and deeply personal, is condemned as a "thing of the past" and doomed to disappear. Yet it is clear that the world is held together by its diversity—the essential condition of its unity and integrity. Diversity, and not unification, makes the world whole. If we obliterate diversity, we will destroy the world. Consequently, the West's all-encompassing desire for unification is disastrous. Yet unification is the dominant form of globalization.

With this simple trick, globalism acts as the ideology of globalization, forcing everyone and everything to become the building material of globalization: if you wish to exist, to go on in the realm of being, you must integrate into the global process, find a place for yourself, be active in generating new global forms of development, and take part in the race.

> This situation did not arise all of a sudden; both theorists and practitioners of the modern world order have worked on it for a long time. Now, the globalists have built a world that is very profitable for them. This world is manageable—not to say that it is easy to manage, but it is highly manageable. Getting hold of all the "threads" by which to manipulate it, the key players in modern world politics have gained the ability to generate threats and manipulate them, achieving their goals and solving their own problems. They have the ability to manage conflicts. This would be quite difficult without globalization.[1]

What is it that enables us to speak of "managing humanity"? This becomes possible because the world process is moving too "unidirectionally": if it had multiple sources and multiple, different goals, no such "unidirectionality" would exist, since unification was carried out precisely in order to make the life of very different states, societies, and communities uniform. It is difficult to manage the diversity of social and state life: diversity requires a variety of management methods. Unification, however, makes it possible to manage humanity uniformly. This is the key to increasing the efficiency of management; uniformity makes it easier to arrive at the necessary decisions and to achieve the desired results. In other words, it makes it easier to manage the world—and this is the rationale of unification. Global unification does not arise from nowhere; its implementation requires purposeful efforts, conscious and deliberate actions of influential forces.

---

1 Anatoliy Kossichenko, "Философия в ее ответах на вызовы глобализирующегося мира" ["Philosophy in Its Responses to the Challenges of the Globalizing World"], in *Философия в контексте глобализации* [*Philosophy in the Context of Globalization*] (Almaty: Institute of Philosophy and Political Studies, Ministry of Science and Education of Kazakhstan, 2009), 135–36.

Globalization has been criticized, almost since the first moments of its manifestation, as a specific historical phenomenon that is not reducible to integration or unity on generally accepted grounds.[2] What is the reason for the widespread rejection of globalization and of its effects, which is already so apparent? Is globalization not just a natural stage in the progressive development of humanity, generated by all of its previous development? It is precisely the *naturalness* of the process of globalization that we intend to question—the idea that globalization is a new stage in the development of human society and humankind, arising from historic causes. Many critics of globalization blame it on the rupture of the natural course of history and on the introduction of a new strategy of self-interest and oligarchy into the process of human development.[3]

Globalization, in its economic aspects, is developing successfully in countries that share a market ideology and that are approximately equal in terms of gross domestic product. It is developing less effectively in the poorer countries that have joined the first group. These countries lag behind in a number of economic positions. Globalization manifests its worst sides in poor countries that have been seduced by the dream of developing alongside the rich. Despite the fact that globalization focuses on the economic development of the world, there are plenty of problems to be found in the economic aspects of globalization.

The range of political problems of globalization is even wider, and those problems are gravely significant in their consequences for the fate of the world. There are also positive assessments of globalization, associated with the possibility of integration into the world community, in particular with respect to specific countries. To what extent such integration is really possible is an extremely difficult question for most countries; they prefer not to discuss it, but the very prospect compels them to join the supporters of globalization, thereby strengthening its momentum. Thus, the competition for leadership in global processes provides globalization with the energy it needs to grow and deepen.

Nevertheless, the predominant attitude to the impact of globalization in the modern world is overwhelmingly critical. In 2017, Sergei Lavrov, the Russian Minister of Foreign Affairs, focused on the negative aspects of globalization in its current forms, stating:

---

2 Anatoliy Kossichenko, "Alterglobalism," in *Global Studies Encyclopedic Dictionary*, edited by Alexander Chumakov, Ivan Mazour, and William Gay (Boston: Brill, 2014), 16–17.
3 See: Samir Amin, *Capitalism in the Age of Globalization* (London: Zed, 2014).

> The world has not become more stable or more predictable. We have repeatedly spoken about the reasons for the degradation of the international situation, about the unviability of the concept of unipolarity, about the counter-productiveness of unilateral actions, about the danger of undermining international law and the associated growth of the power factor in world affairs. Today it is obvious that the liberal model of globalization, rooted in the early 1990s, and primarily its economic component focused on ensuring the leadership and prosperity of a small group of states at the expense of the rest of the world, has exhausted itself. It has demonstrated its vulnerability to various challenges and inability to effectively cope with numerous problems, although, outwardly, its slogans might seem to be noble.[4]

The political component of globalization (in this case, americanization) was well explained by George Soros, although he himself considers globalization to be a process of the development of global markets. To paraphrase the views expressed by Soros in *The Bubble of American Supremacy*, the United States cannot do whatever it wants, but nothing can be achieved in international cooperation without its leadership, or at least its active participation. The United States, more than any other country, has the right to decide what the world should look like. Other countries must yield to American policy, but America also needs to be judicious in its choice of policies to thrust upon the others. This imposes a unique responsibility on the United States: this nation must be concerned with the welfare of the world.[5]

Whereas the economic and political aspects of globalization have been studied in sufficient detail, its spiritual aspects—for instance, the problems of moral and spiritual attitudes towards globalization—remain in the shadows; these are the questions of the spiritual essence of globalization. It is generally accepted that the economy itself will be likely to bind all participants of the global process through a commonality of interests. But this is far from the case. Take Russia, for example. It also strives to become a richer country. But recent decades have shown that it cannot fully share the values and spiritual principles of globalization, mainly because of the difference in Russia's moral and spiritual assessment of globalization. Russia does not sacrifice its traditions and values, although they have undergone a very strong distortion

---

[4] Sergei Lavrov, "Либеральная модель глобализации полностью себя исчерпала" ["The Liberal Globalization Model Has Exhausted Itself"], *Kolokol Rossii*, June 30, 2017, http://kolokolrussia.ru/novosti/lavrov-liberalnaya-model-globalizacii-polnostu-sebya-ischerpala.

[5] See: George Soros, *The Bubble of American Supremacy* (New York: Public Affairs, 2004).

in Russia itself of late. Justified or not, Russia considers itself the guardian of centuries-old Christian values. This is apparent in the idea of Moscow as the Third Rome—"and there shall be no fourth"—and in the feeling that Russia is a country of God, therefore different from the rest of the world or possibly even opposed to it. (In terms of its attitude toward the processes of the destruction of evangelical morality, it clearly supports the values of Christianity.) The spiritual aspects of globalization processes should not be ignored: in some cases, they can prove to be decisive. Still, the spiritual and moral aspects of globalization remain on the periphery of research devoted to globalization and globalism.

One of the most powerful theorists of globalism, Aurelio Peccei, wrote, back in 1976, that the nation-state interferes in the progressive development of the world. He argued that the largest multinational corporations are quite capable of replacing nation-states in all their functions, although he understood perfectly well that the companies' desire to maximize profits casts doubt on their fulfillment of social obligations and their adherence to the principles of social justice. In this regard, Peccei wrote that social responsibility of the modern production system has become so dominant that it can no longer be sacrificed to profit motives—which, of course, must also have a right to exist.[6] He was echoed by Jacques Attali, whose ideas we shall discuss in greater detail. Attali wrote that humanity would need to acquire new political views and establish new institutions that would help compensate for the constraints and restrictions of the market inherent in the nation-state. A vision of global service would require, in his mind, that political leaders recognize the need for limitations and have the courage to abandon traditional notions of national sovereignty.[7]

In December 2020, Pope Francis, the largest transnational banks, and a group of IT companies' owners all came forward with the project of "inclusive capitalism" and announced their intention to implement Peccei's longstanding ideas. Of course, the initiators of the concept of "inclusive capitalism," who declared as the goal of their future activity the rejection of profit and a fair distribution of material wealth, are not philanthropists: they reserve the power to distribute these benefits, making it a condition of obedience of societies and people to the rules of behavior they propose to develop and impose.

Once again, we are faced with a mechanism of domination masquerading as justice; only this time, planned management is to apply to all mankind. Arnold

---

6   See: *Aurelio Peccei, Human Quality* (New York: Pergamon, 1977).
7   See: Jacques Attali, *Millennium: Winners and Losers in the Coming World Order* (New York: Random House, 1991).

Toynbee's "world without nations," Karl Popper's "open society," Peccei's "production of necessary human qualities," Alvin Toffler's "post-industrial society," Kosuke Koyama's and Claude Shannon's "information society," Immanuel Wallerstein's "capitalism in its dynamics and world-system content," Samuel Huntington's "globalization capitalism based on liberal democracy and the struggle of civilizations," Jaques Attali's "new nomadism," Klaus Schwab's "digital economy" and "fourth industrial revolution and the great reset," and, finally, "inclusive capitalism"—all this is the ideology of globalism and globalization in its dynamics. None of these ideologies have any spiritual content in a positive sense, and this is symptomatic, for they do not recognize spirituality as the immanent essence of human beings and as a reality of the modern world.

Nevertheless, the ideology of globalism is not devoid of a certain spiritual bias. All processes occurring in the world have a spiritual component, but their spiritual content is hidden behind external manifestations in other forms, hidden partly "naturally," partly deliberately.

In this regard, it is worth taking a closer look at the predictions and semi-prophecies, appearing seemingly out of nowhere, made by such theorists of the new world order as Attali. In a number of books, he describes with a kind of discouraging ease a picture of the already-realized future that he had seen. Attali does not predict this future, he simply conveys it. Here is an example of Attali's style:

> State formations will weaken. Nanotechnology will reduce energy consumption. There will be changes in healthcare, education, security, sovereignty. New means of personal monitoring will appear, enabling people to measure their own health indicators and to control their deviation from the norm. Everyone will be one's own doctor, teacher, and supervisor.
>
> Self-control will turn into the highest form of freedom, limited by a fear of non-compliance with the norms. Transparency and openness of information will become mandatory: people who hide their origin, social status, health status or level of education will arouse suspicion a priori. Life expectancy will increase, power will be concentrated in the hands of older people who prefer to live on credit. States will weaken in the face of corporations and cities. Hyper-nomads will rule a hyper-empire—an open empire with no clear boundaries and no definite center.... People will stop trusting each other.
>
> Laws will be replaced by contracts, the judicial system by arbitration, the police by mercenaries. New orders will emerge. Performances and sports will become part of the entertainment industry and will be broad-

cast to residents, who will almost permanently stay at home without ever going out. The rest of the population—infra-nomads, representatives of the poorest group of the population—will wander in the backyards in search of food. The world management will pass into the hands of insurance companies, establishing their own laws, which states, corporations, and people will have to obey. Compliance with these laws will be monitored by private security agencies. Resources will be depleted, and many robots will appear.... One day, everyone will be able to self-medicate, make prostheses for different parts of the body, and finally, clone.[8]

A prediction that happens to align with the plan. Or take the following fragment, from another of his books, *Millennium*:

In the coming new world order, there will be both winners and losers. The number of the losers will, of course, exceed the number of winners. They will strive to get a chance for a decent life, but most likely they will not be given such a chance. They will face outright prejudice and fear. They will find themselves in a corral, suffocating in the poisoned atmosphere, and no one will pay attention to them out of simple indifference. All the horrors of the twentieth century will fade in comparison with such a picture.[9]

Attali does not speak directly about the spiritual content of his "prophecies." Nevertheless, it can be easily reconstructed. Humanity in its highest manifestations (spirituality corresponding to such a highest manifestation) has no place in his "history of the future." This once again indicates that the global world needs the standardized person. A spiritually developed person, in other words, does not fit into this world. Globalization treats the spiritually developed person as unnecessary, harmful, and dangerous. It dissolves a person into the rules of modern life constructed by globalization itself, and with the help of the mass media.

The negative role of globalization in the spiritual sense is manifest also in the fact that today's world history is anonymous. Nearly all the people in all the countries are removed from real opportunities to influence the course of events. In spite of the outward appearance of frantic activity, people are in fact

---

8 Translated from the Russian edition. See: Jacques Attali, *A Brief History of the Future: A Brave and Controversial Look at the Twenty-First Century* (New York: Arcade, 2011).
9 Translated from the Russian edition. See: Jacques Attali, *Millennium*.

objects of control and manipulation. The behavior of the masses and single individuals is planned and programmed (nevertheless, erupting quite often in so-called "unmotivated" actions—which can also be taken into account when planning). Moreover, the real passivity of the modern person (given the outward appearance of frantic activity) does not depend on the type of state structure or forms of social organization: both totalitarian and democratic systems (each in its own way) remove people from real influence, be it on general processes within society or the processes of personal development. It can even be argued that democratic regimes are distinguished by an even greater sophistication in their removal of the person from control of their own situation.

Globalization is the ultimate form of projection of human passivity on a worldwide scale. This is its main negative characteristic. It encroaches on the essence of the human being—which consists in being a responsible creator of one's own life. Left to the human being are but the most primitive developmental horizons of modernity. As previously expressed by this author, a person "becomes more and more standardized, loses his personal specificity, betrays himself, acts as an opponent of the deepest diversity of being, which is a condition of a person's ability to attain his own essence. Globalization is responsible for these negative processes."

> Under globalization, individual personhood is subjected to a deforming influence, the personality is eroded and standardized, it has few means for self-preservation, and even fewer for its development. By unifying the life-meaning strategies of a person, globalization deprives him of his humane dimension, making these strategies essentially meaningless. Realizing all this, humanistically-minded critics of globalization are trying to give globalization "a human face," to find in it, at least in the prospects of its development, a humane orientation, to discover the personal dimension of globalization. But personal content generally becomes burdensome, both for the average person in the modern world and for the society in which he exists. The unifying logic of globalism has reached the deepest and most intimate layers of the human personality. There is no need to repeat here the well-understood set of means of such unification, from electronic passports (in which all personal data, down to the most intimate ones, are encrypted) to the terrible prophecies of Jacques Attali. The individual himself has already agreed to the

loss of personal specificity—it is easier than waging an exhausting daily struggle for personal dignity.[10]

The global processes of our time are characterized by the fact that a person loses his or her own sense of reality. What becomes real is not what is, what is objectively present, but what is called real. Here, we witness a global manipulation: instead of being, we are offered an opinion about this being. The ideology of absolute relativism is launched and begins to prevail. It does not matter what obtains in reality; it only matters how we perceive it, how we evaluate it, and how it is presented by the "creators" and imitators of reality—its interpreters. Everything is rendered relative, all positions equal.

In the context of this ideology, it is absurd to talk about values as the individual's guide. This value apathy is the result of conscious work aimed to destroy the primordial human values; considerable forces applied themselves to their destruction for a long time, under the aegis of globalism. "All this convincingly demonstrates the value anarchy in the modern world, which is called pluralism for the sake of convenience and justification, but it means only one thing: the modern world has lost the value foundations of its life."[11]

The spiritual content of globalization has been carefully analyzed by Christian hierarchs and theologians. Here is what His Eminence Agafangel, Metropolitan of Odessa and Izmail (a hierarch of the Ukrainian Orthodox Church of the Moscow Patriarchate), says about the spiritual essence of globalism:

> At the present historical moment, absolutely everything that happens in the world has spiritual causes, and the consequences are apocalyptic. Without taking this into account, it is impossible to correctly understand the essence of the events taking place in the world... In the history of mankind, there have been many different state and political

---

10 Anatoliy Kossichenko, "Личностные аспекты глобализации" ["Personal aspects of globalization"] in *Материалы II Международного научного конгресса "Глобалистика-2011: Пути к стратегической стабильности и проблема глобального управления"* [Proceedings of the Second International Conference "Globalism 2011: Paths to Strategic Stability and the Problem of Global Management"], edited by I. I. Abylgaziyev and Ilya Ilyin, v. 1 (Moscow: Max, 2011), 48–53.

11 Anatoliy Kossichenko, "Влияние глобализации на духовные основы, ценности и идеалы казахстанского общества" ["The Influence of Globalization on the Spiritual Foundations, Values and Ideals of Kazakhstan's Society"] in *Казахстан в условиях глобализации: философско-политологический анализ* [*Kazakhstan in the Conditions of Globalization: A Philosophical and Political Analysis* (Almaty: Institute of Philosophy and Political Studies, Ministry of Science and Education of Kazakhstan, 2006), 198.

> systems: monarchic, republican, totalitarian, democratic, based on the dictatorships of ideology, individuals, and parties. But now, the global society is being built. This has never happened before, with the possible exception of the Babylonian pandemonium. This path is undoubtedly regressive, dead-end; it leads to the self-destruction of civilizations. The current process of globalization will undoubtedly lead to the reign of the Antichrist and the end of the world... The political, economic, ethical and ideological base of the future kingdom of the Antichrist is already under construction, and the entire process of building this base is denoted by the term "globalization." In exposing the lies of globalism, we must declare that globalism is an anti-Christian ideology. This is a system of the world evil, from which not only one cannot expect any mutually beneficial relations, but also one with which peaceful coexistence is impossible. Any compromises with this evil will be used by it only to expand its influence in the world.[12]

This fragment clearly presents a view of globalization as a controlled process, moreover, one controlled by destructive forces with the aim of the spiritual destruction of humanity. For all the rational insufficiency of this view, it is surprisingly productive in explaining the widest range of spiritual problems found in globalization. As with other approaches to globalization, its main spiritual aspects remain in the shadows, presented as a natural consequence of the economic, political, and other dimensions of globalization.

Metropolitan Ioann (Snychev) of St. Petersburg and Ladoga holds a similar position, starting with his criticism of the essence of the economy of globalism.

> The economic basis of democracy is financial, speculative capital. It was this capital that shaped the modern, spiritless "technological" civilization, in which a person is deprived of the last remnants of conscience and mental health, turning into a half-animal, half-mechanism—an impersonal cog in a giant machine... This democratic "civilization" instills a cult of violence and depravity, tolerance for evil and for the perversions of human nature. Sins and passions of a fallen man are inflated to incredible proportions, are deliberately stimulated and ... corrode public morality.

---

12   *Архипастыри, пастыри и монашествующие Русской Православной Церкви о глобализации и цифровом кодировании людей* [*Archbishops, Pastors and Monastics of the Russian Orthodox Church on Globalization and Digital Coding of People*] (Moscow: Vector, 2004), 22, 24.

The people's national self-consciousness deteriorates, the state is criminalized, entangled in all-pervading mafia ties, and inevitably careens towards disintegration.[13]

Pope Francis—who is difficult to suspect of openly criticizing the spiritual foundations of globalization, as he has repeatedly demonstrated his commitment to it—was also forced to concede:

> The thirst to rule and to possess knows no boundaries. In this system, which seeks to swallow everything for the sake of multiplying the profits, any fragile sphere, for example, the environment, is defenseless against the interests of the deified market that have become the absolute law.[14]

He also says:

> Behind such an attitude, there is a rejection of ethics and a rejection of God. Ethics is usually viewed with sort of a mocking disdain. It is considered unproductive, too humane, because it speaks of the relativity of money and power. It is perceived as a threat, as it condemns personality manipulation and personality degradation. Ultimately, ethics refers to God awaiting a binding response, to God who does not fit into the category of the market.[15]

These critical assessments of the spiritual essence of globalization illustrate that the spiritual content of globalization is destructive and poses a threat to an already spiritually weakened humanity. In this regard, it should be noted that spirituality can only be positive. The idea that both good and evil give rise to their own spirituality is logical, but it is not true. There is a direct analogy here with good and evil in their essence. It is impossible to equate good and evil, in that it is impossible to understand them as independent phenomena

---

13 Metropolitan Ioann, "Самодержавие духа" ["Autocracy of Spirit"], in *Русская симфония. Очерки русской историософии* [*A Russian Symphony: Essays on Russian Historiography*] (St. Petersburg: Tsarskoe Selo, 2004), 344–45.

14 "Апостольское обращение *Evangelii Gaudium* Святейшего отца Франциска епископам, пресвитерам и диаконам, людям, посвященным Богу, и верным мирянам о возвещении Евангелия в современном мире" ["Apostolic Address *Evangelii Gaudium* of Pope Francis to Bishops, Presbyters and Deacons, People Devoted to God, and Faithful Laypersons on Proclaiming the Gospel in the Modern World"], *Bezopasnost Evrazii*, 2014, No. 2.

15 "Апостольское обращение."

equally rooted in Being. Evil does exist; moreover, it is widespread. But it is not ontological, meaning that it was not created simultaneously with the good, and is not ontologically equal to the good. Evil is a distortion of good and a product of this distortion. Thus, good is primary and ontological, rooted in Being in an essential way, while evil is a product of pride and the rejection of good, or its denial; therefore, evil is insignificant in comparison with good, although, we repeat, that evil is widely present in the world, for "the world lies in evil."

The ratio of good, "light," positive spirituality and of the spirituality of evil are similar. The former is essential to being and to humans, and the latter is a deviation from the "spirituality of light," and should therefore be treated as a parody of spirituality. Therefore, the proposition that there are equivalent spiritualities of good and evil is nothing more than a metaphor. Although, for those who do not attach importance to the spiritual, the equality of positive and negative spirituality is natural and obvious. But this is a mistake in the view of the ontology of the spiritual.

No person is obliged to share the distorted spirituality on which globalization is based. Despite the powerful impact of globalization, a person can value spirituality and strive to gain it in its true vision, to strive for good. At the same time, this person will not receive the special benefits of globalization, but neither will he lose his spirituality. There is an opinion that a person will inevitably be "drawn" into globalization against his will. But this is not the case. Even St. John Chrysostom said: "Nobody's soul can be harmed by anyone—if we ourselves do not harm our soul."[16] He also said: "Even if the entire universe sought to harm you and you do not harm yourself, you will not be harmed. There is only one betrayal—the betrayal of conscience; do not betray your conscience, and no one will betray you."[17]

Globalization is tightly connected with the ideology of universal consumption. This ideology makes a person dependent on things and on primitive forms of behavior. Thus, by justifying the consumer ideology and its perpetuation, globalization enslaves a person. This method of enslaving a person has been known for a long time, but the ideology and practice of globalism brought it to perfection. St. John Chrysostom wrote, back in the fourth century: "Truly, nothing makes a person a slave like a multitude of needs; and nothing makes you free like contentment with the necessary.... Truly, nothing

---

[16] St. John Chrysostom, *Collected Works* in 12 vols. (Sergiev Posad: Svyato-Troitskaya Sergiyeva Lavra, 2013), v. 2, 272.

[17] St. John Chrysostom, *Collected Works*, v. 3, 410–11.

gives the soul so much strength as freedom from worries, and nothing makes it so weak as the burden of worries."[18]

Now that our analysis has been presented, we might pose the question: What is the spiritual essence of globalization? This question harkens back to a more general one: What is the spiritual dimension of a phenomenon or process, and how to determine the spiritual content of a process? Today, this is not easy to determine, because modern man has lost the purity of the perception of the spiritual. But there are criteria: "You will recognize them by their fruits." Apostle Paul listed these criteria in detail. "But the fruit of the Spirit is love, joy, peace, forbearance, kindness, goodness, faithfulness, gentleness and self-control. Against such things there is no law." (Gal. 5: 22–23). We find none of this in globalization. Consequently, globalization is destroying the spirituality of the modern world. The spiritual is the highest manifestation of human essence. But it is precisely this pinnacle that is being destroyed by globalization. Human beings are being primitivized by globalization, as globalization has no need for the spiritual in its high dimensions.

The modern world is so spiritually weakened that even Christianity, which attempts to hold on to the truths of the Gospels, has plunged into ecumenism, which is globalization "in a Christian way." Yes, Jesus Christ said: "Let all be one" (John 17: 21), but He said "one in faith" and not in the agreements of church diplomacy. Not by diplomacy, but by standing in the unity of truth shall all "be one."

There is no unity of truth in today's Christianity, and one should not unite outside of truth and at any cost, for the sake of formal unity, for such a unity would be meaningless.

> The ecumenical movement has taken shape in the World Council of Churches, whose documents are written in a deliberately indistinct language; ambiguous terms and phrases are introduced; the religious issue itself fades into the background, the secular vision of solving the urgent problems of our time dominates.[19]

Ecumenism, as the implementation of the ideas of globalism in the religious sphere, convincingly demonstrates the spiritual sterility of globalization.

When speaking about the future of humanity (that is, about our present), Apostle Paul described it as follows:

---

18   St. John Chrysostom, *Collected Works*, v. 5, 297.
19   Anatoliy Kossichenko, "Религиозная идентичность в эпоху глобализации" ["Religious Identity in the Era of Globalization"], *Vek globalizatsii*, 2020, No. 3, 109.

> But mark this: There will be terrible times in the last days. People will be lovers of themselves, lovers of money, boastful, proud, abusive, disobedient to their parents, ungrateful, unholy, without love, unforgiving, slanderous, without self-control, brutal, not lovers of the good, treacherous, rash, conceited, lovers of pleasure rather than lovers of God—having a form of godliness but denying its power. Have nothing to do with such people. (2 Timothy 3: 1–5)

It cannot be said that globalization is to blame for this state of humanity, but it has contributed significantly to the negative state of the modern world.

It will not be superfluous to emphasize here that it is not entirely correct to associate everything negative that happens to humanity with globalization alone. But globalization does act as the main "platform" on which everything negative manifests itself and which thereby forces us to be critical. At the same time, globalization should not be demonized. In terms of spirituality, the role of globalization is undoubtedly negative, forcing us to look closely at its ultimate goal, if it is indeed appropriate to talk about the ultimate goals of globalization. But is it only the ideologists of globalism that are responsible for the growing lack of spirituality in the modern world?

It seems to me that the following judgment of Metropolitan Ioann (Snychev) is quite reasonable:

> The frequent mention of the deliberate and planned participation of certain forces, organizations or religious movements in destructive, disastrous processes that put today's world on the brink of a spiritual, cultural, political, and military catastrophe needs some commentary.... Evil, in whatever form it tries to realize itself, no matter how it extends its influence and power among mankind, has never determined and will not determine the life of people ... The ideas of the omnipotent, incomprehensible, unknown God and the free will of a man—these are the two forces driving the world historical process! Yes, there are people, communities, religious systems, and entire states that abuse the freedom of moral choice and incline—consciously or unconsciously—to evil as their spiritual and active source. Yes, their political, social, and religious practices are historically successive and can be retrospectively traced back to ancient times. There are also technologies of this destructive practice that have been polished over the centuries. But there is not a force in the world, and it cannot exist, that is capable of controlling the course of social development, and even more so—of predetermining its result. The forces of evil are gaining more and more power in the mod-

ern world. But this is not due to the fact that their carriers are somehow particularly smart and prudent. No, evil grows as we ourselves (!) deviate from the commandments of God, voluntarily cutting ourselves off from the life-giving Source of goodness and truth, of justice and love. This is not the result of a "conspiracy," but a sad consequence of the worldwide apostasy, and can be correctly understood and appreciated only within the framework of Christian eschatology, not through a primitive search for a "conspiracy" to blame.[20]

The brilliant ideologue of globalization, Jaques Attali, overturned his terrible predictions on humanity and was also forced to admit the following: "In order to create a solid civilization, humanity must somehow come to terms with nature and with itself. It must embrace a pluralistic and politically tolerant culture imbued with a deep sacred meaning."[21] He also says:

> But first of all, a new sacred covenant must be consummated between man and nature, so that the Earth continues to live in the future, so that everything ephemeral and superficial would give way to the eternal, so that diversity could resist monotony. Dignity must prevail over power, and the spirit of creativity must be opposed to violence. It is in this new spirit that the wisdom of humanity must be developed, not the mind of machines. Every person must be given the means to choose his own destiny. No one should be relegated to the role of an observer of their own consumption process. Individuals must be empowered to contribute to the legacy of civilization, determining its direction through the exercise of their own freedom, seeking to turn their lives into a work of art, instead of a boring reproduction.

Even if the leading ideologists of globalization appeal to "the wisdom of mankind, not the mind of machines" (and today this topic is more relevant than ever before), the future of mankind is not hopeless. Moreover, the spiritual essence of a person is fundamentally indestructible. Taken together, this gives rise to a reasonable hope for retaining spirituality within the developmental horizons of human beings and humanity.

---

20   Metropolitan Ioann, *A Russian Symphony*, 285–86.
21   Translated from the Russian edition. See: Jacques Attali, *Millennium*.

Religion in the Globalized World

Philosophical Reflections

Mikhail Y. Sergeev

1   Introductory Remarks

When discussing religion in the globalized world, scholars usually operate under several standard assumptions. First, they proceed from the modern supposition that religion should be separated from the state and, therefore, should not engage in public discourse but rather limit its sphere of influence to personal spirituality and salvation. Second, they usually discuss well-established religious traditions that have been evolving for centuries while paying less attention to new religious movements since their membership is relatively low and so, as they think, is their impact on the global stage. Third, those scholars focus their analysis on the "religious disruptors" (i.e., those sects and groups that defy social norms and represent a threat to civilization). As a result, examining Islamic terrorism or various apocalyptic cults often stands at the center of religious studies in the global context.

It is easy to show that all those assumptions largely oversimplify the role that religion and religious beliefs play in society, whether on a local, national, or global level. Catholic views on the death penalty and abortion, for instance, are an inalienable part of public discourse on governmental policy in the United States. Modern religious movements, like Mormonism, with its almost two hundred years of existence and now more than sixteen million adherents worldwide, have a growing impact in society's life. The American politician, businessman, and LDS minister Mitt Romney was the Republican Party's 2012 presidential nominee. Finally, in our global world, torn apart by cultural divisions and prejudice, religious scholars should undoubtedly pay closer attention to the unifying and value-oriented aspects of spiritual teachings rather than their harmful and militant elements.

There is one more factor that implicitly influences the discussion of religious issues in the contemporary era. It is the collapse of the USSR that took place several decades ago and was entirely unexpected, for both the communist-bloc countries and their liberal-democratic opponents. The whole past century passed under the banner of "the death of God," which resulted in the collapse of organized religion and in the flourishing of secular culture. Religious scholars of the twenty-first century talk, instead, about the resurrection of faith in a "post-secular age." However, no one seems to propose a plausible explanation for the seventy-five years of the existence of the Soviet Union—the only irreligious empire in the entire human history. Theodore Adorno famously remarked about the Nazi Holocaust's horrors that "to write a poem after Auschwitz is barbaric."[1] What about pursuing theological studies after the Gulag, then? After all, the Soviet atrocities vastly surpassed the crimes of the Nazi regime. Yet, the existential mystery of the atheist outburst in Russia did not receive, in my opinion, adequate and exhaustive explanation, neither in its native land, nor in the rest of the intellectual world.

2   Religion after the Gulag

Contemporary Russian philosophers are well aware of this problem, since Russia's national identity in the post-Soviet times is directly related to it. The solutions they propose are fourfold. Russian communists, who survived the USSR's downfall and reorganized under Marxist-Leninist banners, regard the Soviet period mostly with pride and praise the advantages of the planned socialist economy. In contrast, Orthodox nationalists view the communist theory and practice as a social disease that Russia contracted from the degrading West, which is rapidly moving toward its own inevitable decline. In contrast to communists and nationalists, postmodernists in Russia look at the Soviet ideology as the Grand Narratives' last bastion. Their final demise signified the victory of irreducible human diversity and pluralism. Finally, Russian globalists argue that the Soviet experiment, although it ultimately failed, was one of the first practical attempts to create a planetary human society.

All those approaches, in my opinion, vastly underestimate the spiritual dimension of the Soviet period in Russian history, which I explore through the prism of my theory of religious cycles.[2] According to my hypothesis, religion is an organic system that, in the course of its evolution, passes through six typical phases—formative, orthodox, classical, reformist, critical, and postcritical. A particular correlation between any religious system's fundamental

---

[1]   Theodor Adorno, "Cultural Criticism and Society," in *Prisms*, translated by Samuel and Shierry Weber (Cambridge, MA: MIT Press, 1967), 34.

[2]   What follows is a summary of my interpretation of the evolution of religions and the Soviet Union phenomenon. For a detailed exposition of my theory of religious cycles, please see my article "The model of religious cycle: theory and application," *SENTENTIA. European Journal of Humanities and Social Sciences*, 2017, No. 3, 71–92, http://e-notabene.ru/psen/article_23930.html; or my book *Theory of Religious Cycles: Tradition, Modernity, and the Bahá'í Faith* (Boston: Brill, 2015).

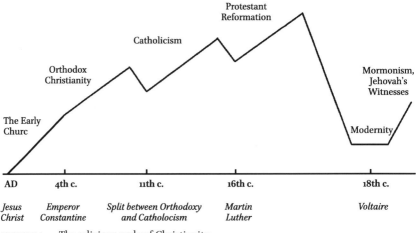

FIGURE 1   The religious cycle of Christianity

components—its sacred scriptures and sacred tradition—characterizes each of those steps or stages. An imbalance between the two elements leads to a structural crisis of religion, marked by the doubt in the sacred tradition. Such a situation results in the appearance of novel branches within the established faith, and signals its transition to a new development stage. Unlike the structural problem that transforms the sacred tradition but leaves untouched the holy scriptures, the systemic crisis of religion questions the system's very foundations by casting doubt in its scriptural texts. The creation of new religious movements within their mother-faith usually resolves this matter.

Christianity serves as the best illustration of this model of religious cycles. The formative, orthodox, classical, reformist, and critical phases are expressed in the early, Orthodox, Catholic, Protestant, and modern forms of Christianity respectively. Let us specifically focus on the European Enlightenment of the seventeenth and eighteenth centuries, which laid the foundation for the Christian Church's modern period and marked the beginning of the systemic crisis of Christianity. Whether critically-minded theologians, deists, agnostics, or atheists, the Enlightenment thinkers questioned the Bible's absolute authority. For the first time in European history, they conceived an all-embracing worldview that was not of divine but purely human origin.

The rational approach to nature and social reality signaled the dawn of modernity, eventually leading to the establishment of democratic political institutions, the spread of secular culture, and the momentous rise of scientific and technological innovations. The Enlightenment paradigm proved so vital and appealing that it conquered the hearts and minds of people all over the globe in the course of the nineteenth and twentieth centuries. Regrettably, the modern way of life is at best neutral and at worst suspicious of, if not entirely opposed to, religion. Members of modern societies often regard religious beliefs as old, pre-scientific, and outdated prejudices. As a result, the collapse of traditional moral values and the steady decline of religious affiliation and practices often accompany the advantages of political, social, and cultural modernization.

Not being confined to the Christian confession sphere of influence, its systemic crisis deeply affected other cultures and world religions, most notably Hinduism, Confucianism, Buddhism, and Islam. In the twentieth century, it already became a full-blown crisis of religious consciousness, which led to the establishment of the Soviet Union. This atheist empire aimed to exterminate religious belief in general, and persecuted traditional and modern religious groups and sects. The Soviet system's subsequent collapse significantly changed the political, economic, and social situation in the countries involved and in the whole world. But it did not resolve the spiritual dimension of the crisis that is still deepening and producing religious tensions and threats of a different kind. According to my theory, religion's systemic problems are resolved only with the appearance and maturation of new religious movements capable of regenerating former spiritual traditions. We know from the history of religions that this is a long process, usually up to four centuries. That is why, being at the epicenter of profound religious transformation, we have to consider the spiritual dimension of globalization, which is as complicated as its economic, political, or social components.

3   Culture vs. Civilization

In the second of his trilogy of monographs devoted to the subject, *Metaphysics of Globalization*, Alexander Chumakov, one of the leading contemporary Russian specialists in global studies, discussed the philosophical aspects of this worldwide process from the standpoint of two basic categories—"culture" and "civilization." According to Chumakov, "every human being, every community of people, be it a certain group, state, or public association, including global humanity, represents a unique cultural-civilizational system."[3] Those two components, which are always interlaced with and tied to one another, perform,

---

3   Alexander Chumakov and Mikhail Sergeev, "Religion and Globalization: Crossroads and Opportunities," *Occasional Papers on Religion in Eastern Europe*, 2018 (38), No. 5, 112, https://digitalcommons.georgefox.edu/ree/vol38/iss5/7.

he argues, quite different functions. Religious beliefs, traditional customs, and standard language usually constitute the foundation of every cultural entity. But it is precisely because of their social nature that cultures are inherently distinctive and varied. As Chumakov puts it, "all human beings and their communities are special, different from other cultural formations that produce, separate, and make them unique and inimitable." These, he writes, "are the natural roots of that cultural diversity and religious pluralism with which we are dealing in reality."[4]

In contrast to various and unique cultures, the civilizational component of human societies, he posits, represents a real and effective instrument of achieving a unity of opposing and even conflicting cultural formations. Chumakov's position here is apparently at odds with that of the American political philosopher Samuel Huntington and his assertion of the irreducible diversity not only of cultures but of different civilizations as well. According to Huntington, the Western civilization, with its focus on parliamentary democracy, the rule of law, and individual rights and freedoms, is unique to the West. It cannot, and should not, be exported to other civilizational regions like the Islamic East, China, or Russia, for instance. Huntington writes:

> Some Americans have promoted multiculturalism at home; some have promoted universalism abroad, and some have done both. Multiculturalism at home threatens the United States and the West; universalism abroad threatens the West and the world. Both deny the uniqueness of Western culture. The global monoculturalists want to make the world like America. The domestic multiculturalists want to make America like the world. A multicultural America is impossible because a non-Western America is not American. A multicultural world is unavoidable because global empire is impossible.[5]

Another American political philosopher and Huntington's famous opponent, Francis Fukuyama, argues precisely the opposite in his volume *The End of History*. Fukuyama analyzes the twentieth-century political and military battles and the post-soviet world's prospects in terms of the Hegelian view of history. According to Hegel, universal human history consists of the progress toward

---

4 Chumakov and Sergeev, "Religion and Globalization," 111.
5 Samuel Huntington, *The Clash of Civilizations and the Remaking of World Order* (New York: Simon & Schuster, 2011), 318. Huntington often uses the terms "culture" and "civilization" interchangeably, and when he writes about American or Western cultures, he assumes that civilizational institutions represent an inalienable part of their cultural identity.

a fully realized freedom. In "the universal and homogenous state" of the future, he believed, "the contradiction that existed in the relationship of lordship and bondage [is fully reconciled] by making the former slaves their own masters ... each individual, free and cognizant of his own self-worth, [will recognize] every other individual for those same qualities."[6] For Fukuyama, we may as well be living at the peak of this historical process. The closest to the Hegelian idea humanity ever stood is in Western republican societies. As he put it, the "two parallel historical processes, one guided by modern natural science and the logic of desire, the other by the struggle for [equal] recognition ... conveniently culminated in the same end point, capitalist liberal democracy."[7]

In his take on cultural and civilizational identities, Alexander Chumakov is much closer to Fukuyama than to Huntington. While accepting the unique cultural-civilizational systems in the world, Chumakov argues that they produce "opposition and conflict ... due to the discrepancy of cultures," but may reach "agreement and mutual understanding on civilizational grounds." By "civility and civilization," he means, of course, not something abstract but very specific features of modern western societies, which holds universal value in Chumakov's estimation. Namely, "the recognition and respect for human rights, tolerance, separation of powers, the rule of law, and the equality of all before the law." As he emphasizes, "the higher the level of civility of the interacting parties and the more of common experience they share, the more effective and fruitful will be mutual understanding and cooperation."[8]

In this ongoing dialogue between the proponents of the uniqueness of Western civilization and those who emphasize its universality and applicability to all cultures, the author of this essay would maintain the middle ground's position. I would agree with Huntington that Western civilization, like any other civilizational construct, is unique to the West and would face enormous challenges and difficulties when imposed by force on non-Western cultures. The outside powers should not compel any governmental system, including democracy, which usually grows from the inside, on other sovereign states. Otherwise, it would seldom take roots on the foreign soil. The latest historical examples that readily come to mind are the results of the American invasion and wars in Iraq and Afghanistan.

At the same time, I would agree with Fukuyama, and Chumakov for that matter, in their assertion of the universal value of Western civilization. Capitalist democracy is indeed the most efficient economic and political system

---

6 Francis Fukuyama, *The End of History and the Last Man* (New York: Free Press, 2006), 300.
7 Fukuyama, *The End of History and the Last Man*, 289.
8 Chumakov and Sergeev, "Religion and Globalization," 112.

humanity was able to develop in several thousand years of its history. The ideology of the European Enlightenment, which laid the foundation for Western liberalism, was formulated as a purely rational enterprise that could successfully be applied to all of humanity in theory.

However, I would also disagree with Chumakov, who argues that it is not culture but civilization that could bring humanity together. Namely, Western civilization, focusing on liberal democratic values, is the surest way to minimize and eventually exterminate social, political, and economic conflicts that tear humanity apart and pose a real threat to its global survival. My argument refers not to Huntington's position about the irreducible plurality of civilizations and the West's uniqueness. It is about the origin of any civilizational construct, which typically does not come out of nothing.

Civilizations grow and flourish by developing from the seeds sowed by the founders and heroes of cultural revolutions. Contemporary Western civilization, for instance, is the product of Christian culture. At the same time, it reflects the crisis of Christianity, in being based on pure rationality. When this modern civilization penetrates other cultural formations' strata, let alone imposes itself on them, it undermines those cultures by challenging their intrinsic, and especially moral, values.

Fukuyama believes that humanity has two aspirations—the satisfaction of desires and the yearning for equal recognition. But he completely disregards the third one, which is universal, and lies at the center of any cultural organism—the search for divine liberation, enlightenment, or salvation. Modern Western civilization cannot offer any meaningful collective response to that spiritual longing, because of its empiricist philosophical and rational scientific foundations. Such a civilizational pattern could be extended to all of humanity, but it will still not be able to satisfy its profound spiritual needs and challenges. That is why, I believe, the global society of the future should be built on cultural foundations rather than civilizational grounds, no matter how progressive and unique they might appear.

4 Globalization and Modern Religions

As a case study of a modern religious movement that promotes the global unity of humankind and the building of an "ever-advancing civilization," I take the Bahá'í Faith, a religion that was conceived in Persia (nowadays Iran) in the middle of the nineteenth century with the declaration of the Báb, born Siyyid 'Alí Muḥammad Shírází (1819–1850) whose prophetic mission lasted for six years. After the Báb's assassination in 1850 by the Persian authorities, his religion was continued and renewed by Bahá'u'lláh, born Mírzá Ḥusayn-'Alí Núrí (1817–1892), who proclaimed his divine mission in 1863 in the Najibiyyih gardens of Bagdad.

Since then, the Bahá'í Faith developed into a distinctive and independent religion with millions of adherents worldwide:

> *Encyclopædia Britannica* and the *World Christian Encyclopedia* have listed Bahá'í membership as over seven million. More conservative estimates produced by the Bahá'í World News Service report a Bahá'í membership of more than five million worldwide, in "virtually every country" and many territories. As such, the Bahá'í Faith is recognized as the second-most geographically widespread religion after Christianity, and the only religion to have grown faster than the population of the world in all major areas over the last century.[9]

Every religion holds a critical notion that is associated mainly with its doctrines. Christianity is known for preaching universal love; Buddhism—for promoting selflessness. The Bahá'í focus on the concept of unity or oneness, which occupies the central position in their teachings. The followers of Bahá'u'lláh differentiate between three levels of unity—those of God, religion, and humanity. Since our Creator is one and the purpose of progressive revelation is to bring people together on an ever-increasing scale—from clans and tribes to national and international communities—the time has finally come for all humanity to be integrated on a global scale.

The exposition of various principles, doctrines, and strategies, both individual and collective, that aim to unite humankind into a scientifically and technologically advanced, while at the same time peaceful, moral, and humane planetary community, constitute the nerve of Bahá'u'lláh's message. I want to explore further in this context some of the themes that run throughout his tablets and epistles. The first one concerns the relationship between the Bahá'í teachings and the ideology of the Enlightenment.

In many important ways, the Bahá'í worldview represents a re-affirmation of most of the Enlightenment ideas but in a distinct religious setting, thus adding a spiritual depth to those theories and transforming modern civilizational practices into genuinely held cultural beliefs and norms. The Bahá'í reassert as sacred such principles as the rule of law, the freedom of conscience

---

9 "Bahá'í Faith by Country," Wikipedia, https://en.wikipedia.org/wiki/Bah%C3%A1%CA%BC%C3%AD_Faith_by_country.

and expression, the freedom of association, the advancement of human rights, the equality of men and women, and so on. In "Glad Tidings," Bahá'u'lláh proclaims:

> In former religions such ordinances as holy war, destruction of books, the ban on association and companionship with other peoples or on reading certain books had been laid down and affirmed according to the exigencies of the time; however, in this mighty Revelation, in this momentous Announcement, the manifold bestowals and favors of God have overshadowed all men, and from the horizon of the Will of the Ever-Abiding Lord, His infallible decree hath prescribed that which We have set forth above.[10]

In politics, Bahá'u'lláh rejects autocratic and oppressive governments, which he condemns as unjust and unfair to the people. He approves of republican democracies but favors constitutional monarchy as a political system that combines the commoners and aristocrats' interests with the kingship, which represents the divine sanction. In his "Epistle to Queen Victoria," Bahá'u'lláh praises the queen for having "entrusted the reins of counsel into the hands of the representatives of the people … for thereby the foundations of the edifice of [her] affairs will be strengthened, and the hearts of all that are beneath [her] shadow, whether high or low, will be tranquillized."[11] And in "Glad Tidings" he counsels political scholars:

> Although a republican form of government profiteth all the peoples of the world, yet the majesty of kingship is one of the signs of God. We do not wish that the countries of the world should remain deprived thereof. If the sagacious combine the two forms into one, great will be their reward in the presence of God.[12]

When discussing future global government, Bahá'u'lláh does not provide many specifics about the executive and legislative branches, except for the general

---

10 Bahá'u'lláh, "Bishárát (Glad-Tidings)," in *Tablets of Bahá'u'lláh*, Bahá'í Reference Library, https://www.bahai.org/library/authoritative-texts/bahaullah/tablets-bahaullah/1#030537471.

11 "Epistle to Queen Victoria," in *The Summons of the Lord of Hosts*, Bahá'í Reference Library, https://www.bahai.org/library/authoritative-texts/bahaullah/summons-lord-hosts/1#264287944.

12 Bahá'u'lláh, "Bishárát (Glad-Tidings)."

importance of equity and justice, consultation, collective decision-making, and so on. His judicial power proposals are much more detailed—perhaps because the independent and fair court system is the backbone of any stable and long-lasting society. Bahá'u'lláh envisions the establishment of the Supreme Tribunal, whose purpose would be to resolve territorial disputes and international conflicts, thus preventing the brutality of warfare. The eldest son of Bahá'u'lláh and the leader of the Bahá'í Faith after his father's passing, 'Abdu'l-Bahá outlined a concrete plan for the world judiciary, which is yet to be fulfilled by the nations. To form such an organization, he advised:

> The national assemblies of each country and nation—that is to say parliaments—should elect two or three persons who are the choicest men of that nation and are well informed concerning international laws and the relations between governments and aware of the essential needs of the world of humanity of this day. The number of these representatives should be in proportion to the number of inhabitants of that country. The election of these souls who are chosen by the national assembly, that is, the parliament, must be confirmed by the upper house, the congress, and the cabinet and also by the president or monarch so these persons may be the elected ones of all the nation and the government. From among these people, the members of the Supreme Tribunal will be elected, and all mankind will thus have a share therein, for every one of these delegates is fully representative of his nation. When the Supreme Tribunal gives a ruling on any international question, either unanimously or by majority-rule, there will no longer be any pretext for the plaintiff or ground of objection for the defendant. In case any of the governments or nations in the execution of the irrefutable decision of the Supreme Tribunal be negligent or dilatory, the rest of the nations will rise up against it because all the governments and nations of the world are the supporters of this Supreme Tribunal.[13]

Overall, 'Abdu'l-Bahá promoted eleven social principles based on the teachings of Bahá'u'lláh, which should guide humanity toward a sustainable global civilization. For the Bahá'í, those precepts serve as a modern equivalent of the Ten Commandments. Like those earlier divine instructions, they can be fulfilled by anyone, no matter religious affiliation or lack thereof. Most clearly

---

[13] 'Abdu'l-Bahá, *Selections from the Writings of 'Abdu'l-Bahá*, No. 227, Bahá'í Reference Library, https://www.bahai.org/library/authoritative-texts/abdul-baha/selections-writings-abdul-baha/.

and systematically 'Abdu'l-Bahá discussed those teachings during his European missionary journey, when he stayed in Paris from October to December 1911. The eleven principles that he enunciated during his meeting at the Theosophical Society of Paris are as follows:

1. *The Search for Truth:* "Man must cut himself free from all prejudice and from the result of his own imagination, so that he may be able to search for truth unhindered. Truth is one in all religions, and by means of it the unity of the world can be realized."
2. *The Unity of Humankind:* "All men are the leaves and fruit of one same tree, they are all branches of the tree of Adam, they all have the same origin ... Holy Writings tell us: All men are equal before God. He is no respecter of persons."
3. *Religion Should be the Cause of Love and Affection:* "Religion should unite all hearts and cause wars and disputes to vanish from the face of the earth ... If religion becomes a cause of dislike, hatred and division, it were better to be without it, and to withdraw from such a religion would be a truly religious act."
4. *The Unity of Religion and Science:* "Any religion that contradicts science or that is opposed to it, is only ignorance ... Whatever the intelligence of man cannot understand, religion ought not to accept. Religion and science walk hand in hand, and any religion contrary to science is not the truth."
5. *Prejudices of Religion, Race, or Sect Destroy the Foundation of Humanity:* "The whole world must be looked upon as one single country, all the nations as one nation, all men as belonging to one race. Religions, races, and nations are all divisions of man's making only, and are necessary only in his thought."
6. *Equal Opportunity of the Means of Existence:* "Every human being has the right to live; they have a right to rest, and to a certain amount of well-being ... Nobody should die of hunger; everybody should have sufficient clothing; one man should not live in excess while another has no possible means of existence."
7. *The Equality of Men—Equality Before the Law:* "The Law must reign, and not the individual; thus will the world become a place of beauty and true brotherhood will be realized."
8. *Universal Peace:* "A Supreme Tribunal shall be elected by the peoples and governments of every nation, where members from each country and government shall assemble in unity. All disputes shall be brought before this Court, its mission being to prevent war."

9. *Religion Should Not Concern Itself with Political Questions:* "Religion is concerned with things of the spirit, politics with things of the world ... It is the work of the clergy to educate the people, to instruct them, to give them good advice and teaching so that they may progress spiritually. With political questions they have nothing to do."
10. *Education and Instruction of Women:* "Women have equal rights with men upon earth; in religion and society they are a very important element. As long as women are prevented from attaining their highest possibilities, so long will men be unable to achieve the greatness which might be theirs."
11. *The Power of the Holy Spirit:* "It is only by the breath of the Holy Spirit that spiritual development can come about ... for it is the soul that animates the body; the body alone has no real significance. Deprived of the blessings of the Holy Spirit the material body would be inert."[14]

Now, more than a century from the initial unveiling of these principles in Europe, many of them have become the animating spirit behind social progress and change worldwide and an intrinsic part of the fabric of life in Western societies. Of course, those teachings envision such a profound social transformation that it will require more time and effort to put them all together in practice. Nevertheless, the ideal image of the future they offer to humanity is so spiritual in quality and global in scope that it has no parallel in world history.

5 Remarks in Conclusion

In *The End of History*, Francis Fukuyama argues that liberal democracy may constitute the "endpoint of mankind's ideological evolution" and the "final form of human government," and as such constituted "the end of history."[15] Fukuyama's position was not based solely on the historical successes of liberal democracy and the collapse of its main rival, the Soviet Union, at the end of the twentieth century. His philosophical inquiry went deeper into the internal worth of a liberal democratic political system coupled with the capitalist free-market economy. Are modern Western societies fully satisfying to their citizens, or, maybe, those systems have some hidden defects that will

---

14 'Abdu'l-Bahá, "Paris Talks: Addresses Given by 'Abdu'l-Bahá in 1911," Bahá'í Reference Library, https://www.bahai.org/library/authoritative-texts/abdul-baha/paris-talks/1 #733601770.
15 Fukuyama, *The End of History and the Last Man*, xi.

eventually lead to their demise as it had happened with all former cultures? In other words, could Western civilization sustain itself without any external competitors or enemies? Fukuyama answers those questions positively. He writes:

> There is no doubt that contemporary democracies face any number of serious problems, from drugs, homelessness, and crime to environmental damage and the frivolity of consumerism. But these problems are not obviously insoluble on the basis of liberal principles, nor so serious that they would necessarily lead to the collapse of society as a whole, as communism collapsed in the 1980s.[16]

Bahá'í teachings address the same issue implicitly, by distinguishing between the so-called Lesser and Most Great Peace. The Lesser Peace may come about through political unification of the world. As the Guardian of the Bahá'í Faith and leader of the Bahá'í community from 1922 until 1957, Shoghi Effendi wrote that

> some form of a world super-state must needs be evolved, in whose favor all the nations of the world will have willingly ceded every claim to make war, certain rights to impose taxation and all rights to maintain armaments, except for purposes of maintaining internal order within their respective dominions.

This global super-state would most likely be built based on modern ideology, including the election of officials, various branches of power, and the separation between religion and politics. As Shoghi Effendi continues:

> Such a state will have to include within its orbit an international executive adequate to enforce supreme and unchallengeable authority on every recalcitrant member of the commonwealth; a world parliament whose members shall be elected by the people in their respective countries and whose election shall be confirmed by their respective governments; and a supreme tribunal whose judgment will have a binding effect

---

16   Fukuyama, *The End of History and the Last Man*, xxi.

even in such cases where the parties concerned did not voluntarily agree to submit their case to its consideration.[17]

Nevertheless, the cessation of war, however remarkable and progressive it might be, does not equal the establishment of peace among nations, which might still be torn apart by internal strife and conflicts on the ethnic, national, racial, political, social, and religious levels. Hence, the difference between the Lesser and Most Great Peace may be likened to the distinction between external unification and internal unity, a matrimonial arrangement, which is based on convenience or love. In Bahá'í Writings, the Most Great Peace stands as the ideal of spiritual rather than material harmony, a cultural rather than civilizational project. The Bahá'í believe that in those distant times, "Bahá'u'lláh's mission will be fully recognized by the peoples of the earth and its principles consciously accepted and applied by the generality of humankind."[18] The ensuing "ultimate fusion of all races, creeds, classes and nations"[19] will firmly secure the long-term stability and flourishing of global humanity. Shoghi Effendi describes this future civilization as a

> World community in which all economic barriers will have been permanently demolished and the interdependence of Capital and Labor definitely recognized; in which the clamor of religious fanaticism and strife will have been forever stilled; in which the flame of racial animosity will have been finally extinguished; in which a single code of international law—the product of the considered judgment of the world's federated representatives—shall have as its sanction the instant and coercive intervention of the combined forces of the federated units; and finally a world community in which the fury of a capricious and militant nationalism will have been transmuted into an abiding consciousness of world citizenship—such indeed, appears, in its broadest outline, the Order anticipated by Bahá'u'lláh, an Order that shall come to be regarded as the fairest fruit of a slowly maturing age.[20]

---

17 Shoghi Effendi, *The World Order of Bahá'u'lláh: Selected Letters*, Bahá'í Reference Library, https://www.bahai.org/library/authoritative-texts/shoghi-effendi/world-order-bahaullah/1#369510938.
18 William S. Hatcher and J. Douglas Martin, *The Bahá'í Faith: The Emerging Global Religion* (Wilmette: Bahá'í Publishing Trust, 1998), 144.
19 Shoghi Effendi, "The Promised Day is Come," Bahá'í Reference Library, https://www.bahai.org/library/authoritative-texts/shoghi-effendi/promised-day-come/1#617979506.
20 Shoghi Effendi, *The World Order of Bahá'u'lláh*, 19.

Appendix: Globalization and Religion in Bahá'í Studies

Selected Bibliography

Books
Bahá'í and Globalisation. University of Copenhagen, 2005.
Bahá'í-Inspired Perspectives on Human Rights. Edited by Tahirih Tahririha-Danesh. Hong Kong: Juxta Publishing Co., 2001.
Danesh, H. B. *Unity: The Creative Foundation of Peace*. Ottawa: Baha'i Studies Publication, 1986.
Human Rights, Faith, and Culture. Rosebery, Australia: Association for Baha'i Studies Australia, 2001.

Articles
Abizadeh, Sohrab. "Will Globalization Lead to a World Commonwealth?" *Journal of Bahá'í Studies*, 15 (2005): 1–4.
Ayman, Rama. "Addressing the Rising Tide of Globalization and Amorality in the Present World Order and Its Implications on Extremes of Wealth and Poverty." *Lights of Irfan*, 17 (2016).
Badee, Hooshmand. "Some Reflections on the Principle of Unity/Oneness." *Lights of Irfan*, 19 (2018).
Buck, Christopher. "The Eschatology of Globalization: The Multiple Messiahship of Bahá'u'lláh Revisited." In *Studies in Modern Religions, Religious Movements and the Babi-Bahá'í Faiths*. Edited by Moshe Sharon. Boston: Brill, 2004.
Ewing, Sovaida Ma'ani. "Collective Security: An Indispensable Requisite for a Lasting Peace." *Lights of Irfan*, 14 (2013).
Fish, Mary. "Economic Prosperity: A Global Imperative." *Journal of Bahá'í Studies*, 7 (1997): 3.
Hanson, Holly. "Global Dilemmas, Local Responses: Creating Patterns of Action that Make the World Different." Bahá'í Library Online, 2000.
Huddleston, John. "Just System of Government: The Third Dimension to World Peace." In *Bahá'í Faith and Marxism: Proceedings of a Conference Held January 1986*. Ottawa, ON: Bahá'í Studies Publications, 1987.
Karlberg, Michael and Cheshmak Farhoumand-Sims. "Global Citizenship and Humanities Scholarship: Toward a Twenty-First Century Agenda." *International Journal of the Humanities*, 2 (2006): 3.
Karlberg, Michael. "Discourse, Identity, and Global Citizenship." *Peace Review: A Journal of Social Justice*, 20 (2008): 3.
Karlberg, Michael. "Education for Interdependence: The University and the Global Citizen." *Global Studies Journal*, 3 (2010): 1.

Kavelin, Chris J. "Individual Bahá'í Perspective on Spiritual Aspects of Cultural Diversity and Sustainable Development: Towards a Second Enlightenment." *International Journal of Diversity in Organizations, Communities, and Nations*, 8 (2008): 1.

Kazemi, Noojan. "Global Prosperity for Humankind: The Bahá'í Model." In *75 Years of the Bahá'í Faith in Australasia*. Rosebery, Australia: Association for Baha'i Studies Australia, 1996.

Landau, Richard. "The Bahá'í Faith and the Environment." In *Encyclopedia of Global Environmental Change, Volume 5: Social and Economic Dimensions of Global Environmental Change*. Edited by Peter Timmerman. Medford, MA: Wiley, 2002.

Locke, Alain. "Four Talks Redefining Democracy, Education, and World Citizenship." *World Order*, 38 (2008): 3.

Lopez-Carlos, Augusto. "Challenges of Sustainable Development." *Journal of Bahá'í Studies*, 22 (2012).

Mahmoudi, Hoda. "Human Knowledge and the Advancement of Society." *Journal of Bahá'í Studies*, 22 (2012).

McGlinn, Sen. "A Difficult Case: Beyer's Categories and the Bahá'í Faith." *Social Compass*, 50 (2003).

Merchant, Ali K. "Religious Challenges in the Twenty-First Century and the Bahá'í Faith." *Global Religious Vision*, 1 (2001): 4.

Meyjes, Gregory Paul P. "Language and Universalization: A 'Linguistic Ecology' Reading of Bahá'í Writings." *Journal of Bahá'í Studies*, 9 (1994): 1.

Moane, Eamonn. "Perspectives on the Global Economy at the Dawn of the Twenty-First Century: An Irish Bahá'í View." *Solas*, 1 (2001).

Nicholson, Graham. "Towards the New World Order: A Bahá'í perspective." *Bahá'í Studies in Australasia*, 3 (1996).

Saiedi, Nader. "From Oppression to Empowerment." *Journal of Bahá'í Studies*, 26 (2016): 1–2.

Schaefer, Udo. "Ethics for a Global Society." *Bahá'í Studies Review*, 4 (1994): 1.

Index

Abkhazia
    ethnic self-consciousness   25, 27, 33
    national language   25, 33–4
    traditional Abkhaz thought and philosophy   25, 27, 30, 33–5
Academy of Sciences of the USSR   xv, 327, 328
Aksakov, Konstantin   308, 309
All-Union Scientific Research Institute for System Studies   xv
alter-globalism
    as an alternative to the global hegemony of capital   154–6, 157
    internal contradictions of   158–9
    movement   148–52, 156
    principles of   156–8
    program of   159–62
    term   140–1, 148
    use of information-network technology   152–4, 156
anthropocene, term   68, 286
anthropogene
    pressure on the biosphere   182–5, 211, 222
    term   68
anthroposociogenesis   54–5
anti-globalism movement   140, 141, 148, 149–50
Arnason, Johann Pall   372, 373, 375
Attali, Jacques   391, 392–3
Avtonomova, Natalia   31–2

Babur, Zahiriddin Muhammad   382–3, 385
Belov, Vladislav   135
Benhabib, Seyla   249
Berdyaev, Nikolai   229–30
Bganba, Vitaly Reshevich   33
bioecology   275–6, 286–90
biogeochemistry   102
biosphere
    adaptation potential   184–5
    anthropogenic pressure   182–5, 211, 222
    biodiversity   214, 221
    biospheric evolution   211
    carrying capacity   185–9, 218
    definition   182
    harmonization with the technosphere   196
    human ecology and   99–100, 279
    humanity's responsibility for   100, 219–22, 223, 281, 282, 289
    man as a geological power   66, 100, 219, 281
    maximum population size   188, 218
    net biota primary production (NBPP)   187–8
    technological solutions for the preservation of   100–1, 183, 218–19, 221, 223, 281
    transformation of natural environments   211–13, 222
    See also noosphere
Bogdanov, Alexander   273–4, 283, 289
Braudel, Fernand   37, 69, 374
Budyko, Mikhail   xvi

Chile   127–8
China
    within the BRICS   265–6
    within competing globalization   40, 42, 43
    core cultural values   263, 268–9
    economic growth   264–5
    economic impact of American unipolar globalization   255–6
    EU's China strategy   112
    financial power   42, 43, 46–7, 261–2
    global development model for the South   45–6, 262
    military-political alliance with Russia   259, 260
    modernization strategies   39, 260–3, 302, 305–6
    research and development funding   266–7
    Russia-China-India alliance   259, 265–6
    Sino-American relations   43, 46–7, 48, 111, 114–15, 242–3, 259, 265
    social credit system   263
    technology industry   46, 261
Chizhevsky, Alexander   100, 326, 327, 330

Chomsky, Noam   146, 148
Chumakov, Alexander   65, 69, 126, 169, 272–3, 376, 377, 405–6, 407
civilization
   as anthropocentric   335
   characteristics of   336
   civilizational values   336–8, 343–5, 377–9
   civilization/culture relationship   52–4, 373–7, 405–8
   clashes between   38–9, 338, 343, 373, 375–6, 377
   common mentalities   285, 335, 338, 372–3, 377
   concept   373–5
   definition   335
   dialogue among   338–41
   ecological imperative   285–6
   global civilization concept   373, 385–6
   globalization and   341–2
   globalization's transformation of civilizational values   342–5
   global security strategies   347
   historical stages of   377–80
   mutual exchange of values   343–4, 345
   Ottoman Empire   384
   possible trajectories for   348–9
   Russia's civilizational choices   271, 274, 289–90
   in Seyyid Nasimi's thought   381–2, 385
   Turko-Islamic world   380–5
   world civilizations/plurality of   335–6, 373, 375
   in Zahiriddin Babur's thought   382–3
climatology
   anthropocene era and   68
   Budyko-Sellers model   xvi
   planetary-scale changes   67–8
Club of Rome   xv, xvii, 9, 11, 99, 105, 181–2, 286, 323–4, 331
Cohen, Jean   249
Communards   315
communication
   cultural information transmission   53, 54–8
   in the digital age   24, 224, 227, 228–35, 284, 350–1
   information-network technology of the alter-globalist movement   152–4, 156

competing globalization
   China's role   45–6
   development of the South   45–6, 48
   economics of   41–3, 44
   ideological models of   39–40, 43–4, 47–8, 49–50
   the North's global predominance   44–5
   as Third Colonialism   43–4
conflict
See also global security; nuclear weapons
cooperation
   characteristics of   79–84
   defined   78
   evolutionary development   271–2, 273
   features of international cooperation   79, 84–90
   human cooperative practices   80–4
   international cooperation in globalization   78–9, 90–5
   military alliances   87–8, 91–2
   in the natural world   79–80
   Self/non-Self distinction   90, 93–5, 96
   within the Sport for All movement   368
cosmopolitanism
   as an alternative to the hegemony   246
   as an alternative to the nation states   14, 248–9
   characteristics of the new cosmopolitanism   244–6
   globalization and   13, 237
   human rights issues   247, 248–9
   Kant's cosmopolitan order   13, 237–8
   philosophical thought and   21–2, 27, 29, 249–52
   sovereignty issues   247–9
   of the United Nations   238–9
COVID-19 pandemic
   causes   287–8
   EU economic responses to   117–21
   future risk analysis and   347
   geopolitical trends, post-pandemic   110–15, 125–6, 130–2
   global civil society   136–7
   global elites attitudes, post-pandemic   137–9
   global inequalities   117, 129
   global institutions responses   132–3

INDEX

human behaviour, post-pandemic
    115–17
  impact on political economies 111, 113,
    132–6
  impact on the global community 124–5,
    217
  primacy of the nation-state 133–5, 136
  Russian economic challenges 122–3
culture
  analysis of globalization 77
  China's core cultural values 263, 268–9
  civilization/culture relationship 52–4,
    373–7, 405–8
  definition 373
  in digital age 229, 231
  ethnic cultural self-reflectivity 30, 32
  Gaia hypothesis and 67
  within the global digital society 229, 231
  global-historical role of 65–6
  globalization's impact on minority ethnic
    groups 24, 25, 30–2
  hegemonic aspects of globalization 24,
    30, 32, 237, 341–2, 343–4, 390
  heterogeneity 236–7
  informational conception of 53, 54–8
  philosophical thought and 26–7
  societal trends of competing globalization
    42
  UNESCO Universal Declaration on
    Cultural Diversity 339–40

Dallmayr, Fred 251–2
de-globalization 113, 125
Derrida, Jacques 30, 31–2, 250–1
digital age
  Big Data analytics 349–52, 357
  communication in 24, 224, 227, 228–35,
    284, 350–1
  culture in 229, 231
  education in 233
  the global digital society 224, 227,
    228–35, 261, 284–5, 350–5
  human rights in 284–5
  politics in 231–2

ecology
  bioecology 275–6, 286–90
  ecological humanism 225–6, 234

ecological production 278–9
field of 275, 277–8
global ecology 102, 182, 189, 283, 286
globalization of 275
human ecology 279–80
modern conservation practices 219–21
population strategies 215
public perceptions of environmental
    problems 190–3
within Russian global studies xvii
society/nature relations 8, 99–100,
    276–9
species extinction 214, 221
transformation of natural environments
    211–13, 222
economics
  analysis of globalization 23, 24, 25, 51,
    54, 77, 389
  civilization and 53–4
  of competing globalization 41–3, 44
  of competing westernizations 40–1,
    42–3
  decline of social market economies 113
  EU economic responses to COVID-19
    pandemic 117–21
  global economy, post-COVID 111–12, 119
  global hegemony of capital 141–3, 147,
    154–6, 157
  the green economy 207–9, 218–19
  impact of American unipolar
    globalization 255–6
  money within historical evolution 73,
    379
  2008-9 economic crisis 110, 111, 118, 124,
    128, 134
  See also finance; neoliberalism
education
  in China 265–6
  civilizational values and 337
  within the global digital society 233
  global education 107
  global security and 108
  globalization of 106–7
Effendi, Shoghi 414–15
Einstein, Albert 6–7, 8
environment
  concept 194
  environmental pollution 213, 221

environment (cont.)
  See also ecology
ethics
  civilizational values 378–9
  development and use of AI technologies 350–1, 352–7
  ethical bonds in pre-state communities 308–9
  informal civil society structures 314–15
  social volunteering networks 320–1
ethnicity
  Abkhazia 25, 27, 30, 33–5
  cultural self-reflectivity 30, 32
  ethnic self-consciousness 25, 27, 29, 32
  globalization's cultural-historical impact 24, 25, 30–2
  minority ethnic groups 24–5
europeanization, term 37
European Union (EU)
  economic tensions, post-COVID 117–21
  new regional industrial strategy 111–13
evolution
  biospheric evolution 211
  civilizational/cultural evolution 52–5
  cooperation-based approaches 271–2, 273
  developmental algorithm 57–8
  earliest state formations 61–2
  evolutionary globalistics 104–5
  extraterrestrial exploration 57, 75
  geo-bio-socio-epo-metamorphosis 65–6
  global resettlement 58–61, 70
  globalization as a process of 51–2, 56
  global-universal evolutionism 52, 57–8, 63–4, 325
  information transmission for cultural genesis 53, 54–8
  Neolithic Revolution 61, 71–2, 182, 211
  social stage of 54, 55–6
  spatial expansion 55–6, 57, 58–61, 63–4, 70, 75
  species formation rate 184–5, 214
  sustainable development 63–4
  technical abilities 198, 199
  universal evolutionism 51–2, 57–8

Fadeyev, Evgeny 278, 288

finance
  advantages/disadvantages of innovative banking 227–8
  China's financial power 42, 43, 46–7, 261–2
  China's social credit system 263
  features of innovative banking 224–5, 226–7
  homogenization of financial rule 92–3
  money within historical evolution 73, 379
Francis, Pope 391, 397
Frank, Andre Gunder 69
Frolov, Ivan xvi, 169, 288
Fukuyama, Francis 39, 241, 372, 406–7, 413–14
Fyodorov, Nikolai 100, 325, 326, 327, 330

Gaia hypothesis 66–7
geopolitics
  analysis of globalization 23, 25
  Greater Eurasia project 256–9, 268
  post-Cold War 241, 242–3
  revolutions as geopolitical weapons 302–4
  trends, post-pandemic 110–15, 125–6, 130–2
  See also international relations; politics
Girusov, Eduard 276, 282, 288
global challenges
  concept 169
  global political challenges 169–76
global community
See also world community
global ecology 102, 182, 189, 283, 286
globalistics
  as distinct from global studies 99, 102–3, 105
  evolutionary globalistics 104–5
  field of xvi–xvii, 99, 103–5
  focus on global development 103–4
  interdisciplinarity of 102–3
  political globalistics 164
globalization
  analysis of 23–4, 35–6, 51–2
  definitions 3, 4, 37, 51, 58, 140, 163, 210, 296, 323, 373, 387–8

INDEX 423

disintegration of hyper-globalization 111–13
hegemonic aspects of 24, 30, 32, 237, 341–2, 343–4, 390
as a holistic phenomenon 23, 27–8
natural-historical approach 210
negative consequences 5–7, 8–9, 15, 107, 165–6, 169, 389–90
philosophical thought and 3–7, 8–9
replacement of westernization 37–40, 42–3, 48–9
scholarship on xv–xvii
socio-natural aspects 65, 67
spatial characteristics 90–1
spiritual aspects 390–401
stages of 3–5
transformation of the World System 296–7
at the World Congress of Philosophy 9–17
See also competing globalization; history of globalization; political globalization
globalization challenges, term 169
global security
American hegemonic ambitions 243–4
as asphatronics 346
civilization's development strategy for 347
cosmopolitanism and 237–9
definition 346
development and use of AI technologies 352–7
as distinct from international security 348
existential threat of nuclear weapons 239–40
as a global political challenge 173
increased potential for conflict under globalization 77–8
military geopolitical balance 347
nuclear winter concept xvi, 240
post-Cold War 240–4
predictive analytics and 352
risks to 107–8
scholarship on 346–7, 352
US-China military tensions 114–15, 123, 242–3
See also nuclear weapons

global studies
alternative global studies 323–5
Department of Global Processes, Lomonosov Moscow State University xvii, 108
as distinct from globalistics 99, 102–3, 105
field of xvi–xvii, 17–18, 99, 103, 323
focus on global development 103–4
global security and 107–8
mathematical modelling 99
multidisciplinarity of 102–3
philosophical thought and 3–7, 8–9, 17, 18–19, 21–2, 26, 35–6
Vladimir Vernadsky as the founder of 99–102, 106
Gorshkov, Victor 187–8
Gromyko, Alexey A. 134–5
Gumilyov, Lev 325
Gvishiani, Dzhermen xv

Habermas, Jürgen 14, 247
Hegel, Georg Wilhelm Friedrich 29, 30, 94, 198, 380, 406–7
Heigegger, Martin 28
history
global history 70, 71–4
great revolutions 291–4
inter-local systems 72
local community formation 71–2
macro-regional systems 73–4
philosophy of history 292–4
regional systems 72–3, 111
history of globalization
definition 70
early mankind's development 58–61, 70
Gaia hypothesis and 66–7
humanity's impact on the planet 67–8
inter-continental systems 74
latent/cover globalization periods 71–4
as a objective-historical process 65–6, 69
periodization of 68–70
the unified social whole 74–5
See also competing globalization; evolution
Hobbes, Thomas 80–1

humanism
    ecological humanism   225–6, 234
    the global consciousness and   19–20
    humanistic dimensions of globalization
        23, 225
    universal human values of   20–1
    in Zahiriddin Babur's thought   382–3,
        385
human rights
    within cosmopolitanism   247, 248–9
    in the digital age   284–5
    UN Declaration of Human Rights   21, 39,
        238–9
Huntington, Samuel   343, 345, 373, 375, 392,
    406

identity
    globalization and identity loss   24, 32, 34
    national identity and cosmism   325
    national self-consciousness   29, 30, 32,
        33
    role of national philosophies   34
    Russian Idea   325
    Turko-Islamic world   380–1
Ilyenkov, Evald   353–4
India
    modernization strategies   264–5, 302
    Russia-China-India alliance   259, 265–6
    the thought of Zahiriddin Babur   383
Inozemtsev, Vladislav L.   255–6
institutions
    civilizational values and   337
    the family   70, 309, 310, 311–13, 317–18
    global institutions responses to COVID-19
        132–3
    marriage   70
    money   73
International Independent
    Ecological-Political University   xvii
international relations
    bipolar world order   76, 165, 256, 298–9
    earliest state formations   61–2, 73
    global political challenges   169–76
    post-COVID   111–12
    as a process of globalization   62
    See also geopolitics

Jaspers, Karl   8–9

Kant, Immanuel   237–8, 376–7
Karaganov, Sergei   257–8
Kardashev, Nikolai   325
Karpinskaya, Regina   288
Kaznacheyev, Vlail   279
Kefeli, Igor   288–9
Kobylyansky, Victor   276–7, 288
Kolin, Konstantin   347
Kropotkin, Pyotr   271–2, 273, 289
Kulpin-Gubaidullin, Eduard   279, 288

labor
    under the global hegemony of capital
        142
    objectification of   205–6
    slave labor   202
Laszlo, Ervin   6
Lavrov, Sergei   389–90
Lee, Myung-Hyun   12
Leonhard, Gerd   284–5
liberalism   377, 379–80
Lomonosov, Mikhail   102
Lovelock, James   66–7

Marx, Karl   22
Matsuura, Koichiro   12
Metropolitan Agafangel   395–6
Metropolitan Ioann (Snychev)   396–7,
    400–1
Moiseyev, Nikita   xvi, 52, 57–8, 285, 289

Nasimi, Seyyid Imadaddin   381–2, 385
nation-states
    cosmopolitanism as an alternative to   14,
        248–9
    decline of social market economies   113
    earliest state formations   61–2, 73
    erosion of sovereignty under
        globalization   77
    global power   130–2
    human cooperative practices   80–1
    international cooperation   78–9, 84–95
    military alliances   87–8, 91–2
    national identity and cosmism   325
    national philosophy within global
        philosophy   24–5, 28–30, 34–6
    national self-consciousness   29, 30, 32,
        33

INDEX

non-state actors 6
   primacy of, post-pandemic 133–5, 136
   structures of social solidarity and 308–10
Navoi, Alisher 383, 385
Nazaretyan, Akop 226
neoliberalism
   Chilean experience of 127–8
   crisis in 111–12, 113, 125, 128–30, 132, 146
   rise of 113, 125–8
   See also ultra-imperialism
noosphere
   concept xv, 8, 100, 272–3, 281
   human ecology and 279
   human responsibility for the biosphere 100, 219–22, 223, 281, 282, 289
   scholarship on 66
nuclear weapons
   existential threat of 5, 6–7, 14, 181, 239–40
   post-Cold War geopolitics 241, 242–4
   in World War II 239
nuclear winter concept xvi, 240

Orudzhev, Zaid 272, 377–8, 379
Outer Space Treaty 85

Pavlov, Alexei 68
Peccei, Aurelio 9, 20, 99, 181–2, 391, 392
philosophy
   within alternative global studies 324
   cosmopolitanism and 21–2, 27, 29, 249–52
   culture and 26–7
   global studies and 3–7, 8–9, 17, 18–19, 21–2, 26, 35–6
   ideality 353–4
   regional/global relations within 24–5, 28–30, 35–6
   role of national philosophies 34
   worldviews and 13, 19, 26
philosophy of history 292–4, 325
political globalization
   defined 163–4
   global political challenges 169–76
   global political processes 164–5
   trends within 166–8

politics
   analysis of globalization 76–7, 105, 163, 164, 389, 390
   cooperation as a political concept 79–84
   within the global digital society 231–2
   global power 130–2
   international cooperation in 78–9
   political globalistics 164
   regional systems, post-COVID 111–13
   Self/non-Self distinction 90, 93–5, 96
   See also geopolitics; international relations
Popper, Karl 392
population
   anthropogenic pressure 182, 183, 330–1
   the biosphere's carrying capacity for 188, 218
   dynamics of the human population 3–4, 5, 215–16, 217–18, 222–3
   globalization's impact on demographic processes 215–18
   global resettlement 58–61, 70
   population strategies, definition 215
   threats to the *Homo sapiens* population 194
Putin, Vladimir 258, 259

religion
   Bahá'í Faith 408–16
   civilizational values and 337, 378–9
   development of the mythological worldview 199–201
   ethical bonds in pre-state communities 309
   faith communities in contemporary Russia 318–19
   within a globalized world 402, 408–15
   Orthodox-Christian civic associations 309–10, 311
   post-Soviet spirituality 317–19
   religious cycles 403–5
   the Russian Idea and 325
   Soviet secularism 402–3, 405
   spiritual aspects of globalization 390–401
revolutions
   as geopolitical weapons 302–4

revolutions (cont.)
    globalization and   295–6, 305–6
    socio-historical impact of the great
        revolutions   291–4, 379–80
    See also Russian Revolution of 1917
Russell, Bertrand   8, 239
Russia
    civilizational choices   271, 274, 289–90
    economic challenges, post-COVID   122–3
    economic impact of American unipolar
        globalization   255–6
    family institution   317–18
    Greater Eurasia project   256–9, 268
    military-political alliance with China
        259, 260
    modernization strategies   266–8, 269–70
    non-state solidarity structures of   317–22
    nuclear disarmament   241
    Orthodox-Christian civic associations
        309–10, 311
    post-Soviet spirituality   317–19
    pre-state communities   308–9
    Russia-China-India alliance   259, 265–6
    social volunteering   320–1
    spiritual aspects   390–1
    Sport for All movement   359
    state socialization   310, 314
    See also Soviet Union (USSR)
Russian Cosmism
    alternative global studies and   325
    contemporary discussions of   330
    cultural significance of   326–7
    national identity   325
    new worldview systems and   330–1
    outer-space research   328–9
    representatives of   100
    research philosophy and   324
    the Russian Idea and   325–6
    Soviet Cosmism   327–8
    Vladimir Vernadsky and   325, 326, 327,
        328
Russian Ecological Academy   xvii
Russian Idea   325–6
Russian Revolution of 1917
    historical significance of   291
    impact on globalization   296, 305–6
    impact on the World System   297, 298–9,
        305–6

phases of influence   304
political regime changes and   297–8

Sakharov, Andrei   188–9
Scholarly Council on Philosophy and the
    Social Problems of Science and
    Technics   xv–xvi
Schwab, Klaus   284, 346, 392
science
    biogeochemistry   102
    globalization of   106, 274–81
    global security and   108
    the interdisciplinary approach   101–2
    knowledge of human beings   280–1
    naturalistic/socio-humanistic split
        282–3
    role of scientific thought for the
        biosphere   100–1, 183
    scientific-technological revolutions   66,
        74–5, 201–5
    See also technology
securitology   347
security
See also global security
Shpet, Gustav   29–30
Skvortsov, Lev   374–5
social solidarity
    in contemporary Russia   307, 317–22
    faith communities in contemporary
        Russia   318–19
    the family institution   70, 309, 310,
        311–13, 317–18
    historically   307
    informal civil society structures   314–15
    non-state solidarity structures of   317–22
    Orthodox-Christian civic associations
        309–10, 311
    Russian pre-state communities   308–9
    socially destructive groups   315–17
    social volunteering   320–1
    Soviet *blat* networks   316–17
    Soviet-era non-state solidarity networks
        310–17
    state socialization   310
    structures of   307–10
society
    feminization of   216

INDEX 427

the global digital society 228–35, 261, 284–5
social ecology 276–9
societal trends under globalization 42
society/nature relations 8, 99–100, 276–9
socio-cultural diversity 236–7, 342–3
socio-natural history 279
Soviet Union (USSR)
    anti-disciplinary, socially destructive groups 315–17
    bipolar world order 298–9
    blat networks 316–17
    Communards 315
    destruction of the family institution 310, 311–13
    influence on social processes 301
    informal civil society structures 314–15
    phases of influence 304–5
    role of the state 301–2
    secular culture 402–3, 405
    socialization of the state 314
    social security system 311–12
    Soviet Cosmism 327–8
    support for Third World states 299–300
    traditional family institution 309
space
    extraterrestrial exploration 57, 75
    outer-space research 328–9
    See also Russian Cosmism
Sport for All movement
    concept behind 359–60, 362–3, 370–1
    positive aspects 361
    principles for competition within 366–9
    programs 360–1
    SPART Games 366–8
    substantive problems 361–9
    terminological problems 361, 369–70, 371
sports
    elite sport 359, 364
    mass sports 359, 364
    modern sports competitions 364–6
    positive/negative aspects 358–9
    Sport for All movement 359–60
St. John Chrysostom 397–8
Stychinsky, Maxim 376
Styopin, Vyacheslav 283

sustainable development
    concept 66, 104, 220
    concept of the environment 194
    definition 189–90, 194–5
    the green economy 207–9, 218–19
    United Nations adoption of 108, 189–90

Taylor, Charles 307–8, 322
techno-industrial revolution 284
technology
    converging technologies 204
    development and use of AI technologies 350–1, 352–7
    development of natural resources 218
    foundations of 197–9
    goods of status/belonging 44
    the green economy and 207–9, 218–19
    human development and 20, 196–7, 198, 199, 230–1
    human ecology and 280
    impact of the mythological worldview 199–201
    information-network technology of the alter-globalist movement 152–4, 156
    innovative banking 224–5, 226–8
    logic of technological development 205–7
    microchip development 46
    for the preservation of the biosphere 100–1, 183, 218–19, 221, 223, 281
    scientific thought and development of 66, 74–5, 201–5
    solutions to environmental pollution 221
    techno-humanitarian balance 225–6, 228–35
    See also digital age
technosphere 196, 208, 279
tectology 273–4, 283, 289
Teilhard de Chardin, Pierre 8, 325, 328
Toynbee, Arnold 8, 336, 373, 374, 392
transhumanism 281, 284
Tsiolkovsky, Konstantin 100, 325, 326, 327, 328, 330

ultra-imperialism
    the proto-empire's threat to 145–7
    rise of 143–5

ultra-imperialism (cont.)
　term　144
UNESCO Universal Declaration on Cultural Diversity　339–40
United Kingdom (UK)　113, 125–6, 130
United Nations (UN)
　Charter　238–9
　formation of　238–9
　principle of collective security　238–9, 242
　sustainable development concept　108, 189–90
　Universal Declaration of Human Rights　21, 39, 238–9
　World Conferences on Environment and Development　189, 190–1, 193–4, 207
　Year of Dialogue among Civilizations　338–9
United States of America (USA)
　disintegration of hyper-globalization　113
　economic impact of American unipolar globalization　255–6
　as a global power　125–6, 130, 131–2
　hegemonic ambitions　243–4, 390
　human rights discourse　247
　post-Cold War security strategies　241–2
　Sino-American relations　43, 46–7, 48, 111, 114–15, 242–3, 259, 265
universal evolutionism　51–2, 57–8
Ursul, Arkady D.　104, 288

Vernadsky, Vladimir
　advancement of *Homo erectus*　59
　biospheric evolution　211
　cosmic worldview　67, 100, 272
　as the founder of global studies　99–102, 106
　on the Industrial Revolution　211–12
　interaction between human societies　99–100
　the interdisciplinary approach and　101–2, 272
　man as a geological power　66, 100, 219, 281
　Russian Cosmism　325, 326, 327, 328
　scientific worldview　101–2
　society/nature relations　8, 99–100, 272
　See also biosphere; noosphere

Wallerstein, Immanuel　69, 146, 148, 392
westernization
　age of competing westernizations　38–9, 40–1, 47, 338, 343, 373, 375–6, 377, 406–8
　civilizational values and　341–2, 343–4
　economics of competing westernizations　40–1, 42–3
　as replaced by globalization　37–40, 42–3, 48–9
　term　37
world community
　competing interests within　5–6
　during the COVID-19 pandemic　132–3
　development of　3–5, 19–21, 70–1
　differentiation of　5
　integral system of　5, 7–9
　mass consciousness　190–3
　new humanism for　19–20
World Congress of Philosophy　9, 10–11, 12–13
worldviews
　civilizational worldviews　336–8
　cosmic worldview　67
　early mankind's development　200–1
　globalization and the need for a new worldview　19–20, 216, 225, 323–4, 325, 331
　the ideal and　353–4, 357
　philosophical thought and　13, 19, 26
　problem of doubt　355–6, 357
　scientific worldview　102, 106
　the system of worldview　354–5
　understanding and meaning within　356–7

Yarochikin, Vladimir　347
Youngs, Richard　137

Zagladin, Vadim　169